Collective Choice

Springer-Verlag Berlin Heidelberg GmbH

Jac C. Heckelman · Dennis Coates
Editors

Collective Choice

Essays in Honor of MANCUR OLSON

With 15 Figures
and 21 Tables

Springer

Prof. Jac C. Heckelman
McCulloch Family Fellow
Department of Economics
Wake Forest University
110 Carswell Hall
Winston Salem, NC 27109
USA
heckeljc@wfu.edu

Prof. Dennis Coates
Department of Economics
University of Maryland, Baltimore County
1000 Hilltop Circle
Baltimore, MD 21250
USA
coates@umbc.edu

ISBN 978-3-642-05565-2 ISBN 978-3-540-24711-1 (eBook)
DOI 10.1007/978-3-540-24711-1

Cataloging-in-Publication Data applied for
A catalog record for this book is available from the Library of Congress.
Bibliographic information published by Die Deutsche Bibliothek
Die Deutsche Bibliothek lists this publication in the Deutsche Nationalbibliografie; detailed bibliographic data is available in the Internet at <http://dnb.ddb.de>.

http://www.springer.de

Originally published by Springer-Verlag Berlin Heidelberg New York in 2003
Softcover reprint of the hardcover 1st edition 2003

Foreword

I met Mancur Olson one snowy morning in Colorado Springs, at the U. S. Air Force Academy where I had lectured to the cadets the night before. I had an early plane to catch at Denver, and an Academy car and driver showed up at about 5:30. A uniformed Mancur Olson carried my bag to the car, joined me in the back seat, and began to tell me his thesis. (I had already been assigned his dissertation adviser, in absentia.) Despite snow flurries we made good time, and he had only about one hour to lecture me before we got to Stapleton Airport. I don't think I interrupted him once. He was still expounding as he carried my bag to the gate, where we shook hands and concluded our first "conference."

As adviser, I think I was of some help. Olson, of course, was an economist--at least his Ph D was to be in economics. He had, in my judgment, tried too hard in his written dissertation to impress economists with more paraphernalia than I thought necessary; and I urged him to think of a wider audience, an audience to which technical economic details would be only an obstacle, and to show applications of what was, actually, a fairly simple theoretical idea. Most of the "logic of collective action" would appear familiar to economists--maybe only because it was so comprehensible as, perhaps, to seem "obvious" once brought to one's attention.

What I should have seen, and did not see then, was that Olson was a political theorist using concepts that were beginning to become an important part of economic theory. Those were the days when "public goods" and "externalities" were moving into the mainstream of economics. Olson not only jumped on that bandwagon, but steered it into political (and sociological, and anthropological) theory. His tools were economics; his interest, and his subject, was organization theory. How do professionals--all kinds, laborers, farmers, industrialists, doctors, teachers, fishermen--with common interests overcome the adverse incentives arising in self-interest to achieve some commonality, some cooperation? How do they generate coercive or attractive incentives to get them to do what they all hope to do together but would not individually have any motive to do?

Olson's chief analytical tool was the concept of methodological individualism and rational choice. The basic unit of analysis is the individual, not the group, the class, the polity, the guild. And the individuals are best conceived as behaving in purposive fashion, aware of their values and alert to their opportunities, knowledgeable about their environment and the constraints on what they may choose, and are able to match actions with objectives over time. This assumption is a powerful tool of analysis even if it applies only approximately most of the time and badly some of the time. It allows what I have called "vicarious problem solving": we figure out what a person might do by imagining ourselves in the person's position, as best we understand that position, adopting for the purpose as much as we can know about the person's preferences, and deciding what the person ought to do. By "what he ought to do" we merely mean what the person should decide in accordance with his own aims, values, and objectives, given the alternatives that the person faces. This is an attractive model: when it works we get a lot of output from a minimal input using a standard piece of intellectual machinery.

Using this model of individual behavior Olson, in *The Logic of Collective Choice*, spelled out clearly the difficulties in organizing collectively-oriented, co-operative pursuit of group interests, and with numerous persuasive examples illustrated some of the solutions to this universal problem.

That done, he went on to the next "level of organization." He took up, in *The Rise and Decline of Nations*, the question: if groups with common interests--craftsmen, farmers, industrialists, academics, realtors, physicians--succeed in overcoming the obstacles to collective action in their collective interest, how does that affect the productivity of a society? In the first instance, people will act in their own interests, not in the interests of their group; once they have harnessed their individual incentives to the group, if they ever do, the groups then act in their own interests, not in the interests of the larger society.

Here his interest is in what have come to be called "rent seekers": protectionists, groups devoted to raising their incomes, not their productivity, through some exercise of monopoly power in the marketplace or of political power in the legislature. He analyzes both the "deadweight loss" due to protectionism and the loss of competitive dynamism, the stifling of new enterprise. Thus the "decline" of his title.

I do not have any idea whether Olson, in completing his work on the *Logic*, already anticipated the potentially stifling effect on the "rise" of nations of the successful surmounting of the obstacles to group collective action. He never mentioned to me that there would be a sequel. There are, though, in the *Logic*, adequate hints that overcoming the obstacles to collective action need not be in the overall social interest. I doubt, though, that he fully anticipated the powerful argument he would offer in the *Rise and Decline.*

Through the *Logic* and the *Rise and Decline* Olson was a scholar working alone. In the *Logic* he was a pure scholar; he took no sides, just looked at the abstract subject, exercising scholarly curiosity. In *Rise and Decline* he became concerned; he cared.

In his final career Olson became an activist. He displayed entrepreneurial and managerial skills that most of us would never have expected (and most of us could never have displayed) . For over a decade he devoted himself on a very large scale to bringing ideas of institutional reform and innovation to developing nations and to nations emerging from Soviet economic and intellectual domination. He was convinced that the institutional theory to which he had devoted his entire career could help to release national economies from stagnation. He was a visionary, but with a vision based on the logic of collective action.

Thomas Schelling
Distinguished University Professor of Economics
University of Maryland

Preface

Many years ago Mancur and I attended a dinner with several leading historians working on the economic history of Maryland and Virginia in the eighteenth century. When the historians made some casual comments about the economic strategies of the Chesapeake tobacco planters, Mancur politely objected that the planters couldn't possibly have acted as the historians said because such behavior wouldn't have been rational for maximizing profits. The historians produced statistics; Mancur doubted they could be right. The historians produced case studies, particular examples of planters who acted exactly as they said they did; Mancur replied that they couldn't be representative. We reached dessert with no agreement: the economist and the historians never saw eye to eye that evening.

The dinner was delightful and all of us had a thoroughly enjoyable time, but I sensed that Mancur was somewhat frustrated with the historian's conclusion that eighteenth century Chesapeake planters did not always pursue their economic interests rationally. When Mancur himself studied any occasion or a problem in history, he asked how people would logically have behaved to maximize benefit to themselves. He assumed, in other words, that since people act rationally, it is the economists job to determine what rational behavior would be in any given circumstance. The historians at our dinner, on the other hand, asked not what the planters would have done, but what they actually did do. They assumed that since people do *not* always act rationally, it is the historians' job to explain why they don't. Perhaps it is this discrepancy that accounts for Mancur's "mixed reception among economic historians" that Robert Whaples mentions in the volume.

Our "Chesapeake" dinner highlighted for me another aspect of Mancur's thinking. His sheer delight in debating with a dinner table of scholars illustrated the genuine love of argument he mentioned in *The Rise and Decline of Nations*: "My strategy of research is to attempt to say or write something audacious enough to elicit intelligent criticism, to reflect at length on that criticism, and then to ... make any amendment, abandonment, or extension that could be appropriate." Or take his remarks in *Power and Prosperity*: "I have made strong claims ... [and it is] for reviewers, readers, and the authors of subsequent studies, to judge whether these claims are true." When Mancur died he left (in addition to the nineteen briefcases Chas Caldwell elsewhere mentions being in his university office) several filing cabinets of notes at home. Some folders contained information on miscellaneous subjects (I counted sixty three folders on different subjects in one drawer alone, ranging from "Lawyers in Germany" to "Wage Scales in Russia" to various topics concerned with "Europe, 1870 – 1914"). But others were devoted to argument. A series of folders began with a talk Mancur had given, continued with copious notes he took on criticisms from commentators and the audience, and finished with Mancur's responses developed both on the occasion and later. Still other drawers contained folders with criticisms that Mancur had solicited on various manuscripts. To Mancur, dispute and audacity made economics fun; argument focused his thinking and moved it along.

In his last book, *Power and Prosperity*, Mancur expressed a hope that his argument would have "important implications for economic policy in advanced democracies of Europe, North America, and Japan, as well as in the countries that are or have lately been under dictatorships." He would have been very grateful to Jac Heckelman and Dennis Coates for putting together this volume of essays sizing up some of those implications in *Collective Choice: Essays in Honor of Mancur Olson*. He would have been delighted with the contributions of colleagues and co-authors, and he would have been particularly pleased that former students also contributed. As a teacher, Mancur wanted to provide the tools to help the next generation of students solve problems that the present generation could not. Inspired by Newton's remark that he "stood on the shoulders of giants," Mancur wanted to provide the shoulders on which future thinkers would stand.

Alison Olson
Professor of History
University of Maryland

Table of Contents

Part III Market Augmenting Government

1 On the Shoulders of a Giant: The Legacy of Mancur Olson

Jac C. Heckelman and Dennis Coates

Mancur Olson Jr is probably the only economist to have published two sole-authored books considered seminal in the field of public choice (see Stretton and Orchard's (Stretton and Orchard 1994) overview of the field, chapter 2). Olson's dissertation was published as *The Logic of Collective Action* (Olson 1965), and quickly forced economists and political scientists to rethink their views on group formation and productive capabilities. The publication of *The Rise and Decline of Nations* (Olson 1982), which has subsequently been translated into 11 languages, spawned a series of symposia published in *The Political Economy of Growth* (Mueller 1983) and special issues of *International Studies Quarterly* and *Scandinavian Political Studies*. In between and after, Olson wrote many important papers extending the analysis in these books. Olson is the only scholar to have a separate chapter devoted exclusively to his work and the work it directly spawned, in both the standard graduate text *Public Choice II* (Mueller 1989) and the most recent handbook on public choice scholarship, *The Elgar Companion to Public Choice* (Shughart and Razzolini 2001).

Olson's work was built upon previous scholarship across various disciplines, including that by economists, political scientists, political theorists, sociologists, historians, and others, and made a concerted effort to appeal to a wide range of disciplines, atypical of most academic economists who read and write primarily within their own sub-discipline. Olson was quick to give credit where due for his inspirations, as he was fond of mimicking Isaac Newton by stating he "stood on the shoulders of giants" (*The Rise and Decline of Nations*, p. ix).

Olson's success in reaching across the social sciences is reflected especially in his appeal within political science being even greater than within his own field of economics. *The Rise and Decline of Nations* won the Gladys M. Kammerer award from the American Political Science Association for the best political science publication in the field of U.S. national policy, and as noted above, led to special journal issues in political science. In addition, "Rapid Growth as a Destabilizing Force" (Olson 1963b) was one of the most widely-cited articles ever published in the *Journal of Economic History* but most citations were by historians, rather than economic historians.

The papers in this volume are written by former students, including two former undergraduates, colleagues, and coauthors of Olson on issues related to Olson's interests. Each author, with the following noted exceptions, has a past affiliation with the University of Maryland. In particular, Richard Zeckhauser and coauthors have no direct connection to the University of Maryland, but Zeckhauser did coauthor what would become Olson's most cited and influential journal article (Olson and Zeckhauser 1966) when both were early in their careers. Likewise, David Colander coauthored a paper with Olson on collective action which appeared in Colander's (1984) edited volume. The remaining chapters are all authored by scholars who were either faculty or students at the University of Maryland, some of whom also have coauthored papers with Olson. Although he did not direct many dissertations, Olson's presence at the university for over 30 years left its imprint on many graduate students who attended his classes and seminars, or simply had the opportunity to discuss their own work with him. His ability to reach outside of economics is reflected in the fact that many of the students who graduated through the Government and Politics department consider themselves to be Olsonian students. Indeed, almost half the former students contributing to this volume received their degrees from the Government and Politics department. In addition, many economics students were supported as research assistants through Olson's Center of Institutional Reform and the Informal Sector (IRIS), established in 1990. Many of the faculty at University of Maryland also contributed to Olson's IRIS projects and the center regularly supported outside scholars, including one of the contributors to this volume, Kenneth Koford, and sponsored symposia on the importance of 'good governance' for development prospects. The essays in this volume represent a tribute to a man who at the time of his death in 1998 was still actively pushing the boundaries of economic knowledge in the area of collective choice.

The rest of this introductory chapter provides background on Olson's work and on the essays in this volume. Specifically, the next section outlines the development of Olson's theories concerning the causes and consequences of collective action. Following that, Olson's place within the contrasting schools of thought in collective choice is discussed. Finally, the chapter ends with a summary of the essays collected in this volume with an emphasis on placing them within the context of Olson's research.

1.1 Olsonian Thought

This section details the development of Olson's work in the area of collective action. First we outline his original theory on group formation and related empirical applications. Next we address the importance of collective action to economic growth, and the positive role for government in addressing potential market failures. Our discussion is organized around a major book for each theme.

1.1.1 The Logic of Collective Action

Olson's concern was the provision of goods or services that provide benefits to multiple individuals, even those who do not participate in their provision. Building upon the inherent instability of cartel behavior, Olson argued that group provision of such goods or services confronts the same difficulties as do cartels. Individuals can benefit without incurring costs of provision, or by cheating on the cartel agreement, and will, therefore, opt not to participate. Individual incentives will, in other words, work against the formation of groups whose purpose is to provide these public goods. Olson notes that in this context the free market would under-provide for public-type goods. He emphasized, however, that the extent of this free riding behavior would be a function of group size, so small groups would be more likely to form than would large groups.

Large (in Olson's terms, "latent") groups would have trouble attracting membership, and would need to rely on a system of selective incentives. Special excludable private goods, such as low cost insurance, would be an enticing carrot, while social pressures, such as ostracism or physical harm, would be a threatening stick. However, if a single member (or small group) could obtain a benefit which would exceed the total cost, they may provide the good while others free ride on its nonexcludability. Olson referred to this phenomenon as "exploitation of the great by the small" (*The Logic of Collective Action*, p.3, p. 29). In game theoretic terms, complete free-riding is the Nash equilibrium to a prisoners' dilemma game, but exploitation of the great by the small is akin to the equilibrium in a game of chicken, where even the exploited is better off, although in a personal second-best situation.

Although much of Olson's theory is not directly testable, such as the motivation for group formation, the exploitation theory is. Olson first presented support for the theory in the context of international alliances where it was shown that those with the most to gain from NATO bear more than a proportional share of the costs (Olson and Zeckhauser 1966). This is where the theory has received the most attention. Subsequent analysis revealed the results were specific to the sample time period and typically did not hold for other alliances (Cornes and Sandler 1986). Most recently, the exploitation theory was used to explain free riding by small banks on large bank lobbying efforts to convince the Federal Reserve to set low reserve requirements after it was given control of the reserve ratios in 1935 (Heckelman and Wood 1999). The chapter by Parson, Zeckhauser and Coglianese highlights collective action issues in providing information.

1.1.2 Institutional Sclerosis

Olson's earlier analysis suggests narrow special interests will be more powerful than larger (latent) groups which suffer more from free riding problems. The macroeconomic consequences of interest groups are developed in several places (Olson 1982; 1983a; 1983b). Because the benefits of economic growth are widely dispersed across members of society, the likely gain to any group that advocates faster growth will be only a small share of these benefits. At the same time, this pro-growth advocacy group would incur all of the costs of its efforts. The upshot is that the incentives work against the formation of pro-growth groups. On the other hand, groups that form to advocate excludable redistribution will obtain large benefits for themselves while imposing costs on the broader society. Consequently, groups that encourage redistribution are more likely to form than groups advocating growth. Moreover, since it takes time for even small groups to overcome their collective action problems, over time more groups are expected to form. As these groups form, more scarce economic resources are diverted away from technological advances and other growth enhancing activities that are non-excludable, toward redistributive activities. Thus, Olson predicts economic growth will decline over time.

These sclerotic effects are due to the formation of special interest organizations (SIOs). If the SIOs are destroyed, growth prospects are enhanced. Instability, such as coups and revolutions, destroy the influence of the SIOs and their avenues for controlling social resources. Constant upheaval, although beneficial in preventing sclerosis from settling in, is also harmful, as economic agents lose faith in the existing institutions and will be unwilling to sign long-term contracts requiring a *quid pro quo*. Economies of scale and other economic efficiencies will then be absent. Thus, the best growth prospects should be present where there was recent upheaval, but long-term stability is expected to follow.

In *The Rise and Decline of Nations* (1982), Olson presents narrative histories of the post WWII experience for many nations that are consistent with his theory. The fastest growing nations in the post-war period were those that suffered the most destruction within their society, including especially the eradication of their wartime and pre-war governments. In these countries, Germany, Japan, and Italy, newly installed democratic governments fostered stability in economic and political relationships. Those nations whose governments and institutions were not altered by the war, such as US, Britain, Australia and New Zealand, generated much lower growth after the war. Olson's econometric evidence focuses on the various state economies of the US, where it is shown that a measure of state lifetime is inversely correlated with state income per capita. The length of a state's life is based either on the date of statehood or the end of the Civil War for the states of the Confederacy. He also presents evidence that SIOs are more prevalent in older and more stable states, where SIOs are proxied by the percentage of the labor force holding union membership in the state.

Olson (1990) later extended the analysis to Communist societies by focusing on bureaucratic direction in the policy process. As the state directly controlled resources, bureaucratic interests were in a strong position to seek rents and redistribute toward themselves. As these interests became more entrenched, they became more efficient at siphoning resources away from other needed areas, creating greater and greater harm for the economy overall while continuing to improve their own positions.

The theory of institutional sclerosis has been most frequently tested by comparing cross-national growth rates. Typically, the number of years of stable borders for each country is used to proxy for the sclerotic effect (Choi 1983; Landau 1985; Nardinelli, Wallace and Warner 1987). This does not address Olson's theory or the spirit of Olson's tests very well as wars or internal coups can create upheaval without changing the society's borders, as evidenced by Olson's usage of the Civil War to restart the southern states' SIO formation clock. Others have created "trauma" variables to measure the degree of destruction caused by wars and revolutions (Chan 1987). Olson (1983b) makes the point that political institutions can be altered in such a fundamental fashion that upheaval can occur even without wars and coups. He stresses as examples the 1965 Voting Rights Act and the end of Jim Crow laws, each of which gave the southern states a fresh start, clearing out the existing sclerotic institutions and opening up avenues of influence to new parties and ideas. Thus, to properly test for sclerotic effects on the economy of a country, state, or province, it is necessary to understand the political and institutional histories of that jurisdiction. The chapter by Patrick James represents a case in point by detailing sclerotic forces at work during constitutional reform in Canada. Our chapter relates the number of interest groups in a country directly to the rate of income growth in that country, providing one of the few direct tests of Olson's hypothesis that interest groups are harmful to economic growth.

1.1.3 Market Augmenting Government

The importance of expected long-term stability for economic growth is true for all societies and forms of government. An autocratic government can be viewed as an encompassing interest, since the autocrat is the ultimate receiver of any wealth creation (Olson 1991, 1993). A long term planning horizon will limit coercive takings through taxation and theft, each of which reduces wealth-generating incentives. In addition, the autocrat will use his own resources (or those obtained through trade) to provide public goods as long as the wealth increases that result provide sufficient tax revenues to cover the costs of the public goods. In other words, the autocrat will provide public services to his subjects as long as doing it increases his own wealth. If, however, the autocrat does not expect to retain his power for very long or plans to move on elsewhere (what Olson refers to as "roving bandits"), then he will not be around to benefit from public service provision, including enforcement of contracts, and he has every incentive to plunder the local economy to maximize his immediate wealth. That such behavior lowers wealth in the long run is of no consequence to this type of autocrat. Consequently, only the stable autocrat with a long planning horizon will maximize long run wealth opportunities for the society, and thus himself. Thus, the importance of good governance is not limited to democratic societies, although the stationary autocrat is the least favored form of stable society.

"Super-encompassing interests" are majorities and ruling interests that obtain a sufficiently large fraction of the social income that it is not in their interest to actively redistribute wealth toward themselves at all (McGuire and Olson 1996). Olson argues that *by definition* a majority that earns income from the market is more encompassing than an autocrat. Therefore, it follows that majorities and oligarchies will provide more public goods than any autocrat.

The notion of good governance is further developed in Olson's posthumous publication *Power and Prosperity* (Olson 2000), where the term "market-augmenting government" is coined to capture the idea that complex markets are needed for growth but are unable to properly develop without impartial governmental enforcement of property rights and contracts, and the absence of predation. Governments function best when they are encompassing but, as developed in *The Rise and Decline of Nations*, tend to focus on special-interest groups at the expense of general welfare. Thus, Olson's policy prescription is for institutions to ensure that authoritative control is given to encompassing rather than narrow interests. This builds upon his earlier theme that less developed nations suffer from poor institutional control, rather than simply a lack of factor endowment or technology (Olson 1996).

Simple markets that involve immediate exchange of goods or services, and from which both parties benefit instantly, will develop spontaneously. However, without proper governmental assistance, complex markets will not emerge. Public goods, for instance, will be lacking due to free-riding in large group settings (Olson 1965). Insurance and futures markets that require outside enforcement will also fail in the absence of government assistance, since credibility is absent (Olson and Kahkonen 2000). While there remain concerns that SIOs will capture the power of strong central government to redistribute, thereby distorting the proper incentives to enhance production, good governance that assists in the enforcement of long-term contracts and the provision of public goods is important for growth.

On net, the power of government can be good or bad, and which it is makes a crucial difference for economic growth (Olson, Sarna and Swamy 2000). Second and third world nations do not suffer simply from low potential, but rather they produce well below what they could due to bad governance in the form of socially gratuitous taking, missing markets, and other poorly designed economic policies (Olson and Kahkonen 2000). The chapter by Christopher Clague develops this theme for a variety of nations.

1.2 Public Choice Schools of Thought

Economists working within the Public Choice paradigm are generally classified according to one of two schools of thought. The first, following the path set forth by the pioneering work of James Buchanan and Gordon Tullock, focuses on the normative aspects of political choice and typically argues government regulations and restrictions on individual transactions hinder the efficiency of free markets. In their view, constitutional provisions are needed to properly limit the potential for a runaway Leviathan government. Buchanan gives Olson credit for first using the phrase "Virginia School" to contrast this line of inquiry from the "Chicago School" represented by Nobel Laureates George Stigler, Gary Becker, and Ronald Coase (Buchanan 1999). The Chicago School tradition focuses on equilibrium outcomes, both economic and political. Although government policies may distort the allocative mechanisms, a form of Pareto efficiency is achieved in the sense that no changes are possible that will not harm at least some individuals. In the Chicago view, rational individuals already would have adopted any institutional change that would improve the welfare of all.

While there is much in the way of overlap between these schools of thought, especially skepticism concerning the idea that public policy is about improving the general welfare, important distinctions remain. Indeed, the two schools share the notion that most political policy is designed to redistribute income. They disagree, however, on how efficient such redistribution is. It is not always clear, of course, whether any given piece of scholarly work fits into one school or another. Placing an entire body of research into a school is even more difficult, and Olson's work is a case in point. While many consider Olson to be part of the Virginia School (Jankowski 2001; Mitchell 2001), Dennis Mueller, Olson's long-time colleague, does not agree (Mueller 1993). However, Mueller does not indicate into which school he would place Olson. Others trace the Chicago views on the role of interest groups to Olson (Alston, Thrainn and North 1996; Moe 1997) and consider Olsonian assumptions to be Chicagoan in the extreme (Stretton and Orchard 1994). Schmid (1996) considers Olson distinct enough to refer to a "Maryland School". We believe this is the first usage of the term, and it appears apt to recognize Olson separately, as well as the large body of work that has followed in his tradition.

Olson's research certainly has aspects of both Virginia and Chicago. An issue that runs throughout his work is the importance of rent-seeking, primarily associated with Gordon Tullock of the Virginia School. At this point, however, the notion of applying rent seeking to the political process is a fundamental postulate to all public choice analysis, and is well accepted within the Chicago School line of research as well. In addition, Olson does not seem to rely as heavily on equilibrium outcomes, separating himself from the Chicagoans. His policy implications, however, are clearly at odds with the Libertarian perspective of the Virginians (Olson 1986). Consider *The Logic of Collective Action* (Olson 1965) and Buchanan's (1965) treatise on club goods. Both understood the potential problem of nonexcludable and nonrival goods. Buchanan argued that for some goods the nonrivalness would expire after a relatively small number of individuals jointly consumed the good, but that individuals' benefits from the good were far too small to make provision economical. Consequently, clubs would form expanding membership until the benefits of spreading out the cost were balanced by the costs of sharing the good with an additional consumer. There is really no discussion of the circumstances under which the club will form, but the implication is that some public goods can be efficiently provided without governmental involvement. Olson, however, stressed those circumstances under which the group would or would not form. Specifically, the production of some goods would require a large group, but no individual would have the incentive to join. Thus, if these public goods are to be provided, government is necessary. Further development on the contrast between Olson and Buchanan is undertaken in the chapter by Keith Dougherty.

Olson often tried to dissociate himself from the Virginia Libertarian attitude that strong governments are necessarily harmful. Believing the term Public Choice had become too closely associated with this perspective, he eschewed it in favor of what he felt was the more neutral terminology "Collective Choice". The Virginia School, similar to the Austrians, also places much less emphasis on econometric analysis, whereas Chicago is rich in empirical analysis. Olson is not an econometrician, and much of his own empirical analysis is fairly basic, but he understood its important role in economic analysis, and always highlighted empirically testable hypotheses and especially encouraged others to further develop this avenue of his work.

Unlike either of the other schools, Olson does not put his faith in the infallibility of free markets. Olson sees a positive role for government to produce public goods, limit externalities, and reduce uncertainty. In fact, much of Olson's analysis is an argument about transaction costs, in line with Ronald Coase and Douglas North. Government can either increase or decrease transactions costs. Successful economies are those where good governance is the rule, keeping transactions costs low, while the poorer economies suffer from poor institutions that hinder efficient markets and make inefficient markets worse, raising transactions costs.

Another important distinction between Public Choice scholarship at the Universities of Chicago and Virginia, compared to the University of Maryland, is that both economists and political scientists at the University of Maryland actively participated in the outgrowth of research in Public Choice. In the Economics department, graduate study in the Public Choice program was led by Olson, Dennis Mueller, and Peter Coughlin, each of whom brought a different area of expertise to the program. Mueller's approach was solidly in the Virginia camp, focusing on normative constitutional political economy, but he also created the classic graduate text *Public Choice* (1979, 1989) and the recent *Perspectives on Public Choice: A Handbook* (1999) which surveys the entire field covering both Virginia and Chicago school approaches, and of course Olson's influence, as well as the rational choice political science inspired Rochester School, following from the work of William Riker. Coughlin's emphasis was on social choice theory, formalizing and extending mathematical spatial voting models in the Downsian tradition. Olson taught not only in the Public Choice field sequence but occasionally in the Macroeconomic Theory courses, exposing a greater number of graduate students to his line of inquiry. The Collective Choice Center (CCC) was developed because of the overlapping interests of the economics and political science faculty. Recently, the Olson Memorial Lecture Series was established as part of the CCC to highlight continuing research in the Olsonian tradition. That the Collective Choice Center is headed up by a political scientist and housed in the Department of Government and Politics is further evidence of Olson's broad influence outside of economics. While many of the faculty in both Economics and Government and Politics contributed to the development of Public Choice at the University of Maryland, as Distinguished University Professor and past president of Public Choice Society, Southern Economic Association, and Eastern Economic Association, Mancur Olson was at the forefront, spreading his ideas the farthest, and is the member most closely associated with and most influential within Public Choice scholarship.

1.3 The Contributions in This Volume

As developed earlier in this chapter, Olson's work in collective action can be split into three periods of analysis. Likewise, the contributions to this volume are sorted into sections organized around these three periods with each section containing four chapters. The three sections are, in order, Collective Action, Institutional Sclerosis, and Market Augmenting Government. The various chapters also represent the diverse style of Mancur's methodology. Olson is typically associated with purely descriptive analysis (see the chapter by Robert Whaples) and several of the chapters follow this tone, but he also occasionally incorporated basic and straightforward regression analysis to test his theories (Olson 1982, 1983a), a framework utilized in the chapters by Charles Enis, Dennis Coates and Jac Heckelman, and Phil Keefer and Steven Knack. A few of Olson's coauthored papers were also quite technical in nature (Olson and Zeckhauser 1966, McGuire and Olson 1996, Dixit and Olson 2000). The previously unpublished chapter by Olson and Jack included in this volume, and the new contribution from Marek Kaminski, are written in this vein.

Opening the Collective Choice section is the contribution by Keith Dougherty entitled "Precursors of Mancur Olson". Dougherty reviews the major theories concerning public goods and free-riding behavior that had been developed prior to Olson's *Logic of Collective Action.* He concludes that Olson's most original contributions were in his specific claims as to how groups behave, including his discussion of selective incentives, equilibrium predictions, and the application of collective action to a wide variety of settings.

Another prediction from Olson's model in the *Logic of Collective Action* entails 'exploitation of the great by the small' where those with the most to gain bear a disproportionate share of the burden. In contrast, Warr's (1983) neutrality theory predicts the provision of a public good is unaffected by the distribution of income, and thus a redistribution of income leaves each person with exactly the same amount of public and private goods as before the redistribution. Bryan Jack and Mancur Olson have revisited this issue in "Warr Neutrality and the Natural Egalitarianism of Voluntary Public Goods Provision".[1] In their chapter, they first compare the testable implications of the neutrality theory with observed reality and then develop a more general graphical analysis of voluntary public goods contributions that allows them to consider all possible income distributions. They conclude that voluntary contributions to public goods have a strong tendency toward natural egalitarianism by which they mean an equalizing of the distribution of real welfare.

---

[1] This chapter represents an older working paper that was to be updated by Bryan Jack specifically for this volume, before his death as a passenger on board American Flight 77 from Dulles on September 11, 2001. We have decided to include the paper with minimal editing in deference to both Jack and Olson. We have corrected typographical errors, added some section headings, and reworded two sentences that described the Nash equilibrium.

A particular type of public good in many instances is the provision of information. In "Collective Silence and Individual Voice: The Logic of Information Games," Edward Parson, Richard Zeckhauser, and Cary Coglianese address the circumstances under which society's interests in information revelation or lack of revelation are best satisfied. Although the framework differs from Olson's analysis in that targets are deciding to provide or conceal information rather than make monetary contributions, and their interest in revealing information depends on how they expect the regulator to utilize the information, the targets still face a form of prisoners' dilemma that generally leads to under-provision of the public good.

Concentrating on political developments in Poland, Marek Kaminski describes "The Collective Action Problems of Political Consolidation: Evidence from Poland". The discussion centers on efforts of the many small rightist parties to work together. At issue was the division of the seats in parliament among the individual parties should the coalition win electoral support. Solving the collective action problem was especially important for these groups because their fragmentation contributed to the return to power of post-communists, weak cabinets and parliaments, and the slowing of institutional reforms. Kaminski documents the problems and provides a simple game-theoretic model to explain the observable outcome.

The four chapters in the section on Institutional Sclerosis each attempts to assess or extend the idea of institutional sclerosis first advanced in *Rise and Decline of Nations*. Olson's theory of institutional sclerosis is based on the notion of special interests attracting resource use to engage in redistribution toward themselves and stifling innovation, typically through government regulation. Charles Enis applies Olson's macroeconomic theory to a microeconomic setting in "An Empirical Analysis of Institutional Sclerosis and Managerial Incentives: The Case of Motor Carrier Deregulation". Enis argues that under regulation, managers had little control over rates, routes, and freight they could haul, leaving little left for them to do in attempting to maximize profits. Deregulation allowed for greater flexibility on the parts of managers and, consistent with self-sorting theories of labor economics, carriers that offer incentive compensation plans should attract managers with greater expertise. In the context of motor carriers, deregulation serves as the "upheaval" that in Olson's theory would destroy those growth-retarding institutions that have developed over time and whose destruction will free the industry for greater profitability and efficiency. As it turns out, improved efficiency after deregulation did not translate into greater profitability. Enis' conclusion is that a sclerotic effect of the former regulatory environment was to dissuade the best managers from seeking employment in the trucking industry to begin with.

In "Developing the Canadian Government's Bargaining Position on the Constitution, June-July, 1980: An Application of Olson's Argument from *The Rise and Decline of Nations*," Patrick James extends Olson's analysis in a new direction and to a new country. From Olson's famous set of seven implications in *Rise and Decline*, James develops hypotheses and corollaries with respect to the nature of the politics of constitutional reform in Canada. Evidence is gleaned from the newly released minutes of the Constitutional reform meetings in June and July 1980, to corroborate his specific hypotheses and corollaries.

An alternative to detailed case studies employs cross-national empirical regression analysis to explain variation in national growth rates. In "Absolute and Relative Effects of Interest Groups on the Economy," Dennis Coates and Jac Heckelman follow this vein of the literature by testing for the impact of interest groups among the OECD nations, using the absolute number of interest groups per capita, and the number of interest groups relative to the size of the national government. This chapter extends the empirical literature on institutional sclerosis in two ways. First, the government size variable is recast as properly measuring government rent creation, in line with recent neo-classical institutional growth models. Second, it is argued the marginal sclerotic effect of an additional group is expected to decline as the number of existing groups rises, and that the effects will diminish over time. Empirical evidence supports these notions and reveals a greater absolute effect from the number of groups per capita than a relative effect of the number of groups compared to the size of government.

Much of Olson's work showed his interest in how political and economic forces interacted to influence historical long-run economic growth patterns. Robert Whaples' chapter on "If I had a Hammer: Mancur Olson as an Economic Historian" examines Olson's contributions to economic history, summarizing and examining his historical findings and arguments, but its main focus is on the reception of Olsonian thought by economic historians in their writings, including reviews of Olson's work, textbooks, reference works, journal articles, monographs, and survey responses. It appears that Olson had a mixed reception among economic historians. Reviews of *The Rise and Decline of Nations* appearing in economic history journals, for example, were often critical, but the book has been assigned to students by many economic historians, and generated a great deal of research designed to test the central hypotheses in a variety of settings, and economic historians have applied his theories to explain developments in Latin America and Africa.

Except in the rare cases where interest groups are encompassing, Olson has argued interest group lobbying would make public policy less efficient. He has also argued that government may, under certain circumstances, be able to augment or facilitate the working of markets to the advantage of the society. The chapters in the Market Augmenting Government section each contribute to our understanding of how government can help the market.

The ability of government to enhance the workings of the market will be related to the "encompassingness" of special interest organizations. Interest groups are likely to be particularly non-encompassing in societies where policy preferences are more polarized. One important policy application is in the honoring of debt commitments. In more polarized societies, building a consensus on how various groups will share economic sacrifices to manage and repay sovereign debt should be slower and more difficult, resulting in a greater likelihood of defaulting on foreign debt payments. Philip Keefer and Steven Knack examine the generality of this result in two important ways in "Social Polarization, Political Institutions and Country Creditworthiness". First, they argue that the effects of polarization will vary with the degree of political competition. For example, they suggest that a highly polarized country with little political competition will be more likely to be a high-risk borrower than an equally polarized country where politicians must reach across groups for electoral support. However, they also suggest that the flexibility to address financial problems will be lower where political competition and polarization are high than where polarization and political competition are both low. Second, they are able to include a much larger set of nations than in the existing literature by using an index of sovereign default risk based on surveys of international bankers. The evidence supports their hypothesis that the effects of polarization and political competition are highly intertwined.

Christopher Clague applies many of Olson's ideas concerning collective action, encompassing interests, devolution of power, and stationary banditry to "Corruption and Economic Development". In developing a taxonomy of public-sector corruption, Clague shows there is a wide gap between the kinds of conduct and practices that arouse moral outrage, and those that seriously impede economic and social development. Examples abound to distinguish between civil service construction, reform, and decay; grand corruption in developmental autocracies; corruption in laissez-faire environments; corrupt dealings with an entrepreneurial minority; dirigisme and corruption in postwar Europe and the Third World; and corruption and government performance.

John Wallis stands Olson's hypothesis of institutional sclerosis on its head while contributing to Olson's hypothesis that good governance is beneficial to economic growth and development in his chapter, "The Public Promotion of Private Interest (Groups)". From his analysis of state constitutions, Wallis suggests that the early 19th century promotion of the formation of private groups by American state governments contributed to the rapid growth of that era.

Finally, in "Macroeconomic Policy and Collective Action," David Colander, Kenneth Koford and Jeffrey Miller consider an overall framework for macroeconomics that integrates Olson's coordination failure of collective action into the core macroeconomic models. They argue that macroeconomic policy should focus on the fundamental principle of internalizing macroeconomic externalities, just as is done for microeconomic policy, and that this means that encompassing interests must find ways of inducing special interests to act in the best interests of the entire economy rather than in their own particular best interests. They suggest that the current approach to fiscal and monetary policy should be replaced with methods of internalizing inflation and aggregate demand externalities. Using incentive based approaches relies upon the microeconomic foundations of the macroeconomy and follows from Olson's (1982, p.233) early insight that "the best macroeconomic policy is a good microeconomic policy".

Olson's stature as an academic and the generosity he showed throughout his life is made clear in the multitude of "In memoriam" tributes that appeared in *Southern Economic Journal, Eastern Economic Journal, Public Choice, Journal of Public Choice and Public Finance, Economic Journal* and *The Economist.* This volume represents another form of tribute through a collection of new essays devoted to Olson's work on collective action, and is long overdue. Mancur surely deserved such a retrospective while he was still with us.

This volume would not have been possible without the efforts of each of the contributors, for which we are grateful. Only their devotion to the concept of honoring Mancur can explain their willingness to put up with, in some cases, repeated requests for revisions, and the extra work associated with inclusion in this volume. We also thank Alison Olson and Barbara Rachko for permission to include the previously unpublished chapter by Mancur Olson and Bryan Jack. Finally, at Springer-Verlag Martina Bihn showed enthusiasm for this project from the start and was patient with us in delivering the manuscript, and Markus Richter provided additional technical support for some of the formatting issues.

Part I

Collective Action

2 Precursors of Mancur Olson*

Keith L. Dougherty

Mancur Olson wrote four books during his career. He wrote *The Economics of Wartime Shortage*, which studied food shortages in wartime Britain; the *Rise and Decline of Nations*, which dealt with "institutional sclerosis" caused by interest groups; and *Power and Prosperity*, which described the formation of government from roving bandits to democracy. But his most seminal work was *The Logic of Collective Action* (hereafter *Logic*). In it, Olson laid the foundation for free-riding behavior, created a taxonomy of groups, and extended the problems associated with collective action to a broad class of economic and non-economic phenomena. Olson wrote with simplicity and clarity. This work was so persuasive that several authors attributed the discovery of the free-rider problem to him (Alt 1999; Brand 1983; Baldwin 1989). Others were more critical of his work. They argued against his claimed relationship between group size and the successful provision of collective goods (Frohlich and Oppenheimer 1970; Chamberlin 1974; Esteban and Ray 2001); against the exploitation of large actors by small ones (Sandler 1992); and against the importance of selective incentives in the formation of groups (Marsh 1976; Moe 1980). Some scholars even went so far as to claim that *Logic* was merely a popularization of earlier ideas (Dowding 1997; Chamberlain 1966).

This chapter studies Olson's work from a different perspective. It reviews the major theories of public goods and collective action before *Logic* and notes the contribution of Olson's predecessors to the theory of collective action. It then compares their theories to those laid out in *Logic*. In doing so, it attempts to unravel the legacy of Mancur Olson's greatest work and to determine why it was so successful.

2.1 Olson's Primary Arguments

Introducing the major themes of *Logic* up front will help the reader compare Olson's work to that of his predecessors. Although the following list is not exhaustive, it highlights the central themes:[1]

1. Free-rider hypothesis: when actors benefit from collective goods, they are likely to free ride.

* I thank Jac Heckelman for careful comments and editorial suggestions.
[1] See Sandler (1992, pp. 8-9) for a similar list.

2. Group size hypothesis: larger groups are more likely to fail than smaller ones.
3. Exploitation hypothesis: group members who receive larger benefits are more likely to contribute than group members who receive smaller benefits. Hence there is an "exploitation of the great by the small" (Olson 1965, p. 35).
4. Asymmetry hypothesis: groups with asymmetric benefits are more likely to succeed than groups with symmetric benefits.
5. By-product hypothesis: the successful provision of a collective good, such as lobbying, is often the by-product of selective incentives in large groups.

Several terms should be defined before launching into a history of collective action theory. First, Olson used the term collective good, in a general sense, to refer to any good that provides benefits to more than one individual. When individuals benefit from collective goods, coordinated effort, and sometimes enforcement, is required to assure provision. Second, a public good refers to any good that is nonexcludable and nonrival (Sandler 1992). Private goods have the opposite qualities. Although both terms will be used throughout this work, it is important to note that they were rarely used prior to the mid-1950s. When they were used, these terms had somewhat different meanings.[2]

2.2 The Theory of Public Goods before Olson

2.2.1 Valuing Public Goods

Although Adam Smith is best known for his study of free trade, he also investigated the allocation of governmental goods. Smith concluded in Book V of *The Wealth of Nations* that if governments raised revenues through user fees, they could allocate the costs of public goods to those who benefited from them the most. In making this argument, Smith indirectly recognized the difference between nonexcludable goods, that benefited everyone, and excludable goods, that benefited some to the exclusion of others. Although he never used the terms public and private, nor did he make the distinction explicit, he did argue that some goods -- such as roads, bridges, education, and religious instruction -- could be paid out of tolls and fees. Other goods -- such as defense and supporting the dignity of the sovereign -- would require general revenues. Smith separated the two simply because he could not figure out how to apply user fees to defense and the dignity of the sovereign, but he could figure out how to apply them to roads, bridges, education, and religious instruction. In other words, thinking about user fees led Smith to a loose notion of excludability.

[2] Samuelson described "private consumption goods" and "collective consumption goods" in Samuelson (1954). A year later, he changed the terminology to "private consumption goods" and "public consumption goods" (Samuelson 1955), which he later shortened to its current form in Samuelson (1958). The meanings of these terms were still in dispute when Olson wrote *Logic* (Head 1962).

This is the extent of Smith's contribution to the modern understanding of public goods. He did not describe the free-rider problem nor make any prediction about whether defense and dignity of the sovereign could be maintained optimally. He did, however, lay the foundation for later explorations.

Almost a century later, German and Italian economists embraced Smith's quest of tying public good quantities and tax shares to individual valuations. Indirectly, they discovered bits and pieces that would later influence Olson. Richard Musgrave (1939) dubbed them "The Voluntary Exchange Theorists" because they believed that processes similar to voluntary exchange would lead governments to accurate levels of demand.[3] Theorists, such as Antonio de Viti de Marco, Eric Lindahl, Ugo Mazzola, Emil Sax and Knut Wicksell, argued that governments established tax shares and expenditures "as if" they were responding to voluntarily negotiations among individuals. With some modifications these negotiations could produce optimal results.[4]

For example, Lindahl argued that if two asymmetric parties negotiated over a governmental expenditure, they would end up at a variety of optimal and sub-optimal outcomes. This was because "each party naturally tries to shift the equilibrium, within that interval, to its own advantage" (Lindahl [1919] 1967, p. 171). If the two parties had the same bargaining power, however, the outcome would settle in on "the standard position" where one party's marginal valuation of the last dollar spent equaled the other party's marginal valuation of its last dollar spent. In other words, democratic forces, such as negotiations between parties, could lead to optimal results.

Lindahl then suggested that his description was a good approximation of real world processes. He wrote, "This proves that the actually existing graduation of taxation is in a sense the result of the same economic principles which cause the same goods to have the same prices on the free market." For Lindahl, as well as the other Voluntary Exchange Theorists, governments mimicked markets. They could produce roughly optimal outcomes through voluntary exchange (ibid., pp. 173-74).[5]

The Voluntary Exchange Theorists focused their attention on optimal taxation, optimal expenditures, and how these optima could be obtained. They did not focus

---

[3] The notable exception to the idea that tax shares could be associated with marginal benefits was Emil Sax who claimed that individual valuations could *not* be determined for many collective goods. For Sax, the correct allocation was determined by looking at the demand of society as a whole. Musgrave groups Sax in with the other Voluntary Exchange Theorists because Sax makes descriptive claims based on voluntary exchange, not because he uses individual valuation (Sax 1924 [1967]).

[4] The seminal works of Mazzola, Lindahl, Sax, and Wicksell can be found in Musgrave and Peacock (1967). De Viti de Marco's *First Principles of Public Finance* ([1932] 1936) is based on his earlier work "Theoretical Character of Pubic Finance," also in Musgrave and Peacock. Although Musgrave clearly describes Wicksell as a Voluntary Exchange Theorist, his "New Principle of Just Taxation" is arguably more normative than descriptive.

[5] Lindahl further claimed that his assumptions are realistic in Lindahl ([1928] 1967).

on whether individuals would voluntarily contribute to governmental expenditures nor on how unorganized groups might respond to nonexcludable benefits. For this reason these scholars made greater contributions to the theory of public goods then they did to the theory of collective action.

They did, however, produce some passages that were directly related to *Logic*. Most notable was Knut Wicksell. In response to Mazzola's suggestion that taxpayers should distribute resources any way they please, Wicksell wrote:

> If the individual is to spend his money for private and public uses so that his satisfaction is maximized, he will obviously pay nothing whatsoever for public purposes (at least if we disregard fees and similar charges). Whether he pays much or little will affect the scope of public services so slightly, that for all practical purposes he himself will not notice it at all. Of course, if everyone were to do the same, the State would soon cease to function ([1896] 1967, p. 81).

Wicksell explained the free-rider problem using a mechanism latter adopted by Olson for large groups. When individual contributions were too small to be noticed, individuals would have no incentive to contribute their unnoticeable shares.

Olson cites parts of Wicksell's passage and praises him for the insight (Olson 1965, pp. 99-100). In Olson's eyes, however, Wicksell missed some major points. Olson wrote, "Wicksell confined his discussion to the special case of government and did not consider the general problem faced by all economic organizations. Nor did he consider how small a 'public' must be before the theory no longer applies" (Olson 1965, p. 100). Mancur was humbling himself. In addition to applying the theory more broadly and creating a size thesis, Olson developed a more elaborate mechanism to explain free-riding than Wicksell asserted in two paragraphs.

The problem of how to value public goods, which Smith initiated and the Voluntary Exchange Theorists elaborated upon, was making slow progress until Paul Samuelson (1954) showed exactly why the problem was so difficult to solve. His works were so important that many scholars, even today, credit Samuelson with the theory of public goods (Dowding 1997; Downs 1957). Like any great theorist, however, Samuelson's work grew out of others. Henry Sidgwick ([1901] 1969), Eric Lindahl, and Knut Wicksell all distinguished goods that were appropriate for private production from goods that were appropriate for public production, and Richard Musgrave (1939) and Howard Bowen (1943) were making great strides toward establishing the mathematical conditions for optimal production of public goods before Samuelson's work.

None of these theorists made the distinction between private goods and public goods entirely clear, however, but neither did Samuelson -- at least not in his seminal papers (1954, 1955). Samuelson created the public good versus private good terminology, but he based it on "jointness" rather than excludability. Samuelson (1955) defined private consumption goods as those where total consumption equals the sum of each individual's consumption, and public consumption goods as those where every individual consumes the same total. This was the critical distinction needed to derive the optimality conditions, but as Head (1962) pointed out, the indivisibility of a good was not the crucial excludability property that Samuelson sought.[6]

Samuelson's central concern was to derive optimality conditions when individuals consumed both public and private goods. This was similar to the first and second theorems of welfare economics. Discovering these conditions was an enormous contribution to public goods theory and a watershed in valuing goods based on individual utility. It was not, however, a revolution in collective action theory.

Samuelson showed that the Pareto-optimality conditions no longer hold when public goods are present. In the case of two individuals, 1 and 2, and two private goods, the optimality condition are $MRS_1 = MRS_2 = MRT$, where MRS_i is the marginal rate of substitution for individual i and MRT is the marginal rate of transformation. When one of the goods is public, however, the optimality condition changes to $MRS_1 + MRS_2 = MRT$. The new condition has a disastrous effect on the market's ability to allocate goods because markets tend to charge common prices for all consumers, yet these conditions require separate prices for each consumer. Even if producers could adequately price discriminate, consumers would not have an incentive to accurately reveal their demand.

Samuelson noticed that no decentralized pricing system would accomplish this task and voting or signaling systems would fail as well (Samuelson 1954, p. 388; Head 1962, p. 199-200). Self-interested individuals will always have an incentive to give false signals and understate their demand for public goods. In this sense, "the solution 'exists'; the problem is how to 'find' it" (Samuelson 1954, p. 389).

Samuelson had discovered the optimality conditions that Howard Bowen, Richard Musgrave, and the Voluntary Exchange Theorists were working toward. He showed what the optimum would look like, when public goods were present, and created the public good analogue to the fundamental theorems of welfare economics. He did not, however, show how individuals would respond to public goods when they were not behaving optimally. In other words, he did not show whether partial contributions were rational, no contributions were rational, or contributions from only some individuals were rational. Such behavioral equilibria would be developed by later theorists such as Baumol, Downs, and Olson. For this reason the suggestion that Olson popularized Samuelson's work is inaccurate.

If anyone is to be attributed with showing the significance of Samuelson's work, it should be Richard Musgrave, not Mancur Olson. While Bowen and Samuelson were working out the mathematical details of public good production, Musgrave was giving it a broad stroke. He was prodding into the nature of collective goods, arguing against the claims of the Voluntary Exchange Theorists, and trying to piece together the separate tasks of government that were needed for the proper production of public goods.

Musgrave (1959) suggested that the allocation problem should be handled by voting mechanisms that were both demand revealing and capable of selecting

[6] It is important not to confuse "jointness" and "joint products". The former is a good where each unit is indivisible. The latter is a good that produces both private and public benefits.

among Pareto optimal allocations. He considered majority rule, plurality rule, and point voting as contenders then rejected each as failing to accurately reveal demand. Although his book did not fully resolve the allocation problem, it moved the emphasis away from voluntary exchange and toward demand revealing mechanisms. It also put greater emphasis on fairness issues and clarified the importance of Samuelson's work.

With regard to a theory of free-riding Musgrave showed how far he was from the mark. In an article published twenty years earlier, Musgrave wrote that everyone free riding on the provision of a public good should be considered a "pathological case" one which he would assume only for the sake of argument (Musgrave 1939, p. 219, n. 5). Olson later drew the opposite conclusion. He claimed that free riding would be the norm.

2.2.2 Allocating Club Goods

When it seemed as if the valuation problem could not be solved, James Buchanan (1965) and Charles Tiebout (1956) offered a twist that would allow market forces to allocate a particular type of collective good to those who demanded them most.

To obtain such a result, Buchanan and Tiebout focused on club goods that excluded non-members. For example, individuals that did not pay user fees could be excluded from communally shared bathrooms and privately owned pools (Buchanan 1965).[7]

Buchanan's insight was to recognize that a club owner could fix her prices and expect new members to join as long as each member's marginal benefits were at least as great as his marginal costs. This would cause those who valued the good to pay for it and partially solve the allocation problem.

Unfortunately, Buchanan did not solve the problem completely, even for the case of club goods. Club owners could not exclude those whose marginal benefits exceeded marginal costs, nor would they want to. Hence, club goods would not be allocated according to marginal rates of substitution.

Tiebout (1956) offered a means of closing the gap. Tiebout argued that competition among communities producing club goods could determine the right goods to produce at the right price. As long as there were a wide variety of communities providing the same goods, individuals could choose a community that best fulfilled their preferences. If there were enough communities, individuals might receive a club good that roughly matched their marginal rates of substitution. Such an argument could require as many clubs as there were individuals, leaving this argument still as only a partial solution.

Buchanan and Tiebout applied market mechanisms to a sizeable class of collective goods, but they did not describe collective action problems within clubs, nor

---

[7] Buchanan's (1965) seminal work on clubs was published the same year that Olson published *Logic*. Although neither work was based on the other, it is clear that both men exchanged drafts before they published their works (Olson 1965, p. 38 n. 58)

study free riding behavior at any length.[8] Such studies were conducted by different authors with a different focus.

2.3 The Theory of Collective Action before Olson

The collective action problem was first studied by modern philosophers, such as David Hume ([1739-40] 1978, pp. 538-39) and John Stuart Mill ([1848] 1965, pp. 947-69). These authors offered short descriptions of the free-rider problem, but they did not tie their findings back to a general theory of groups. When the topic resurfaced in the twentieth century, some of the first scholars to study it were institutional economists such as John Commons (1934, [1950] 1970) and Selig Perlman (1949). These scholars argued for the importance of collective action in corporations, trade unions, political parties, and society in general. They noted that collective bargaining was more effective than individual bargaining and seemed to go so far as claiming that collectives, such as interest groups, were the ultimate champions of fairness. However, despite the title of Commons' book, *The Economics of Collective Action*, institutional economists did not consider the possibility of free riding nor the factors that would affect group formation. Instead, they merely showed the importance of acting collectively and created frameworks based on successful collective activities.

2.3.1 Free Riding in the Welfare State

William Baumol ([1952] 1969) was among the first economists of the twentieth century to re-visit the free-rider problem.[9] Baumol, like many other economists, wanted to determine the proper role of government in light of "external economies" (ibid., p. 52). He criticized earlier claims that defense, police enforcement, and postal services were within the governmental realm. Although he did not disagree with the conclusion, Baumol argued that previous theorists had not adequately justified this conclusion. Baumol wrote, "since no general yardstick is developed with which one can determine whether some activity is or is not properly within the sphere of governmental operation, one can always wonder whether the exclusion of some items is based on whim or oversight" (ibid., p. 51). Developing such a yardstick was one of Baumol's concerns.Baumol argued that a series of conflicts between individual and collective interests created a significant role for government. To illustrate the point, Baumol described the process of seeding

[8] It is interesting to note that Olson (1962b) chided Buchanan and Tullock for missing the free-rider problem in *The Calculus of Consent*. Although Buchanan was clearly aware of the problem when he wrote his article on clubs, he did not elaborate on the point in *The Calculus of Consent*.

[9] See Sidgwick ([1901] 1969) for a similar, but slightly less thorough, example.

clouds and asked whether farmers who gained from cloud seeding would be willing to pay the costs of seeding them. He wrote:

By contributing, each farmer benefits the others as well as himself, but if he contributes only a small amount he will gain just as much as if he were contributing more. The result is that each farmer may try to keep his payments as low as possible, with the danger that ultimately there will not be enough funds to pay for the process (ibid., p. 130).

His description foreshadowed the descriptions made by Olson. Both saw the problem as a quasi-prisoner dilemma game, where individuals would have no incentive to contribute regardless of the contribution of others.

Baumol believed this problem applied to the collective provision of parks, public health, and national defense (ibid., pp. 130-31). He also noticed that such incentives might be embedded in more traditional market relationships. For example, several labor unions might have a collective interest in keeping wages low during periods of inflation, but they did not have a unilateral incentive to keep the wages of their own union low. Likewise, firms in an oligopoly might desire higher prices from limited supply, but they would not have an incentive to restrict their own supply.

Other problems differed in nature, though Baumol seemed to claim they were the same. In his analysis of two countries imposing tariffs on each other's goods, Baumol described a process that appeared more like the tit-for-tat behavior of an iterated prisoners' dilemma than the dominant incentive to defect in a one-shot game. Baumol wrote, "where a truce is the order of the day, a nation may find it unprofitable to initiate such a chain of events – for in this case the policy of other nations may be to a considerable extent dependent on her own" (ibid., p. 146). Baumol lumped such descriptions into one theoretical box, but clearly described different game theoretic structures.[10]

Baumol had understood the free-rider problem and applied it to a variety of settings. He showed why the problem existed and how it would upset market forces. He did not, however, develop formalisms that could explain the free-rider problem in general contexts and he did not distinguish problems with a dominant incentive to defect from problems with conditional incentives to defect. This limited both the depth and clarity of his ideas.

Moreover, Baumol never completed what he set out to do. He never produced the general yardstick that distinguished activities requiring government intervention from those that did not. Since his theories were couched in a study of government intervention and never tied to established literatures, the greater significance of his insights went almost unnoticed.[11]

---

[10] For another example that differs from his analysis of cloud seeding, see Baumol's ([1952] 1967, p. 147, n. 1) description of currency conversion. This example appears to be more similar to an assurance game yet Baumol claims that the "same" theory applies.

[11] Baumol also claimed that there was a relationship between group size and group success. In his example of farmers attempting to seed rain clouds, Baumol argued that a small group might pool their resources to seed the clouds. A large group should not be ex-

2.3.2 Free Riding in Elections

Anthony Downs developed a much more thorough explanation of free-riding behavior than Baumol, but he applied his explanation in a more narrow context. In *An Economic Theory of Democracy* (1957), Downs described the free-rider problem with blistering clarity:

> [P]rovision of national defense is a boon to every citizen; even if one citizen paid for it solely out of his own pocket, all the others would gain from it. Where citizens are numerous, each man finds it advantageous to refuse to pay for such indivisible benefits. Instead he assumes that other men will bear the cost and he will benefit. . . . This situation means that voluntary action cannot produce a Paretian optimum in a large society when collective goods exist (ibid., p. 170).

Downs attributed this insight to Samuelson (1955), even though the theory of free riding existed before and Samuelson did not discuss it.[12] Using the nonexcludability of election outcomes as his starting point, Downs explained how rational ignorance and rational abstention arise among voters.

With regard to the former, Downs concluded that it is frequently not rational for individuals to obtain enough information to differentiate candidates. The reason they do not seek information is because information is costly (in terms of time; verifying reliability of sources, etc.) and because the probability of affecting the outcome is small (Downs 1957, p. 244). Hence, many individuals would not seek the type of information that will give them clear preferences, and "it may be rational for a man to delegate part or all of his political decision-making to others, no matter how important it is that he make a correct decision" (ibid., p. 233).

Downs applied the same idea to rational abstention. He viewed the decision to vote as an expected value calculation, where the probability of affecting the outcome was so small that the expected benefits from voting would not outweigh the costs. In other words, the rewards from voting were $R = b(p) - c$, where b was the benefit from the outcome, p was the probability of the individual's vote altering the outcome, and c was the cost of voting. With small probabilities, expected benefits would never exceed costs and rational individuals would never vote.[13]

pected to work together because "it is not easy to get the bulk of the inhabitants of an area to contribute a 'fair' share towards such a project, even where some sentimental attachment is involved" (Baumol [1952] 1969, p. 131). This was the extent of his explanation for the failures of large groups. In other words, Baumol asserted a size thesis, but did not explain why it would occur, outside of suggesting that it was somehow related to sentimental attachment.

[12] The concept of a free rider dates back at least as far as John Stuart Mill, James Madison, and David Hume, though none of these authors used this term (see Baumol [1952] 1969; Dougherty 2002).

[13] This conclusion differs from that of Samuelson, Musgrave, and even Buchanan, since all three studied goods that produced optimal output as a function of individual contributions. Output in an election is due to the policies of the winning candidate, not to the total

Although Downs developed his ideas around a prominent public good and created a clear rationale for why this good would not be provided, he did not extend his ideas to other public goods. Social scientists at the time might apply his work to other step-goods, but they could not easily draw conclusions about other types of goods. Step-goods are public goods that produce benefits only when a critical mass of contribution has been reached, such as an election where a voter receives benefits from his favorite candidate winning when the candidate receives a plurality of the vote. Such benefits are not produced when a favorite candidate loses.[14] Other public goods, such as police protection, are incremental in nature, where each unit of contribution produces an additional unit of the public good.

Moreover, after claiming that it is not rational for individuals to vote, Downs attempted to save himself from this conclusion by claiming that rational individuals would be motivated by a desire to support democracy. He wrote, "voting is a necessary prerequisite for democracy; hence democracy is in one sense a reward for voting" (Downs 1957, p. 270). Supporting democracy, however, was a public good with all the same incentive to free-ride. By replacing one public goods problem with another, Downs demonstrated both his understanding and misunderstanding of the problem in the same chapter.[15] Perhaps this is why Downs did not have the final say on collective action theory.

2.4 The Logic of Collective Action

The proceeding summary illustrates the development of public goods and collective action theories before Olson. Bowen, Samuelson, and Musgrave had shown that public goods would be under supplied, Buchanan and Tiebout showed why club goods would be produced more efficiently, and Baumol and Downs developed the free-rider problem. Olson went further. He argued that the nonexcludability of collective benefits would cause wide-spread free riding in a variety of settings. "Just as it was not rational for a particular producer to restrict his output in order that there might be a higher price for the product in his industry, so it would not be rational for him to sacrifice his time and money to support a lobbying organization to obtain government assistance for the industry" (Olson 1965, p. 11). Cartels, unorganized labor, and interest groups were afflicted with the same

number of voters supporting the winning candidate, hence the optimal number of contributors cannot be analyzed the same way.

[14] For more, see Hardin (1982).

[15] Although civic duty could explain voting if Downs defined civic duty as benefits received from the *act* of participating (Riker and Ordeshook 1968), Downs clearly rejects this notion. He states that "the difficulty with such arguments is that they rationalize everything. If it is rational to vote for prestige, why is it not rational to vote to please one's employer or sweetheart? Soon all behavior whatsoever becomes rational because every act is a means to some end the actor values. To avoid this sterile conclusion, we have regarded only actions leading to strictly political or economic ends as rational" (Downs 1957, p. 276).

problem. Not only would they produce sub-optimal amounts of collective goods, as Samuelson and Musgrave had argued, Olson showed the level at which rational actors would contribute.

Olson started with costs and benefits, as did Downs, but he allowed his costs and benefits to vary across all positive quantities of a collective good. Downs focused on costs and benefits that were all or nothing in nature. In addition, since Olson assumed public benefits would increase for each unit of contribution, the probability of altering the outcome was fixed at 1. This reduced the rewards from collective action to $R = B(1) - C$, where B and C are continuous benefits and costs functions, respectively, with various quantities of the public good in the domain.

For Downs the probability of altering the outcome was the cause of universal free riding. Olson went one step and showed that there was a strategic component to the problem. Even when the probability of altering the outcome was certain, Olson could show that some actors would free ride when their benefits from the public good exceeded costs. Generally, everyone would free ride off the actor with the greatest net benefits, even when all (or some) actors benefited in excess of costs.[16] Of course, universal free riding would still occur if costs exceeded individual benefits as Downs had noted. In this sense, Olson took the analysis one step further.[17]

Although the big picture in *Logic* was clear, Olson admitted that the details were somewhat muddied. Based on the fraction of group benefits that individuals obtained, Olson concluded that rational contributions depended upon group size and group symmetries. In large, symmetric groups (such as labor unions) everyone would free ride. In small, asymmetric groups (such as cartels) actors with the greatest net benefits would contribute while others would free ride.

---

[16] At one point Olson refers to the privileged individual and at another point he refers to the privileged group. Contrast his statements on pp. 28-29, which describe the response of a single actor, with his statements on pp. 35-36, which describe the rational response of actors in plural. In honor of Olson, Dougherty (2001, pp. 183-92) attempts to sort out what followed from Olson's framework. Using the initial framework of Olson's cost and benefit analysis, it is rational either for a single actor to contribute or for no actor to contribute -- regardless of group size. Which result holds depends on whether benefits exceed costs for positive quantities of the good, whether the single actor has more benefits than all other actors, and whether actors have sufficient endowments to make such contributions. Actors, in plural, would contribute only when more than one of them gain the same benefits and these same benefits are the largest obtainable benefits for the group. Such results apply to public goods with summation technology and no income effects. They would not apply to public goods with weakest link aggregation, negative income elasticities, some leader-follower behaviors, and other strategic assumptions (Sandler 1992).

[17] Another aspect of Olson's theory which may be considered superior to that of Downs is the use of endogenous factors to explain collective behavior. As Barry ([1970] 1988) pointed out, Downs used the value of supporting democracy (an exogenous motive) to explain individual cooperation. Olson used selective incentives and privileged actors (endogenous factors) to explain individual cooperation. Although Olson's explanations may be inaccurate on occasion, they have the advantage of being consistent with narrow self-interest which both authors assumed.

Since asymmetries in individual benefits might encourage some individuals to contribute while others free rode, Olson also concluded that there was a tendency for smaller actors to exploit larger ones (referred to above as the exploitation hypothesis).

He also made some interesting conjectures about the importance of selective incentives (referred to above as the by-product hypothesis). Olson argued that the benefits obtained from collective goods, such as lobbying efforts, were mere by-products of the selective incentives that encouraged individuals to join in the first place. For example, the American Medical Association (AMA) provided valuable lobbying efforts for doctors within the medical industry, but these benefits were nonexcludable and would not encourage individuals to contribute (1965, pp. 138-41). The reason that individuals joined the AMA, Olson argued, was to obtain private inducements, such as lower malpractice insurance, a copy of their professional journal, and admittance to educational conferences. These benefits only came with membership and they were the true explanation for its success.

Olson made several contributions that his contemporaries had not. In addition to showing the broad implications of free-riding behavior, Olson developed an equilibrium prediction for a large class of collective goods. He created a reasonable series of hypotheses about asymmetric benefits and exploitation that had not been introduced before. Only his free-riding hypothesis, group size thesis,[18] and arguments about selective incentives (which usually arose in the context of government compulsion) appeared before *Logic*. When they had appeared, they were applied more narrowly than Olson applied them and frequently contained weak explanatory mechanisms. For these reasons Olson made a major contribution to collective action theory.

2.5 The State of Group Theory

However, the new parts of Olson's theory were not the sole reason for his success. Part of the reason that *Logic* succeeded was because it applied free-riding behavior to new settings. The Voluntary Exchange Theorists, Samuelson, and Baumol focused their attention on governmental allocation of public resources; the club good theorists concentrated on local clubs; and Downs limited his attention to elections. These works contained major insights, but they did not provide the same type of marginal improvements for their fields that *Logic* provided for organizational behavior, studies of pluralism, and international relations. In other words, the demand for Olson's theory contributed to his success as much as the quality of the ideas he supplied.

[18] For example, Hume ([1739-40] 1970, p. 538) presented a group size thesis but offered almost no explanation for it. Downs' voting formula produces a size thesis since the probability of altering outcomes is affected by group size. Downs did not make this point, however, since p always approximates zero in mass elections.

2.5.1 Organizational Behavior

One of the fields that greatly benefitted from Olson's work was Organizational Behavior. Organizational Behavior focuses on the internal processes of corporations, bureaucracies, and other organized groups. Central to the study is a consideration of information flow and how it affects the efficiency of organizations.

For example, in a classic study, March and Simon (1958) argued that organizations needed internal incentives. They wrote, "Each participant will continue his participation in an organization only so long as the inducements offered him are as great or greater (measured in terms of *his* values and in terms of the alternatives open to him) than the contributions he is asked to make" (ibid., p. 84, emphasis in the original). Employees had no interest in expanding company profits unless they received payments based on profits. Such arguments were based solely on private interests. They were not based on conflicts between individual and collective interests.

Other examples illustrate the point more clearly. Marschak (1955) considered different networks with various combinations of one-way communication, such as mail, two-way communication, such as a telephone, and no communication. He found that the optimal network depended on the cost of information transfer as well as the variation in external information. In Marschak's framework, all individuals gained a common reward, as two teammates would playing bridge. There were no rewards for pursuing unilateral interests. In other words, collective action problems were not allowed.

In his suggestions for further research, Marschak recognized the shortcoming and wrote that separating "the diversity of interests of the individual members" from the interest of "an organization [was] another gap to be filled by a realistic theory" (ibid., p. 137). Olson helped to fill that gap.

2.5.2 Interest Group Politics

Political science was in a worse condition with regard to its understanding of collective action. Political scientists addressed questions that contained non-excludable benefits at the core yet failed to see the free-rider problem that these benefits implied. For example, Arthur Bentley ([1908] 1967) argued that individual motivation could be inferred from group behavior for methodological reasons. Workers in a labor group would want to advance labor interests because they had similar feelings and ideals. This was exactly the opposite of what Olson had claimed. Bentley took this stance, not because he believed it was the most accurate, but because he thought it was a useful simplification.

Bentley emphasized the importance of observable theory -- one in which the causes of human action could be tested (ibid., p. 21). He favored assuming socially minded individuals because it allowed him to map observable social behavior to individual intention. In other words, he ascribed feelings and ideals to social characteristics in order to conduct his research (ibid., pp. 166-72). For Bentley this provided an observable motivation. For Olson this simplification was an empirical error.

Forty years later, David Truman (1951) was making a similar mistake. Drawing from anthropology and social psychology, Truman claimed that individuals were socialized into groups "from infancy onward" (ibid., p. 18). This gave them shared attitudes, which ultimately constituted the interest of a group.

Since individuals always behaved within groups, Truman claimed that there could be no conflict between individual and collective interests. He wrote, "The argument that the individual is ignored in any interpretation of politics as based upon groups seems to assume a differentiation or conflict between 'the individual' and some such collectivity as the group. . . . These distinctions simply do not square with the kind of evidence concerning group affiliations and individual behavior that we presented in the preceding chapter" (ibid., 48). Rather than connecting the two for methodological reasons, Truman believed individual and collective interests were empirically the same.[19]

Logic flew in the face of these arguments. Individual interests could no longer be inferred from group interests, as Bentley had claimed, and individual and group interests could no longer be considered empirically inseparable, as Truman had claimed. The two could conflict and the conflict might be so systematic that individuals would never advance their collective needs.

This created a conundrum for pluralism -- a theory about the interaction of groups. Before Olson, political scientists had always thought that competition among interest groups would identify the most intense interest. Interest groups would compete for the legislative ear and the largest interest groups, or at least the one with the most aggregate individual benefits, would win (Dahl 1956).

Logic changed these interpretations. Olson showed that even though members had common interests, they also had purely unilateral interests that pulled against their common goals. If Olson's postulates about group size were correct, large interests (such as American sugar consumers) might fail to form, while small interests (such as American sugar beet farmers) might succeed. This could explain why American sugar beet farmers were protected in Washington when they were clearly the smaller of the two groups. *Logic* put pluralism on the defense.

2.5.3 International Relations

Similarly, Olson's exploitation hypothesis and Olson and Zeckhauser's (1966) application of it to the NATO alliance, launched a series of studies on burden sharing in international relations. Before Olson's contribution, there was no simple explanation for why alliances repeatedly failed and no reasonable arguments about how to encourage international cooperation.

[19] It should be noted, however, that Truman does not claim that groups have monolithic interests. He argues that many interest groups have federal structures and that subinterests may be more responsive to individual interests than the overall group (1951, pp. 104-6).

Hegemonic Stability Theory developed out of Olson's work. Hegemonic Stability Theory claimed that the largest state (a hegemon) not only carried the brunt of international burdens, but that these states were *necessary* for maintaining world economic order (Kindleberger 1981; Gilpin 1987). In other words, a really big actor committed to world defense, free-trade, or monetary stability was necessary for the provision of these goods. Without a hegemon, the world would become less stable. Although *necessity* was not claimed by Olson, it is clear that his exploitation hypothesis, like his group size hypothesis for pluralism, engendered a new body of research in political science.

2.6 Conclusion

Many of the details of *Logic* are now treated as special cases, while the big picture is seen as affecting a variety of studies in political science and sociology. *Logic* focused on the parts of the public good problem that were relevant to a wide variety of research. Prior to *Logic*, Samuelson and Musgrave had derived the conditions for optimal allocation of pure public goods. Buchanan and Tiebout looked at exclusionary mechanisms that could be used to allocate club goods more efficiently. Baumol and Downs noted that individuals did not have an incentive to contribute to their collective interests. It was Olson, however, who was the first to create a behavioral equilibrium that applied more generally. He noted why some groups failed and offered solutions to their failures.

The reason that Olson's contribution is remembered and his name is associated with public goods is not because he was more careful than his predecessors, nor more original. It was because he applied the collective action problem to areas that had never been exposed to the collective action problem before. Perhaps this explains why his contribution was valued more outside of economics than within it (McLean 2000). Organizational Behavior was not as central to economics as interest groups and international relations were to political science. Hence, Olson's work had a greater affect outside economics than within it.

Olson did not simply popularize an idea that other economists had fully worked out, rather he advanced new parts of the theory into new areas where collective action problems had never been applied before. In addition to being thorough and creating reasonable hypotheses about group size, exploitation, asymmetry, and by-products, applying his works broadly made *Logic* mostly original and fully deserving of its legacy.

3 Warr Neutrality and the Natural Egalitarianism of Voluntary Public Good Provision*

Bryan Jack and Mancur Olson

One of the more intriguing logical discoveries in economics in recent years is the result, due to Peter G. Warr (1983) and foreshadowed and developed by others,[1] of "neutrality"; the finding that "when a single public good is provided at positive levels by private individuals, its provision is unaffected by the distribution of income." A redistribution of income among the set of individuals voluntarily contributing to the provision of a public good leaves each person with exactly the same amount of both the public and the private good as before the redistribution because the beneficiaries of the redistribution increase their expenditures by exactly the same amount by which the losers from the redistribution reduce theirs.

Bergstrom, Blume and Varian (1986) describe Warr's result as "striking" and offer generalizations of it. B. Douglas Bernheim (1986) calls the result "startling" and argues that, even as generalized by Bergstrom, Blume and Varian, it is "only the tip of the iceberg"; maintaining Warr's assumptions, he demonstrates that any public policy of contributions or transfers to a privately provided public good, whether financed by lump-sum or discretionary taxes, has no effect on the amount provided or on resource allocation generally. When rigorous deductions lead to conclusions as puzzling as these, it often turns out that there is more to the story. We shall see in this chapter that this is, indeed, the case here.

When the recent discoveries are properly understood and combined with some older theory, this leads to more general results that are both intuitively and practically satisfying. This chapter will initially compare the testable implications of the neutrality theory with observed reality and then develop a more general conception.

Empirical testing of the theory growing out of Warr's work is trivially easy, since the theory predicts a pattern of behavior that almost certainly could not arise

---

* We are grateful to Peter Coughlin, Dwight Lee, Martin McGuire, and Todd Sandler for helpful comments, and Olson is thankful to the U.S. Agency for International Development for support of his project on Institutional Reform and the Informal Sector (IRIS).

[1] At the time that Warr's paper on neutrality was published, a number of other economists had independently been heading toward this result. Shibata (1971) approached the result in his study of Pareto-efficient provision of public goods. Becker (1974), in his "rotten kid" theorem, demonstrated a type of neutrality in the presence of a redistributive parent. And, Cornes and Sandler had by 1983 discovered a form of the neutrality result in working papers preceding their 1985 article on the analytics of public good provision.

from other causes. This amazing pattern is also most unlikely to pass unnoticed. Yet our survey of the literature did not reveal even one example of the change in the pattern of contributions to a public good that the theory tells us would result from a redistribution of income among the contributors to a public good. No one we have talked to has been able to think of any observation or empirical test that is likely to support the theory. This does not, however, mean that the neutrality literature has no value -- when it is properly combined with other work, we obtain a more general theory that is in full accord with the empirical evidence.

The neutrality theory, especially as extended by Bernheim, also makes startling and testable predictions about whether the governmental provision of public goods will increase the total amount of public goods provided or instead be wholly offset by a reduction in private provision. Warr (1982) appeared to demonstrate that, though the free rider problem implies that private charity leads to a less than Pareto-optimal level of provision, governmental redistribution will simply reduce private giving dollar-for-dollar and will change the level of provision only if it exceeds the level where private charity ceases. Roberts (1984) deduced similar conclusions.

Bergstrom, Blume and Varian's aforementioned analysis, which makes a major advance over the rest of the neutrality literature by emphasizing that the neutrality results hold only if the set of contributors remains unchanged, points out that the Warr and Roberts results apply only if all the taxes are collected from people who are contributors to the public good. Bergstrom, Blume and Varian contend that, in fact, those who privately contribute to the provision of the public good are normally only a subset of the taxpayers, so that the taxes paid by contributing consumers are less than the total tax collections, and governmental provision can then increase the total level of provision of a public good. Bernheim, on the other hand, demonstrates that if there is sufficient overlap among contributors to different public goods, then government provision of a public good adds nothing to the supply even if some taxpayers had not been contributing any of the public good.

Thus the neutrality theory in some formulations implies that the increase since World War II in governmental expenditures on public goods, whether for welfare state or military purposes, has had no effect on the amount of welfare or defense that has been provided! Bernheim is much too prudent to draw this bizarre conclusion. He argues instead that the real implication of the theory is that individuals who contribute to the provision of a public good do not do so simply because they care about the aggregate level of expenditures on that public good -- they must instead contribute to the provision of public goods at least partly for other reasons.

Whatever other reasons Bernheim has in mind must be quite different from the motives that economists normally suppose govern resource allocation. Possibly citizens contribute to the provision of a public good not only to increase their consumption of it, but also because they gain moral satisfaction from making voluntary sacrifices to provide a public good that others also enjoy. They then contribute even more than they would when they are motivated only by their desire for more consumption of the public good. This would make the purely private provision of public goods even larger than the Bernheim-Warr type of analysis implies and the contrast between the theoretical predictions and the observed facts even starker.

A number of writers, such as Bergstrom, Blume, and Varian (1986) and Cornes and Sandler (1986), trace the literature on the private provision of public goods back to Olson's *Logic of Collective Action* (1965). But at least in most cases previous writers do not relate the results growing out of Warr's discovery to the theory in that book and in Olson and Zeckhauser (1966), even though this earlier theory also makes predictions about the sharing of the burden of a voluntarily provided public good. Most notably, the older theory predicts that the voluntary provision of a public good leads to what Olson (1965) called the "exploitation of the great by the small" -- to a sharing of the burden of providing a public good that is dramatically unfavorable to the party with the largest absolute demand for it. Thus, for example, in a defense alliance such as NATO or in a cartel such as OPEC (where a higher price is a collective good to oil exporters) the country with the largest absolute demand for the collective good at issue is predicted to bear a disproportionate share of the burden of obtaining it. There have been many empirical studies of this implication of disproportionality and almost all of them provide at least some support for it (for citations to this literature, see Oneal and Elrod (1989) and Sandler (1992)).

The Warr-neutrality theory and the theory implying disproportional burden sharing seem to contradict each other, but in fact they do not. Both theories use the same behavioral assumptions and they can readily be integrated into a more general theory. When this is done, it is immediately evident why it is so difficult to find real-world examples of the neutrality result. The more general conception of the matter also reveals a remarkable "natural egalitarianism" in the voluntary provision of public goods -- that is, a powerful tendency for this type of provision to reduce inequalities in real income or welfare.

To derive the more general theory and even to obtain a full understanding of the Warr literature, we must consider the *entire range* of possible distributions of resources in a group that can enjoy the voluntary provision of a collective good. Warr considers only redistributions that leave the set of contributors unchanged, and Bergstrom, Blume and Varian show most impressively how crucial this restriction is. But none of the articles on the neutrality result explores what would happen across all possible allocations of the wealth in the group that consumes a public good. In a group of two individuals, for example, one of the two might have (or in a redistribution be given) all of the wealth, or the other might possess (or obtain) all of it, or there could be any one of the infinite set of divisions of endowments between these two polar extremes.

We must also define and compare the "unilateral" and the "full income" quantities of a public good demanded by each of the parties in a group and then compare each of these quantities with the corresponding quantities demanded by each of the others. The unilateral demand for a public good is the amount that a party would purchase in isolation or when no amount of this good is provided by any other party, and it has been analyzed at least since Olson's (1965) account of the "privileged" group. The full-income quantity demanded by a party is the level of provision it demands when its opportunity set is enlarged by the free provision of the public good by one or more of the other parties, and it has also often been analyzed in the literature.

3.1 Basic Model

In considering the quantities of a public good that are demanded by each of the parties it is convenient to start with only two parties. The implications of our analysis for larger groups will be obvious. We also assume, as do Bergstrom, Blume and Varian (1986), that the public good is a normal good, i.e. has an income elasticity of demand greater than zero.

With two parties, i and j, each of which could in the appropriate circumstances demand either a unilateral or full-income quantity, all the logical possibilities can be dealt with quickly:

1. The quantity of a public good demanded unilaterally by i exceeds the full income demand for this public good of j, $U_i > F_j$. In this case, even though j's income has been increased by the free provision of the public good by i and the public good is a normal good, j does not wish to purchase any of the public good. Party j might, if this were possible, like to sell some of the public good and use the income received to purchase more of the private good, but with a public good this is impossible by definition. Thus we have in this case a stable Cournot-Nash equilibrium with disproportional burden sharing -- i is stuck with the full bill.
2. The exact opposite of the above case: $U_j > F_i$. This is also a perfectly possible Cournot-Nash equilibrium and there is again disproportionality in burden sharing, with j instead of i being stuck with the entire burden.
3. Crucially, there is *no possible* two-party Cournot-Nash equilibrium with either party demanding a greater full-income quantity than the other. By the definition of a public good, both parties get the same amount, so if one party were to demand a larger full-income quantity than the other, the other party would then have this larger amount of the public good and then provide none at all, in which case the relevant provision of the first party would be the quantity it would provide unilaterally.
4. Obviously, two (or more) parties cannot, by the definition of unilateral provision, simultaneously provide unequal quantities.
5. There is only one remaining logical possibility: the two parties might have exactly the same full-income standards for the public good, $F_i = F_j$.[2]

[2] If there are three (or more) parties, it is possible for two (or more) of them to have the largest full-income demand, $F_i = F_j$, for the public good, so that each provides some positive amount of it, while one (or more) other party has a lesser full-income demand $F_k < F_i = F_j$, and thus provides nothing.

As we shall soon see, there is normally only a quite restricted set of circumstances in which this condition is satisfied, and that is the reason the neutrality result has apparently not been observed.

Our analysis builds upon an analytical and expository technique developed by Bryan Jack (1990), which can simultaneously explain the neutrality result and the logic of disproportionality in burden sharing with a simple set of diagrams.[3] Jack supposes there are two actors, *i* and *j*, who value a public good, and that the production functions and factor prices of *i* and *j* are the same, so that a unit of the public good has the same cost, at every level of output of the public good, to each of them.

Figure 3.1 depicts an allocation of initial wealth such that *j* will provide none of the public good and will free ride on *i*'s level of provision. If *j* were to provide his isolation output of the collective good, *OA*, this amount would be available to *i*, and *i*'s budget constraint would be shifted out so that he could buy whatever he bought before plus *OA* of the public good. With this budget constraint he would purchase *OC* of the public good, or much more than *OA*. With this level of provision, *j* would provide none, so the pair of contributions (*OC*, *OA*) is not a Nash-Cournot equilibrium.

If *i* were to purchase his isolation output of the public good, *OB*, then this amount would be available to *j*, who would then choose to spend all of his disposable income on private goods and be in equilibrium at point *D*, wishing that it would be possible for him to consume a larger proportion of his income in the form of private goods. The pair of contributions (*OB*, 0) is a Nash-Cournot equilibrium. Obviously, Figure 3.1 can be modified to treat the case of a wealthy *j* and a more modestly endowed *i*, with the same utility functions and Engel curves as before, to show an outcome where *j* provides all the public good and *i* free rides.

If, as we continue to assume, the collective good is never an inferior good, then the full-income demand of a party must exceed its unilateral demand, simply because its full income exceeds its isolation or unilateral-provision income. Thus if one party's unilateral demand for a collective good exceeded the other party's full-income demand, the first party's full-income demand would also exceed the other party's full-income demand. Therefore, we need no further analysis of cases where the unilateral demand for the collective good of one party exceeds the full-

[3] Just as several researchers converged upon the neutrality result in the 1970s and early 1980s, there are several diagrams in the literature, each expressing neutrality in a different context. Shibata (1971, figure 6) uses an asymmetrical diagram, with reaction curves, showing Cournot-Nash equilibria; it can easily be used to illustrate the neutrality result. McGuire (1974, figure 1) offers a diagram to show the impact of adding a second potential public-good contributor to a one-member "group", and the neutrality result can be seen in that diagram as well. Cornes and Sandler (1985) presented a simple diagram, in public-good space, that demonstrates neutrality by means of a sliding X-Y intercept. The important thing is that each of these diagrams has a different intended application from those presented here. The diagrams developed in this chapter are intended to explore neutrality in the spectrum of all possible distributions of a given community endowment.

income demand of the other; these cases involve unsymmetrical burden sharing but do not lead to a neutrality result.

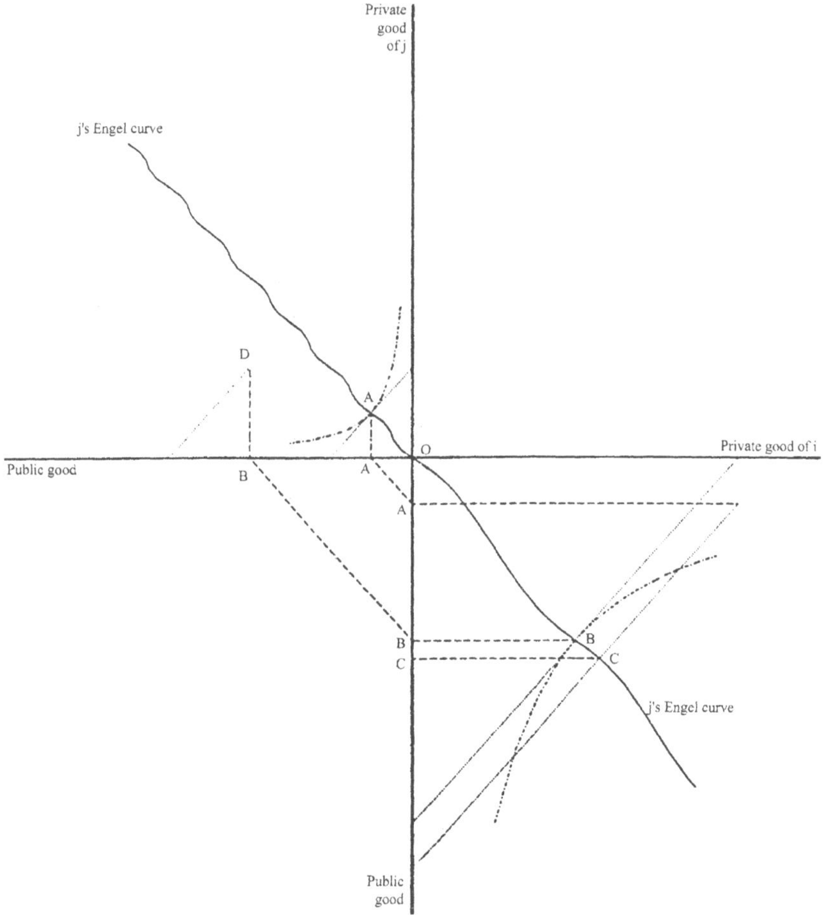

Fig. 3.1. Free riding behavior

3.2 Neutrality

With this exposition, we can explain the neutrality results in the literature growing out of Warr's work in an astonishingly simple and intuitive way. Let us suppose that there are two parties and a fixed endowment of private goods, which may be divided in any manner between the two parties. Let us shift the distribution of the initial endowment in Figure 3.1 in the direction of the free riding party, and shift it to such an extent that the unilateral provision of the provider party no longer exceeds the full-income provision of the other. Indeed, let us shift it just enough to ensure that both *i* and *j* have exactly the same full-income demands for the public good. This leads to the situation we depict in Figure 3.2, which is the same as Figure 3.1 except that, in the northeast quadrant, all possible allocations of the private good of the society are given along the dashed line with a slope of -1; any point on this line (W_i, W_j) will depict the private good wealth of each of the parties. At point *D* in Figure 3.2 the distribution of initial endowments for *i* and *j* is such that it will give both parties precisely equal full-income demands; the point *D* may conveniently be found by arbitrarily starting with the level of public good provision that has both parties providing positive amounts of the public good in equilibrium and then finding the initial endowments of each that are consistent with this double interior-solution equilibrium.

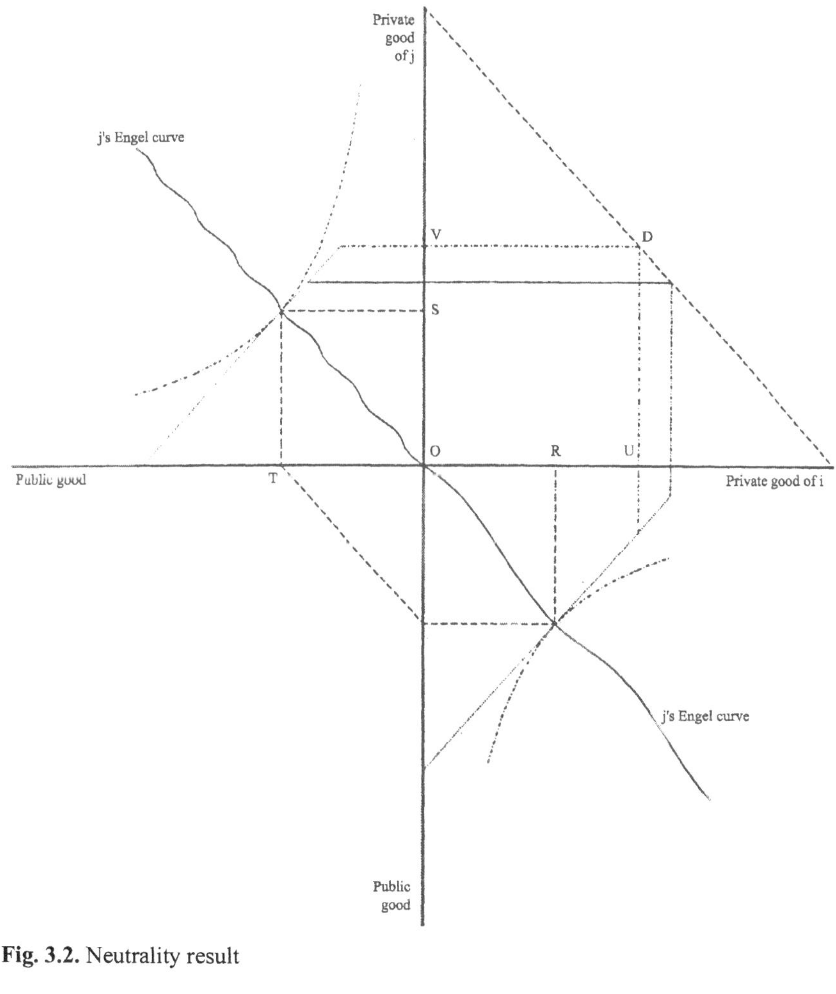

Fig. 3.2. Neutrality result

At the level of public provision depicted, party i consumes OR and party j consumes OS of the private good. Party j spends SV on provision of the collective good and i spends RU on it. These expenditures respectively exhaust the endowment income of each and the budget constraints are drawn to reflect the fact that neither party can possibly consume less of the public good than the amount provided by the other.

The intuitive essence of the Warr result may be seen with striking simplicity by examining the impact, at this distribution of endowment income between the two parties, of a transfer of private goods from one party to the other. Suppose, as shown on the figure, a small transfer of private goods from j to i occurs. The result is that, as j is made "poorer" and i made "richer" by this transfer of the private good, j "exploits" i's public good provision to get a "public good" transfer of exactly identical value, so that there is, in fact, no change in the distribution of income or welfare. Party i becomes "greater" and party j "smaller" just enough to exactly compensate, both in distribution and allocation effects, for a transfer of private good from j to i.

The most important implication of this point is evident only when it is integrated with earlier findings. As we shall see, the voluntary provision of public goods is inherently egalitarian. The familiar result from the neutrality literature arises, in the special cases where it does in fact arise, only because the "egalitarian" or exploit-the-bigger-demander burden sharing logic exactly offsets the impact of a redistribution of the private good. In our example in Figure 3.2, individual j was made "poorer" and individual i "richer" by a small transfer of private goods. But the party made poorer is not even a trifle worse off, since the party made richer increases his provision of the public good by exactly the amount the loser reduced his, and both have precisely the same level of public and private good consumption as before. We shall see that this is just a snowball on the tip of an iceberg of natural egalitarianism.

3.3 Natural Egalitarianism and Neutrality

Exactly when can the result that the Warr literature has made famous occur? It is already clear that both (all) parties must demand exactly the same level of public good provision, but when will this happen? This is shown in Figure 3.3, drawn from Jack (1990), which in the northeast quadrant contains projections of both the Engel curves and the enlarged-opportunity or full-income demands for i and j.

The Engel or endowment-consumption curves are constructed by taking points on the locus of possible distributions of endowments and plotting each member's isolation expenditure on the private good as a function of the other member's endowment. From any given endowment point one can read across to determine i's isolation expenditure levels and read down to determine j's. At the illustrative point (W_i, W_j) shown, the isolation expenditures of each of the respective parties are depicted in the northwest and southeast quadrants.

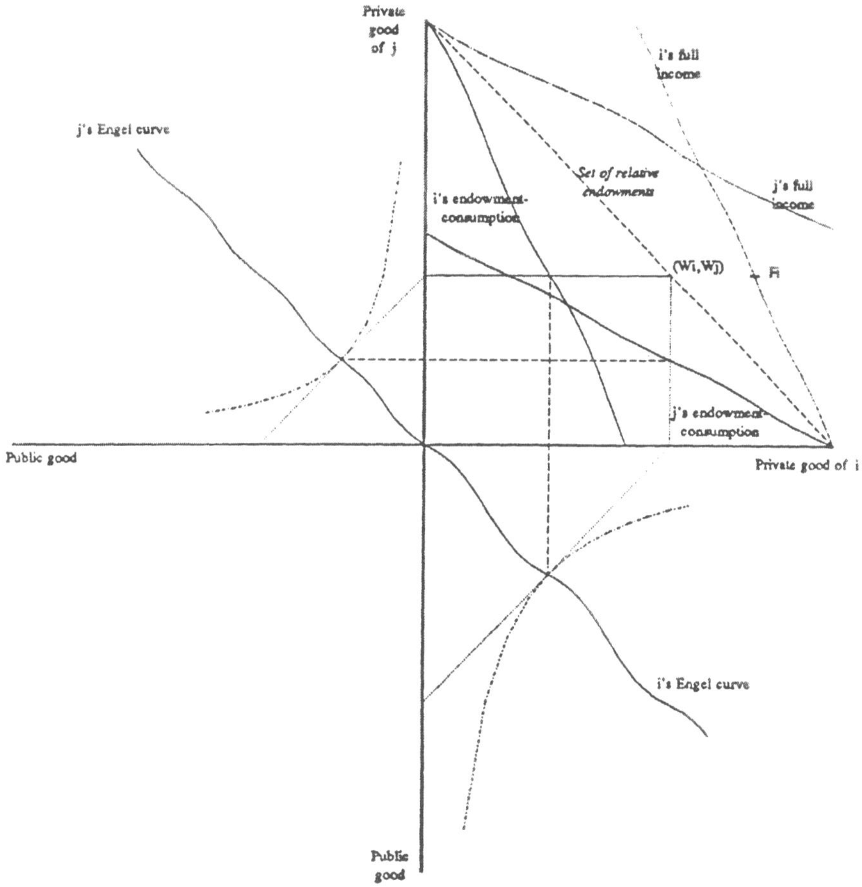

Fig. 3.3. Construction of endowment consumption curves

From the endowment-consumption curves we can also calculate the resource cost of whatever amount of the collective good each party would get at each point because of the other's provision. By going outward from the 45-degree line by this amount we are able to depict the "full income" that each party would have at each distribution of the endowment. To calculate *i*'s full-income curve, we reflect *j*'s endowment-consumption curve in the 45-degree line. The vertical distance from *j*'s endowment-consumption curve to the 45-degree line represents the amount of *j*'s income that it has spent on the public good rather than the private good.

Thus it indicates the portion of *i*'s income that is due to *j*'s provision of the public good. At the endowment point (W_i, W_j) shown, the hypothetical or isolation public good output that *j* is depicted as producing at that endowment point would have given *i* a full income greater than that at (W_i, W_j) by an amount that can be represented as a horizontal distance to the right of (W_i, W_j) equal to the vertical distance between *j*'s endowment-consumption curve to that point, *i.e.* to point F_i.

This point is on *i*'s full-income line, which obviously starts at the point on the 45-degree line where *i* has all the income and *j* thus necessarily produces no public good. Naturally *i*'s full-income curve goes further to the right of the 45-degree line as *j*'s endowment income and hypothetical public good provision increase.

We shall here leave aside certain complexities that have no importance for the issue at hand, such as those that can arise from decreasing or varying marginal costs of producing the public good or preference orderings in which the public good over any range is an inferior good. Thus, in keeping with most of the literature growing out of the Warr result, we assume that all parties have the same constant marginal costs of production of the public good and that there are no discontinuities in production or utility functions. These assumptions entail that the consumption-income and full-income functions are smooth and cross only once.

Since we are considering all possible distributions of endowments for the two individuals, our assumptions also imply that there are an infinite number of possible levels of provision of the collective good. There could be one distribution of income at which *i* unilaterally provided a given quantity of public good and another more or less opposite distribution of income at which *j* unilaterally produced exactly the same quantity of public good. But apart from this there would be, under the assumptions we have made, a different level of public good provision for each distribution of income. At each level of public good provision, whether it is provided unilaterally or with contributions from both parties, there is at least one distinct pair of quantities (one for *i* and one for *j*) of private good consumption. Since we have excluded discontinuities there is an infinite set of these pairs of private good consumption levels as well as this infinite set of levels of provision of the public good.

3.4 Limits to Neutrality

3.4.1 Identical Preferences

We can see how often the type of result analyzed in the neutrality literature comes up by going to Figure 3.4. It will be helpful at this point, especially for our later discussion of natural egalitarianism, to suppose that the two parties have identical preference orderings. This will conveniently rule out the possibility that the party with the lower income would have the larger demand for the public good and make it possible to identify the "richer" party as the one with the larger demand for the public goods.[4]

We begin at the point where *i* has all of the income and then see what happens as we shift the distribution progressively toward *j*. When *i* has all the income his private good consumption is shown at the point where his endowment-consumption or Engel curve intersects the horizontal axis. His spending on the

[4] Figure 3.4 does not, however, depend upon an assumption that parties *i* and *j* have identical preference orderings.

public good is the remainder of the social income and is measured by the horizontal distance to the 45-degree line. This means that *j* gets a large amount of the public good as a free rider. Of course, *j* would like to trade the public good for the private good, but this is impossible by definition for a public good.

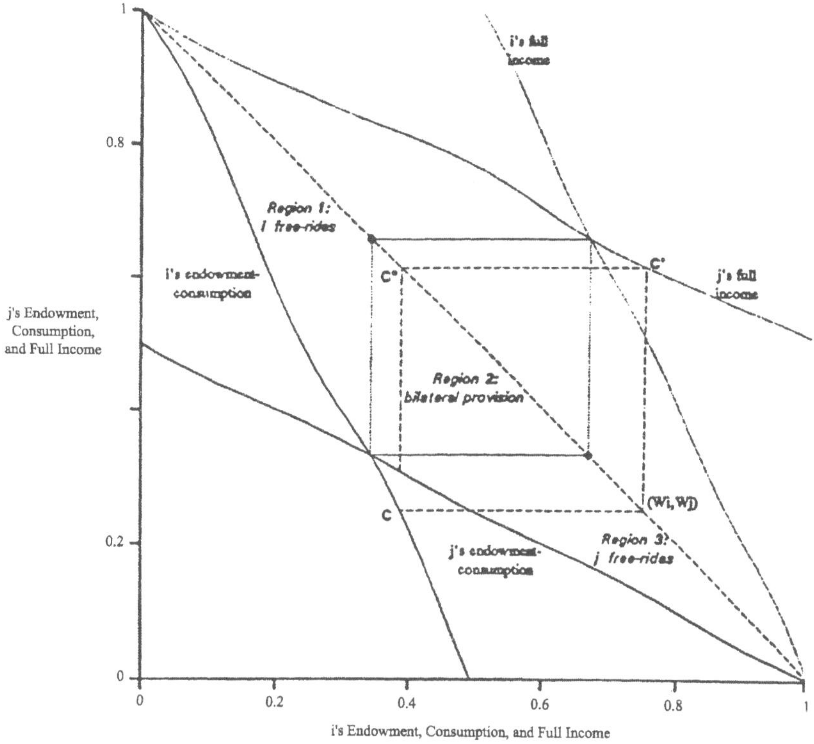

Fig. 3.4. Cournot-Nash public good provision regions

As we move to a less unequal distribution of endowment such as point *C*, then *i*'s free public provision to *j* is decreasing (the horizontal distance to the 45-degree line is shortening), and *j* obviously has more private good. But *j* still does not have an equilibrium amount of the private good, as we can see by considering his full income, which is the amount of private good -- the amount given by the (W_i, W_j) locus corresponding to point *C* -- plus the substantial gift of the public good from *i*, which takes *j* to point *C'* on his full-income curve. As the dotted lines show, at *C'*, *j* is as well off as he would have been had he been at *C''* on the 45-degree line but received no gift of the public good.

How much public good would *j* have purchased at *C''*? We can see from *j*'s endowment-consumption curve that his equilibrium private good consumption would have been at the point on his endowment-consumption curve directly below *C''*. This is an amount that is a little greater than *j* is in fact consuming at allocation *C*. So it follows that *j* is consuming a larger proportion of his income in public goods than he would like to. Thus, to go back to our earlier exposition, the unilateral demand of one party for the public good exceeds the full-income demand of the other and there is no neutrality result.

Now let us shift the distribution of endowment away from *i*, and by just enough to bring him to the point on his endowment-consumption curve where it intersects *j*'s corresponding curve. Here the same procedure as we used at point *C* will take us to a point on *j*'s full-income curve such that, if he had endowment income just equal to this and no gift of a public good, he would have ended up purchasing precisely the amount of private good he is now consuming. So *j* now has an equilibrium supply of the public good. This is the very amount that *i* is demanding, so we have reached a situation in which both happen to demand exactly the same level of provision of the public good.

This is just the point where the natural egalitarianism that, as we shall see, characterizes the whole range of voluntary Nash-Cournot public good provision, takes on a new form. At the point we have just considered, *i* has more of the endowment than *j*; to a casual observer he would be "richer". But the natural egalitarianism ensures that *i* isn't really any richer than *j*; at the point we have just considered *i* pays the whole bill for the public good. And, given our temporary assumption of identical preferences, the two have precisely the same level of real income or utility. The modest difference in endowment income is totally offset by the incentive that the "richer" party has to pick up the entire check for the public good!

Now, let us shift the distribution of endowments in favor of *j* just enough to make him "richer" than *i* by the corresponding amount -- that is, put him at the allocation of endowment such that *i* is right on the margin between joining in providing the public good and being a total free rider. Of course, at this point the exploitation of the great by the small goes in just the other direction; *j*'s additional endowment is totally offset because he now has an incentive to pay the whole bill for the public good, so the two incomes are still exactly equal. The natural egalitarianism is such that, so long as one stays inside the "square" introduced by Jack (1990), any redistribution of endowment will have no effect on real income or welfare; the exactly equal distribution will prevail over the range.

This is, of course, also the Warr result. If we rule out the possibility that the poorer party has the greater taste for the public good, we can restate the Warr result in a way that gives a very different impression. It then comes down to the idea that, in the special circumstance when more than one party is providing the public good, the burden of the costs of the public good will always be such as to reduce any inequality of real income or welfare among the contributors. *If tastes are identical, the Warr result applies only when the distribution of income or welfare is exactly equal.* We shall see later that other manifestations of natural egalitarianism with voluntary public goods are normally much more important than the one that has just been described.

3.4.2 Different Preferences

Let us now drop the assumption of identical tastes and return to the same assumptions that are typical of the rest of the Warr literature so that we can meaningfully ask how often the Warr result applies. Our analysis luckily makes it possible for us to explain why no one has evidently been able so far to find a real-world example of this phenomenon.

Our exploration of the implications of the whole range of possible income distributions between two people has revealed that the Warr result holds at only *one* level of public good provision. It also holds at only one pair of consumption levels for the private good; the endowments change within the square in Figure 3.4, but neither the level of public good provision nor the private good consumption of either party. There is also only one distribution of real income or welfare -- the one that is consistent with the level of public good provision and the pair of private good consumption levels given by the intersection of full income curves or (what is the same thing in this analysis) the intersection of the endowment-consumption curves.

The neutrality result is therefore normally applicable in only a restricted set of circumstances. Of course, different cost and utility functions could make the endowment-consumption and full-income curves intersect more than once, and sometimes also in ways that would give more than one intersection that is a stable equilibrium. But even when this is the case there will be at most only a few levels of public good provision, pairs of private good consumption levels, and real income or welfare levels at which the Warr result will hold.

These results are easily extended to groups with more than two members. The Warr-neutrality result can occur in a group of n members only if there is one level of public good provision and set of private good consumption levels that leaves every member of the group in Nash-Cournot equilibrium. Otherwise, the only Nash-Cournot equilibrium with provision of the public good occurs when the party with the largest absolute demand for the public good is at its unilateral optimum and all the other parties enjoy a free ride. Thus the likelihood that there will be a Warr-neutrality result that applies to all members of a group gets ever smaller as the group gets larger. (As Olson (1965) demonstrated, the group also falls farther and farther from achieving a group optimal level of provision as the number of members increases.)

3.4.3 The Importance of Endowments

There is, however, a limited *range* of *endowments* that is consistent with each level of public good provision and pair of private good consumption levels. The Nash-Cournot private provision of public goods is *never* independent of the distribution of *income* -- that is, it is never independent of the distribution of real or true income or welfare at which the neutrality result holds -- but it can, within a range, be independent of the distribution of *endowments*. Though this range is normally rather narrow, there are certain circumstances when it is wider. Even for a two-member group, modest (and, possibly, ordinary) levels of interest in consuming a public good imply very egalitarian income-distribution conditions for the neutrality result. For example, suppose that the two members have identical tastes in the form of Cobb-Douglas utility functions. If the tastes are such that each party (in isolation) would spend 90% of income on the private good and 10% of income on the public good, then the only distributions of income that produce the neutrality result are those where the poorer party has at least 47.4% of the total endowment. In a more extreme case of preference for public goods, suppose that each party has Cobb-Douglas utility functions giving equal weight to private and public goods. Thus, in isolation, any member of the group would spend 50% of his or her endowment on the private good and the other 50% on the public good. In that case, the neutrality result occurs only if the poorer party has no less than 33.3% of the total endowment.

It is also important to understand that as the population size increases, the already limited likelihood that the Nash-Cournot equilibrium exhibits the neutrality result becomes vanishingly small. Andreoni (1988) has shown, in a simulation of income distributions and charitable contributions, that in large populations the large majority will free-ride. A simple numerical example can demonstrate how any neutrality is extinguished when group membership increases. Let us continue to suppose that every member of an n-member group has identical tastes, amounting to a Cobb-Douglas utility function that gives equal weight to the private and to the public good. This means that no income distribution in which any member has less than $1/(n+1)$ of the total income will produce the neutrality result. If we further assume that all income distributions are equally likely (i.e., that the density function of income for an n-member group distribution is uniformly distributed over the $(n-1)$-dimensional unit simplex of relative income), then the likelihood of neutrality for a group of n members is $[1/n+1]^{(n-1)}$. For $n = 2$ this likelihood is 1/3, but for $n = 3$ it is 1/16, and $n = 4$, it is 1/125.

3.5 Discussion

Natural egalitarianism is, if anything, more striking in the more common cases where the Warr-neutrality result does not occur than it is in those special cases. To understand this natural egalitarianism in all its simplicity, it is useful to abstract once again from differences in preferences. The natural egalitarianism is also normally important when there are differences in tastes, but it can be obscured or on occasion even offset by a tendency for the "exploitation of the zealous by the apathetic." We will analyze this tendency later and so we return now to Figure 3.4 and again consider the entire range of possible distributions of income. It is immediately obvious that when i has all of the income he will bear the entire cost of the public good and that this will reduce the inequality in welfare.

The more important point is that, at all distributions of the endowment except an exactly 50-50 split, the party with the larger endowment will either (in the more common case) reduce inequality by bearing all of the cost of the public good, or (in the less common cases with neutrality) bear whatever share of the cost he needs to bear to ensure that the distribution of true income becomes perfectly equal. In any society (unless it already has perfect equality in endowments) the Nash-Cournot private provision of public goods is always inequality reducing; it either reduces the degree of inequality or else generates an exact equality of welfare out of an inequality of endowments. It will also partly or (in the less common case where there is continuing neutrality) totally countervail any inequality-increasing redistributions of the endowment. The "winner" in any redistribution of sufficient size is also the total loser who gets stuck with the whole cost of the public good.

Under our assumption that the public good is a normal good, moreover, *the level of voluntary provision of the public good will be greater the more extreme the inequality of wealth.* The provision will be *lowest* when *both* contribute. If we drop the assumption that there are only two contributors, we get the paradoxical result that *the greater the number of Nash-Cournot voluntary contributors, the lower the supply of the public good.* The greater provision of public goods when there is greater inequality will also prove to be an important point in our later analysis of an ideology that was common in "feudal" times and is by no means absent today. This consideration also makes it obvious that the greater the inequality, the greater the resource cost of an inequality-reducing gift of the public good to the poorer party.[5] Thus the natural egalitarianism of public good provision is in some sense stronger the greater the degree of inequality.

The situation is usually the same when there are differences in preferences, but the natural egalitarianism is complicated or occasionally even offset by a neglected tendency for the exploitation of the zealous by the apathetic. Suppose that the parties have identical initial endowments of private wealth but differ in their preferences for the public good. Then the party with the strongest preference for the collective good will necessarily bear a disproportionate share -- and often all -- of the costs of providing it. The greater the difference in tastes for the public good, the larger the amount that will be provided. This logic helps explain the importance of fanaticism for collective action.

Nonetheless, so long as collective goods have a positive income elasticity of demand, the natural egalitarianism of voluntary public goods provision will tend to apply, and it will necessarily apply in any situations where the differences in wealth are great enough for the richest party to have the largest absolute demand for the public good. In any such situation, the richest party will necessarily bear a disproportionate share -- and often all -- of the cost of providing the collective good.

We have now been able to see why the Warr neutrality result has rightly been described in the literature as "startling" and "striking", and also why no empirical illustrations of it have been recounted in the literature. We have also now been

[5] We cannot analyze the value of the public good gift in terms of the poorer party's willingness to pay, for he is not willing to pay anything for additional amounts of the public good. When his income is very low, even his willingness to pay for private goods is constrained by his poverty.

able to see the sweeping character of the natural egalitarianism in voluntary burden sharing with public goods. Natural egalitarianism applies not only to the situations where the party with the largest absolute demand for the collective good bears all of the costs, but even in the special cases where the Warr neutrality result holds.

The foregoing analysis also bears on a number of historic and contemporary debates about public policy. In prior centuries it was often argued, as it is on some occasions even today, that arrangements that generate huge fortunes are desirable, not simply on grounds of incentives, but also on the grounds that the super-rich will voluntarily provide public goods for the society, such as philanthropy, patronage of artists, and so on. Aarts and Lieshout (1986) have, for example, made this point. In some earlier times, the richest sometimes also financed the police power needed to maintain order.[6]

Quite apart from the obvious distributional objections to such arrangements, they are not efficient, since Nash-Cournot voluntary provision undoubtedly does not supply Pareto-optimal quantities of public goods, even when inequalities are so great that there is some voluntary provision. It is nonetheless true, as this chapter has shown, that the level of public goods provision does increase with the degree of inequality.

Another policy implication of the argument here has a more contemporary ring. The theoretical demonstrations in the literature cited earlier in this chapter, to the effect that the governmental provision of public goods will offset private contributions dollar for dollar, are almost certainly not relevant to the world we live in -- they assume, as a starting point, the conditions needed for Warr's neutrality result. Both empirical observation and the theoretical argument offered in this chapter indicate that this result, if it occurs at all, is applicable only in rare cases. Thus many of the conclusions about public expenditures and private charity that are offered in the neutrality literature normally have no pertinence for the real world. Most notably, there is no warrant whatever for the conclusion that the high levels of public expenditure on welfare and defense in the present century have not brought about any net increase in aid to low income people or in military expenditures. Neither is it reasonable to conclude, as Bernheim (1986) does, that the implausibility of the predictions of his model is a sign that individuals do not have normal economic motivation with respect to public goods; the predictions are, instead, implausible because they take the conditions for Warr's neutrality result, which rarely if ever hold true for any country, as a starting point. A proper understanding of the issues raised in the Warr literature does not in any way call into question the familiar idea that *laissez faire* will lead to the severe under-provision of public goods, and that government provision can increase the supply, even if there are at the same time private contributions to the provision of these public goods.

[6] Once the richest person buys the coercive power needed to maintain order, he also has an incentive to tax the rest of the population for his own benefit. Historically, this has been a common occurrence.

4 Collective Silence and Individual Voice: The Logic of Information Games

Edward A. Parson, Richard J. Zeckhauser, and Cary Coglianese

In its original formulation, the Prisoners' Dilemma concerned the decision whether or not to reveal information: two prisoners being interrogated separately had to decide whether or not to confess to a crime they had both committed. Subsequently, virtually all study of the Prisoners' Dilemma game (and of related formalizations of collective-action problems) has examined two other classes of decision-making, unrelated to decisions to reveal or conceal information.[1] These games have been used to study strategic decisions by parties in conflict, such as price-cutting by competing firms, arms build-ups or military attacks by antagonistic nations, or negative campaigns by candidates for political office; and decisions to undertake costly individual action in support of collective welfare, such as decisions to reduce pollution, restrain exploitation of common resources, or contribute to military alliances.

Olson's primary contribution to these studies was to demonstrate that the strong propensity for voluntary efforts to lead to under-provision of conventional public goods such as open space and clean air also applied to the organization of groups to pursue their political objectives. Thus, despite their strong economic concerns with government policy, neither repairers of automobiles nor consumers of food have found the way to organize themselves to be strongly represented in Washington, DC. Olson also identified two major mechanisms to resolve the problem of under-provision. The first was to bundle the public good with a private good provided to contributors. The American Medical Association used this mechanism effectively for many years. Members supported the organization's political activities through their dues, but also gained professional status and a referral network (Olson 1965). The second mechanism was disproportionate provision: those who value the public good the most – in simple formulations, the largest actors – provide the lion's share of it (Olson and Zeckhauser 1966). Examples are the disproportionate spending by the largest corporations to secure influence over public policy through campaign contributions, and the vast military expenditures of the United States (exceeding those of the next six nations combined), which as the sole superpower acts as policeman of the world (U.S. Department of State 1998).

This work on under-provision and the means to cope with it has focused overwhelmingly on the provision of material resources. Often, however, as in the original story of the Prisoners' Dilemma, the critical issue for a group is whether

[1] One exception is Scheppele (1988).

its members reveal or conceal information. This chapter focuses on these situations, which we call "information games". In an information game, there are a number of players – whom we will call "peers" – in similar roles. The peers may be industrial polluters, parties to a crime, faculty members in a department, or partners at a private firm such as Arthur Andersen. Each has private information relevant to some decision to be made, and each must decide whether to reveal or conceal it. Revelation may be to their peers, to a player or players on the opposite side of the table, or to the world at large.

Our purpose in this chapter is to introduce the concept of information games, to identify how they resemble and how they differ from other forms of collective-action games, to undertake a preliminary investigation of their major types, characteristics, and predicted outcomes. While games of information revelation can be as diverse in their payoff structures as any other kind of games, many prominent information games are filled with issues of mixed motives and tensions between individual and collective interest – problems of the kind that intrigued Olson. The constructs of these games can describe a wide range of settings, from unsavory nations cooperating with U.S. intelligence in the fight on terrorism to fairy-tale children noting the nakedness of the Emperor.

Among information games whose payoff structures resemble traditional collective-action problems, we distinguish two broad classes. In the first, the collective interest of the peer-group is to maintain silence; in the second, it is to promote individual voice. For each type, we identify broad regularities in the pattern of interests and resultant behavior that we expect, and identify numerous real-world examples. Part 1 places information games in the context of the general literature on collective-action problems, in particular the games of Prisoners' Dilemma, Assurance, and Chicken. Parts 2 and 3 discuss the two broad types of information games we highlight, those in which collective silence and individuals speaking up, respectively, provide a collective benefit for the group. Part 4 summarizes the principal characteristics of information games, and identifies directions for elaborating the concept further. Table 4.1 provides a schematic preview of what follows, presenting the main features of our argument in summary form.

4.1 Prisoners' Dilemma and Assurance Games as Information Games

We treat peers' decisions to reveal or withhold information as binary choices: reveal honestly and completely, or not at all. This allows the information game to be defined simply in terms of peers' payoffs from whose information is and is not revealed. This approach abstracts from a great deal of complexity in the character of information that actors hold and might choose to reveal, and in how others may interpret information that is revealed. With this simplification, we need not describe the character of each agent's information in detail. Similarly, we need not concern ourselves with whether the information that actors reveal is accurate or biased, steering clear of the vast literature on honest revelation in various contexts. Nor do

Table 4.1. Information games vs. traditional collective-action games: principal features

		Information games where the collective good is:	
	Standard public good provision	Silence	Voice
Status Quo	Past level of provision	Silence (full cooperation)	Silence (zero cooperation)
Principal cost of cooperation	Direct	Indirect	Indirect
Principal source of indirect cost	N/A	Actions by outsider	Actions by outsider; group norms of conformity or obedience
Costs to cooperate, as function of level of cooperation	Constant	Rising if first few talkers are bribed; falling if last few silent holdouts are punished	Falling
Collective costs of defection, as function of level of defection	Significant throughout (shape depends on +/- returns to public good)	Falls sharply after first few defections	Exhibits critical level (S-shaped)

we consider the possibility that actors will engage in signposting, the partial or selective revelation of accurate information (Zeckhauser and Marks 1996).

As we will relate the payoff structures of the information games we discuss to the well-known collective-action structures of Prisoners' Dilemma, Assurance, and Chicken, we briefly summarize those here, in both their two-player and multi-player forms. In the two-person Prisoners' Dilemma game, both players have a strictly dominant strategy that yields a jointly inferior outcome. Each has an individual interest in "defecting" (confessing to the crime), whether the other is defecting or cooperating (where "cooperating" means with the other prisoner, i.e., not confessing). But the outcome when both defect is worse for both than the outcome when both cooperate, if they could only bind themselves to that outcome. Payoffs in the two-person case are shown in Table 4.2, with higher numbers denoting more preferred outcomes and the equilibrium outcome shown in bold.

Table 4.2. The Two-Player Prisoners' Dilemma

		Player 2	
		Cooperate	Defect
Player 1	Cooperate	(3, 3)	(1, 4)
	Defect	(4, 1)	**(2, 2)**

Schelling developed an elegant graphical representation of collective-action problems with multiple actors, which allows us to illustrate the N-person generalization of the Prisoners' Dilemma as in Figure 4.1 (Schelling 1978). In this representation, the vertical axis shows players' payoffs as a function of their own choice and the aggregated choices of all others. The horizontal axis shows the total number of other players (other than the one whose payoffs are being represented) making the cooperative choice, while the two sloping lines show the payoff to a player who cooperates, and to one who defects, as a function of the number of others cooperating.

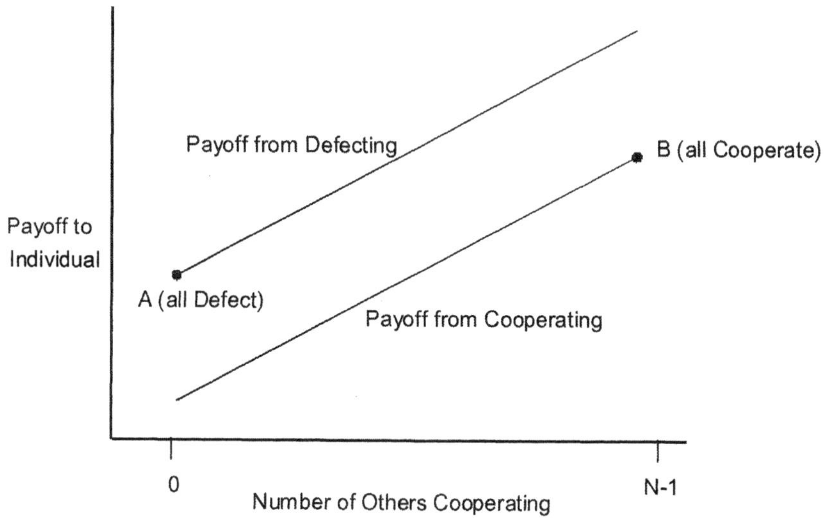

Fig. 4.1. N-Person Prisoners' Dilemma

Table 4.3. Two-Person Assurance Game

		Player 2	
		Cooperate	Defect
Player 1	Cooperate	**(4, 4)**	(1, 3)
	Defect	(3, 1)	**(2, 2)**

As in the two-person case, every player prefers maximal cooperation by others, but for any given level of cooperation by others each one would rather defect than cooperate. The situation might be a group of firms deciding whether to collude on a price increase. Each prefers that the others raise prices, but each prefers not to raise his own price whether the others raise theirs or not. The standard prediction in both the two and N-person cases is that all players will defect – they will reach the lower-right cell of the two-person matrix and point A on the N-person diagram – even though all would rather be at the point of unanimous cooperation, the upper-left cell of the matrix or point B on the N-person diagram. Absent some way to bind themselves, bind each other, or change their payoffs (e.g., lowering the payoff for defecting or increasing that for cooperating), players cannot reach these preferred joint outcomes.

The game of Assurance makes one crucial modification to the Prisoners' Dilemma payoffs. Each player still prefers to defect if the other defects, but now prefers to cooperate if the other cooperates. The game consequently has two equilibrium outcomes, one in which both players cooperate and one in which both defect, and both strictly prefer the equilibrium in which they both cooperate. The generalization to N players makes each player prefer to cooperate if enough others do so. The payoffs for Assurance with 2 and N players are shown in Table 4.3 and Figure 4.2 below.

The game of Chicken modifies the Prisoners' Dilemma structure in a manner opposite to that of Assurance, as shown for the two-person case in Table 4.4 and the N-person case in Figure 4.3. In this game, each player prefers to cooperate if and only if the other defects, because defection by both is the worst possible outcome (e.g., cars crashing head-on at high speed because neither player would turn off first, as in the test of nerve for which the term "playing chicken" was invented). With N players, each prefers to Cooperate if and only if few others are doing so, yielding equilibrium C in which some fraction of players cooperate. (Since this formulation does not distinguish among individual players, however, it says nothing about who cooperates at equilibrium.)

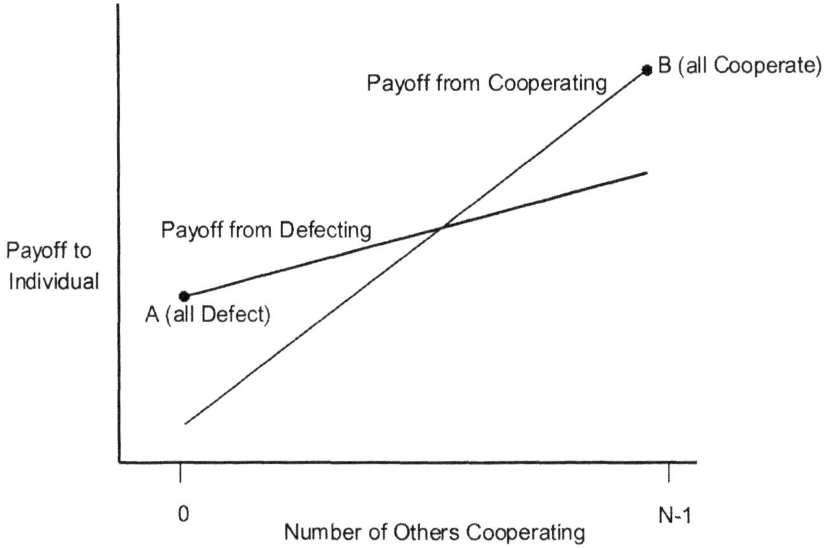

Fig. 4.2. N-Person Assurance

In Assurance, both the lower-right and upper-left cells (points A and B in the figure) are equilibria. The preferred equilibrium (the upper-left cell in the table, point B in the figure) gives the best outcome to both players and neither has an incentive to deviate from it. But can the players reach it? This depends on how agents are able to communicate and coordinate their choices; their expectations of how others will think and act; and their willingness to risk bad outcomes. A player who has strong enough doubts about others' cooperation, or who cannot endure any risk of reaching the worst outcome (cooperating when others defect) may rationally choose to defect. An example might be two merchants in a run-down district deciding whether to relocate. If both move, both are better off, but if only one moves the new district does not get established and the mover suffers.[2]

The information games we discuss have important points in common with the problems of providing public goods through costly efforts that were studied so insightfully by Olson. In both, individual rational choice runs counter to the achievement of collective gains. Information games also have significant differences from standard situations of voluntary provision of public goods. In the standard setting, the tension between private and public interests arises because pro-

[2] The firm that stays behind will gain a larger share of a smaller total volume of business, so the net effect might be a gain or a loss, or perhaps a short-term gain followed by a longer-term loss. Our payoffs show the total effect as a gain, but the game remains one of Assurance in either case, since this does not affect either firm's preferred choice given the other's choice.

viding the public good or taking action for the common welfare is intrinsically costly. In information games, this tension arises not from the direct cost of either revealing or concealing information, which is usually very small. Rather, it arises indirectly, from the actions that others (members of the peer group or outsiders) are expected to take based on the information revealed. Any player's payoff from revelation of information by any specified set of peers (possibly including herself) reflects her expectations of who will do what based on the information revealed. We take these payoffs to subsume her knowledge of other actors' information, as well as the confidence with which other actors will view it, and the ease with which it can be verified, since these all contribute to her expectations of how others will act in response. Her payoff also reflects some expectation of how her own choices will change in response to the information revealed and others' responses to that information.

Table 4.4. Two-Person Chicken Game

		Player 2	
		Cooperate	Defect
Player 1	Cooperate	(3, 3)	**(4, 2)**
	Defect	**(2, 4)**	(1, 1)

As a class, information games are sufficiently rich that they may violate three simplifying assumptions that are essential to Schelling's compact representation of multi-party interactions shown in Figures 4.1 to 4.3. That representation assumes that all players are identical, so only the total number of players making a particular choice matters, not their identity; that the order in which players make their choices does not matter; and that the marginal effects of additional players making a particular choice are constant (i.e., the payoff curves are linear). As discussed below, any of these assumptions may be too restrictive.

Situations illustrating the collective-good aspects of information games are numerous, and the associated payoffs can vary greatly. We consider two broad types of information games. In the first, maintaining silence is a collective good for the peers. In the second, individuals provide a collective benefit to their peers by revealing information they hold – or alternatively, by securing information and then revealing it. In both cases, we assume that silence is the status quo, so advancing group welfare requires maintaining the status quo in the first case, and breaking it in the second. It is also possible in either case that what benefits the peer group may harm outsiders, as when captives facing a Prisoners' Dilemma do not confess.

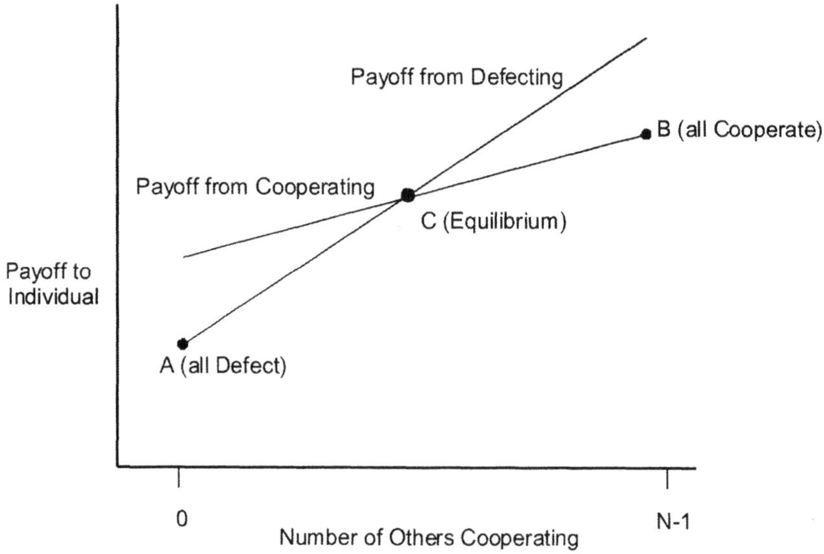

Fig. 4.3. N-Person Chicken Game

4.2 When Silence is a Collective Good

In many situations silence can be a collective good for the peer group. Perhaps information that is revealed can be used against the group by an outside authority or adversary with interests opposed to those of the group. For example, such information might concern past or present wrongdoing by some or all members of the group. Individual members of the group may have various reasons for wanting to reveal their information, but doing so is likely to harm the other members of the group. This is the problem faced by individuals involved in a conspiracy deciding whether to turn states' evidence in criminal prosecutions, and by firms deciding whether to reveal potential environmental or health risks that are not yet known to regulators or the public.

Similarly, supporters of a group engaged in a conflict must decide whether or not to reveal errors or wrongs of their group that might jeopardize its support. Supporters of the U.S. Democratic Party faced such a choice in deciding whether to censure President Clinton's personal misconduct. The need to stand with the President, the Party, or the nation in a time of conflict can be a powerful tool to suppress both internal criticism and external revelation of wrongdoing. As Lyndon Johnson once put it, "I'm the only President you've got." Individuals' information can also give an outside adversary an advantage in future dealings with the group, even if there was no past misconduct. For example, regulators can use information about individual firms' technological capabilities to tighten requirements on the industry, while procurement authorities or other major customers can use information about firms' costs to bargain harder on future contracts.

The collective benefit of silence can also arise from the way revelation affects members of the peer-group themselves, either through their actions if the information is revealed, or through changes in their shared ideology, self-image, behavioral norms, or trust relations. One such group of situations, commonly known as "opening a can of worms", concerns controlling the agenda for contentious group decision-making. If a group has settled, or provisionally settled, some controversial issue – frequently involving the distribution of benefits or burdens – many individuals or sub-groups might wish they had gained more favorable treatment. But reopening the issue would pose the risk of extended conflict or deadlock as many individuals and sub-groups try to claim more favorable outcomes for themselves, sacrificing the often substantial collective benefits that accrue to the group from having an agreement – any agreement – in place. Prominent examples include any comprehensive constitutional negotiations, such as proposals to amend the Charter of the United Nations. Re-opening the Charter to pursue even a single high-priority change, such as adding new permanent members to the Security Council to reflect postwar shifts in national importance, would risk an extended deadlock as all parties try to add the rule changes that they want to the agenda.

Individuals' revelation of information can also cause group harm directly, by harming group-level assets such as reputation, self-image, or trust, important components of the group's social capital. This case is close in spirit to those in which the harms follow from the response by authorities or other outside actors, but differs from them in the mechanism through which the group harm occurs. Individual revelation can cause such harms by exposing hypocrisy and undercutting widely endorsed (but violated) principles that provide the social glue needed to restrain the much more extreme violations that would occur if the principles were publicly discredited.

These "silence is golden" situations can have a diverse range of payoff structures. Indeed, they may not always represent collective-action problems at all. If there are no conditions under which any individual's interest in revealing his information outweighs his share of the collective harm from breaking silence, then there is no conflict between individual and collective interests and we would expect peer groups to maintain silence.

When individuals do derive larger benefits from revealing, these are likely to arise in two distinct ways. In the first case, most of the group damage is done by the first few revelations. Additional revelations cost the group little, but can substantially benefit the individuals who make them if it is costly or dangerous to be in a small minority of non-revealers. If all but a few conspirators or parties to a shameful secret are confessing, those few will face much more pain than those who are confessing, whether from prosecutorial pressure or moral censure. In this case the information-revelation game is a game of Assurance, in which all individuals prefer collective silence, but prefer to speak if more than some critical number of others has broken their silence.

In the second case, a single revealer or small group may be able to draw some reward that is depleted if larger numbers speak. Such a reward may be offered by an outside adversary, such as a prosecutor or regulatory authority seeking to promote revelation. Alternatively, an individual who threatens to reveal might be able to exact a reward from the rest of the peer group as the price of his silence. This will be especially significant when the value of unanimity is large, either because even a single revelation greatly harms the group in its dealings with an outside adversary, or because some group norms or decision rules mean that any voicing of dissent or complaint greatly impairs the group's ability to function. These situations can all be formalized in terms of the power of various sub-coalitions of the whole peer group. When a single defector can greatly harm the group or greatly benefit an outside adversary, the remaining coalition of (N-1) players may be too weak to prevent such exploitation – particularly when many individuals are in the position to make such demands. In these cases the information-revelation game can be a game of Chicken, in which individuals prefer to reveal their information (or equivalently, demand a reward for not doing so) if few others are doing the same. Further revelations may bring additional harm to the group but, critically, offer no benefit to individuals to tempt them to reveal.

In the Assurance and Chicken payoff structures, individuals prefer to reveal under specific conditions of others revealing. In Assurance, they prefer to reveal when many others are doing so. In Chicken, they prefer to reveal when few or none are doing so. A Prisoners' Dilemma structure – where each individual strictly prefers to reveal regardless of how many (or few) others are doing so – could occur if processes similar to both the Assurance and Chicken cases were in operation: sole or minority revealers gain large rewards, and minority non-revealers suffer censure or punishment. The combination of these conditions, and consequently the Prisoners' Dilemma structure, may be relatively uncommon in real-world information games despite the Prisoners' Dilemma being the best known model of collective-action problems.

Several factors will determine which of these payoff structures apply in realistic situations. First, when the peer-group's payoffs are determined by its interaction with an outside actor, this actor's ability and willingness to manipulate payoffs to individual group members will be crucial. Second, the symmetry or asymmetry of individuals' payoffs from revelation will also be crucial: Do all oppose revelation to an equal degree, or do some care less, not care at all, or actively prefer to reveal? Such asymmetries may be intrinsic to the interests of differently situated individuals, or they may arise from the order in which individuals reveal. When an outside actor has some ability to manipulate individual payoffs he may seek to augment such asymmetries, focusing inducements on those who are most inclined to reveal. Expected outcomes may also be significantly influenced by peers' knowledge – and uncertainty – about others' payoffs, and by any history of similar interactions among these peers in the past, which will contribute to the shared sense of the status quo for the interaction in question. The following sections consider how these factors can interact to determine the peers' payoff structure.

4.2.1 External Manipulation of Individual Payoffs

When the group's collective interest in silence arises as a consequence of its adversarial interaction with an outside actor, that outside actor can frequently tailor its response to individuals who reveal information. For example, prosecutors routinely grant immunity from criminal prosecution, or at least reduced sentences, to those who turn states' evidence. They may even provide elaborate protection for witnesses who fear reprisals from their peers. Similarly, a regulatory agency has discretion over the details of regulatory requirements, and can frequently craft or enforce these requirements so as to vary the burden imposed on particular industries or firms. Discretion in such regulatory matters, like prosecutorial discretion, can be used to reward players that come forward with information.

If the outside authority is able to tailor its response, it should be most willing to do so when its marginal benefit from different individuals' revealing is not constant. Sometimes one peer's information will serve as a close substitute for any other person's information. For example, any party to a crime may be able to provide the same testimony or identify the same evidence, while firms in the same business, using the same technology, are likely to have fairly similar information about risks, costs, and potential alternatives. In the extreme, a single revelation might give the outsider all it needs to prevail against the group. In these cases, if allowed, the outsider would reward one party or a few for speaking but not offer similar terms to others even if they did reveal. If, on the other hand, the strength of the outsider's case or its ability to craft an appropriate response increases with further revelations, or depends on the specific identity of who reveals, we would expect the outsider's disbursements of benefits to adjust accordingly. In any case, since what the outsider is offering is a limitation or modification of its pursuit of its own goals, these benefits can be offered to at most a few individuals. No prosecutor offers immunity to all conspirators in return for their confessions, since the purpose of eliciting confessions is to use them to convict other, more important conspirators. If the peer group has some ability to distribute benefits internally, it may attempt to do so to prevent initial defections, particularly when the cost of the first breach of unanimous silence is high.

More complex situations arise when there are multiple outsiders, who are not unified or indeed necessarily opponents of the group. They may even be unaware of when information is revealed. Consider two high-tech firms seeking to protect their products. Each amply rewards its employees for technological breakthroughs. This creates a situation where secret-tellers from rival organizations have an incentive to collude, promoting their careers at the expense of their organizations. Thus, two engineers from high-tech competitors may help each other with their company-specific technical problems, but in the process some proprietary information is spilled, possibly even to the general marketplace (Schrader 1991). It has even been alleged that members of national intelligence organizations sometimes trade secrets, so each looks like he is bringing home good information (Epstein 1989).

4.2.2 Asymmetries among Peers

Although we have stipulated that the players in an information game are peers, their payoffs from silence and revelation need not be identical. It is easiest to maintain silence under complete symmetry of interests, but such symmetry is uncommon in reality. Even when peers' payoffs are the same, the group's efforts to maintain silence will depend on what peers know and guess about each other's payoffs. Efforts to maintain silence may be thwarted if peers are sufficiently uncertain about each other's payoffs. For example, if the peers' true payoffs are all those of an Assurance game (Figure 4.2), then all prefer to maintain silence if enough others do. But if some or all peers are not confident about others' payoffs and think that others may strictly prefer to reveal, they may seek to avoid the risk of loss from being one of few non-revealers by revealing preemptively. Carrying the analysis one level deeper, they also have to be concerned about their peers' confidence about their payoff structure, and so on ad infinitum.

More frequently, peers' interests will truly be asymmetric. All conspirators may be implicated in a past crime, but to different degrees. A group of firms may all employ the same environmentally harmful technology, but may differ in size or in the fraction of their business that depends on the technology, or have disparate opportunities to replace it with alternatives. The firm that can reduce pollution at lowest cost may prefer to reveal information that will promote regulation, expecting to gain a competitive advantage. In the extreme, the asymmetry of benefits from silence may be so strong that some peers strictly prefer to reveal, because their individual benefit exceeds their share of the group harm. This may have been the case, for example, when the smallest and most financially precarious U.S. tobacco company, the Liggett Group, reached a deal with state Attorneys-General in 1997 to release long-secret studies on the health harms and addictiveness of cigarettes (New York Times 1997).[3]

Similarly, in the 1975 controversy over environmental harm from certain chemicals used as propellants in aerosol spray cans (chlorofluorocarbons, or CFCs), firms marketing aerosol products initially tried to maintain a uniform front denying the harm. But when consumer activism began to cut sales of all aerosol products – both those using CFCs and other propellants – the Johnson's Wax Company broke with the industry by announcing that it was eliminating CFC propellants from its products. While some other firms, particularly marketers of toiletries, used CFC propellants in nearly all their products, Johnson's Wax Company was able to gain marketing and PR advantages at nearly no cost, as it used CFCs in only two of the dozens of aerosol products it marketed (Dotto and Schiff 1978).

When such asymmetries are strong, a group that wishes to enforce silence on all its members needs selective internal incentives strong enough to outweigh individuals' interests in revealing. Groups might achieve this by bribing the members most tempted to reveal, or by threatening punishment to those who do reveal.

[3] The terms of the settlement also gave Liggett certain advantages in its search for a merger partner.

In Figure 4.2, these possibilities correspond to shifting the payoff upward for those for not revealing (co-operating), and downward for those revealing (defecting). If the group seeks to defend itself by bribing potential defectors to stay, then the group can benefit from asymmetry. Only if individuals are highly asymmetric can the few most inclined to defect be bribed not to do so without risking that the group's solidarity will unravel completely in the face of a cascade of demands for equivalent payments by others.

If the group seeks to defend itself by punishing, or threatening to punish, defectors, the incentives can include some combination of the approval or disapproval of other group members, and real material rewards and punishments (Loury 1993). When peers identify strongly with the group, the border between these measures blurs, as group disapproval can be very painful and can carry direct material harms as second-order consequences. "Codes of silence" have long been used by criminal organizations to suppress revelation, with punishment of death to "canaries" who "sing". The entire Boston neighborhood of Charlestown followed such a code of silence prior to the early 1990s, as fearful residents refused to share information with the police about crimes by local gang members (U.S. Department of Justice 1994; U.S. v. Houlihan 1996). Sanctions that are similar in style, although less draconian, are used by various social groups. For example, some religious groups have used threats of exclusion or denial of rites to enforce conformity or obedience to community authorities, and to prevent individuals opposed to or harmed by the group's practices from going public with their complaints. Examples include the shunning of deviants by Jehovah's Witnesses, persecution of apostates by Moonies and Scientologists, social sanctions against deviant and outspoken Mormons in the Church's Utah heartland, and the Catholic Church's demands for silence about clerical pedophilia. These mechanisms can be extremely subtle, both in how the borders of acceptable dissent are drawn and in how violators are treated. For example, American political parties harbor legislators with such divergent views that they may appear to be in disarray, but nevertheless manage to secure party unity on particular important votes. In contrast to the use of bribes, punishments of shame and exclusion will in general be most effective when peers are most similar, and will grow less effective as the asymmetry among peers increases.

In regulatory settings, an outside actor may be particularly able to benefit from the asymmetric interests of the peers it oversees. A firm might learn that its products or processes (and those of its competitors) carry risks to health, safety, or the environment that were not previously realized, or may learn of some potential alternative to present conduct that could reduce an already recognized harm. Regulators seek to exploit the resultant asymmetries to elicit information about risks and capabilities from the firms with the least to lose from potential controls, or those that might even stand to gain – at least in relative terms.

A firm that learns of a previously unrecognized risk of its operations must decide whether to continue or revise its practices, and whether to conceal or reveal its new knowledge. Being first to learn of a risk may hold the prospect of competitive advantage, but only if this early knowledge gives the firm a lead in developing less risky alternatives. Moreover, the discovery itself may imply an increased liability risk, since the firm may later be judged liable for harms done during the period when it knew but did not act. Changing the risky practice without explicitly revealing the information may not be feasible, since the behavior change itself may be taken as a signal that something is known to be wrong. For example, marketers of aerosol hair-care products containing vinyl chloride decided not to switch to available alternatives, judging that since the alternatives were known to be costlier, regulators and potential litigants would infer from the switch that the manufacturer had discovered a health risk from vinyl chloride.

Conversely, a firm may hold information about technological or managerial ways it can change present operations and reduce a known external risk or harm.[4] Although an industry may be collectively served by silence – in this case, maintaining the status quo position that any change in operations will be difficult and costly – a firm that learns more about a benign alternative to present practices may perceive a competitive advantage in revealing what it knows and encouraging regulation based on this new capability that will differentially burden its competitors. It may even expect a regulation to bring new revenues, if other firms are forced to license its innovation. For example, U.S. automakers for many years resisted federal requirements for the installation of air bags, but when Chrysler Corporation perceived a competitive advantage in such safety systems in the late 1980s, it broke from the other manufacturers, began installing air bags on most of its models, and shared its engineering performance data with the government.

In regulatory settings, exploitable asymmetries of interest may also arise simply because firms differ in their judgments of the likelihood that collective resistance against regulations will succeed. When resistance begins to appear futile, second-order interests in being perceived as a good citizen and having some influence over regulatory details can override the preference for no regulation at all. Hence, it will not be just the firms least dependent on present practices and most confident of their ability to develop alternatives that are most inclined to reveal information, but also those least confident in the success of the industry's collective efforts to oppose regulation.

4.2.3 Effects of the Order of Revelation

Our formulations above have assumed that all cooperators receive the same payoff, as do all defectors, however they settle on their strategy. Thus, either the order of choice did not matter, or all players had to choose simultaneously. Simultaneous choice could be imposed through a deadline, suggesting that players might not know what others were choosing, or as part of an equilibrium process, where no choice becomes final until no player wishes to change. Though simultaneous-play processes are sometimes observed in the real world, and their study forms the backbone of traditional game theory, for many information games the order of choice matters.

---

[4] If no associated risk is yet known, then information about such options has no collective significance.

Even if peers' interests in silence and revelation are symmetric or close to it, the game is much more complex if players' payoffs depend upon the order in which they reveal. The outside authority might make special deals with those who speak first, but exhaust its ability or willingness to do so as more speak. Similarly, the group's ability to deploy payoffs for maintaining silence or punishments for breaking it may be limited in total, with the strongest incentives – positive or negative – being applied to those who move first. If the first to speak benefits the most from outside inducements, then the threat to speak can be used to extort a special internal accommodation. This possibility compounds the group's difficulty in enforcing collective silence, since peers who are unsure how much they can rely on each other's silence, or who fear there will be no resources left to accommodate them, may rush to avoid being a late speaker.

The opposite situation, in which it is preferable to speak last, will ease the group's problem of maintaining silence, since even players with dominant strategies to reveal may delay in the hope of gaining an even larger payoff if others reveal first. This situation is likely to be less common than that in which early speakers gain the most, since early speech will usually reveal the most. When this situation does occur, however, it will make it easier for the group to maintain silence in both Assurance and Prisoners' Dilemma situations.

As the foregoing discussion suggests, the effects of both intrinsic asymmetry of interests among peers and order-of-revelation effects are increased when outside actors can split the group by tailoring their responses to different players. Outside authorities will wish to target weak links. For example, prosecutors of criminal conspiracies gain the most from their ability to grant immunity if they target the informants with the strongest individual interests in revealing (whether due to moral scruples, disgruntlement at their treatment within the group, or lesser guilt). If they succeed, prosecutors gain the information they need to obtain the convictions they most value, while foregoing prosecutions of lower value that represent the least reduction in enforcement effectiveness.

To summarize, we make the following conjectures regarding situations in which silence is both the status quo and a collective good for the peer group. If revealing information imposes net costs on the revealer, the group will usually succeed in maintaining silence. If revealing can bring individual net benefits to the revealer at the group's expense, then the group must create incentives to maintain collective silence. Outside actors seeking to break the group's silence may deploy opposing incentives, such as selective individual rewards to those who reveal. In general, groups in which the peers' interests and perceptions are more symmetric will be better able to maintain silence. The less confident peers are that they all share the collective interest against revealing, the more likely that some will reveal. Particularly if individual interests are structured as an Assurance game, attempts to increase confidence through mutual reassurance may be thwarted, because the communication between peers that this requires can itself reveal at least some of the information that the group wishes to conceal. As peers' interests grow more asymmetric, maintaining silence grows more difficult, as some individuals have stronger intrinsic interests in revealing, more susceptibility to inducements from an outside actor, less susceptibility to the threat of internal group sanctions, and less commitment to group norms. The only countervailing effect is that the group is better able to maintain silence by bribing potential revealers if asymmetry means that bribes need only be offered to the few individuals most likely to reveal. If payoffs to those who reveal also depend on the order of revelation, then revelation grows more likely if, as seems likely, those who reveal first benefit most.

4.3 When Revelation is a Collective Good

Sometimes voice -- the revelation of individually held information -- provides a collective benefit for the peer group.[5] Privately held information may be needed to guide a group decision, perhaps to prevent herding to sub-optimal collective choices based on limited information. For example, some individuals may purchase Product A, though their personal information suggests that B is better, because A's purchase by many others suggests that it is superior. But if even a few doubters expressed their thoughts, the whole group might tip to Product B. Herding to an inferior equilibrium can even occur in two-player games. A mutually unsatisfactory romantic relationship may persist because neither party is willing to take the lead in revealing their unhappiness.

In most such situations, the information held by different individuals will be distinct, but will reflect on common issues. Thus, each revelation will bring additional, usually declining, marginal benefit for the group. Even multiple revelations of nearly identical information can bring collective benefits, if they establish conditions of common knowledge that are necessary for better group decisions. These may take the form of helping a latent group to identify, organize, or empower itself, or of allowing the revision or abandonment of a dearly valued collective endeavor whose results do not merit the sacrifices being made for it. As discussed above for maintaining group silence, encouraging individual voice can be a collective-action problem if the individuals who speak bear a cost from doing so.

A common situation in which revelation is collectively beneficial concerns research and innovations. The creators of such works provide collective benefits by revealing them, indeed, by disseminating them widely. In order to profit from their creation, however, they must be able to control subsequent use and reproduction; absent this opportunity, many desirable innovations would never be produced. This problem is so widespread and important that it has been addressed through the creation of rights in intellectual property, such as patents. Few such situations have been so systematically addressed, however. The individual costs that obstruct revelation can come from several sources, and can be imposed by actors outside the group, or by the peers.

Sometimes an individual's voice enhances the group's identity, empowerment, or reputation, while an outside authority wishes to suppress the group. For example, if individuals are deciding whether to identify themselves as members of a group that opposes a repressive regime, the risk to those who speak comes from

[5] In using the term voice in this context, we follow the lead of Hirschman (1970).

the outside authority. Even if the authority lacks the power to punish the whole group, those who speak – or more particularly, those who speak first – can bear substantial personal cost. In such situations, asymmetries can be crucial in promoting the revelation of collectively beneficial information. Kuran (1991) has argued that the 1989 revolutions in Eastern Europe gained momentum from asymmetry in individuals' willingness to take the risk of speaking out against the regimes, and from the visibility of even small demonstrations. The numbers grew day by day as more citizens became willing to risk participating, producing a rapid tipping phenomenon.

Alternatively, the cost of revealing can come from actions of the group itself or of some of its members, or from norms that individuals have internalized that act as surrogates for a narrow or partial view of the group's interests. These situations typically arise when individuals' information implies the need for an uncomfortable change in the group's conduct or self-image. Individuals may, for example, present unfavorable factual news about the group's performance or prospects, specific challenges it faces, or the strength of its adversaries. The way the group or its leaders express chagrin at the content of the bad news – at least initially – might be to "kill the messenger." As in some of the collective silence situations discussed above, this is an Assurance game, with the difference that the status quo equilibrium of silence is inferior. Anyone who speaks out suffers costs, unless enough others also do so. Moreover, participating in punishing the messenger may also be an Assurance game. Others might know the messenger is right and prefer to spare him, but fear they cannot do so lest they be taken to endorse his message – and share his fate. If punishment of deviance is the norm, then not only is courage required to speak out, but so to a lesser extent is courage required to argue that someone who has spoken out should not be punished.

In related situations, individuals may face such costs when they ask the group to take note of comfortably shared delusions, erroneous conventional truths, or bad conduct. The group may greatly benefit from having these exposed and corrected, but may still forbid or discourage individuals from doing so or punish those who do – or individuals may police themselves in the same way. Those who speak up suffer costs from breach of social norms, shame, or censure, or alternatively from concrete punishments against deviance applied by the group, its leaders, or the members most strongly opposed to the revelation and its implications. A contemporary analogue to the ancient treatment of diplomatic messengers is the treatment of whistle-blowers who "betray" their peers by exposing illegal or unethical conduct by their organizations. Whistle-blowers suffer substantial personal and professional costs, including widespread hostility and mistrust – even when the conduct they report is egregious, and despite the existence of laws seeking to protect them and principles declaring that they have done right. These costs are smaller when more people blow the whistle, but coordinating such a group of defectors can also be risky since the first to propose doing so exposes himself nearly as much as if he had gone to the authorities by himself.

Similar forces discourage individuals from adopting unpopular positions when they are among the first to recognize that the group's long-term welfare requires taking costly action that others would prefer to avoid or delay. Even raising doubting questions can be costly. Ibsen's play "An Enemy of the People" describes the persecution of a local physician who tries to alert his town to dangerous contamination in a local mineral spring. Similarly, in the recent Argentine economic crisis, it was obvious for months (or longer) that the fixed-exchange system had to be abandoned, but whichever political leader said so and acted accordingly was bound to be sacrificed. In the Japanese financial crisis, a similar fate confronted those who declared the widely known fact that many banks were already bankrupt under mountains of bad debt, and that fixing the problem would require a shakeout in which many banks would fail. A common theme in these situations is that the group fails to act in accordance with its true interests. The group is served by revelation, yet acts to discourage it.[6]

These forces that repress dissenting voices can be magnified when the group is in a situation of conflict or adversity. Self-censorship or collective censorship can extend to the point that group members refuse to acknowledge things that are obviously true and known, but are favorable to the adversary. That is one reason why mutually destructive wars of attrition, whether military or political, can persist for so long. When the shared belief of the group has a strong normative character, the problem is more severe. For example, a group may hold strong and perhaps simplistic views of who is good and who is bad, or who or what is responsible for ills the group is suffering. Group sanctions against individuals who deny or question these beliefs, and individuals' inclination to avoid these sanctions through self-censorship, can operate especially strongly. Parties to conflict can thereby not only obstruct beneficial decisions and opportunities for mutually beneficial accommodation with their adversaries, but can also discredit themselves in the eyes of outside authorities or neutral third parties. When the possibility of outside neutral intervention or the importance of the opinion of neutrals is uncertain, groups in conflict then face a classic strategic dilemma: Should they continue to maintain cohesion and inflame supporters through simplistic propaganda to demonize their opponents, or should they compete to be at least minimally more reasonable than the opponents (or to trick the opponent into being more extreme) in dealings with outside neutrals or potential arbitrators? Both Ariel Sharon and Yassir Arafat have extreme factions on their sides whose support they must retain, but each must also try to maneuver to appear more reasonable and less belligerent than the other, so that the greater censure and pressure from external parties falls on his adversary.

Even if the group does not punish people who speak out, desirable revelation can be suppressed simply if individuals holding information anticipate a cost from revealing, even one as minor as the embarrassment of saying something incorrect or foolish in public. Such weak anticipated costs can have force, particularly when individuals are not fully confident of their information. A classic fictional treatment of this phenomenon is Hans Christian Andersen's story "The Emperor's New Clothes" (1837, 1948), in which all the courtiers and citizens saw (or thought they saw) that the Emperor was naked but feared to say so. The swindlers who sold the Emperor his nonexistent robe anticipated how the game would play out. They announced at the outset that those who were stupid or unfit for their office

[6] This is similar to the problem of "groupthink" discussed by Janis (1972).

would be unable to see the robe. Given such expectations, the plausibility of the mechanism that kept all the adults from saying what they saw gains force. Not only did they doubt their own eyes when they heard everyone else praising the beauty of the robe, but they feared that revealing they saw nothing would also reveal (or be taken to reveal) that they were stupid or unfit for their office. Each individual's information would have gained credibility had people known how many others were seeing the same thing, but they could only gain this knowledge at the price of exposing themselves to ridicule or shame. This was a straightforward example of herding behavior. No citizen had enough information to overcome what was implicitly learned from others' silence. Only the child, who presumably understood neither the game nor the inference process, was willing to state the obvious.

Whether the collective interest in voice comes from the group's identifying and organizing itself or from overcoming a shared delusion, the marginal benefits the group derives from voice are likely to be first increasing, then decreasing. When very few people are speaking, not only are the speakers more likely to suffer harms but they are unlikely to attain the force or volume required for the group to overcome its collective inferior state. At some higher level of voice, the speakers will succeed at making their case heard or mobilizing the group, bring a sharp increase in collective benefits. Beyond that point, the group's benefit is largely achieved and further voices bring little additional gain. This structure of collective benefits suggests an S-shaped curve.

A common theme in these situations is that the payoffs to speakers are likely to depend on the order of speaking, even more strongly here than in the cases discussed above where silence is the collective good. Many people may perceive the group's need for voice, or may even wish to speak themselves, but be unwilling to bear the cost of being among the first to do so. Early speakers may bear especially high costs because they are conspicuous, individually identified, and easy to isolate for reprisals. The first person to flout an external authority is more likely to be punished than the fifth or the twenty-fifth (and is also usually less confident that others will follow). The first to question a dearly held group view is especially likely to suffer censure or stronger punishments. In a far less consequential but structurally similar example, the first person to move onto an empty dance floor may simply suffer embarrassment (or more aptly, expect that they will when considering whether to move or not). The typical result is that the dance floor is empty for a long time. Ultimately, the most confident dancers venture out, after which the floor rapidly fills. The analogy extends to groups awaiting voice. They hold to old behaviors, arguments, and beliefs long after these have ceased to be functional. Once a critical mass for change is achieved -- possibly quite small -- they suddenly convert.

In sum, we make the following conjectures regarding situations in which revelation is a collective good for the peer group. In these situations, we still presume that silence is the status quo, so the group's problem is to motivate individuals to change their behavior. Early speakers are likely to suffer the most severe costs, while the group's benefits from voice increase slowly at first until some critical level is reached. In contrast to the silence case, asymmetry of interests makes the group's problem easier, because it can lead to "cascading revelation," starting with those who bear the smallest cost from revealing, or who are the most disgruntled, the most inclined to seek fame or notoriety, or the least risk-averse.

4.4 Elaborations and Conclusion

Information games, which are widely found in our society, bear strategic similarities with the more commonly studied games where direct actions are costly, but they have distinctive elements as well. We have only sketched some characteristics of information games, some conjectures about expected outcomes, and some applications to real settings. Our principal findings were summarized at the outset in Table 4.1, which outlines typical but not exclusive patterns in different types of collective-action games. Here we lay out four areas for future development.

First, study of information games should enrich the characterization of the information that agents hold, and the range of choices they have regarding its revelation. Actors may hold information of different levels of accuracy and precision, may attempt to shade information to their advantage in choosing what to reveal, or may selectively reveal accurate information (Zeckhauser and Marks 1996).

Second, the treatment of actors' knowledge and uncertainty about others' information and payoffs must be enriched. Players should be allowed to have uncertainty about what information others hold, and consequently the expected consequences of others' decisions to reveal it. In addition, players might be uncertain about others' payoffs, for example over whether others have Assurance-game payoffs or prefer to reveal regardless of what others do.

Third, we have dealt only with the two polar cases in which silence and voice respectively are the collective good. There are also mixed situations, where some peers desire silence and others voice, or where voice and silence are beneficial over different portions of some range. To illustrate the latter, consider the insider peers who know about an excellent but out-of-the-way restaurant. If the secret stays too well kept, the restaurant may die, but once it becomes widely known the restaurant is likely to become both congested and more expensive. Voice is desirable only until an appropriate scale is reached, at which point the (now enlarged) peer group will desire silence. Metaphorically this subtle game resembles many information games, where peer membership shifts and consists of those who are informed.

Fourth, we can consider cases in which more than one level of aggregation of actors into groups is important, and the collective payoffs of different groups go in different directions. One major consequence of asymmetric interests is that the same action can have opposite values for two groups, even when they are closely related to each other. For example, a division of an organization might benefit from silence, while the whole organization benefits from revelation; a gang might prefer silence, while the neighborhood in which it operates prefers revelation. As we have framed the relationship between the peer group and an outside actor in this chapter, the outside actor wants the group not to solve its collective-action problem, whether that problem is maintaining silence or encouraging voice. A more interesting case arises when individual interests go one way, group interests the other, and the outside authority has the same interest as the individual: For example, individuals want to talk; the gang wants silence; the neighborhood (and the authorities) want revelation. The larger group or its agents are the "outside authority" trying to extract information from the smaller group.

In the reverse situation, the group of oppressed citizens wants speech, but the state wants to keep them silent. Individuals remain silent out of fear of punishment by the state. In reply, the group deploys internal norms and sanctions to foster speech. Recognizing this, the outside authority tries to identify those with strongest interest in maintaining silence, and encourages them with rewards to go along with punishments to those who speak. The outcome may well be a tussle between the group and the outside authority to identify critical focal points in Assurance game situations.

In his most famous work, *The Logic of Collective Action* (1965), Mancur Olson was primarily concerned with groups mobilizing for political action. Olson's principal focus was the provision of resources to the group, most easily thought of as money or effort. Frequently, however, groups seeking collective action, including those promoting political agendas, are most concerned with the concealment or revelation of information.

We have looked at situations where collective benefits came from silence (concealment) or voice (revelation). In some instances, the spirit of Olson's primary observations – notably under-provision of a public good that is costly for each to provide – are directly applicable. For example, if a new product is coming on the market, the advertising (voice) of one firm may bring positive spillovers for competing producers. However, for a range of additional situations, information games yield different results than resource provision games, even though the information or its absence is a public good.

Information settings require generalizing Olson's results. In these settings, private actors' decisions to produce information, and to reveal, bias, or conceal what they hold, will reflect their calculated attempts to influence the knowledge and perceptions of other group members and outside authorities to promote decisions that avoid costs or bring them benefits. Judged from the standpoint of the peers, the essence of the problem is to align individual and group interests.

Asymmetry of size was the primary determinant of individual willingness to contribute to collective goods in Olson and Zeckhauser's (1966) formulation of alliance theory. In information games, the effects of asymmetries are both stronger and more diverse than in conventional collective-action problems, and the range of possible interests in revelation, at both the group and individual level, are much broader. The group's interest may be in either concealment or revelation. Individuals' interests in revelation can range from large benefits to large costs, since these are consequences of the reactions of others and are not bounded by the direct cost of revelation, which is usually very small. Consequently, the relationship of individual to collective interests can range from being strongly aligned to strongly opposed.

Asymmetries in the quality of individuals' information or their capability to acquire it can further broaden the range of possible outcomes. If those best able to produce collectively beneficial information have interests that are strongly opposed to the consequences of its being revealed, then the problem of getting socially efficient revelation to support policy-making may be even more severe. This situation may be common in regulatory contexts, as the best technical information relevant to crafting regulatory standards is often held by the firms that are the potential targets of regulation.

The resolution of the group's problem in information games still requires aligning individual and collective payoffs, as in Olson's classic result. When the group benefits from revelation this means rewarding early revealers, or at least reducing their expected penalty so revealing becomes their individually preferred choice. When the group wants silence, this means penalizing early talkers, or bribing those most at risk of talking to keep them silent. When there is an outside actor opposed to the group's silence, that actor will want to deploy opposing individual incentives. While conferring private rewards on early talkers may look like corruption or regulatory capture, it may be advantageous in social-welfare terms if the improvement in outcome for the society at large (e.g., enacting socially beneficial regulation of an externality that would otherwise not be feasible) is worth more than any costs of the payoff.

5 The Collective Action Problems of Political Consolidation: Evidence from Poland*

Marek M. Kaminski

The problem of collective action, while noticed early by Rousseau and Hume, received its first model in the 1950's in the celebrated Prisoner's Dilemma introduced by Flood and Drescher and motivated by Albert Tucker's familiar story. Later, with the development of game theory, problems of collective action were thoroughly formalized as variants of the Prisoner's Dilemma, coordination games, or just strategic games with a unique Nash equilibrium that is strictly Pareto dominated (Hardin 1982; Sandler 1992). Among the early social scientists who analyzed social dilemmas with simple models was Thomas Schelling. Mancur Olson, Schelling's student, focused in his dissertation on the intersection of economics and politics. He made studying the problems of collective action his lifetime research program. He applied his framework and its variants to the workings of professional associations and labor unions (1965), maintaining the NATO (1966, with R. Zeckhauser), interest group formation and their impact on the aggregated welfare (1982), revolution-making (1990), or incentives facing various rulers to cultivate economic growth (2000). He demonstrated that political and economic collective action problems are not mere curiosities, paradoxes, or aberrations of otherwise efficient markets. They underlie every aspect of human activity and have profound political and economic consequences.

Since Olson's seminal dissertation-turned-book on collective action, systematic failures of various social, economic, and political players to coordinate on mutually beneficial solutions received increasingly more attention from political scientists and economists. The 1989 Eastern European revolutions produced a new crop of such failures. The old institutional grid - political, economic, and social - was destroyed and the new institutions were still in the making. The collective action problems born in this institutional vacuum contributed to political instability, economic under-performance, and social inefficiencies. One of the most persistent problems plaguing transitional societies was the huge number of small entities such as companies, political parties, foundations, universities, etc., that emerged quickly and then "froze" at what seemed to many observers as an inefficient level of consolidation.

* Comments of Jac Heckelman, Frank Lovett, Monika Nalepa and the late Mancur Olson are gratefully acknowledged. The usual disclaimers apply. A part of this chapter was earlier published in the *American Journal of Political Science* 45, 294-312.

5.1 The Fragmentation of Eastern-European Party Systems and Collective Action

The end of communism in Eastern Europe brought the free competition for votes that almost immediately resulted in a proliferation of parties. In Poland, the effective number of parliamentary parties (ENPP) after the 1991 elections reached an astronomical value of 10.45.[1] Perpetual splits, coalitions, and the formation of new parties made the emerging party systems in Eastern Europe quite dissimilar to their mature counterparts in Western Europe. Parties focused at least as much on negotiating electoral coalitions as on cabinet coalitions. Coalitional negotiations became the crucial component of party politics in Bulgaria (Waller 1995), the Czech Republic (Kopeckỳ 1995), Estonia (Grofman, Mikkel and Taagepera 2000), Hungary (Lomax 1994), Poland (Kaminski 2001), Russia (Filippov, Ordeshook and Shvetsova 1999) and other transitional democracies (Cotta 1996; Kaminski 1998).

Political fragmentation creates an Olsonian setting of a great number of relatively small players whose ability to enter binding agreements with the others is limited. When such players face decisions in which a joint action could benefit all as opposite to individual maximization, i.e., if there are dominant or locally dominant strategies for everybody that jointly produce an inefficient equilibrium, they may visualize the game as non-cooperative and act separately. This is the famous Olsonian prediction that in various settings "*rational, self-interested [players] will not act to achieve their common or group interests*" (Olson 1965, p.2; emph. in orig.). In public decision-making, fragmentation slows down the decision process, makes political players more vulnerable to pressures from main economic players, increases political tensions through misrepresentation of large chunks of the electorate and often facilitates unexpected political consequences. One of the most important such political consequences was the enabling of post-communist parties return to power in some Eastern European democracies. In October 1992, a post-communist party regained power in Lithuania. In September 1993 a similar comeback took place in Poland, and in May 1994, in Hungary. The electoral victories of these post-communist parties were much more spectacular than one could have predicted from the size of their popular support alone. In Lithuania, 46.6% of the popular votes resulted in 56.7% of lower house seats whereas in Hungary the corresponding numbers were 33% and 55%. In Poland, the disproportion between popular votes and seats was even greater. A mere 20.4% of popular votes for a post-communist party resulted in a total of 37.2% of Sejm (Lower House) seats. Another big winner in the elections was a successor of a communist puppet-ally,

---

[1] The ENPP, the most popular indicator of parliamentary fragmentation, is defined as $1/\sum_{i=1}^{n} p_i^2$ where p_i^2 is seat share of party i (Laaksa and Taagepera 1979). Greater values represent greater fragmentation. ENPP is equal to the inverse of the Herfindahl ratio, widely used by economists as a measure of market concentration. For most western democracies, ENPP assumes values between 3 and 4. For the United States, it is roughly equal to 2. The value of 10.45 implies that at least 11 parties had political representation.

the peasant party (PSL) with 15.4% of votes and 28.7% of seats. The electoral success of both old regime parties in Poland resulted in a coalition that turned out to be very stable and ruled Poland from 1993 to 1997. The most important economic consequences of the post-communist come-back included the halting or slowing down of multiple institutional reforms, privatization, and the restructuring of the most heavily unionized branches of state economy.

The post-communist comebacks following the economic difficulties of early transition were ultimately made possible by a deep fragmentation of anti-communist rightist parties. The increase in electoral support of the post-communist parties was insufficient for their electoral victory. In the 1993 Polish parliamentary elections, six sibling rightist parties commanded 26.2% of votes and only 3.5% of seats. Simulations show that the united coalition of the rightist parties could win about 35% of seats, enough to form a cabinet with other non-communist parties (Kaminski, Lissowski, and Swistak 1998). In fact, in the next elections in1997, the post-solidarity rightist parties coalesced and jointly with one more anti-communist pre-solidarity party, won 39.4% of votes and 45% of seats.

Electoral coalescing creates multiple collective action problems for the affected parties. Such problems are often different from political puzzles found in mature democracies. Consider a simple example of two similar small parties that can capture 10% of Lower House seats each when competing separately. Assume further that the estimates show that when the parties form a common list of candidates, then, due to the properties of the electoral law rewarding larger coalitions and attracting additional votes, they win 30% of seats. At first, it seems that seat-maximizing parties would have strong incentives to coalesce and a natural prediction would be that they would coalesce. However, the parties may engage in an attrition-game by bargaining over how to divide the 10% surplus and may end up not coalescing (Zielinski 2000, 2002). They may also be discouraged from coalescing by a prediction that their coalition will facilitate consolidation among their opponents, and eventually will make them worse off.

With more parties, the picture may become even more complicated. For instance, even when there are gains from forming a grand coalition, there may be non-empty subsets of parties with incentives to leave such a coalition (the core of the corresponding cooperative game may be empty).

The general analysis of electoral coalitions requires a complex framework of partition-function form games (Kaminski 2001). The three collective action problems of electoral coalescing in Poland and their political consequences are analyzed in this chapter in a less formal fashion. The consequences were of utmost importance and the solutions to consolidation problems worked out by the political actors shaped Polish politics for many years.

The next section describes the consolidation dilemma that the rightist parties faced in the 1993 elections after an electoral reform. In this first situation, the rightist parties did not coalesce and entered the elections with separate lists of candidates. Then, a special case of the dilemma is analyzed. This special situation arose in the Polish 1993 elections after the August 10 deadline for registration of candidate lists. After this deadline, the coalitional structure was fixed and the six parties and coalitions of parties helplessly watched their poll results oscillating just below the minimum threshold required for seat distribution. While it was common knowledge that defeat was inevitable, there was a solution to the dilemma, namely a lottery among all parties determining who would stay and who would withdraw from the elections. This collective action problem was not solved successfully. Finally, Section 5.4 describes how the defeated rightist parties were able to overcome their differences, coalesce, and win almost half of the seats in the 1997 elections despite the total proportion of votes similar to that of 1993 elections. The grand rightist coalition, AWS, became the dominant force in Polish politics for four years.

5.2 The 1993 Dilemma of Electoral Consolidation

The story of the Left's spectacular comeback begins on May 28, 1993. On that day a new electoral law was adopted by the Polish parliament, the Sejm. The new law was more friendly to larger parties, and accordingly almost all larger parties in the Sejm supported the change whereas almost all smaller parties voted against it. The voting on the new law took place in a fervent situation due to another major political problem, a non-confidence vote, that was put on the agenda for the same day. The cabinet fell by one vote, and on the next day, unexpectedly, President Lech Walesa dissolved the Sejm and called for new elections in September.

The new electoral law provided strong incentives for coalescing.[2] The relatively homogeneous bloc of the rightist parties immediately started coalitional negotiations. The media thoroughly analyzed the poor prospects of the fragmented right and it was the common knowledge among all the players that fragmentation would be equivalent to defeat.

Then, in June and July, the picture changed. Figure 5.1 shows poll results of the rightist parties and coalitions between the dissolution of the parliament and the new elections. The height of the graph represents the mean support for a party or coalition computed from ten OBOP and CBOS polls. Merged graphs represent coalitions of corresponding parties created at the time the poll was conducted. BBWR entered the race as a new party in June.[3]

[2] The new law introduced country-level thresholds of 5% to 8%, required using the d'Hondt-Jefferson divisor method , which is more friendly towards larger parties, instead of the largest remainder Hare-Hamilton method with Droop quota, and substituted 37 districts with 52 smaller districts. The average district magnitude decreased from 10.6 to 7.3 (Kaminski, Lissowski, and Swistak 1998). In an electoral system with relatively small districts, the choice of a particular proportional representation (PR) method may strongly influence the distribution of seats among parties. For detailed discussion of various PR methods, see Balinski and Young (1982), and Taagepera and Shugart (1989).

[3] Figure taken from Kaminski (1998). For each poll, the number of respondents js between 1083 to 1376. 'Undecided' voters are excluded.

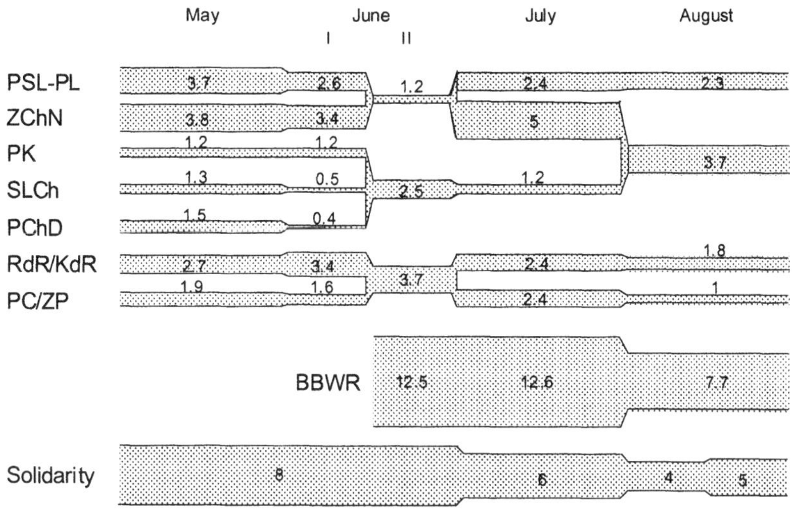

Fig. 5.1. Poll results of the rightist parties and their coalitions before the 1993 elections

Surprisingly for almost all commentators, estimates showed that instead of generating more votes, coalescing in fact subtracted many votes from the partners of two largest coalitions. In addition, a new rightist party, the Walesa Bloc, was formed and the Solidarity trade union decided to compete in the elections. The presence of two new entrants further dissipated the rightist parties' vote share.

Coalitions that showed weak performance in the polls were quickly dissolved. The deadline for registration of candidate lists on August 10 was approaching fast and the rightist leaders seemed to be paralyzed. Most commentators concluded that the coalescing did not work, and that the unsuccessful unifications made the electorate disappointed. The polls showed the popularity of post-communist parties skyrocketing and the nightmare of a reestablishment of the communist order started to haunt the rightist leaders.

The August 10 registration deadline was a crucial date. After the deadline, the coalitional structure of parties competing in elections was almost frozen. No further coalescing or adjustment of candidates' positions on the lists was allowed. The only option remaining to parties was the withdrawal of its list of candidates from the electoral race.

The leaders of the rightist parties did little to prevent what seemed at that time to be their inevitable defeat. They were appealing to the *other* leaders and *other* parties for withdrawal from the election, or to voters to coordinate on their own parties (Sulek 1995, p. 114). Not surprisingly, there were no altruists, and the voters did not coordinate efficiently. The rightist parties entered the elections divided and lost.

5.3 The Dilemma of Electoral Participation or Withdrawal

The collective action problem that the rightist parties faced during their final weeks was of a peculiar nature. Only the withdrawal from the elections of some of the rightist parties could give a reasonable chance of winning seats for the other rightist parties. Had the parties been able to solve the dilemma, they could have received an *ex ante* better seat share even in this supposedly hopeless situation. A possible solution to the problem is a lottery. A randomly selected party or coalition would have most likely attracted the entire rightist electorate and prevented the post-communist victory. A simple model is outlined below that represents the dilemma of this situation.

A lottery among parties competing for the same chunk of the electorate could have been arranged in a variety of ways. The game introduced below represents one such a possibility, with players choosing between unconditional participation and entering a lottery.

The model is a symmetric n-player non-cooperative game with risk neutral players and $n \geq 2$. Players are interpreted as a set of virtually identical parties clustered closely in the issue space, 'the rightist parties'; no other players are present. Every player i has two strategies: $s_i = 1$ is interpreted as "run" in the electoral race independently of decisions of others and $s_i = 0$ is interpreted as "negotiate withdrawal" from the race.

Payoffs are interpreted as expected seat shares and are driven by the following story: the total expected seat share of the rightist parties when exactly k of them are running is equal to $f(k)$, where $k \in \{1,..,n\}$ and $f(k) \in [0,1]$. As a result of the electoral law that punishes fragmentation, the total seat share decreases as the number of rightist players entering the elections increases:

(a) f is decreasing.

However, everybody has a chance of getting some seats, even if the probability associated with winning a positive seat share when everybody competes is low. Thus, if everybody enters, then the expected total seat share remains positive:

(b) $f(n) > 0$.

Each player can decide to enter elections independently of the other players' decisions. Alternatively, a player may join a subset of parties that try to negotiate withdrawal and win a 'lottery ticket' that gives him the right to run as the subgroup's representative. By convention, assume that when a single player 'negotiates,' this means that the player unilaterally quits the race and gets nothing. When at least two players negotiate, all such players draw fair straws, and exactly one of them, the winner, enters the race.

Every player who enters the race receives his expected share of seats, which depends on the total number of entrants and his own decision whether to run or withdraw.

Let s denote any strategy profile and let s_i be the strategy of player i. The total number of players running when the strategy profile is s is denoted by r_s. The formula representing payoffs is given below:

$$P_i(s) = \begin{cases} 0 & \text{if} \quad s_i = 0 \text{ and } r_s = n-1; \\ \dfrac{1}{(r_s+1)(n-r_s)} f(r_s+1) & \text{if} \quad s_i = 0 \text{ and } r_s < n-1; \\ \dfrac{1}{r_s+1} f(r_s+1) & \text{if} \quad s_i = 1 \text{ and } r_s < n-1; \\ \dfrac{1}{r_s} f(r_s) & \text{if} \quad s_i = 1 \text{ and } r_s \geq n-1. \end{cases} \tag{1}$$

Consider the strategy profile $s^E = (1,...,1)$ representing the case of all players running independently of the decisions of the other. To evaluate the payoff of player i for both of his strategies, note that $P_i(1, s^E_{-i}) = \frac{1}{n} f(n) > 0$ by assumption (b), where s^E_{-i} denotes the strategy profile of all players except i, and $P_i(0, s^E_{-i}) = 0$ by definition of payoffs in equation (1). Thus, s^E is a Nash equilibrium and, in addition, since $P_i(1, s^E_{-i}) > P_i(0, s^E_{-i})$ for any player, the equilibrium strategy of running is not weakly dominated by this player's withdrawal.[4]

Compare the equilibrium payoff vector with the payoffs resulting from cooperation $s^* = (0,...,0)$, i.e., when all players negotiate withdrawal and draw straws in order to select a single rightist contender. By equation (1) and assumption (a), $P_i(s^*) = \frac{1}{n} f(1) > \frac{1}{n} f(n) = P_i(s^E)$. Thus, the payoff vector corresponding to s^* strictly Pareto dominates the equilibrium payoff vector corresponding to s^E.

Running strictly dominates negotiating when no more than one other player decides to negotiate withdrawal, regardless of n. Thus, for a two player game, running is a dominant strategy. For $n > 2$, this is not necessarily the case. If the function f decreases very steeply for a certain number of players, then a player may have incentive to join the negotiators, decrease the total number of runners and have some chance of winning a big reward instead of winning a small reward for sure. However, as the calculations below show, such situations are rather implausible empirically.

Denote the number of other players who chose running, excluding player i, by r'. By definition, for player i, running is a strictly better response than negotiating to s_{-i} when the payoff from running is greater than the payoff from negotiations. This condition arises, after simple algebra, when

$$\frac{f(r'+2)}{f(r'+1)} > \frac{(r'+2)}{(r'+1)(n-r')} \;. \tag{2}$$

---

[4] This is an important property that constitutes a very simple and natural refinement of the Nash equilibrium solution concept. An example of a Nash equilibrium with weakly dominated strategies is provided by a 2×2 game with payoffs for both players equal to 0 in three cells, and equal to 1 in the fourth cell.

Equation (2) reveals that the total expected seat share does not increase too steeply when one more player decides to enter negotiations instead of running. For $n = 6$, (the actual number of sibling rightist parties in the 1993 elections) the values of the expression on the left-hand side are approximately equal for $r' = 0, 1, 2$, and 3 (specifically, the values are 0.33, 0.3, 0.33, 0.42, respectively). These numbers are small and rather unlikely to represent the properties of our actual function f. For instance, to generate the ratio of $1/3$, the total seat share of the rightist parties would have to jump from the actual 3.5% for six parties to 10.5% for only five parties. The simulations from Kaminski, Lissowski and Swistak (1998) show a possible jump from $f(6) = 3.5\%$ to $f(1) = 26.2\%$. This means that if we define the geometric average ratio as $q = [f(6) / f(5) \times f(5) / f(4) \times f(4) / f(3) \times f(3) / f(2) \times f(2) / f(1)]^{1/5} = [f(6) / f(1)]^{1/5}$, then we can estimate that $q \approx 0.67$. Thus, under empirically plausible values for the f function, running without attempting negotiated withdrawal is a strictly dominant strategy for all parties.

A qualitative analysis of the collective action problem of the 1993 Polish elections reveals a number of relevant factors that supplement the simplified model presented above. The problem arose under strong time pressure. In the first stage, before the August 10 deadline for the registration of candidate lists, coalescing was allowed. In the second stage, the parties could only withdraw from the electoral race.

It seems that the surprising poll results discouraged the rightist leaders from coalescing at the first stage. The polls were most likely misinterpreted by party leaders. In fact, when three new coalitions of the Right were introduced simultaneously with the new entrant, Walesa Bloc, the total number of rightist parties or coalitions decreased from eight to five and the polls showed a strong gain in the total share of seats of the Right, from 21.1 in early June to 27.9% in late June, as shown in Figure 5.1. There is no evidence in the poll data that the coalescing actually subtracted votes. However, since the new entrant captured a sizable portion of the rightist electorate, the effects of coalescing for the coalition's partners could not be easily separated from the loss of votes caused by the effect of a new entry.

At the second stage, after the August 10 deadline the candidate lists were closed, an agreement for sharing spots on the joint list of candidates ceased to be a viable option. The payoffs became non-transferable. Under these constraints, no selective incentives of any conceivable kind were available in order to induce cooperation. The possibility of solving the dilemma through a lottery system was not explored.

When the rightist parties were given more time to negotiate a sharing scheme, they were able to solve the dilemma. In 1996, before the 1997 elections, the descendents of all six coalitions united and formed one large coalition AWS and one smaller party ROP. These parties commanded a solid 39.4% of votes and 45% of seats in the 1997 elections. The AWS then became the senior partner in a cabinet that survived four years. The next section analyzes this process.

5.4 The 1993-1997 Consolidation Dilemma

5.4.1 Background

The Right's failure helped two parties with a communist ancestry. The return of the Polish post-communists, along with similar comebacks in Lithuania and Hungary, was declared a surprising "shift-to-red" in Central European politics.

The 1993 election taught the Right's politicians a tough lesson. The Right faced the next election united into one large coalition, the AWS, except for a minor party, ROP. After the election, the AWS and the centrist party UW formed a majority cabinet. Many political commentators considered the results of the 1997 elections to be surprising again. However, the popular votes obtained by major ideological clusters of parties in the 1993 and the 1997 elections were surprisingly similar. The real difference was only in the distribution of seats.

The remainder of this section is based on Kaminski (1998, 2001) and tells the story of what happened on the Right between 1993 and 1997. A complex model of coalition-formation that uses partition-function form games is developed in Kaminski (2001). The narrative is organized around the dilemmas that coalescing parties face; i.e., *payoff estimation*, *promotion* of the new entity on the political market, and *sharing the expected seats*.

5.4.2 Payoff Estimation

The *estimation* problem is caused by the deficit of reliable information. In a transitional party system, prospective coalescents do not know the partition function, i.e., the distributions of seats following all possible coalitional structures, but rather form proxies based on popular support. Polls provide estimates of popular support under the existing coalitional structure, but estimates for other hypothetical structures are infrequent and less reliable. Such estimates are often plagued by methodological problems that do not appear in standard polls.

The Right's coalitional failure before the 1993 election is a good illustration of estimation problems. The threat of a poor votes-to-seats translation ratio was evident, and the talks started soon after the parliament was dissolved. In early June of 1993, three Right coalitions were formed and further coalescing was expected. However, the surprising poll estimates showed that two of the new coalitions were deeply vote-subadditive and that only the smallest one was approximately vote-additive. Both subadditive coalitions were soon dissolved. (See Figure 5.1.) Political analysts concluded that a large part of the electorate was lost due to coalescing (CBOS 1993). Polls clearly halted further negotiations (Kaminski, Lissowski and Swistak 1998).

The election results of the Right were poor but still better than the polls suggested. Some politicians believed that the polls were used to initiate a self-fulfilling prophecy. The leader of PC, Jaroslaw Kaczynski, inferred that "so-called public opinion polls are manipulated" (quoted in Sulek 1995). Though fragmentation-based explanations are more plausible, the predictive failure of polls seems unquestionable.

Over time, polling companies managed to better understand the methodological problems of poll estimates in a fragmented party system. Politicians learned how to interpret polls as well. Calculations based on estimates of the partition function were substituted for the ideological language of early negotiations. Obviously, estimates of different politicians were sometimes inconsistent. When Jan Olszewski, the leader of ROP, suggested a grand coalition with the AWS, he implicitly assumed superadditivity and argued that such a coalition could win a qualified majority of seats. Marian Krzaklewski, the AWS leader, was more conservative. He responded that, "We have to check first whether our electorates are additive" (Zdort 1997a). In fact, polls showed a 2% vote loss for a potential grand coalition which, possibly, prevented any agreement between the ROP and AWS.[5]

5.4.3 Name Recognition

Votes come from voters who must *recognize* the political entity for whom they are voting. The brand name of a new entity must be implanted in voters' ears and hearts. In a transitional multiparty system, the successful promotion of a new brand name is a complicated endeavor – particularly amidst the informational noise of splits, mergers, coalitions, negotiations, withdrawals, defections, and entries.

The first coalitions on the Right — PJL, SUC, and PdP — formed soon after the defeat in 1993 in order to compete in the 1994 local election. All three coalitions assumed new names that were entirely unknown to the supporters of their members. No intra-coalitional mechanisms promoting the new names were created, and no popular politician advertised these new entities. None of the competing coalitions created a well-recognized identity. As a result, it was no wonder that their political life was short. In May 1994, "about half the Poles had not heard about the main organizational force on the Right [PdP]" (OBOP 1994). Analysts were heard to complain that, "many respondents do not recognize differences among the PdP, PJL, and SUC, and do not know which parties comprise these coalitions" (OBOP 1995). In fact, the first three years of coalitional adjustments brought a dizzying informational noise of frequent splits, mergers, and changes of names.

[5] After the 1993 election, parties actively sought estimates of the partition function. During intensive coalitional negotiations of the Right in early 1996 and mid-1997, polling companies conducted surveys on potential gains from coalescing. In April 1998, one of the largest parliamentary parties performed a secret survey, designed similarly to the survey used in this research, to measure potential benefits from coalitions with various partners.

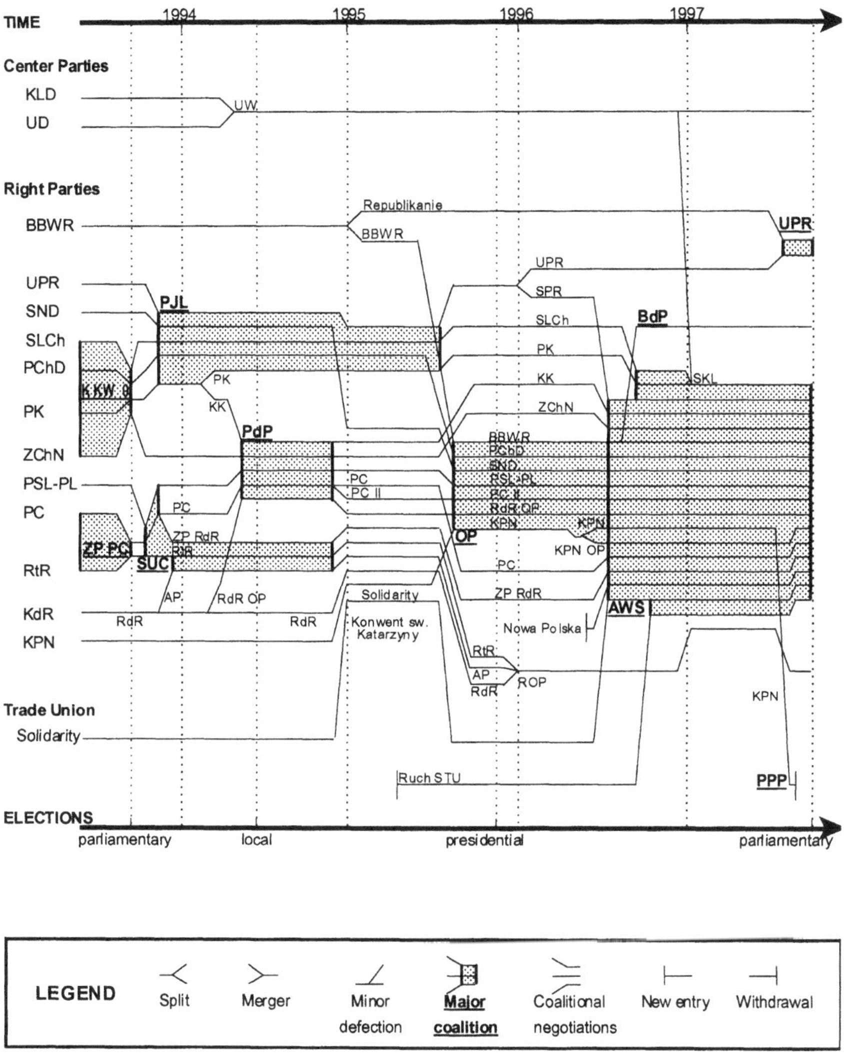

Fig. 5.2. Major coalitions and other transformations of the rightist and centrist parties between 1993 and 1997

Figure 5.2 shows major splits, mergers, coalitions, entries of new parties, coalitional negotiations, defections, and withdrawals from race of the Right and Center parties in Poland between the 1993 and 1997 elections. Every line represents the story of coalitional, split, merger, etc. activity of a non-ephemeral political party or coalition on the Right or Center.[6] Consider for illustration a convoluted life path of one of the more interesting parties, PC. It formed the coalition ZPPC before the 1993 parliamentary elections that dissolved quickly after. Next, the PC joined another coalition, SUC, but it soon quit and joined PdP for local elections. When PdP dissolved in late 1994, PC split. The smaller faction joined the coalition OP in mid-1995. When this coalition was transformed into the AWS, the larger faction joined as well as an AWS founding member in mid-1996. Both PC's remained in the AWS coalition until the 1997 parliamentary elections.

The first serious attempt at consolidation, the long negotiations at St Catherine's Church, failed with no joint presidential candidate selected. The subsequent victory in the 1995 presidential election by a post-communist candidate provided a strong stimulus for consolidation. A relatively popular presidential candidate, Jan Olszewski, accomplished the first success of the rightist parties. Olszewski's popularity attracted considerable support in the polls for his new party, the ROP. The ROP's entry mobilized the remaining players on the Right who formed another broad coalition around the Solidarity trade union. The name AWS, Electoral Action Solidarity, included the magical word "Solidarity," which proved to be an excellent vehicle for promotion. In 1996, the AWS emerged as a focal point for the rightist electorate.

The consolidation of the Right resulted from a three-year search for a credible brand-name. The dynamics of learning explained in McKelvey and Ordeshook's model (1984) shows how an uninformed voter might use a poll to make an informed decision. When spatial positions of a cluster of small parties are virtually identical, voters are virtually indifferent among the parties and ready to vote strategically for the party which seems to be the most serious contender. Well-promoted coalescing offers them a "focal coalition". The existence of such a coalition induces more voters to strategically declare their support in polls, and the coalition gradually takes over a larger share of the cluster. Voters coordinate their intentions by learning about a new coalition's strength from polls or through media hype. A successful coalition displays a characteristic pattern of monotonic growth of support over time. For the ROP and the AWS, the support increased monotonically over the first several months since inception from 9% to 14%, and from 22% to 28%, respectively (OBOP 1996a, 1996b, 1997).

5.4.4 Sharing Seats and Stabilizing the Coalition

Even if parties figure out the benefits of coalescing and establish a solid name for their coalition, they still have to divide seats among themselves. Even if a sharing scheme is in place, heavy internal and external bargaining are inevitable. Until the deadline for registration of candidates, conflicts over the seat-shares can tear the coalition apart.

[6] Figure taken from Kaminski (1998). Minor players, minor changes of players' identities or names, and players other than political parties (except for the Solidarity trade union) are omitted. Dates are approximate. Relative players' strength not shown.

In all negotiations after the defeat in the 1993 elections, bargaining over seat-shares was the central part of the dispute. Marian Krzaklewski, the leader of the Solidarity trade union and the AWS coalition, worked out a marvelous solution to the sharing problem. Instead of proposing an exact sharing scheme in advance, Krzaklewski designed a set of institutions for intra-coalitional decision-making, with voting power allocated on the basis of a transparent scheme.

In the chief legislative and coordinating body of the AWS, the National Council, votes were allocated by a formula measuring the relative input of every partner to coalitional power. Krzaklewski, a computer scientist, operationalized the input of the partners with his own additive formula based on several variables, including poll estimates.[7] The essence of the scheme was that Solidarity had blocking power, but not winning power, in all national and regional executive and legislative bodies. To assure decisiveness, Krzaklewski assumed a dictatorial power to break the tie in the event of two voting stalemates over an issue (Krzaklewski and Raina 1997, p. 253; Graniszewski 1997).

Krzaklewski's solution offered to all members of the AWS coalition important Olsonian 'selective incentives' in the form of better media exposure that was associated with the brand name 'Solidarity'. Moreover, Solidarity was perceived as roughly equidistant to all Right parties, the political appetites of its activists were constrained by the trade union's internal rules, and Krzaklewski was regarded as an unbiased arbiter. His almost-dictatorial voting power was curbed by every member's exit power. Thus, all members of the coalition could reasonably expect that their seats under the AWS umbrella would be no smaller than under any of the alternative arrangements or unilateral action. Not specifying seat shares in advance moved potential conflicts and bargaining into the future when candidates were to be selected. In the meantime, the coalition focused on promoting the AWS brand name.

When positions on the AWS lists were allocated just before the 1997 elections, they disappointed many coalescents. Solidarity trade-unionists sneaked smoothly into the world of politics. With blocking power in all voting games, Solidarity's local branches formed minimal winning coalitions in districts with other AWS members and grabbed a disproportionate share of best places on district lists.[8] The position of trade-unionists was further improved by an ad hoc Solidarity-dominated Election Committee with a line-item veto power over the candidates.

---

[7] Variables included membership, numbers of representatives in legislatures at all levels, territorial span, media access, know-how potential, input to local AWS organizations, votes in recent presidential and parliamentary elections, and the mean support in recent polls for parties and leaders. The weights given to different variables in the Krzaklewski's formula were not released to the public.

[8] A high position on a list greatly improved the 'electability' of a candidate. In the 1991 elections candidates on the top of alphabetical lists (i.e., lists considered random with respect to candidates relative popularity) received an average of 31% votes for the entire list; while for the next places the numbers were 19%, 13%, 10.5%, and 8% (Raciborski 1997, p. 235).

The victory of Krzaklewski's heresthetic was not easy. During the final weeks before the registration deadline for candidates, an extraordinary spectacle of threats took place. Almost every major partner threatened to exit. However, the exit threat of any single party turned out to be incredible. The AWS built such a strong brand name that a defection of one or two parties would not change its support. Solidarity spokesman Piotr Zak announced that "he did not expect any major deserters that might weaken the AWS [since] most such politicians would face oblivion outside the AWS umbrella." (CEO 1997)

The only somewhat successful threat was carried out by a large subcoalition parties that included PC, Ruch STU, KPN, BBWR-SwW, PN, KK and ChD-SP, whose leaders submitted names of candidates who should be removed, added, and moved up on the lists (Zdort 1997b). Some of the group's suggestions were accepted.

The second attempt to mobilize a strong sub-coalition failed. A KPN leader declared, "we got offers from the UPR [a minor libertarian coalition]. If BBWR-BdP and BBWR-SwW join us, we will pass the five percent threshold. Now, the seven-eight percent for us means 10-15 percent less for the AWS" (Zdort 1997c). However, the prospective partners accepted small advances from the AWS and the sub-coalition soon broke down. After failed negotiations with the UPR, the lonely dissenter, KPN, withdrew from the elections in face of a total defeat.

5.5 Conclusion

The dilemmas of political consolidation in new democracies are probably the most spectacular transition-specific phenomena. The features of 'collective action' problems arising among parties are strongly sensitive to the particulars of the electoral situation, such as electoral laws, numbers of parties, or the ideological locations of parties. One of such possible models was analyzed in Section 5.3.

The students of transitional politics gathered a lot of empirical material and worked out a few models that analyze various aspects of consolidation. However, we still know too little to build a full-scale, empirically testable general model of coalition formation that could help us to predict with reasonable accuracy whether the parties could solve their collective action problem. Nevertheless, we can offer some comparative statics and name the main variables facilitating consolidation. In Poland after the 1993 elections, one could notice the fast learning of politicians, the ample time that the parties had before the 1997 elections for evaluating the consequences of their actions and the marketing of their new coalitions, and the development of new estimation techniques by polling companies. Despite the shortage of theory one could re-interpret the apparently chaotic actions of politicians depicted in Figure 5.2 as a trial-and-error search for a most beneficial coalitional structure. The search resulted in a large political coalition that successfully competed in the elections and seized the political power until the next elections.

Appendix

Acronyms and English Names of Major Parties, Coalitions, and Organizations

AWS	Electoral Action Solidarity
BBWR	Non-Partisan Bloc for Supporting the Reforms
BdP	Bloc for Poland
CBOZ	Center for Social Opinion Study (polling company)
KdR	Coalition for the Republic
KKW O	Country's Electoral Committee "Fatherland"
KLD	Liberal-Democratic Congress
KPN	Confederation of Independent Poland
MN	German Minority
NSZZ S	Solidarity Trade Union
OBOP	Center for Public Opinion Study (polling company)
PC	Centrum Alliance
PdP	Alliance for Poland
PJL	Alliance of 11th November
PSL	Polish Peasant Party
PSL-PL	Polish Peasant Party-Peasant Alliance
RdR	Movement for the Republic
ROP	Movement for the Reconstruction of Poland
SLD	Alliance of Democratic Left
SUC	Secretariat of Parties of the Right
UD	Democratic Union
UP	Labor Union
UPR	Real-politik Union; in 1997 election: Union of the Republic's Right
UW	Freedom Union
ZChN	Christian-National Union

Part II

Institutional Sclerosis

6 An Empirical Analysis of Institutional Sclerosis and Managerial Incentives: The Case of Motor Carrier Deregulation*

Charles R. Enis

According to Olson's (1982) theory of institutional sclerosis, politically stable societies such as the United States foster the formation of special interest groups whose collective actions can lead to rent seeking behavior and formation of market structures that resemble cartels. The consequences of this process are often deadweight losses to society and a retardation of innovation and economic growth. Government regulation of trucking, railroads, airlines, and public utilities in modern American economic history offer examples of this process (Olson 1982, p. 63). The sclerotic effects of motor carrier regulation and the subsequent mitigation of these effects through deregulation serve as the setting for this study.

According to Olson, institutional sclerosis is brought down when a major upheaval disrupts the stability that allowed the special interest groups to flourish. The government itself through the regulatory process became the agent that established the institutions through which special interest groups in the transportation and public utility industry obtained their monopoly power. Therefore, the abolishment of such institutions by the government through deregulation served as the major market upheaval that began the reversal of sclerosis in these sectors. During the period of regulation, institutions also developed within member firms of these industries. Such firm-specific institutions are characterized by a command and control leadership style that is unresponsive to change and discourages innovation. A major premise of the present study is that in addition to an industry-wide upheaval at the macro-level, firm-specific upheavals must occur at the micro-level to expedite the reversal of sclerosis. Thus, an expectation of this study is that firms that have experienced a micro-level upheaval are those firms that have jettisoned the internal institutions that stifle innovation. These less stable and more innovative firms will more successfully adapt to the competitive market environment brought about by deregulation.

* The author acknowledges the helpful comments of participants in sessions at the annual meetings of the Public Choice Society in conjunction with the Economic Science Association, the University of Nebraska Accounting Research Colloquium, the Temple University Accounting Research Colloquium, and the Pennsylvania State University Department of Business Logistics Research Colloquium. The comments and suggestions of Dennis Coates and Jim McKeown were also most appreciated. The author takes responsibility for any remaining errors.

The adoption of incentive compensation plans is the event used to identify motor carriers that have experienced some firm-specific upheaval that facilitated such a major change in compensation policy. Stable carriers that are resistant to innovation would be much less likely to adopt such plans. Trucking companies that have adopted incentive compensation plans are expected to be better positioned to handle the challenges and opportunities of market reform in two respects. First, such firms are better able to adjust to changing conditions because of the innovative climate that allowed the adoption of incentive plans to begin with. Second, trucking firms that offer incentive contracts that compensate managers based on the economic performances of their firms are those carriers that are likely to attract executives with the skills necessary to achieve such performances. Superior managerial talent should enable a firm to better compete after the removal of market restrictions. Success in a deregulated market requires the incorporation of greater strategic planning into a formerly strict command and control management style. This study hypothesizes that managers with greater expertise will self-select into the more innovative firms that offer incentive plans, and that such firms will out perform other firms to a greater degree after deregulation.

The data are analyzed using regression models covering pre- and post-deregulation periods. The dependent variables are measures of firm performance including the operating ratio, net earnings, revenue growth, and maintenance expenditures. While maintenance expenditures are not strictly a measure of performance, such captures the extent to which incentive plans encourage managers to achieve short-run performance by reducing such expenditures. This issue has important public policy implications as the public is concerned about sharing the highways with unsafe, poorly maintained vehicles. The independent variables are carrier size, whether the firm adopted an incentive plan, and the length of time (if any) the plan has been in effect.

The remainder of this article is organized as follows: the Background section discusses the origins of trucking regulation within the framework of institutional sclerosis, trucking industry deregulation, other empirical work related to managerial expertise and incentive compensation contracts, and certain unique features of the motor carrier industry; the Method section describes the variables, regression models, data configuration and sources employed in the empirical work; the Results section presents the findings; and finally, the Conclusion section summarizes the salient points of the study.

6.1 Background

6.1.1 Institutional Sclerosis and Regulation of the Trucking Industry

Olson's (1982) theory of institutional sclerosis suggests that societies that have had freedom of organization without upheaval the longest will experience the greatest consequences from growth-repressing coalitions. In describing this theory, Olson enumerated nine implications (1982, p. 74), six of which relate directly to the origin of and/or the manner of government regulation of the trucking industry. Implication 2 states that stable societies such as the United States accumulate more special-interest organizations for collective action over time. Special-interest groups representing agriculture, railroads, trucking, labor, and the federal bureaucracy all were stakeholders in instituting and prolonging trucking regulation.

Trucking regulation began with the Motor Carrier Act of 1935 (MCA35), (U.S. Congress 1935), and was the result of depression era economic policy and lobbying pressure from the railroad cartel (Snow 1977). The unexpected disinflation during the depression years motivated policies that would restrict competition, and artificially set prices above market levels to increase profits whereby firms could afford to hire idle workers. Hence, minimum rate restrictions became an earmark of trucking regulation.

The rail industry had been regulated by the Interstate Commerce Commission (ICC) for over thirty years in response to the collective action of farmers who sought protection from the railroad monopoly. Railroad regulation without corresponding trucking regulation rendered the pricing structure of the former less flexible than that of the latter. During the depression years, sectors with flexible pricing and low entry barriers became attractive to unemployed workers (Olson 1982, pp. 211-14). Many idle workers purchased used trucks and competed against established trucking firms as well as against railroads by offering low cost transportation service to shippers of high unit value freight. Thus, coalitions of both motor and rail carriers lobbied Congress for legislation that would establish higher shipping rates for trucking services and restrict entry into the motor carrier industry. It was also argued that minimum trucking rates and restricted entry created a public good in the sense that prices could not be driven so low that trucking firms could not afford adequate maintenance on their vehicles, or that roads would be congested with trucks thereby endangering the safety of public highways.[1] In short, although the special interest groups representing motor and rail carriers are non-encompassing organizations[2] that usually compete vituperatively for greater shares of the nation's transportation services, these distributional coalitions[3] colluded to obtain monopoly rights for established trucking firms to be administered by the ICC. In other words, motor carrier regulation represents use of government

[1] Other aspects of trucking regulation that may be regarded as public goods would be price and service stability, guaranteed service to rural markets, information reporting benefits, national defense, and a more favorable environmental impact; see Wallin (1975).

[2] Motor and rail carrier special-interest groups are non-encompassing organizations with respect to the American economy because they represent a relatively narrow segment of society. Non-encompassing organizations have little incentive to consider the effect of their policies on the efficiency of society as a whole; see Olson (1982, pp. 47-53) for a discussion of differences in the incentives of non-encompassing versus encompassing special-interest groups.

[3] Distributional coalitions are special-interest groups that engage in rent seeking activities to obtain greater shares of social output for their memberships while disregarding the social costs their efforts impose on the remainder of society (Olson 1982, pp. 43-47).

to adopt policies designed to reduce the vulnerability of trucking firms to the consequences of market competition.

MCA35 and subsequent related legislation transformed the motor carrier industry into a textbook cartel. Trucking firms under the auspices of the ICC organized rate bureaus to collectively set prices for transportation services. The ability to collectively set rates enabled the teamsters union to negotiate favorable wages for its members as increased labor cost could be passed through to shippers in higher rates (Goodman and Dolan 1982). Thus, this labor organization acted in support of prolonging motor carrier regulation. The existence of rate bureaus reflects Implication 6; distributional coalitions make decisions slowly and more often fix prices than quantities. The unanimous-consent bargaining procedures typical of rate bureaus resulted in sticky prices, and the process of gaining ICC approval to enter a market was slow and cumbersome given the entry restrictions of MCA35.

The entry restrictions that reduced the ability of trucking firms to compete with railroads and the ability of new truckers to compete with entrenched motor carriers illustrate Implication 7; distributional coalitions slow down innovation. The emergence of larger, faster and more reliable trucks and an expanding network of improved highways were innovations that could position trucking as a formidable competitor to railroads. Trucks can transport freight anywhere there are public highways. In contrast, trains can only serve markets where the railroad owns and maintains track. Although the rail industry could not directly thwart technological progress in trucking, the structure of the entry barriers served to nullify these advantages.

MCA35 required a new firm wishing to enter the trucking industry to apply to the ICC for an operating authority or a "certificate of public convenience and necessity". An operating authority gave a carrier the right to haul specified freight over designated routes. In short, whereas a railroad is physically restricted to haul freight between points where its tracks are located, a trucking firm became legally restricted to haul freight between points specified by the operating authority. Trucking firms in existence at the time of MCA35 received "grandfather" operating authorities. New operating authorities had to be obtained if a carrier wanted to serve a new market or haul a different commodity.

To obtain an operating authority from the ICC, the applicant had to prove that entry into a given market would not hurt existing carriers, that existing carriers could not adequately handle the traffic volume on the given route, and there was a compelling public need for another motor carrier to serve that route. This application procedure was very cumbersome, costly and hence consistent with Implication 8; distributional coalitions once successful are exclusive. Because these onerous entry restrictions protected both rail and motor carriers from new competition, one can also tie in Implication 9; the accumulation of distributional coalitions increases the complexity of regulation. A substantial resale market for existing authorities developed as the result of the complex process involved in obtaining new operating authorities from the ICC. Prior to deregulation the value of operating authorities increased substantially each year. The Council on Wage and Price Stability estimated the total market value of operating authorities to range from three to four billion dollars during the mid-seventies (U.S. Senate 1976). Even bankrupt carriers were able to sell operating rights for large sums. Associated Freight Lines, for example, received 20 million dollars for their operating rights in a liquidation sale held on July 9, 1976 (Wilson 1980). Interest in buying Associated's operating rights was so keen that about 300 participants were attracted to the auction that was marked by intense bidding, and various individual certificates selling for high values (Aug 1976).[4] Such values were evidence of rates of return that exceeded those necessary to raise capital and, in effect, were the capitalized monopoly rents attributable to protected markets (Breen 1977).

Implication 4 states that special-interest organizations reduce efficiency in the societies in which they operate. There are many aspects of trucking regulation that reduce efficiency. For example, a trucking firm may have the authority to haul freight from point A to B, but not from B to A. This situation results in idle capacity as the truck must return empty to its point of origin. Furthermore, the operating authority may specify that the truck must travel through point C (a "gateway") on its way to point B rather than using a direct route, a requirement also wasteful in time and fuel. In addition, a shipper that wants to transport commodities X and Y from point A to B may have to hire two different trucking firms as operating authorities impose freight as well as route restrictions. According to Moore (1978), trucking regulation had cost society an estimated four billion dollars in regulatory inefficiency, and in economic rents accruing to trucking firms and the Teamsters union for 1972 alone. In summary, the economic environment in which trucking firms operated prior to deregulation was demonstrative of the consequences of institutional sclerosis.

6.1.2 Market Deregulation

Government regulation of trucking and other industries has continuously been a concern to economists and policymakers. Critics of motor carrier regulation often contend that regulatory rate and entry controls restrain competition, raise the price of transportation services, redistribute income from consumers to carriers, misallocate traffic among transportation modes, and allow firms to achieve economic rents (DeVany and Saving 1977; Wilson 1980).

In addition to the criticisms of economists, several other factors lead to the unraveling of trucking regulation. To begin with, the first regulatory domino fell when airlines were deregulated several years earlier. As the unexpected disinflation of the depression years lead to regulation, the unexpected inflation of the seventies played a role in the deregulation movement as policy makers in the Carter administration believed deregulation would result in lower costs and an abatement

[4] For example, Ryder Truck Lines acquired New England operating certificates for $1.3 million. Great Coastal paid $1.6 million for certain rights to serve the Mid-Atlantic region. The largest single purchase was Leeway Motor Freight's acquisition of operating rights in the Carolinas for $5.4 million. About 17 groups acquired portions of Associated's operating routes throughout most of the Eastern half of the United States (Aug 1976).

of inflation. The Carter administration's commitment to neutralize the regulatory establishment resulted in appointments to the ICC of pro-competition "outsiders" that had no vested interest in prolonging regulation (Goodman and Dolan 1982). Also, to make deregulation less unpalatable to the trucking coalitions, motor carriers were subsequently granted a tax write-off of the book values of their operating rights over five years (U.S. Congress 1981).

Because of continuing doubts over the efficiency of regulation, the U.S. Congress enacted the Motor Carrier Act of 1980 (MCA80) (U.S. Congress 1980), which significantly increased competition in the motor carrier field. MCA80 was a legislative attempt to promote competition among motor carriers and to remove barriers to efficient operations as a means of providing better quality and more flexible service to shippers at a lower cost. Thus, in relaxing entry controls, the ICC has allowed a proliferation of less restrictive versions of operating rights (ICC 1981). For example, prior to MCA80 (in 1979) there were 17,000 regulated carriers in the nation while soon after deregulation the figure grew to 28,000 certificated carriers (ICC 1980, 1984). More importantly, for both new and existing operating authorities, MCA80 mandates that certain certificate limitations be eliminated or reduced. Among the limitations lifted are back-haul restrictions, the number of shippers to be served, intermediate points to be served, types of commodities to be handled, geographical scope, gateways to be observed, and highways to be traveled. Specifically, carriers became free to ship a wider variety of goods along the most direct route from origin to destination, to solicit back-haul traffic, and to serve intermediate points along a particular route (Harper 1980). In terms of pricing policy, carriers can now more quickly adjust freight rates to compete with railroads, to utilize excess capacity, or to attract new customers without rate bureau interference (Enis and Morash 1986). In short, MCA80 was aimed at reversing the consequences of institutional sclerosis.

6.1.3 Market Competition, Innovation, and Managerial Skills

MCA80 offers a natural quasi-experiment to study the impact of a change in a macro-economic setting on micro-economic phenomenon. The institutional sclerotic aspects of market regulation neutralized any competitive advantage attributable to motor carriers that embraced innovation and employed executives with superior managerial skills. Market restrictions inhibit managers from using their talents to be innovative in attracting new customers and to be effective in allocating resources in response to changing conditions because regulators control many of the variables that are critical to such strategic decision-making.

Prior to deregulation most decision-making was operational such as scheduling trucks for maintenance, meeting shipping deadlines, supervising drivers, controlling costs, issuing freight invoices, and complying with voluminous federal, state and local regulations. It is questionable as to whether the skills needed to cope with such a strict command and control environment would be applicable to the opportunities and challenges of a competitive market. In short, some firm-specific upheaval is needed to free carriers from the command and control institutions that inhibit innovation for such firms to succeed in a competitive market.

The research question investigated in this study requires the identification of those motor carriers that are innovative and employ managers that have the skills needed to succeed in a market moving towards greater competitiveness. Such skills, however, are unobservable; hence, a surrogate is needed to indicate the presence of an atmosphere conducive to developing superior managerial potential (Heckman 1976). Self-sorting theories in labor economics suggest that job seekers are drawn to situations that offer compensation contracts that reveal their capabilities (MacDonald 1980). Firms that pay-on-performance are more likely to attract higher quality employees than those that offer only a flat salary (Jovanovic 1979). In short, executives who have greater expertise to improve economic performance (i.e., increase earnings) by reducing expenses and embracing competitive market opportunities will accept employment contracts with motor carriers that reward such performance, and also provide the environment needed to exercise their decision-making skills.

One can make the proposition that leadership innovations, such as pay-on-performance contracts, are more likely to attract a class of managers who are risk-seeking and who possess skills compatible with the uncertainties inherent in an unregulated market. The present study hypothesizes that motor carriers that offer incentive compensation plans are free of the institutions that inhibit change and are thus better able to incorporate into the existing command and control structure the strategic planning necessary to gain a competitive advantage over more stable carriers in the new deregulated market. Earnings-based compensation is used to identify carriers that behave in a manner consistent with the strategic performance objectives of firms operating in a free market.

6.1.4 Earnings-Based Compensation

Much of the literature on earnings-based compensation plans indicates the adoption of such plans has an influence on managerial behavior.[5] In other words, managers are purported to take actions that will influence the reported earnings variable in their incentive schemes so as to maximize their compensation. Managers can influence reported earnings in several ways. First, executives can choose accounting alternatives that will affect earnings in their favor; e.g., choosing to either capitalize or expense certain asset improvements (Healy 1985). Secondly, managers can manipulate events such as allowing inventories to rise or fall to shift earnings from one period to the next. Thirdly, managers can make decisions that affect the economic performance of their firms. For example, maintenance expenditures can be increased or decreased to produce profits more in concert with their desired incentive awards.

[5] Specific details of earnings-based and other types of executive compensation plans are covered in Larcker (1983), and Smith and Watts (1982).

Many studies of earnings-based compensation plans postulated a direct relationship between reported earnings and managerial incentives (Watts and Zimmerman 1978; Holthausen 1981; Bowen et al. 1981). Tehranian and Waegelein (1985) observed positive unexpected earnings associated with the adoption of an earnings-based bonus plan. Tehranian and Waegelein (1985) concluded that managers either were motivated to increase earnings following plan adoption or that they adopted bonus plans in anticipation of higher than expected earnings. Waegelein (1988) showed that earnings-based plans were linked to increased capital expenditures but not to discretionary expenditures on advertising and research and development. In contrast, Larcker (1987) found a negative relationship between incentive plans and discretionary expenditures. The empirical work cited in this section on incentive plans has as its theoretical underpinnings the principal-agent framework (Jensen and Meckling 1976). Here principals (owners) offer agents (managers) incentive contracts to induce goal congruency between the two groups. Alternatively, incentive contracts attract managers that possess the skills necessary to meet the performance demands of owners.

6.1.5 The Motor Carrier Industry

Trucking firms offer several features as subjects for a micro-level study of institutional sclerosis. In discussing Implication 7, Olson (1982, p. 63) specifically mentioned trucking as a coalition that obtained monopoly rights through public regulation. Thus, this industry is a setting where the consequences of institutional sclerosis should be observed. Trucking has also undergone the upheaval of deregulation, which provides the opportunity to study firms in this industry before and after the reversal of the regulatory process. Unlike railroads and airlines that have also experienced deregulation, the trucking industry is dominated by many small privately held firms thus providing an observation-rich setting for a micro-level study. A common theme in Olson's work is the extension of micro-economic principles to macro-economic issues. Furthermore, focusing on a single industry with many firms, as opposed to several industries with fewer firms, reduces the confounding effects and noise from variations in production functions, asset mixes, and accounting procedures that exist across industries (Ely 1991; Murphy 1985). Finally, the behavior of trucking firms has social implications in that the failure to adequately maintain trucks results in externalities such as poor highway safety, fuel inefficiency, noise and air pollution.

Because the motor carrier industry has had a history of regulation and has numerous privately held firms in its ranks, earnings (as opposed to share price performance) play a dominant role in incentive compensation schemes. Managers of trucking firms do not have as much freedom to manipulate reported earnings as managers in other industries. To begin with, the regulatory requirements of the ICC resulted in relatively uniform accounting methods to accompany the consistent asset mix found in the industry. Inventories and manufacturing processes are not factors in trucking operations. Thus, managers cannot influence reported earnings in their favor by adjusting inventory levels or manufacturing overhead allocations. Such uniformity and consistency tend to control for potentially confounding factors that have been reported to influence the relationship between executive compensation and performance measures (Healy et al. 1987; Lewellen et al. 1987). However, managers of trucking firms can manipulate events to influence reported profits in their favor such as cutting maintenance expenditures by ordering cheaper tires and parts, delaying routine maintenance and hiring lesser skilled mechanics. Such behavior can be detrimental to the economic health of the firm in the long run and create social cost on the macro-level.

On several occasions the broadcast media has drawn attention to the public safety risk, pollution, and energy inefficiency that dilapidated trucks pose on the nation's highways.[6] Thus, factors that encourage motor carriers to maintain operating equipment are important public policy issues in that rights-of-way for this transportation mode are public highways. Any industry that fails to make appropriate maintenance expenditures is likely to create adverse externalities. However, few industries create externalities with the political visibility of those associated with the motor carrier industry in that trucks are part of the daily environment faced by many Americans.[7]

A justification for regulating markets is to prevent the deleterious consequences of ruinous competition. Unbridled competition is alleged to drive down profits to the point that firms sacrifice their long run economic health as a means of cutting cost to survive in the short run. Such behavior raises the specter that motor carriers may be induced to sacrifice truck maintenance as a cost cutting tactic. Furthermore, earnings-based compensation plans may even exacerbate this possibility as managers strive to maximize bonuses linked to contemporaneous profits. Thus, this study also tests whether earnings-based compensation plans are associated with reduced maintenance expenditures in the motor carrier industry.[8]

---

[6] Truck accidents account for over 4,000 highway deaths and several billion dollars in economic losses each year. In 1986, heavy commercial motor vehicles were involved in 4,888 fatal accidents, representing 9.3 percent of such accidents. However, these trucks account for only 4.3 percent of vehicle miles traveled and less than 1 percent of registered vehicles (U.S. General Accounting Office 1989).

[7] The frequency of GAO studies is evidence of a substantial degree of political visibility and public scrutiny associated with truck safety issues (U.S. General Accounting Office 1987, 1989, 1990a, 1990b, 1991).

[8] Managers can increase profits in the short run decreasing discretionary expenditures. Maintenance expenditures are discretionary to the extent that less expensive inputs can be substituted for more expensive inputs (i.e., parts and labor), and scheduled maintenance can be delayed for short periods. This study does not suggest that carriers will eliminate any required maintenance. Also, managers can reduce discretionary expenditures such as advertising in lieu of maintenance reductions. This study focuses on maintenance expenditures because of the social cost implications they entail.

6.2 Method

6.2.1 General Description

The research design is a two-by-two that uses a series of ordinary least squares regressions. This difference in differences design is specified to ascertain the influence of incentive plan adoptions (an indicator of micro-level upheavals) and deregulation (an indicator of a macro-level upheaval) on the economic performance of motor carriers. The dependent or performance variables are efficiency, profitability, market growth, and maintenance expenditures. Within Olson's framework, the adoption of incentive plans identifies firms that have jettisoned institutions that inhibit innovation and the ability to adjust to changing conditions. Such firm-specific upheavals are expected to compliment the industry-wide upheaval of deregulation in expediting the reversal of institutional sclerosis.

The regressions are pooled cross-section time-series models with fixed effects. Observations for these models are 1,600 firm-years, consisting of ten consecutive years of data for 80 carriers that adopted incentive plans, and 80 similar carriers that never had an incentive plan. Extending Olson's Implication 2 to the micro-level predicts that stable organizations are more susceptible to stagnation than unstable organizations.[9] A premise of the present study is that motor carriers can be

[9] The terms "upheaval" and "unstable" as applied to motor carriers that adopted incentive plans do not necessarily mean that these firms were undergoing destructive turmoil or financial distress. Instead, these carriers were unstable in that entrenched institutions that stymied innovation (as suggested by Implication 7) were sufficiently neutralized to allow innovation. A relatively radical event such as a major change in executive compensation is evidence that such an innovation has occurred. The change agent responsible for such a "shake-up" in the *status quo*, and whether this catalyst was favorable or unfavorable, is unobservable and beyond the scope of this study.

Two important stakeholders in business enterprises are owners and managers. In large publicly traded corporations these stakeholders may be very distinct groups. However, these groups overlap in small privately held firms such as the trucking companies sampled in the present study. In these firms, top level officers are likely to also be owners while middle and lower level executives constitute the managerial stakeholder group. The form of upheaval that leads to the adoption of incentive plans is often a conflict between owners and managers (Jones and Hill 1992; Lenz and Lyles 1986). Owners may be dissatisfied with firm performance and look to incentive plans to motivate managers to make strenuous effort on behalf of the company to increase the value of the firm (Brozovsky and Sopariwala 1995). Alternatively, managers that are responsible for outstanding performance may demand that owners share the fruits of their efforts by paying on performance.

The adoption of pay-on-performance contracts also signals an increase in the level of risk that owners share with managers. Increased levels of risk and/or risk sharing are also indicative of some form of firm-specific upheaval. Example of such upheavals that could usher in incentive plans include changes in ownership and/or leadership styles, increased

grouped into stable and unstable organizations based upon whether or not the firm adopted an incentive plan. Each "unstable" or plan adopting carrier is paired with a "stable" or non-adopting carrier over the same ten-year period. The ten-year period for each carrier-pair was determined by the year of plan adoption, and consisted of the five years prior to adoption through the four years following adoption. These ten-year periods are staggered from 1958 to 1987. Thus, some of the firms that experienced a micro-level upheaval, as indicated by plan adoption, also experienced the macro-level upheaval of deregulation that was in place during the 1980-1987 period. Other plan-adopting carriers did not experience deregulation during the ten years in which they are represented in the sample. Ninety percent of the firm-years are within the 1968-1984 period. Table 6.1 shows the frequency of firm-years within the two-by-two design.

Table 6.1. Distribution of firm years

Compensation policy	Market environment		Row totals
	Pre-deregulation (before 1980)	Post-deregulation (after 1979)	
Plan	622	178	800
No plan	622	178	800
Column totals	1,244	356	1,600

6.2.2 Dependent Variables

Operating Ratio (OR): The operating ratio is operating expenses divided by revenues expressed as a percentage. Because extraordinary expenses, income taxes, and interest are excluded, individual peculiarities are eliminated. The operating ratio is an inverse measure of managerial efficiency that is characteristic of trucking firms, closely followed by industry analysts, and a frequent variable in earnings-based incentive plans in the trucking industry. The popularity of the operating ratio as an important performance measure in trucking reflects the operating command and control orientation of management in the industry given its history of regulation. Managing cost is critical in a tightly regulated market because there is little else to manage.

Net Earnings (NE): This is "bottom – line" reported accounting income, and is examined because all incentive plans in this study are based on one or more variants of earnings measured over one or several years. Net earnings like all other monetary variables in this study are adjusted using the Consumer Price Index for all Urban Consumers (CPI – U) to obtain values expressed in constant 1967 dollars in thousands. This adjustment was performed to remove the effect of changing price levels to measure variables in real terms. Unlike the other variables ex-

degrees of separation between owners and managers, shifts in organization structure from centralized to decentralized management, and increased competition from railroads.

pressed in monetary terms that follow, the net earnings variable is never expressed in natural log form as it may take on negative values.

Revenues (REVE): This dependent variable is the natural logarithm of gross fees from freight transportation in 1967 dollars, and is a measure of market growth. Prior to deregulation, carriers had little control over *REVE* as most of the usual determinants of market growth were controlled by regulators. Deregulation transfers market control from regulators such as rate bureaus to the individual carriers that compete in the market. Innovative carriers are expected to be better positioned to exploit market expansion opportunities as the managerial talent selected by such firms is expected to be better skilled at setting optimal rates and selecting markets to enter.

In spite of the new market expansion opportunities, aggregate revenues for the trucking industry are expected to decline following deregulation. Consistent with Implications 6 and 9, rate bureaus and ICC entry controls were part of a system that tended to support higher rate levels and rate stability than would otherwise exist. This system will unravel as greater competition exerts downward pressure on rate levels, and the freedom to adjust rates to competitive conditions increases rate variability.

Maintenance Expenditures (MATN): Values of this variable consist of the natural logarithm of the total amount spent on vehicle repairs, parts, tires, tubes, etc. The inclusion of this variable addresses the issue of whether managers sacrifice truck maintenance as a means of attempting to improve performance measures.

6.2.3 Independent Variables

This research employs three main and two interaction independent variables that relate to the existence of earnings-based compensation plans and/or a regulated versus a deregulated market. The former measure the extent to which carriers sustained a micro-level upheaval that should attract executives with greater risk-taking propensities and other strategic decision-making attributes, while the latter indicate the market environment in which such talents can be advantageous.

Incentive Plan (PLAN): This dummy variable is equal to one if a carrier adopted an earnings-based compensation plan and zero if a carrier did not adopt such a plan. Ten years of data are observations for each of 80 plan-adopting carriers and 80 no-plan carriers. Obviously the *PLAN* variable is equal to zero across all ten years for the no-plan firms. The ten years of data for the plan-adopting carriers begins with the five years prior to plan adoption. However, the plan variable is coded one for all ten of these years, even those years prior to adoption. The purpose of the *PLAN* variable is to capture information about a carrier that is associated with a predisposition to adopt an incentive plan as well as the effects of the plan once it is in place. Given that some carriers changed compensation policy while others in similar circumstances did not, it is possible there are differences in the innovative climate between these two types of firms. Consistent with Implication 7, the innovative climate of the former trucking firms is presumed to be the product of some unobservable upheaval that destabilized the *status quo*. The pre-adoption years reflect the destabilizing processes that led up to implementation of the plans, while the remaining years capture changes in managerial behavior induced by the pay-on-performance contracts. Thus, the firm-specific operating environments of the plan-adopting carriers versus those of the more stable no-plan carriers likely differed throughout the ten-year window.

Length of Plan (PLGH): This variable is one in the year prior to adoption of an incentive plan, two in the year of adoption, three in the year following adoption and so on post adoption. The variable is zero otherwise. Thus, six is the maximum value for the *PLGH* variable. The reason for this coding is that proposed incentive plans can affect managerial behavior in the year prior to formal adoption as actions are taken in anticipation of the plan. Values for the *PLGH* variable are obviously zero across all ten years for the non-adopting carriers. *PLGH* measures whether changes in the dependent variables that are associated with the *PLAN* variable are attributable to the innovative climate responsible for the incentive plans or to the managerial behaviors induced by the plans. If the estimated coefficients for *PLAN* and *PLGH* are both significant in the same direction, then the plans selected for managerial capabilities that enhanced the performance measures of innovative firms. If the estimated coefficient for *PLAN* (*PLGH*) is significant (insignificant) then the performance measure is more attributable to the innovative climate responsible for the plan than to the plan itself. Signs in opposite directions suggest that the plans motivated managers to change performances that persisted prior to plan adoptions. For example, the upheavals responsible for the new compensation policy may have had a deleterious effect on profitability, and the incentive plans in turn selected for managers that improved profitability.

Differences in the signs of the estimated coefficients for *PLAN* and *PLGH* could also mean that the initial effects of the incentive plans were not sustainable. For example, a new compensation scheme may at first trigger above average performance. However, the principle of "regression toward the mean" predicts that above average performance is often followed by declines in performance; see Tversky and Kahneman (1974). Furthermore, the upheavals responsible for the incentive plans could have displaced old institutions with new ones. Overtime these new institutions could slow down the progress initiated by the incentive plans.

Market Regulation (DEREG): This dummy variable equals one if the year of an observation is after 1979, and zero otherwise, and hence is an indicator of the macro-level upheaval of deregulation.

Market and Plan Interaction (PLREG): This dummy variable is equal to *PLAN*DEREG* and represents the interaction between the micro- and macro-level upheavals indicative of incentive plan adoptions and deregulation, respectively. *PLREG* addresses the issue of whether plan-adopting carriers outperformed no-plan carriers to a relatively greater degree after deregulation than before deregulation.

Market and Plan Length Interaction (LGREG): This dummy variable is *PLGH*DEREG*. The estimated coefficient for LGREG determines whether the incentive effects of pay-on-performance contracts are more sustainable in a deregulated versus a regulated market.

Revenue Equipment (SIZE): This variable is investment in trucks, trailers and equipment, and controls for carrier size. The natural logarithm of *SIZE* captures much of the variance in operating features that exist among motor carriers. For example, the larger a firm is the greater is its expected earnings, revenues, number of employees, etc. It is important to control for firm size in executive compensation research as some studies have reported that the association between pay and performance is related to firm size (Jensen 1989; Jensen and Murphy 1990).

6.2.4 Analysis

6.2.4.1 General Model

Equation (1) is the general form of the pooled cross-section time-series regression model used in the data analysis:

$$Y_{itj} = \hat{\beta}_{0j} + \hat{\beta}_{1j}(SIZE_{it}) + \hat{\beta}_{2j}(PLAN_{it}) + \hat{\beta}_{3j}(PLGH_{it}) + \hat{\beta}_{4j}(DEREG_{it}) + \hat{\beta}_{5j}(PLREG_{it}) + \hat{\beta}_{6j}(LGREG_{it}) + \hat{e}_{itj} \tag{1}$$

where:

Y_{itj} = value for firm i in year t for dependent variable j;

i = firm 1 ... 160;

t = year 1 ... 10;

j = operating ratio, net earnings, revenues, and maintenance expenditures;

$\hat{\beta}_{0j}$ = intercept for model j;

$\hat{\beta}_{1j} .. \hat{\beta}_{6j}$ = estimated regression coefficients for model j;

$\hat{e}_{itj}$ = estimated residual for firm i in year t and model j.

Because each of the 160 firms is represented in the data ten times, and these carriers are matched to form 80 pairs of similar firms that behaved differently regarding incentive plans, Equation (1) also includes 79 dummy variables identifying all but one of the carrier pairs. One pair is omitted to avoid perfect collinearity with the intercept.[10]

Two continuous variables were included in equation (1) to control for trend effects. The first is *YR* and is the raw values for each year (i.e., 58. . .87). The second is the quadratic form of the *YR* variable; i.e., year-squared (*YR-SQ*) which allows the trend to be nonlinear.

[10] Incorporating intercepts for each firm, as opposed to firm-pairs, would make the firm fixed effects perfectly collinear with *PLAN*. Likewise, including intercepts for each year would make these variables perfectly collinear with *DEREG*. Such collinearity would nullify meaningful tests of the main variables.

6.2.4.2 Hypotheses

Significance tests of the appropriate estimated regression coefficients serve as tests of the following general null hypotheses:

H_{01}: Deregulation (i.e., a macro-level upheaval) had no effect on the efficiency, profitability, revenues, or maintenance expenditures of firms in the motor carrier industry. One or more of the $\hat{\beta}_{4j}$ ... $\hat{\beta}_{6j}$ coefficients achieving statistical significance would suggest rejection of H_{01} for the specified dependent variable.

H_{02}: Innovation (i.e., a micro-level upheaval) as evidenced by those motor carriers that adopted incentive compensation plans, is not associated with efficiency, profitability, revenues, or maintenance expenditures either before or after deregulation. Statistical significance reported for one or more of the following: $\hat{\beta}_{2j}$, $\hat{\beta}_{3j}$, $\hat{\beta}_{5j}$, or $\hat{\beta}_{6j}$, would support rejection of H_{02} for the indicated dependent variable.

Rejection of these null hypotheses is evidence that upheavals at the micro and/or macro level impact economic performance in the trucking industry. Because no definitive direction can be specified regarding the alternative forms of these hypotheses, all tests are two-tailed. However, the changes in performance that are linked to upheavals are expected to reflect a mitigation of institutional sclerosis.

6.2.4.3 Expectations

Deregulation ended entry controls and inflexible pricing institutions in the motor carrier industry, and thereby, according to Olson's Implications 6 and 8, initiated a reversal of institutional sclerosis. In other words, deregulation was an upheaval that brought down the institutions that thwarted innovation, growth, and competition in the trucking industry. Deregulation offers motor carriers the opportunity to enter new markets, adjust service offerings to meet shipper demands, to eliminate idle capacity and inefficient route structures, and to set optimum freight rates to maximize revenues. Astute exploitation of these opportunities is expected to increase revenues, efficiency, and profitability. On the other hand, increased levels of competition are expected to dissipate economic rents that are associated with operating authorities, and propped up by rate bureaus. Realization of this scenario is expected to have the opposite effect on performance. The focus of the present study is on the extent to which the more innovative carriers, as evidenced by the adoption of incentive plans, outperform their more stable no-plan counterparts after relative to before deregulation.

6.2.4.4 Data

Data regarding compensation plans were obtained from a direct mail survey that I sent to 1,500 motor carriers selected randomly from the *TRINC's Blue Book of the*

Trucking Industry (hereafter TRINCs).[11] Because motor carriers are largely privately held businesses, proxy statements that contain compensation data for publicly traded corporations were unavailable. The data gathered from the research instrument allowed the determination of those respondent firms that adopted incentive plans, the dates of adoption and the criteria upon which they are based. A respondent firm was classified as having an incentive plan if the plan participants received annual remuneration based upon some measure of earnings. Other data used in this study were hand-collected from TRINCs yearbooks.

Of the 307 responses received, 167 carriers had adopted incentive plans. To have been selected for this study, a plan-adopting firm must have been conducting trucking operations for at least five years prior to plan adoption and four years following the year of adoption. In addition, data for the variables employed in this study for this ten-year period must be reported in TRINCs. Of the 167 adopters, 80 carriers met these conditions.[12] Next, 80 of the 140 carriers that did not adopt an incentive plan were selected for inclusion in the empirical work. These firms had to have the same data availability as the 80 plan firms for the same ten-year horizon.[13]

[11] Motor carriers with operating revenues in excess of specified thresholds must file annual reports with the Federal government. At the time of this study, all carriers with revenues of $1 million or more had to file annual reports (Form M-1, financial and operating data) with the ICC. Data from these annual reports were compiled into annual editions of "TRINC's Blue Book of the Trucking Industry" by TRINC Transportation Consultants, a division of Dun and Bradstreet. Data for this study were hand collected from these annual editions. The earliest TRINC's yearbook was the 1959 edition (reporting 1958 data). Dun and Bradstreet disbanded TRINC in 1985. As a result the 1985 edition (reporting 1984 data) was the last TRINC's yearbook. Data for years after 1984 were obtained from annual volumes of the Motor Carrier Annual Report published by the American Trucking Associations. Form M-1 data does not disclose information regarding incentive compensation plans; thus, these data were collected by survey. The survey instrument was sent during April of 1983 to motor carriers that were sampled from the 1982 edition of TRINCs. Thus, to be included in the study a trucking firm had to have filed Form M-1 with the ICC for reporting year 1981.

[12] Four explanations account for the exclusion of 87 plan adopting carriers from the matched-pairs design. First, 32 firms were dropped for having incentive plans in force since their inceptions. These adoptions were unlikely attributable to micro-level upheavals. Second, 23 adoptions were not timely. Data availability for this study spanned the 1958-1987 period. For a firm to have five (four) years of data availability before (after) adoption, such must occur between 1963 and 1983. Plan adoptions outside of this window were thus not timely. Third, 21 plan adopters were eliminated because insufficient data were reported in TRINCs. Fourth, 11 firms were dropped because appropriate matches could not be found. Data for the 87 plan adopters that were not included in the study were collected for 1981, see footnote 11. Mean operating revenues for the excluded and included plan adopters for 1981 were $14,797 and $25,437 (1967 dollars in thousands), respectively; the difference in means is not statistically significant ($t = 1.02$).

[13] Ten years is an appropriate window to capture the effects of internal upheavals that lead up to and follow incentive plan adoptions. Compiling data for longer durations introduces

Table 6.2. Differences in means between no plan and plan firms one year before adoption

	Plan firms		No plan firms			
Variable	Mean	Std dev	Mean	Std dev	|t| value[a]	2 tail prob> |t|
Operating ratio[b]	93.9	6.8	96.0	5.7	2.13	0.035
Net earnings[c]	526.6	31,320.2	391.6	2,346.0	0.43	0.669
Revenues[c]	12,508.3	1,565.8	15,042.0	40,867.7	0.44	0.661
Maintenance[c]	523.3	637.4	955.1	2,585.6	1.45	0.151
Size[c d]	3,296.8	5,532.1	4,406.1	12,409.1	0.73	0.467

[a]Test that the means of the plan and no plan firms do not differ.
[b]Operating expenses as a percent of operating revenues.
[c]1967 dollars in thousands.
[d]Revenue equipment at cost; trucks, tractors, and trailers owned by the carrier.

The 80 no-plan firms were selected so that each plan adopter could be matched with a no-plan carrier. Gross revenues and freight classification for the year prior to plan adoption were used as matching criteria. The ratio of the smaller firm's to the larger firm's gross revenues had to be at least .2. Paired firms must also have had the same freight classification: general freight, household goods, refrigerated and agricultural products, petroleum products, and other specialized freight. Thus, paired firms served shippers in similar sectors of the economy and invested in like-kind revenue equipment (trucks, tractors, and trailers). Table 6.2 reports descriptive statistics to validate the matching criteria. With the exception of the operating ratio, none of the means for the dependent variables or the matching variable (size) were significantly different between the plan and no plan firms one year prior to the year in which the former carriers adopted incentive plans.

6.3 Results

Table 6.3 reports descriptive statistics for the four dependent variables and the major control variable—size. This table shows means and standard deviations for

a greater risk of survivorship bias. Small privately held firms such as those common in the trucking industry do not have the longevity of large publicly traded corporations.

both plan-adopting, and non-plan-adopting carriers for the five most recent pre-deregulation years (1975-1979), and the first five years of the deregulation period (1980-1984). Table 6.3 shows steady increases in mean net earnings, revenues, maintenance and size during the pre-deregulation period for both plan and no plan firms. In contrast, these indicators were sporadic during the deregulation period, and suggestive of the macro-level upheaval created by MCA80. Similar evidence of the micro-level upheavals attributable to the plan firms can be noted by observing the greater standard deviations for these firms relative to the no plan firms prior to deregulation. Table 6.4 reports in columns (2) through (5) the estimated coefficients, t-values, and significance levels for the variables in equation (1) using operating ratio (*OR*), net earnings (*NE*), revenues (*REVE*), and maintenance expenditures (*MATN*) as dependent variables, respectively.[14]

Table 6.3. Descriptive statistics

		Opearating ratio		Net earnings		Revenues		Maintenance		Size	
Years	N	Mean	Std dev	Mean	Std dev	Mean	Std dev	Mean	Std dev	Mean	Std dev
Plan firms											
Pre-deregulation											
1975	58	97.9	7.7	385	1,514	13,128	35,168	837	2,231	4,706	12,525
1976	64	95.2	4.0	592	2,143	15,530	39,849	941	2,564	4,959	12,745
1977	63	95.6	5.0	646	2.506	17,407	45,722	1,125	2,931	5,346	14,311
1978	59	95.6	4.9	797	3,089	20,935	55,319	1,237	3,449	6,009	16,698
1979	52	95.4	3.3	716	2,753	23,584	58,734	1,389	3,725	6,829	18,342
Deregulation											
1980	46	95.0	3.7	181	1,528	23,896	59,138	1,282	3,400	6,807	17,980
1981	39	96.4	4.9	1,043	3,956	25,437	61,440	1,229	3,183	6,593	18,605
1982	35	98.6	7.5	527	2,222	25,602	62,559	1,134	2,991	6,687	20,350
1983	23	98.2	5.8	422	647	21,036	30,111	822	1,360	4,145	5,982
1984	18	99.5	7.7	518	1,156	26,278	36,504	902	1 622	4,538	7,527
No plan firms											
Pre-deregulation											
1975	58	95.1	6.0	350	1,017	9,075	17,513	377	445	2,880	3,871
1976	64	94.5	4.7	482	1,134	11,484	23,837	455	571	3,033	4,337
1977	63	95.5	5.0	434	1,333	13,130	27,829	574	718	3,600	5,458
1978	59	94.8	5.6	480	1,388	14,182	31,960	619	770	4,071	6,484
1979	52	95.4	5.1	629	1,914	17,252	40,124	645	759	4,577	7,204
Deregulation											
1980	46	95.6	5.4	598	2,374	18,084	43,122	592	698	4,774	7,376
1981	39	95.9	4.2	1,053	2,768	21,403	47,914	565	641	4,813	7,323
1982	35	94.8	5.5	631	2,128	21,030	47,063	562	733	4,826	8,165
1983	23	98.3	7.7	703	1,914	22,973	52,667	629	873	4,937	8,504
1984	18	97.9	8.0	1,305	3,004	29,837	66,446	738	1,014	6,289	11,480

The model shown in Table 6.4, column (2) has *OR* as the dependent variable. As the *OR* increases, managerial efficiency decreases. Thus, estimated coefficients with negative signs are indicative of explanatory variables that are associated with

[14] The number of observations reported in Table 6.4 is 1,582. This figure is less than 1,600 because some observations were deleted because of missing data.

managerial efficiency. The model shown in column (2) is the only such model where the major control variable *SIZE* is not significant (i.e., 2-tail p-value > .05). *SIZE* is highly significant in the other three models because, in general, larger firms have higher absolute levels of income, sales and service revenues, and various classes of operating expenses (e.g., maintenance) than do smaller firms. Also, this is the only model where the *YR* and *YR-SQ* variables are significant. The estimated coefficients for these variables suggest that managerial efficiency in the trucking industry has increased at a decreasing rate over time. *PLAN* is the only main variable that is significant in column (2), indicating that carriers that use incentive plans are less efficient than carriers that don't. The insignificant coefficient on the *PLGH* variable suggests that the length of time over which an incentive plan was in effect did not materially reverse the tendency for firms with incentive plans to be less efficient than carriers that never had such plans. Also, the negative association between incentive plans and efficiency is unrelated to the regulatory environment. Individual and joint tests of the *DEREG*, *PLREG*, and *LGREG* variables failed to reject the null that the estimated coefficients for these variables are zero. In short, the internal upheavals that are associated with motor carriers adopting incentive compensation plans for managers are also linked to lower levels of efficiency for these firms relative to firms without such plans.

Table 6.4, column (3) shows the results from estimating equation (1) with *NE* as the dependent variable. The significant and positive coefficient for the *PLAN* variable in tandem with the significant and negative coefficient estimated for the interaction variable *PLREG* indicate that firms that used incentives were more (less) profitable before (after) deregulation than firms that did not use incentive plans. Although the *DEREG* variable is not significant, the joint test of the *DEREG*, *PLREG*, and *LGREG* variables point to an association between deregulation and lower profits in the motor carrier industry. This downward pressure on profits is consistent with the expected siphoning off of monopoly rents attributable to operating authorities. The positive and significant coefficient estimated for *LGREG* in the presence of the insignificant coefficient for *PLGH* suggest that the length of time a plan was in effect mitigated poorer profitability after deregulation, but did not augment superior profitability before deregulation of the plan relative to the no-plan firms. In other words, before deregulation the micro-level upheavals that lead up to the adoption of incentive plans were associated with greater profitability, and the post-adoption stage of this instability did not alter this association. However, when combined with the macro-level upheaval of deregulation, this firm-specific instability had a negative effect on profitability that was somewhat counteracted by the post-adoption stage. In short, the macro-upheaval of deregulation did not materially impact the profitability of stable firms, and adversely affected the profitability of unstable firms. The managerial behavior induced by incentive plans had a greater influence on profits when instability was present at the macro and micro levels.

Table 6.4. Estimate regression coefficients (|t| values)

Independent variables	Dependent variables			
(1)	(2) Operating ratio	(3) Net earnings	(4) Revenues	(5) Maintenance
Constant	190.34	7,606.15	-0.57	4.57
	(5.16)***	(1.03)	(0.22)	(1.35)
Size	-0.35	436.59	0.42	0.72
	(1.76)	(11.07)***	(30.89)***	(40.09)***
Plan	1.97	193.22	0.172	0.17
	(5.20)***	(2.55)*	(6.61)***	(4.78)***
PLGH	-0.21	-19.33	-0.011	-0.034
	(1.43)	(0.67)	(1.07)	(2.57)**
DEREG	0.34	-18.08	-0.16	-0.17
	(0.48)	(0.13)	(3.38)***	(2.62)**
PLREG	0.13	-1,028.76	0.24	0.086
	(0.10)	(4.11)***	(2.76)**	(0.75)
LGREG	-0.28	148.87	-0.006	0.030
	(0.99)	(2.61)**	(0.30)	(1.15)
YR	-2.83	-313.50	0.13	-0.12
	(2.83)**	(1.56)	(1.89)	(1.26)
YR-SQ	0.02	2.21	-0.001	0.001
	(3.11)**	(1.62)	(1.33)	(1.34)
Adj R-Sq	0.30	0.66	0.93	0.88

*, **, and *** indicate $p < .05$, .01, and .001, respectively.
For all models, N=1,582; d.f.= 87, 1,494.
SIZE = natural log of the cost of trucks, tractors, and trailers in terms of 1967 dollars in thousands.
PLAN = 1 if a firm adopted an incentive plan, 0 otherwise.
PLGH = length of time in years an incentive plan has been in effect.
DEREG = 1 for years after 1979, 0 otherwise.
PLREG = interaction term, *PLAN*DEREG*.
LGREG = interaction term, *PLGH*DEREG*.
YR = time measured in calendar years.
YR-SQ = the square of *YR*.

Table 6.4, column (4) reports the results of estimating equation (1) with *REVE* as the dependent variable. The estimated coefficient for the *PLAN* variable is significant and positive while the estimate of the *DEREG* parameter is negative and significant. The positive and significant coefficient estimated for the interaction term *PLREG* implies that motor carriers that used incentive plans had greater revenues than carriers that never used incentive plans, and this superiority was greater following deregulation. Also, an inspection of column (4) reveals that *PLGH* was not a factor in this finding. In other words, the firm-specific upheavals that lead to the adoption of incentive plans are more responsible for greater revenues than the changes in managerial behavior attributable to the plans themselves. In short, the unstable firms were better able to exploit the market expansion opportunities offered in a freer market than were the stable firms. Alternatively, revenue declines resulting from greater competition brought about by deregulation had a greater impact on the more stable no-plan firms.

A synthesis of the results reported in Table 6.4 establish the following points: (1) the less stable plan adopting firms were less efficient than the no-plan firms and this relationship persisted during deregulation, and is not altered by the length of time such plans were in effect; (2) plan adopting carriers had superior market growth relative to the no-plan carriers and this difference in performance increased following deregulation, and was more related to the firm-specific factors that led to the adoption of incentive plans than to the influences of the plans themselves; (3) plan adopting firms, in spite of their superiority in market growth and greater profitability before deregulation, were significantly less profitable than the corresponding no-plan carriers, and this reversal in performance was less pronounced the longer an incentive plan was in effect.

Greater revenues in tandem with lower profits observed for the plan adopting firms following deregulation points to differences in strategic behavior between firms that differed regarding internal stability. Deregulation gave carriers greater freedom in setting freight rates. Total revenues can be increased by cutting freight rates as a means of competing for additional traffic in markets where the price elasticity of demand for trucking services is less than -1. This strategy of using rate reductions to increase revenues reduces profit margins. Lower profit margins do not necessarily mean reduced profitability; in fact the greater volume of demand resulting from price cuts often more than offsets lower margins to result in greater profitability. However, in the present study, greater revenues were not associated with greater profitability following deregulation. This finding is consistent with the expectation that the greater competition allowed by deregulation dissipated the monopoly rents connected with operating authorities. Also, the poorer managerial efficiency observed for the plan adopting firms in combination with lower profit margins is an additional explanation for the lower profitability of these firms following deregulation.

The internal instability that allowed trucking firms to innovate incentive compensation plans also allowed these carriers to respond more quickly to the changing market conditions of regulatory reform as evidence by the greater market growth of the plan relative to the no-plan firms following MCA80. The insignificant coefficient estimated for the *PLGH* variable in column (4) at first blush suggests that the innovative environment responsible for the plan adoptions, as opposed to incentives created by the plans themselves, deserves credit for the greater superiority in market performance following deregulation. This observation raises questions as to whether the incentive plans selected for managerial talent that did in fact have leadership skills more congruent with a less restricted market. However, the significant positive coefficient estimated for the *LGREG* interaction term in column (3) leads to the conclusion that the incentive plans themselves are associated with a lesser decline in profits resulting from the innovative carriers increasing their revenues. This smaller sacrifice in profits to achieve greater market growth suggests the expected linkage between incentive plans and a more strategically oriented leadership.

The no-plan carriers had greater efficiency as evidenced by lower operating ratios before and after deregulation. This superiority in operating efficiency allowed greater stability in the net earnings for the no-plan relative to the plan-firms in spite of the decline in revenues experienced by the former following deregulation. This observation suggests that the more internally stable firms failed to respond to the new competitive pressure, which resulted in lower revenues. These firms protected their profits by matching revenue losses with expense reductions. This tendency to take a defensive posture by cutting cost rather than to aggressively compete for market share in response to deregulation is consistent with the command and control leadership style that flourishes in a restricted market. This behavior of the less innovative no-plan firms is consistent with Implication 7 which points to the inability of distributional coalitions to reallocate resources in response to changing conditions, and thereby reduce the rate of market growth.

Olson's Implication 6 states that distributional coalitions have a greater tendency to fix prices than quantities. Market entry restrictions and rate bureaus institutionalized this tendency in the trucking industry. Deregulation was a macro-level upheaval that removed these artificial barriers to competition. The movement of revenues and profits in opposite directions observed in this study for the plan-adopting firms is evidence of greater competition and hence an unraveling of institutional sclerosis. The results of this study suggest that micro-level upheavals that are experienced by members of distributional coalitions stimulate the reversal of institutional sclerosis.

According to Implication 4, collusions such as regulated industries reduce efficiency and aggregate income in the societies in which they operate. The monopoly rents that accrued to member firms of the trucking coalition prior to deregulation increased the distribution cost of finished products and raw materials that were shipped by trucks throughout the supply chain. The reduction in profits following deregulation noted in this study suggest an increase in aggregate income for society as a whole as these rents are shifted away from the trucking coalition and diffused to other sectors within society.

Greater competition results in lower freight rates which are private costs imposed on shippers. Trucking operations also impose social costs in the form of energy consumption, safety risk, and noise and air pollution. The issue of these social costs is addressed in the present study by estimating equation (1) with maintenance expenditures as the dependent variable. According to Table 6.4, column (5), the significant positive coefficient estimated for *PLAN* indicates that the firm-specific factors responsible for incentive plan adoptions are linked to greater levels of maintenance expenditures relative to the more stable no-plan firms. However, the opposite and significant coefficient for *PLGH* points to reductions in *MATN* the longer the incentive plans are in effect. Also, the insignificant coefficients estimated for both interaction terms indicate that the association between the two incentive plan variables and *MATN* persisted following deregulation. The joint test of these two interactions, however, rejected the null that the coefficients for *PLREG* and *LGREG* in tandem are zero. The negative coefficient for *DEREG* implies that reductions in *MATN* were a negative consequence of deregulation. Thus, the gain to society from greater competition among trucking firms was somewhat offset by externalities resulting from lesser maintained trucks on the nation's highways. However, reductions in *MATN* after deregulation are more attributable to the no-plan carriers that responded to deregulation by cutting cost than to the plan-carriers that focused more on increasing revenues.

6.4 Conclusions

Olson's theory of institutional sclerosis describes circumstances whereby stable societies offer the setting for the formation of distributional coalitions that extract economic rents through the stifling of competition that retards progress and depresses aggregate income. This theory is used to explain differences in rates of economic growth among industrialized societies. Nations that have had more recent major upheavals tend to have higher rates of economic growth than nations that have had a long history of stability. Major upheavals destroy the institutions responsible for sustaining the coalitions that stagnate economic growth. Although this theory is used to explain macro-economic phenomena, its extension to micro-level issues cannot be ruled out. In fact, Olson (1982, p. 36) points out that most of the economics he uses to argue for the validity of his theory is well-established "microeconomic theory" of individual firms, consumers, and industries. The motor carrier industry served as the setting for the present study as this industry typified institutional sclerosis for 45 years before undergoing a major upheaval as embodied in deregulation. MCA80 was a macro-level upheaval in the sense that all firms in the industry were affected. Thus, the performances of motor carriers before and after deregulation were compared to ascertain the effects of the unraveling of institutional sclerosis. In addition, this inquiry was extended to the micro-level to determine whether there were differential effects on the performances of firms that underwent an internal upheaval. The adoption of incentive compensation plans by carriers that previously did not have such plans was used to identify trucking companies that were subject to some firm-specific upheaval in the sense that these firms were relatively free from institutions that otherwise would have thwarted innovations such as changes in compensation policy. Two factors were hypothesized to account for differences in performance between plan-adopting carriers and their more stable no-plan counterparts; (1) the innovative climate that allowed the plan adoption to begin with, and (2) the more strategically oriented and risk-taking managerial talent that would likely be attracted by such plans.

In summary, the findings point to lower revenues and sharp declines in profits of trucking firms following deregulation. This finding is consistent with the expectation of greater competition driving out economic rents. Differences in the strategic response to MCA80 between the plan-adopting firms and the more stable no-plan firms differed substantially. The former carriers seized upon the new opportunities for market expansion. In contrast, the motor carriers that never had incentive plans were unable to adjust to the more competitive environment. These less innovative carriers offset declines in revenues with corresponding reductions in operating expenses as indicated by the lower and stable operating ratios for these firms both before and after deregulation. This strategy included reductions in maintenance expenditures, which is linked to an increase in social cost borne by society. In short, the no-plan carriers looked inside the firm for cost cutting opportunities, while the plan-adopting carriers looked outside the firm for revenue increasing opportunities. The net result of this difference in strategic response to deregulation was smaller reductions in profitability for the no-plan trucking firms. This finding at first appears counter-intuitive in that firms whose managers are compensated based on profits were the firms with the greater reductions in profitability after deregulation. However, the plan-firms did have greater profitability before deregulation and *PLGH* was a factor that mitigated the fall in profits sustained by the plan-firms after deregulation.

The cost cutting response to deregulation of the no-plan carriers in contrast to the revenue increasing strategy of the plan-carriers suggests that the management of the former remained grounded in the command and control leadership style typical of institutional sclerosis. According to Olson, the institutional sclerosis that gripped the transportation and public utility industries was of a form whereby the distributional coalitions were propped up by the government, through MCA35 in the motor carrier case. Thus, it follows that the government, through the enactment of MCA80, would also institute the type of industry-wide upheaval that would undo such coalitions. The results of this study point to the importance of micro-level upheavals as complimentary to macro-level upheavals in facilitating the reversal of institutional sclerosis. The findings of the present study support the notion that sound macro-economic theory should be linked to micro-level phenomena, a major theme throughout Olson's work.

7 Developing the Canadian Government's Bargaining Position on the Constitution, June-July, 1980: An Application of Olson's Argument from *The Rise and Decline of Nations**

Patrick James

The persuasiveness of a theory depends not only on how many facts are explained, but also on how diverse are the kinds of facts explained.

– Mancur Olson, *The Rise and Decline of Nations* (1982, p. 13)

Can the general arguments about macroeconomics and interest groups put forward in the *Rise and Decline of Nations* (Olson 1982) be used to explain something so specific and seemingly distant as the development of the Canadian federal government's bargaining position in constitutional negotiations with its provinces? The answer offered here is 'yes'. An assessment of the Government of Canada's formulation of a bargaining position for constitutional negotiations with the provinces in the summer of 1980 supports several expectations derived from Olson's arguments. This result, if the case for it proves convincing, would open new vistas for Olson's arguments – from macroeconomics into constitutional order and with respect to formulation rather than implementation of policy.

This chapter is not intended as an in-depth re-examination of the Canadian constitutional process that began in 1980 and culminated in the signing of the Constitution Act and Charter of Rights and Freedoms on 1 July 1982. The literature on the background to this phase of reform, along with the intergovernmental bargaining itself and both short- and long-term consequences of the new constitutional document, is vast.[1] As opposed to a contribution to the history of Canadian politics in particular, the present study focuses more on Canada as one of many cases con-

* The author thanks Jac Heckelman, Jonathan Krieckhaus, Michael Lusztig, Todd Sandler and Doh C. Shin for valuable comments.

[1] While many works might be suggested for reference, those in the lists that follow provide examples of (a) informative treatments from the last decade of Canadian constitutional politics in general (Meekison 1993; Archer, Gibbins, Knopff and Pal 1995; Peacock 1996; Manfredi 2001; James and Lusztig 2002); (b) immediate reactions to the Constitution Act and Charter of Rights and Freedoms (Banting and Simeon 1983a, 1983b; Gibbins 1983; Smiley 1983); and (c) assessments of lobbying and rent seeking in the post-Charter era (Hiebert 1993; Sigurdson 1993; Barnes 1995; Martin 1996; Smithey 2002).

cerning constitutional reform that might have been selected. For example, a survey of 80 states in the mid-1990s revealed that, over the previous 15 years, almost half had been either writing or adopting a new constitution or significantly revising the one already in place (Maddex 1995, p. ix). With so many new states in the aftermath of the decline and fall of the Soviet Empire, it becomes interesting to see whether Olson's classic arguments may be able to explain constitutional reform in Canada, one of the world's oldest and most stable democracies.[2] If so, wider, cross-national application of those arguments could follow.

Obvious issues for the outset of the analysis are why Canada might be selected for study and, in particular, why formulation of a federal constitutional strategy during the summer of 1980 might require special attention. These matters are connected to the epigraph from Olson at the outset of this chapter, which asserts that an argument supported by diverse evidence gains greater value from that experience. Thus the first of the two matters is resolved easily: Aside from its inclusion in cross-national data analysis, as in the case of average industrial tariff levels (Olson 1982, p. 135), Canada is not the focus of Olson's exegesis of the rise and decline of nations. In fact, Canada does not even appear in the book's index. This observation is not meant as a criticism of a book that covered a vast range of subject matter; instead, the purpose is to point out that Canada is relatively unexplored territory for Olson's argument.[3]

The second aspect from above, which pertains to the specific application pursued in this chapter, also is easy to address: Olson's (1982) argument in *The Rise and Decline of Nations* is applied to economic growth among developed democracies, foreign trade, inequality, discrimination and development, and culminates in an evolutionary approach to macroeconomics. While rent seeking plays an important role at various points, analysis of constitutional reform is absent from Olson (1982) and does not appear to play a significant role in the vast literature stimulated by that work.[4] Furthermore, the focus in the present case is on *formulation*, which tends to be neglected relative to the *outcome* of policy. With regard to the Canadian application, the federal proposals of 1980 for constitutional reform clearly are the most important in the country's history since its beginning in 1867, so this case provides an obvious point of departure. In sum, if Olson's argument can help to explain the formulation of a constitutional strategy for the government

---

[2] The more recent arrival of Newfoundland would not seem to create any problems for the validity of Olson's implications. Newfoundland was, and is, a province with a small and impoverished population. Thus it would be fair to say that the political and economic boundaries of Canada did not change in a theoretically significant way throughout the last century.

[3] A wide range of studies have tested Olson's theory on a cross-national basis; Canada typically is included as one of the data points. A recent example of this research is Heckelman (2000).

[4] Sutter's (2002: 109) analysis of rent seeking at the stage of constitutional development implies that the concept is implicit within Olson's (1965, see also Sandler 1992) classic treatment of coalitions and redistributive policy making. Tullock (2001) summarizes the origins and applications of rent seeking within the study of political economy.

of a state that plays only a peripheral role in his major work on the rise and decline of nations, that would seem to meet the imperatives from the epigraph very well indeed.

This chapter unfolds in three additional sections. The next section uses implications from Olson (1982) to derive hypotheses (and sets of corollaries) about democratic constitutional reform in general, most notably with respect to federal formulation of a bargaining position. Section 7.2 provides a brief overview of the case as a whole (for those without a background in Canadian political history) and then assesses the hypotheses and corollaries derived from Olson in the context of how the federal bargaining position developed in the crucial period of June through July of 1980. Third, and finally, the overall performance of the hypotheses derived from Olson's argument is appraised and ideas for future research are put forward.

7.1 Hypotheses and Corollaries about Formulation of a Federal Position on Constitutional Revision as Derived from Olson's Argument

7.1.1 Overview

Hypotheses about formulation of a federal bargaining position on constitutional reform will focus on the familiar economic concept of *rent seeking*, that is, the pursuit of income through redistribution rather than production (Sandler 2001, p. 64; Tullock 2001). Olson (1982, pp. 154-161, 231-237) shows how coalitions that seek to redistribute income can play a key role in explaining such widely diverse things as systems of caste and class and stagflation. The present set of hypotheses will focus more specifically on rent seeking in relation to federal and sub-national governments during the process of constitutional revision. The most general concern is with how rent seeking, which the federal government anticipates from sub-national political units, influences federal formulation of its bargaining position.

Two subjects need to be covered before hypotheses are derived about the constitutional process in light of Olson's implications: (1) the nature of constitutional rent seeking; and (2) rent seeking by political sub-units as an issue of specific concern to the federal government in Canada. Dealing with these matters will help to move the study forward within the Canadian context.

Constitutions typically do not serve as the locus for redistribution of material resources. The possibility of such activity being carried out by *sub-national political units*, however, cannot be ruled out at the stage of formulation. As Sutter (2002) points out, societal groups will be inclined, all other things being equal, to free ride at the stage of constitutional development. Sub-national governments, however, have an automatic place at the bargaining table in a federal system such as Canada. Thus the distribution of powers in a revised national constitution (and even sub-national constitutions (Wallis 2000)) will be of great interest to sub-national political units. These governments will want to gain as much for themselves as they can, with the logic behind that following from Olson (1982) and being put forward explicitly in the next sub-section. Intergovernmental conflict, in other words, is built into the system when it comes to constitutional revision under federalism.

Canada's constitutional order at the time in question created especially difficult conditions and encouraged rent seeking. In particular, one section of the constitution as it existed in 1980 gave provincial governments a disproportionate share of jurisdictional authority over spending issues, even though they had far fewer means to raise revenues. This made provincial governments depend upon transfers from the federal level, thus elevating fiscal issues to the level of constitutional bargaining. Thus respective levels of government had different preferences about a new constitutional order. The federal government would be willing to make concessions but wanted to keep costs down, redistribute income more equitably and retain input into policy areas that technically sat under provincial control (Banting and Simeon 1983a, 1983b). This explains why, for example, the federal government will turn out to have been so concerned about internal trade barriers during the 1980 phase of formulating proposals. Such barriers – both existing and possibly augmented by the provinces in the future – could affect aggregate economic performance, with an important secondary consideration being that the existing constitutional order obligated the federal government to compensate, in effect, for the inefficiency of its sub-national units. The provinces, by contrast, preferred more money and policy autonomy through, for example, powers of taxation (Banting and Simeon 1983a, 1983b). Being aware of this dynamic helps to explain the story that follows in the second section of this chapter.

7.1.2 Deriving Hypotheses and Corollaries

Among the nine implications derived by Olson (1982, p. 74) from his general argument, several can be evaluated, at least indirectly, through analysis of how a federal government formulates its bargaining position on constitutional renewal in relation to sub-national political units. Table 7.1 lists Olson's implications to permit easy reference as needed. Theorizing begins by deriving specific hypotheses about a federal government's development of constitutional policy from Olson's implications. (The label 'hypotheses' is used here in order to prevent confusion with the original set of 'implications' that appear in Olson (1982, p. 74).)

Table 7.2 shows the respective hypotheses and corollaries, along with their connection to Olson (1982) and anticipated form in the Canadian context. It might be noted that the illustrations in the final column of Table 7.2 vary in form; those for corollaries A4 and B1 contain what might be looked for in terms of support, while the others are more specific products that can derived only after examining the documents. Both of Table 7.2's two hypotheses about development of a federal position on constitutional renewal, along with their corollaries, are described in turn.

Table 7.1. Implications from *The Rise and Decline of Nations*

1. There will be no countries that attain symmetrical organization of all groups with a common interest and thereby attain optimal outcomes through comprehensive bargaining.
2. Stable societies with unchanged boundaries tend to accumulate more collusions and organizations for collective action over time.
3. Members of "small" groups have disproportionate organizational power for collective action, and this disproportion diminishes but does not disappear over time in stable societies.
4. On balance, special-interest organizations and collusions reduce efficiency and aggregate income in the societies in which they operate and make political life more divisive.
5. Encompassing organizations have some incentive to make the society in which they operate more prosperous, and an incentive to redistribute income to their members with as little excess burden as possible, and to cease such redistribution unless the amount redistributed is substantial in relation to the social cost of the redistribution
6. Distributional coalitions make decisions more slowly than the individuals and firms of which they are comprised, tend to have crowded agendas and bargaining tables, and more often fix prices than quantities.
7. Distributional coalitions slow down a society's capacity to adopt new technologies and to reallocate resources in response to changing conditions, and thereby reduce the rate of economic growth.
8. Distributional coalitions, once big enough to succeed, are exclusive, and seek to limit the diversity of incomes and values of their membership.
9. The accumulation of distributional coalitions increases the complexity of regulation, the role of government, and the complexity of undertakings, and changes the direction of social evolution.

Source: Olson (1982, p. 74).

Hypothesis A, the more general of the two in scope, asserts that a federal bargaining position will be formulated in anticipation of rent seeking by sub-national units. This expectation is derived from a combination of Olson's Implications 2 and 4. (Each of the other hypotheses and corollaries also depends on these implications, with others from Olson being added in specific instances along the way.) Narrow, redistributive interest groups can be expected to accumulate and these entities should become visible in the process of constitutional renewal. Constitutions are fundamental documents about behavior in a society and, as such, should attract a relatively high degree of attention from rent seeking coalitions. Hypothesis A follows naturally: A rational federal government will be aware of these tendencies and, as it formulates a bargaining position, expect sub-national units to be the 'carriers' of the rent seeking 'disease'. Four corollaries follow from Hypothesis A.

Corollary A1 asserts that the federal government will prefer to limit rent seeking by the sub-national units. The federal government is the most encompassing political unit by definition, so Implication 5 comes into play here.[5] Thus the federal government can be expected to not only anticipate sub-national rent seeking,

[5] This implication, of course, provides an opportunity to recognize the continuing contribution of *The Logic of Collective Action* (Olson 1965) to the study of politico-economic processes. Implication 5 is a product of that still-influential work.

but also to oppose it virtually across the board. In other words, the process of constitutional revision is viewed as a meta-arena in which sub-national units seek to redistribute benefits in self-serving and parochial ways.

Table 7.2. Hypotheses development of a federal position for constitutional bargaining: applications to the government of Canada, June-July, 1980

Hypotheses and Corollaries for Formulation of Federal Position	How is the Hypothesis or Corollary Derived from Olson	Illustrations in the Canadian Context, June-July, 1980
Hypothesis A: the federal position will be formulated with an expectation that rent seeking will be manifested among sub-national units	Implications 2 and 4	Ottawa will be expressed about decentralization, especially in relation to barriers to internal trade and mobility between provinces
Corollary A1: the federal position will reflect its preference to limit rent seeking opportunities for sub-national units	. . .and Implication 5	change will be pursued with respect to non-tariff barriers to interprovincial trade, services and workers
Corollary A2: the federal position will incorporate relatively limited rent seeking in its own favor	. . .and Implication 5	federal measures do not promote additional powers but instead limit provincial rent seeking opportunities
Corollary A3: the federal position will be self-consciously strategic relative to expectations about sub-national rent seeking behavior	. . .and Implication 1	the newly proposed charter of rights will be used as part of a moderate strategy to weaken internal barriers to commerce
Corollary A4: if the federal government seeks consultation with any sub-national unit, it will begin by approaching the largest, if one stands out, or the subset of relatively large units, because those are most likely to support its agenda	. . .and Implication 5	the Province of Ontario will be consulted before others
Hypothesis B: federal proposals are likely to be interpreted by sub-national units in the context of how the distribution of rents might be affected	. . .and Implication 3	provincial leaders will express concern about the distributive consequences of an economic union
Corollary B1: the federal government will attempt to separate general principles from more specific concerns related to distribution of rents between levels of government	. . .and Implication 3	a "People's Package" is separated from initiatives related to power sharing between governments

Table 7.2. (cont.)

Corollary B2: as the federal government develops its position, economic issues will dominate consultations with sub-national units	. . .and Implication 3	the subset of economic issues on the agenda, including resources and power over the economy, will predominate

Implications listed in Table 7.1

Corollary A2 asserts that federal rent seeking, to the extent it is manifested in a package for constitutional reform, is expected to be limited in comparison to what is proposed by sub-national units. This expected difference is a by-product of Hypothesis A in conjunction with Implication 5. As the most encompassing political entity, the federal government should be more restrained with respect to rent seeking in its proposals for a new constitutional order. Thus the tendencies toward myopic self-interest among members of the federal government, which exist in all systems, will be minimal in comparison to those at lower levels.

Corollary A3 notes that the federal government will not behave 'as if' it understood the strategic environment – instead, it can be expected to acknowledge the situation explicitly. In other words, federal leadership will recognize the rent seeking propensities of sub-national units because Implication 1 is understood; the federal government will comprehend that sub-national units are organized and in place to represent parochial interests. Therefore, 'course corrections' are needed throughout the federal government's constitutional journey if a safe and relatively efficient destination is to be reached. In other words, federal leaders recognize that they cannot count on countervailing power to arise automatically, at least in the short-term, to oppose rent seeking groups that are built into the bargaining process through its inherently intergovernmental nature.

Corollary A4 stipulates that the federal government, if it engages in consultation with sub-national governments in putting together its bargaining position, will choose to begin with either the largest unit (if one clearly exists) or a subset of those deemed relatively sizable. This corollary brings Implication 5 into play once again: Relatively encompassing sub-national political units will have a greater incentive to support the national level of government as it engages in institutional design. The largest political unit(s) will be more motivated toward collective action in favor of the general public interest. Thus the corollary is more nuanced than the intuition shared with Marxism, pluralism and probably any other overarching way of looking at things vis-à-vis government consultation with powerful actors. In this context, the difference is that the largest sub-national unit(s) are expected to be disposed *positively*, at least in relation to others, toward the federal position.

Hypothesis B is a product of Implications 2 and 4 in conjunction with Implication 3. Sub-national political units can be expected to show greater sensitivity to the likely reactions of their constituencies – more narrow, by definition, than those of the federal government – with respect to (re)distribution of economic rents. Two corollaries follow from Hypothesis B.

Corollary B1 points out that the way to get around resistance from sub-national units to constitutional reform is to separate out general proposals that will 'sell' to the general public and thereby create momentum for the process as a whole. Opposition by sub-national units to general proposals then can be portrayed as obstructionist, with one possible side-effect being better prospects for specific initiatives as well – this might be referred to as 'going over the heads' of sub-national leaders directly to their populations.[6]

Corollary B2 is straightforward in relation to Hypothesis B. If sub-national political units are inclined toward rent seeking, economic issues will come to the fore in bargaining and stay there. The distribution of rents may not be the only item on the agenda, but it can be expected to pervade intergovernmental consultations.

7.2 Development of the Federal Position on the Constitution, June-July, 1980

7.2.1 Evolution of the Canadian Constitution[7]

Canada's constitutional problems can be traced back to Confederation itself in 1867, with the passing of the BNA Act. Since that time, two interpretations of what Canada means have maintained an uneasy co-existence. One view is that Confederation and its subsequent expansion represented an agreement between peoples, while the other is that it created a pact among *provinces*. Residents of Quebec, who are mostly of French descent and speak that language, favor the former interpretation of the BNA Act, while the vast majority of those in the rest of Canada, who are more diverse in ethnic terms but overwhelmingly speak English, are disposed toward the latter point of view (Archer, Gibbins, Knopff and Pal 1995). This basic disagreement about the country's meaning has been the principal obstacle to obtaining a lasting constitutional agreement between the federal and provincial governments. Evidence exists that the issue of Quebec's sovereignty is expansive in its influence over voter conceptions of Canadian politics (Hinich, Munger and de Marchi 1998).

Various attempts to agree upon proposals to bring the constitution 'home' from Britain and create a formula for its amendment failed, with the usual problem being an ongoing confrontation between a federal government in Ottawa seeking greater authority to govern and the Province of Quebec, which emphasized the need for a more decentralized form of federalism. Constitutional arrangements

[6] Opposition to the general proposals would be expected to focus on specifics that target a given province, although at least some of the ensuing federal-provincial conflict focused on the overarching issue of revenue sharing *per se*.

[7] For a more detailed overview of constitutional developments in Canada, see Carter and James (2002) and Flanagan (2002). McMenemy (2001) provides a guide to possible unfamiliar terms related to Canadian politics.

remained fundamentally flawed because final authority, most notably the ability to amend the BNA Act, remained in Britain – a legacy of the colonial era.

When Quebec elected a government in 1976 with at least a nominal commitment to taking the province out of Canada by one means or another, constitutional politics heated up. The decade of the 1970s also brought increasing alienation in the western provinces of Canada, which saw the Liberal Government, led by Prime Minister Pierre Trudeau, as overly concerned with keeping the central Canadian provinces of Ontario and Quebec happy at the West's expense. Ontario wanted political stability and cheap oil, while, the West had primarily economic grievances, most notably as related to the role of the Alberta oil industry in a changing world economy. Like Ontario, Quebec also wanted cheap oil, but continued to spar with the federal government over issues related to the French language and culture. Province-building collided with the federal state, with competition over tax revenues as a natural by-product.

Matters came to a head with the Quebec referendum, which in May 1980 proposed to voters that the provincial government should have the authority to negotiate "sovereignty association" with the federal government. While voters in Quebec rejected that option by about 20% differential, the intense campaign heightened the sense of urgency in Ottawa for a new constitutional deal that would reduce the centrifugal tendencies that seemed to be picking up in various parts of the country. Furthermore, the federal government hoped to have proposals ready for the scheduled September meeting with provincial premiers, i.e., the First Ministers Conference. Thus the period of June and July 1980 emerges as a crucial one for development of a federal position in a new round of constitutional bargaining and becomes the focal point for the ensuing application of Olson's arguments.

7.2.2 Testing Hypotheses and Corollaries Derived from Olson in the Canadian Context

Minutes from Cabinet meetings in June and July 1980 provide the primary material for this analysis of the formulation of the Government of Canada's bargaining position with regard to a new constitutional agreement.[8] The meetings took place

[8] A more Canadian-centric reason for the choice of this case is the recent availability of federal documents from 1980-81 to permit effective study of how the federal position developed from the inside. The Government of Canada is required after 20 years to provide previously secret documents unless it can show proper grounds for continuing to keep them private. Since the federal government reached agreement on a constitutional reform package with the provinces (aside from Quebec) in November 1981 and went ahead at that point to patriate the constitution, I requested the documents used in this study at the first time of availability, that is, November 2001. (The more than 500 pages of Cabinet minutes and other documents have been obtained from the Privy Council Office (PCO) of the Government of Canada and I am grateful to Ciuineas Boyle, Coordinator, Access to Information and Privacy, for assistance in obtaining the needed materials.) Thus the descriptive section of this chapter is based primarily on previously unreleased materials

on June 3, June 12, July 3 and July 31. In addition to the minutes from the meetings, documents distributed to the Cabinet at and around this important time have proven invaluable. For example, perhaps the most useful item of all is a position paper dated June 27, which spelled out for Cabinet ministers the federal government's tentative approach to each of the major issue areas on the constitutional agenda.

Dated 16 June 1980, a memorandum to Cabinet provides a useful introduction to the constitutional agenda. It conveyed the questions that would need to be answered by a federal position on the twelve "priority items" encompassing constitutional renewal that had been put forward to the provincial premiers at a June 9 meeting (Memorandum to Cabinet (MC), 6/16/80, N-2-4(a)). The agenda is interesting in and of itself because redistributive economic issues are so visible. The twelve items are as follows: (1) statement of principles for a new constitution; (2) charter of rights; (3) a dedication to sharing and/or to equalization: the reduction of regional disparities; (4) patriation of the constitution, the amending formula and the delegation of legislative authority; (5) resource ownership and interprovincial trade; (6) offshore resources; (7) fisheries; (8) powers affecting the economy; (9) communications; (10) family law; (11) the Senate; and (12) Supreme Court.[9] As will become apparent, issues related to rent seeking pervaded the federal documents that are about to be reviewed.

One point should be made concerning method. The evidence used here to assess the hypotheses must be regarded as impressionistic in nature. No attempt is made to engage in a content analysis or other rigorous approach toward quantifying the narrative that appears on the federal record. Passing references that seem to support the hypotheses and corollaries then could be pulled out and cited as evidence, while other material is neglected. This concern, however, becomes minimal because of the relatively clear nature of the hypotheses. This makes the reading of the public record much easier. The decision rules for this reading are simple: Statements that confirm hypotheses are noted and some are produced verbatim later in this section as illustrations. Perhaps the strongest meta-support for Olson's theory comes from the fact that no statements contradicting any of the hypotheses

from the federal cabinet – the forum within which the prime minister and other ministers formulated their proposals. Some material remains confidential and is stricken from the record as provided by the PCO. Sections 13, 14 and 15 of the Access to Information Act of the Government of Canada, which pertain to information obtained in confidence, strategy and tactics of the Government of Canada as related to federal-provincial affairs and international affairs and defence, required the PCO to delete material from the minutes and documents provided to me. Sufficient material remains, however, to assess all of the hypotheses and corollaries included in this chapter.

[9] The list of items reveals that the federal government had an excellent grasp of what would have to be included on the agenda in order to obtain some measure of provincial cooperation. Among the twelve items, the federal government had anticipated eleven and put those forward – the premiers added only the issue of fisheries at the June meeting itself (MC, 6/16/80, N-2-4(a), p. 5).

could be found in the literally hundreds of pages, all of which are now available to be read by anyone. In sum, although it is prudent not to make too much of the evidence that follows, it does tend to point in a positive direction.

Hypothesis A is supported by numerous assertions throughout the documents, so illustrations are provided rather than an exhaustive record. Early in the detailed Cabinet paper of 27 June 1980, which mapped out federal positions across all of the major issue areas, it is clear that the federal government expected provincial rent seeking:

. . .there are grounds for serious concerns about the degree of economic decentralization that has occurred. Evidence of this may be found in the fiscal imbalance which exists between the central and provincial governments, as well as in the barriers to internal trade and mobility which have been established by several provinces (The Federal Government's Approach (FGA), N-2-4(a), 6/27/80, Part I, p. 9).

Barriers to internal trade and mobility at the provincial level result directly from efforts to accumulate rents – a warning of likely resistance in response to federal efforts toward change.

Further evidence in favor of Hypothesis A, along with Corollaries A1 and A2, appears in this statement from the above-noted June 27 document on the federal government's approach to constitutional negotiations:

. . .competing protectionism among province[s] disregarding the imperatives of national economic efficiency is not a "zero sum" game, an economically neutral way of redistributing economic activity among provinces. It can involve significant net costs for Canada as a whole, and hence for each and every one of its parts. It should be noted that costs can also result from injudicious use of the federal government's virtually unrestrained ability, under the present constitution, to derogate from common market principles in areas under its jurisdiction. There are, therefore, valid reasons for specifying in the constitution the basic operation rules of the Canadian common market, and ensuring that both orders of government will abide by these rules (FGA, N-2-4(a), 6/27/80, Schedule XI, Section B, p. 3).

The federal government clearly expected rent seeking from the provinces to continue unless constitutional arrangements could be altered (Hypothesis A). Note further the federal position is that competing protectionism will be harmful regardless of which level of government is engaging in such policies (Corollaries A1 and A2).

Corollary A1 receives support from a memorandum to Cabinet from 16 June 1980. A sub-section on the background to proposed negotiations with the provinces over resource ownership and interprovincial trade is revealing:

The federal intent was to work out a constitutional arrangement for resources which would more clearly recognize provincial control but retain for the Government of Canada, at the same time, the capacity to control prices, allocation, quantities, etc., on interprovincial movements of resources, *in circumstances of compelling national interest*, and the same capacity, *in all circumstances*, on international movements. It was recognized that this capacity to control price was essential if the country was to avoid giving any producing province the ability to dictate to the rest of Canada (both in terms of price to be paid by consumers and in terms of the federal capacity to obtain a reasonable share of the benefits). Without control over price, the Government of Canada could be faced with prices set so high by a producing province that there would be no "space" for the imposition of federal taxes (MC, N-2-4(a), 6/16/80, p. 29;. the emphasis is in the original).

This assessment reveals the federal mind-set. Aimed primarily at Alberta, which had by far the most substantial oil and natural gas reserves in Canada, these words suggest that placing some kind of 'ceiling' on provincial resource-related rent seeking in particular would be a continuing federal priority.

Further along in the memo to the Cabinet on June 16 is a list of the federal government's agenda for economic issues from February 1979, which provided the foundation for development of its position in 1980. At least three of the eight items listed focus to some degree on limitation of rents to be secured by the provinces: "2. The question of non-tariff barriers to interprovincial and international trade and investment."; "3. The question of interprovincial and international movement of goods and services including the right of passage of electricity and oil, gas and other minerals."; and "4. The question of barriers to the movement of persons for employment" (MC, N-2-4(a), 6/16/80, p. 43). In particular, the memorandum urged that an item such as "Freedom of Movement of Goods, Services, Capital and Persons" appear in a new constitutional document (MC, N-2-4(a), 16/6/80, p. 45). The intention of this is straightforward: to limit provincial ability to collect economic rents through imposition of taxes or other means.

More evidence in favor of Corollary A1 is apparent in the list of reasons provided for why constitutional change is needed in a document distributed to Cabinet on 27 June 1980. One statement in the document is representative of the overall tendency in the federal 'paper trail' with respect to provincial dispositions. It refers to the "strong winds of protectionism that are blowing throughout Canada which are undermining the country's capacity to function as an efficient economic Union" (FGA, N-2-4(a), 6/27/80, Part I, p. 5). Further evidence of this view appears at a later point in the same document, when the existing Section 121 of the BNA Act is criticized for not doing enough to limit provincial abilities to seek rent: "[Section 121] has had very limited application, preventing only customs duties and not barriers created by the exercise of regulatory powers of government or by the exercise of other fiscal powers. As such it creates a customs union rather than a common market. One question is whether Section 121 should be extended and made more explicit. . . . " (FGA, N-2-4(a), 6/27/80, Part III, Schedule XI, Part A, p. 2). Specific measures intended to counteract provincial barriers to commerce come out of this discussion and bear upon workers, taxation, regulation of production and trade, financial assets, enterprise and subsidies (FGA, N-2-4(a), 6/27/80, Part III, Schedule XI, Part B, pp. 7-9).

Corollary A2 receives limited support in the documents. Only one prominent example could be located – as noted previously, in the federal government's mapping out of its approach toward the provinces on June 27. Although the federal government certainly took a hard line against provincial rent seeking, its intense competition for power with the sub-national political units may have worked against the expectation of ongoing self-restraint with respect to rent seeking. Explicit evidence of federal rapaciousness is absent from the Cabinet documents, but it is impossible to say much more about this.[10]

Corollary A3 is confirmed at various points in the records of June and July. For example, in the federal position paper of June 27, four "complementary approaches" toward creating a Canadian common market are compared to each other not only in absolute value but also with respect to political feasibility in relation to the provinces (FGA, N-2-4(a), 6/27/80, Part III, Schedule XI, Part B, pp. 4-5). The choice of a middle ground among the strategies noted, with an emphasis on using a charter of rights to limit government power rather than broadening federal influence, reflects an explicitly strategic approach in response to expectations about sub-national rent seeking.

More evidence in favor of Corollary A3 appears in the minutes of the Cabinet's meeting on July 3. At that time Trudeau asked ministers explicitly to comment on a "strategic approach to constitutional discussions" and a page later in the same document it is observed that a "strong challenge from the provinces' deputies on the powers issue would in fact help sell the people's package" (CM, 66-80CBM, 7/3/80, pp. 6-7). The same kind of thinking is revealed in the discussion paper of July 27, in which Cabinet ministers are asked how the government might "sell" its position on constitutional issues in the period leading up to the First Ministers' meeting in September (DP, FPRO-1-80DP, 7/27/80, p. 31). In sum, strategic analysis appears openly at various points throughout the June and July meetings.

Cabinet records concerning initial federal consultations with the provinces offer support to Corollary A4. Herb Gray, the Minister of Industry, Trade and Commerce, met with cabinet ministers from the Ontario provincial government, regarded with confidence as generally sympathetic to the federal government's efforts toward constitutional reform. At the June 3 Cabinet meeting, Gray summarized the advice received from the Ontario ministers:

1. the mood for change will not last and therefore it was best to concentrate on the limited but important people's package including, if possible, an amending formula;
2. in order to assure the Premiers that the federal government took their concerns seriously, discussions should begin on the division of powers noting that this will take time and that it should not hold up progress on the people's package;
3. the division of powers discussion must also include matters relating to the reinforcement of federal powers (CM, 6/3/80,, 63-80CBM, pp. 4-5).

---

[10] Evidence suggests that, as intergovernmental conflict intensified in 1980-81, the federal government engaged in a highly coercive strategy in relation to the province of Alberta in competition for economic rents obtained from highly increased oil and gas prices at the world level. See James (1993) for evidence of heightened federal-provincial conflict as a by-product of the Canadian Government's National Energy Program, which taxed provincial energy revenues very heavily.

The preceding sections make sense in the context of Corollary A4. Two features stand out. First, Ontario, by far the largest province, is the one being consulted initially and most intensively by the federal government – very much in line with the corollary. Second, and also as expected, Ontario's view reads in a friendly way, i.e., 'do this in order to get ahead'.

Justice Minister Jean Chrétien reported on his meetings with the provincial representatives to his colleagues at the Cabinet meeting of June 3.[11] The contents of this report reveal strong support for Hypothesis B, which concerns the likely reaction of the provinces to federal proposals. In general, Chrétien found a willingness among premiers to move forward relatively quickly. However, he also reported "a lingering feeling among the provinces that they would not concur to finalization of any particular agreement unless they received a quid pro quo in return" (Cabinet Minutes, 63-80CBM, 6/3/80, p. 4). The more specific, rent-related aspect of presumed provincial thinking comes out later in the minutes of a Cabinet meeting on July 31:

> Obtaining provincial agreement to a satisfactory position on the entrenchment of the Canadian Economic union principle would require some federal concessions on specific powers issues (e.g., Resources; Offshore), and Ministers should accordingly give careful consideration to the extent of their commitment to the economic union principle vis a vis their position on these individual issues.

In other words, the provinces could be expected to fight for economic rents obtained in areas such as resources in general and offshore resources in particular.

Corollary B1 is supported throughout the documents. The concern with keeping the "people's package" separate from "powers and institutions", which pertained to power sharing with the provinces, is ever-present (CM, 66-80CBM, 7/3/80, pp. 6-7). The People's Package is labeled as such because it consists of the following general issues: patriation and an amending formula, a charter of rights and a preamble with principles. By contrast economic items (resources and interprovincial trade, offshore resources, fisheries, powers over the economy and equalization) and institutions and other items (Senate/second chamber, Supreme Court, family law and communications) focus on government division of powers. The federal government, to the extent that it could, kept these sets of items separate from each other (DP, FPRO-1-80DP, 7/27/80, p. 9).

Corollary B2, which pertains to the centrality of economic issues, is supported throughout the documents from the point of provincial consultation onward. For example, a discussion paper from July 28 reports on federal meetings with provincial representatives. The 'bottom line' is as follows: "The item dealing with powers over the economy dominated the three weeks of constitutional discussions, without a consensus emerging at this stage" (DP, FPRO-1-80DP, 7/28/80, p. 4; see also p. 14 on the Vancouver meeting in particular). This observation is confirmed by the summary of discussions with provincial leaders in the Cabinet minutes of July 31, which list the following as "key items": resource ownership and inter-

[11] This title is used as an abbreviation for Chrétien's full designation as Minister of Justice and Attorney General of Canada and Minister of State for Social Development.

provincial trade, offshore resources, powers over the economy and the Senate. Thus, of the twelve items on the overall agenda, three out of the four that received primary attention are economic in nature.

7.3 Conclusions

Olson (1982, p. 13) asserted that when facts "are not selected because they fit a theory, and they are also numerous and in very different classes, then it is most improbable that a false theory could explain them and at the same time remain parsimonious." The evidence in the present investigation increases the confidence that the argument from *The Rise and Decline of Nations* is correct. An investigation of policy formulation in one state, with an emphasis on constitutional politics, is at some distance from the cross-national analysis of issues related to economic growth and macroeconomics that provided the focal points for Olson's original exposition. The results are favorable to both hypotheses in the Canadian context and all but one of the corollaries, namely A2, which pertains to self-designated federal self-restraint about rent seeking. Even there, weak support exists in that the federal government looks restrained at least in comparison to the provinces with which it negotiated.

This investigation tells only a part of the story of the formulation and implementation of a federal strategy leading up to the Constitution Act and Charter of Rights and Freedoms in 1982. The Canadian case continues to be fascinating because Trudeau's venture, for good or ill, remains the only constitutional initiative to have succeeded in that country during the post-World War II era. The long-term legacy of the constitutional revision of 1982 remains uncertain, but it would be fair to say that it provided only a starting point with respect to limiting the power of government and associated seeking of rents at the public's expense.

Four ideas come to mind readily for future research. First, and most theoretical in nature, it would be an ambitious but potentially rewarding task to transform the hypotheses and corollaries into a set of systematically connected propositions that would form a new theory of policy formulation. A second idea would be to continue with testing and move in a cross-national direction. As noted earlier, many states are engaged in constitutional revision and much might be learned from comparative analysis. A third idea would be to complement the economic analysis of this chapter with a treatment of issues related to ethnic and cultural identity, which played a central role in the process of Canadian constitutional reform. A fourth and final idea would be to focus on further stages of constitutional bargaining in Canada. For example, after 20 years, it would be useful to assess the overall economic impact of the new rules set down in the Constitution Act and Charter of Rights and Freedoms. Learning more about such subjects is fundamental to the study of Canada as well as political economy in general, so much work remains.

8 Absolute and Relative Effects of Interest Groups on the Economy*

Dennis Coates and Jac C. Heckelman

The literature on growth across countries, regions and states has burgeoned in recent years. Mancur Olson's (1982) *Rise and Decline of Nations* represents an early contribution to the new institutional approach to growth. In his important book Mancur argued that special interest groups develop over time and that these groups compete for shares of the economic pie to the detriment of growth in the size of that pie. The harmful effect of interest groups on economic growth is referred to as institutional sclerosis. Olson (1982) provides evidence in favor of this theory using length of time of governmental stability as a proxy for the formation of interest groups.

Olson's approach came under attack from many sides. One of these attacks was from Virginia Gray and David Lowery (1988) who argued that the simple use of time since the last upheaval did not adequately address the depth and richness of the model Olson had developed. For example, Olson's model indicated that some groups might be sufficiently large that greater economic growth would be in the interest of their members. Olson called these groups encompassing groups. Gray and Lowery argued that some groups, such as trade associations, would also favor growth over redistribution. Therefore, they argued that the extent to which pro-redistributive groups could reduce economic growth would depend upon their power both in absolute terms and relative to the power of pro-growth groups. Gray and Lowery may have a valid point in that lots of special interest groups which have no influence surely generate very little institutional sclerosis. On the other hand, a few powerful groups may have substantial effects on the economy. All this begs the question of what it means for a group to be powerful. Gray and Lowery attempted to construct measures of the power of groups in different states. Their measures depended upon the number of groups and group members. This they called absolute power. At the same time, they compared this power of one type of group to the similarly constructed power of another type of group and to the size of the government. These are their measures of relative power.

The contribution of this chapter is that we examine these ideas of absolute and relative power of interest groups in a fresh way. In doing so we provide further testing of the Olson model and find support for his hypothesis. As he states:

* We appreciate comments from participants at the Southern Economic Association and Western Social Science Association conferences.

If we define society in national terms, it follows that the national government encompasses everyone in society. This means that though there are colossal and well-known difficulties in arriving at optimal collective decisions the national government would, if not influenced by lobbies, have an incentive to promote efficiency and growth. The argument here accordingly focuses not only on the absolute power of special-interest groups but also on the *relative* (italics in original) strength of the most encompassing group, the government, versus constituent groups that are much less encompassing. The efficiency of an economy may be increased either by making narrow special-interest groups weaker or by making the government stronger in relation to them. (Olson 1983a, p.23)

To test Olson's hypothesis, we devise alternative measures of the absolute and relative power of interest groups which, we believe, are more in keeping with Olson's insight than are the measures used by Gray and Lowery. Moreover, we argue that the typical test of the Olson hypothesis assumes that the additional effect of interest groups is constant regardless of how many interest groups already exist. We find this assumption implausible and, using data on the number of interest groups in a variety of countries in 1970, show that the marginal effect of the number of interest groups varies with the number of interest groups. We contend that this is evidence that the power of interest groups depends upon their number. Our results suggest quite plausibly that the more interest groups there are, the smaller the power of an additional interest group. The results also suggest that the fewer interest groups that exist for a given level of governmental involvement in the economy, the less harm done to the economy.

Gray and Lowery (1988) argued that the power of interest groups relative to the government is a key component of Olson's theory. Since interest groups are anti-growth and the government, as the largest "encompassing" group, is pro-growth, the stronger those interest groups are relative to the government the greater the institutional sclerosis in the country. Pryor (1983) makes a similar argument, suggesting that the communist party of the Eastern European countries was an encompassing interest group, "one that is strongly committed to high rates of economic growth". Consequently, as the number of interest groups rises relative to the size of the government, growth is slowed.

We find support for this hypothesis that growth slows as the number of interest groups increases relative to the size of government. However, while Olson (1983a) states that in the absence of lobbies the government would "have an incentive to promote efficiency and growth", we doubt that Mancur Olson would have considered governments in the real world to be "encompassing" in this way.[1] It is certainly the case that few public choice economists would make such a

[1] Obviously, lobbies exist, so the premise of the statement is false and Olson's conclusion need not follow. Moreover, his lack of a statement about what would happen in the presence of lobbies suggests that he believed that actual governments do not have this incentive. Indeed, we would contend that federal government by its very nature involves lobbies. These lobbies are the representatives from the various jurisdictions who will press for advantages for their constituents at the expense of constituents from other jurisdictions.

claim. One possible explanation for our result is that lobbying and other efforts at capturing rents are more intense, and therefore more harmful, when the number of interest groups is large relative to the basket of goodies available for the government to distribute.[2] Put this way, the result does not rely upon government as an encompassing group but rather may relate to the costs incurred as government tries to determine which rent-seekers to reward and which to ignore.

The rest of the chapter is organized as follows. The next section discusses in greater detail the role of interest groups in reducing the rate of economic growth. Section 8.2 describes the methodology and data. In section 8.3, we report the estimation results. Finally, section 8.4 represents a brief conclusion.

8.1 Interest Groups and Economic Growth

Mancur Olson (1982) drew several implications from his analysis of interest groups on their formation and activities. His seventh implication (1982, p. 65) is that:

> Distributional coalitions slow down a society's capacity to adopt new technologies and to reallocate resources in response to changing conditions, and thereby reduce the rate of economic growth.

The more distributional coalitions, therefore, the stronger the detrimental effects they exert on economic growth. Olson further argued that the length of time that a region has been politically stable relates to the number of distributional coalitions that exist. Essentially, upheaval destroys these groups and stability allows them to form. The longer in the past is an episode of upheaval, the more groups that will have formed, and the worse the consequences for subsequent economic growth.

Olson (1982) reports a variety of regression results testing the two main hypotheses: time since upheaval has a negative effect on growth, and distributional coalitions grow over time. The extent to which his analysis accurately reflects the growth of distributional coalitions may be called into question. Since distributional coalitions are likely to form at different rates over time and in different areas, a simple linear time measure for number of years of stability is unlikely to properly capture the dynamics involved. In addition, for the U.S. states he proxies the amount of distributional coalitions by the number of union members as a share of non-farm employment in 1964 and in 1970. These union membership data are a poor measure of the amount of distributional coalition activity in an economy since they completely ignore the role of non-labor related distributional coalitions.

Kwang Choi (1983) provides evidence on cross-country growth effects. He constructed an index of institutional sclerosis based on a logistic function. Essen-

[2] The theoretical literature on rent seeking consistently finds that total rent seeking expenditures is expected to be an increasing function of the number of interest groups (Nitzan 1994). Endogenizing the size of available rents does not alter this relationship (Appelbaum and Katz 1987; Yates and Heckelman 2001).

tially, the idea is that early on, the development of interest-groups has a small but growing effect on the extent of sclerosis, but over time, additional groups have a diminishing marginal influence on sclerosis. This index is also adjusted for the length of time during which the given country experienced major disruptions, revolutions, occupation and so on, but does not directly measure interest group formation. Choi states that he believes this "index is close to that implied by Olson's rather general theory."

Murrell (1984), using interest group data from the OECD countries for 1970, finds that of the variables hypothesized to influence the number of interest groups in a country, the average length of time since "consolidation of modernizing leadership" and "economic and social transformation" began is one of three which is consistently significant and of the expected sign. Murrell's estimates include "all non-governmental formal organizations whose members share sectional interests". A "sectional" group is one in which the members have a common economic interest. For example, all the members may work in the same firm, industry or sector of the economy. Murrell's analysis suffers from several problems related to missing data and the small number of observations. In addition, he also assumed a strictly linear relationship to hold between length of stability and interest group formation. Nevertheless, he tests for the relationship between length of stability and the number of interest groups in several ways and finds support for a positive relationship under each method. He does not relate his interest group number to the index created by Choi.

We regressed Murrell's interest group variable on Choi's index of institutional sclerosis. If the length of time since modernization adjusted for the number and duration of upheavals, revolutions and foreign occupations, is positively related to the number of interest groups, then this is support for Olson's theory. Indeed, since Gray and Lowery question the link between interest groups and time, and find no evidence of such a link for the states of the U.S., the lack of statistical relationship between Choi's and Murrell's variables would provide support for Gray and Lowery and be evidence against Olson's theory. In a regression explaining the number of interest groups in a country in 1970, the coefficient on the Choi index is 45.2 with a p-value of 0.025. This, it seems, is strong evidence of a positive link between the time since modernization and the number of interest groups. Taken with Murrell's results, this suggests that there is a strong relationship between the number of special interest groups and the passage of time in a stable environment.

McCallum and Blais (1987) find support for the Olson hypothesis when the institutional sclerosis variable is proxied by Choi's preferred measure of time since modernizing consolidation began, but they do not find a significant relationship between Murrell's interest group variable and growth. Using an instrumental variable technique, Heckelman (2000) does find some support for Olson's hypothesis using Murrell's interest group variable, but his data set includes several non-OECD nations for which Murrell had also created the interest group variable. Because the non-OECD countries for which interest group data are available may not be representative of all developing countries, and because we want as much as possible to use a set of similar countries to keep as close to the Gray and Lowery approach which used data from the individual U.S. states, we

approach which used data from the individual U.S. states, we choose to limit our sample to only include the OECD countries, as in Murrell's original analysis.

8.2 Methodology and Data

In this section, we test the impact of the number of special interest groups per capita (*SIGPC*) on the nation's economic growth rate. We use Murrell's (1984) measure of the number of special interest groups in the OECD nations in 1970 to explain growth rates for the decade 1970 to 1980. Population figures for 1970 and growth rates for 1970-1980 are taken from World Bank (1984).

The use of the number of interest groups per capita is one attempt to address the absolute power of interest groups, that is, about their "encompassingness". Consider two countries with widely divergent populations, such as the United States and Canada, but with about the same number of interest groups. The number of interest groups per capita would be much smaller in the U.S. than in Canada. One hypothesis is that interest groups in the United States would have more absolute power than would those same interest groups in Canada. More generally, absolute power of interest groups falls as the number of groups per capita rises.

Interest groups per capita can also be interpreted as a very rough measure of membership in the average interest group. As groups per capita rises, then, membership in the average group falls, and the "encompassingness" of that group falls. Conversely, as the interest groups per capita falls, membership in the average group rises, and the encompassingness of the average group rises. Increased encompassingness would result in greater emphasis on growth, and less on redistributing the existing economic pie, while decreased encompassingness would result in lower emphasis on growth and more on redistributing the existing economic pie. Consequently, one justification for inclusion of the groups per capita variable in a growth regression is to test Olson's hypothesis about encompassingness.

However, as we have said, interest groups per capita is a very rough measure of average group membership. It is, therefore, a very rough measure of encompassingness at best. For implicitly we are assuming that all interest groups are nearly equal in size and that as the number of interest groups grow parity in memberships is maintained, but with fewer members in each. In other words, established interest groups lose members to newly formed interest groups, reducing the encompassingness of the former. There is no reason that this must be true. Individuals may have multiple memberships, so one very large group may be quite encompassing while its members join many smaller groups that are not encompassing. Alternatively, the vast majority of the population may belong to one group, with the remaining minority split equally among hundreds of groups. The large group is quite encompassing, the small groups are not. Interest groups per capita may not be a good measure of encompassingness under either of these circumstances.

The Olson model describes what happens as the number of interest groups rises, but it makes no mention about the size of the country in relation to the number of groups. Estimating the model with interest groups per capita can be justified on the grounds that a given number of interest groups, for example 1000, would imply rather different levels of sclerosis in Switzerland than the United States. The enormous differences in size, both geographic and population, suggest that those 1000 interest groups may induce less harm in the United States than they would in Switzerland. In this case, interest groups per capita is a rough measure of the intensity or density of interest group activity in a country after normalizing for the country's size. Under this interpretation, the interest groups per capita variable says nothing about encompassingness of groups but captures the intensity of special pleading.

A second issue about the interest group variable concerns the manner in which it enters the regression. If interest groups per capita enter linearly, then an additional group has the same impact if it is the second to form or the thousandth. However, one might contend that the sclerotic effects of interest groups vary with the number of groups. One possible explanation for changing marginal effects of additional groups is a variant of the well known efficiency property of free mobility of resources. Specifically, early groups to form attract the most productive resources (particularly entrepreneurs), who are the most effective at influencing redistribution in their favor and represent the largest opportunity cost to lost productive innovations. Thus, the first groups have large detrimental effects on the economy as they attract the most talented entrepreneurs and lobbyists. As the number of groups grows, less proficient entrepreneurs and lobbyists enter the rent-seeking process. For these later groups, the lobbying is less effective and represents a smaller opportunity cost to the economy, and they therefore have smaller harmful impacts on the overall economy.

Alternatively, the first groups to form may focus on issues that are of broad consequence and later groups may have a more narrow focus. For example, labor unions and professional associations may form before groups whose focus is on specifically local (Save Beaver Creek) or more narrowly defined concerns (Save the Snail Darter). The more wide ranging effects of the labor and professional groups carry with them larger harm to the economy than the more parochial focus of the local, and late forming, groups. Regardless of which explanation one accepts, the intuition implies that the marginal damage to growth of later groups is smaller than that of early groups, which suggests that the number of groups enter the growth equation nonlinearly.

Gray and Lowery emphasize the importance of the power of groups relative to the government. We use the ratio of groups per capita to the government's share of GDP (*GOV*), to capture the relative power of interest groups compared to government.[3] This ratio (*SIGPC/GOV*) is similar in construction to that used by Gray and Lowery (1988) in their state level analysis. A problem rises with its interpretation, however. As noted above, Gray and Lowery suggest that government is the most encompassing group. Consequently, as interest groups grow in power relative to government, the ratio of groups per capita to government share of GDP rises, which they would expect to generate harmful effects on growth. This variable increases, however, if either groups per capita increases or government's

[3] Values for *GOV* are taken from World Bank (1984).

share of GDP falls. Consequently, if government's share of GDP falls, according to the Gray and Lowery argument, growth should be adversely affected. In contrast, Barro (1991, 1997) treats increases in the government's share of GDP as a proxy for wasteful rent seeking activities and finds it to be a strong negative determinant of growth.

There are a few points to note about the difference between Gray and Lowery (1989) and Barro (1991, 1997). First, Barro does not control for the number of interest groups in his analysis.[4] It will come as no surprise that the number of interest groups is positively correlated with government's share of GDP. The correlation coefficient between number of interest groups and government share of GDP in our sample is 0.41 ($p = 0.06$), between the natural logarithm of the number of interest groups and government share is 0.40 ($p = 0.07$), and between the log of interest groups per capita and government share is 0.48 ($p = 0.02$). The direction of causation, if causation exists, is unknown. One might suspect that large government induces growth in interest groups, as the size of the pie to fight over entices combatants into the ring. On the other hand, government may be large because interest groups are individually successful at lobbying for their own particularized programs.

Second, Barro's government consumption variable is net of spending on education and military, treating these as pure public goods and remaining expenditures to be primarily redistributive in nature. However, government expenditures in these areas are surely influenced by the powerful education lobbies and military industrial complex, and their encompassingness is an empirical issue. Our measure of government size includes all government consumption.

Finally, as we remarked above, Olson indicated government would be encompassing if there were no lobbies or lobbyists. Of course there are lobbies and lobbyists, so it seems unlikely that Olson would have considered government an encompassing group. If government is not an encompassing group, then what it means for interest groups to have more power relative to government is unclear and not something to which Olson's model was directed. Given the presence of rent seeking lobbies, government does not strictly act as an encompassing group so it is no longer clear whether increased interest group power relative to government power is growth enhancing or growth reducing. For example, if the interest groups are more encompassing than government, then a rise in interest group power may be growth enhancing. If the reverse is true, then a rise in interest group power will be growth retarding. Consequently, the relevant issue is not about significance versus insignificance of the relative power variable per se, but rather it is about the direction of impact of relative power. Consequently, neither significance

[4] Barro (1991) does account for revolutions and assassinations per year during the period for which the growth rate is determined. For countries with non-zero values of these variables, this suggests a high degree of instability and uncertainty is likely to remain, weakening the growth of interest groups. Countries for which these values are zero may have had revolutions or other instability immediately prior to the start of the period or not for decades or even centuries before the period. The upshot is that Barro's analysis really can not say anything about Olson's hypothesis.

Table 8.1. Data

NATION	SIGPC	GOV	SIGPC/GOV	GROWTH 1970-1980	GROWTH 1980-1990
Australia	1.14	14	0.08	3.0	3.4
Austria	17.87	15	1.19	3.4	2.1
Belgium	9.06	13	0.70	3.0	2.0
Canada	8.20	19	0.43	4.6	3.4
Denmark	9.17	20	0.46	2.2	2.4
Finland	7.36	14	0.53	3.1	3.4
France	3.06	15	0.20	3.2	2.2
Germany	4.00	16	0.25	2.6	2.1
Greece	1.08	13	0.08	4.7	1.8
Ireland	10.14	15	0.68	4.9	3.1
Italy	0.84	13	0.06	3.8	2.4
Japan	0.35	7	0.05	4.3	4.1
Netherlands	6.98	15	0.47	2.9	1.9
Norway	9.78	17	0.58	4.8	2.9
New Zealand	2.38	13	0.18	1.9	1.9
Portugal	2.45	14	0.18	4.3	2.7
Spain	0.76	9	0.08	3.5	3.1
Sweden	5.87	22	0.27	1.9	2.2
Switzerland	17.98	10	1.80	0.5	2.2
Turkey	0.23	13	0.02	5.9	5.1
United Kingdom	5.81	18	0.32	2.0	3.1
United States	2.74	19	0.14	2.8	3.4
Mean	5.78	14.73	0.40	3.33	2.77
Std. Dev.	5.05	3.56	0.42	1.26	0.81

nor insignificance of this interest group relative to the government share of GDP variable is, by itself, necessarily evidence for or against the relative power argument.

Although the number of special interests is expected to grow over time (Olson 1965), we hypothesize that the impact on growth from a given number of special interests weakens over time. We therefore also consider the impact of the special interest groups in 1970 on growth rates from 1980-1990, taken from World Bank (1992). Both Gray and Lowery (1988) and Pryor (1983) criticized Olson (1982) for not being clear about the time frame of his model. By looking at the effects of the number of interest groups on growth in the current and subsequent decade we are able to draw an inference about the appropriate time frame for the analysis.

8.3 Empirical Results

The data are presented in Table 8.1. Switzerland and Austria have by far the two highest *SIGPC* values, and are the only nations to have values more than two standard deviations from the mean. Austria is not quite as much of an outlier for the relative measure, *SIGPC/GOV*. The estimated absolute impact of *SIGPC* on growth for 1970-80 is presented graphically in Figure 8.1, where the potential importance of the outliers becomes more clear. The estimated regression line is downward sloped as expected, but is not statistically significant. The relative measure is also inversely related to growth, and is marginally significant at the 10% level. Regression statistics are given in the first two columns in the upper portion of Table 8.2, and presented graphically in Figure 8.2.

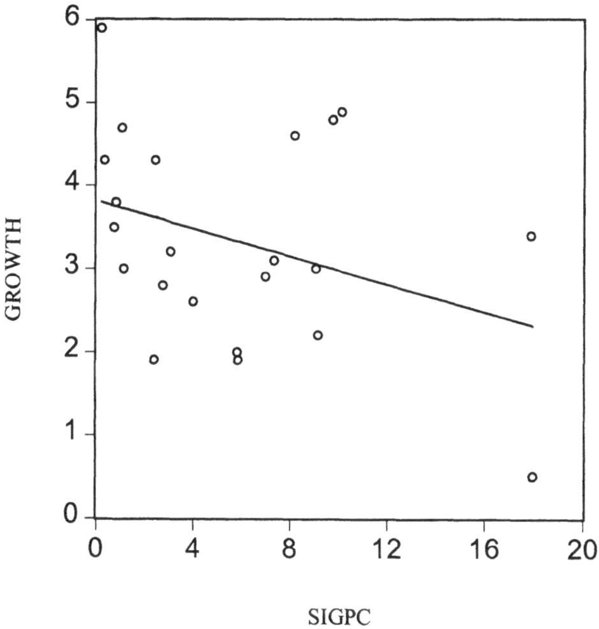

Fig. 8.1. Absolute measure of special interest group effect

At first blush, these results may be viewed as more supportive of Gray and Lowery's relative measure than Olson's absolute measure. It turns out, however, the marginal significance of the relative measure is completely dependent on the presence of Switzerland. Removing this outlier from the sample drops the t-statistic for *SIGPC/GOV* to -0.30. Thus, there is little support for either the relative or absolute effect of interest groups on growth.

However, this conclusion too may be premature. It seems likely that the damage to growth from special interest groups, though potentially severe, would be limited. Although additional groups would further constrain growth, we expect their marginal contribution to growth hindrance would be lessened the more groups already present. Therefore the linear specification, which requires that each

Table 8.2. Effect of absolute and relative measures of SIGC in 1970 on growth

	linear measures			log measures	
			Growth 1970-1980		
constant	3.82** (9.70)	3.82** (10.98)	3.90** (11.15)	2.58** (6.43)	2.28 (0.80)
SIGPC	-0.084 (-1.63)		-0.46** (-2.27)		0.11 (0.10)
SIGPC/GOV		-1.23* (-2.03)		-0.52** (-2.36)	-0.64 (-0.57)
R-sqaure	0.12	0.17	0.20	0.22	0.22
F-value	2.65	4.11*	5.15**	5.57**	2.65*
			Growth 1980-1990		
constant	3.08** (11.88)	3.02** (12.71)	3.19** (14.58)	2.21** (8.73)	2.58 (1.43)
SIGPC	-0.053 (-1.58)		-0.35** (-2.74)		-0.14 (-0.21)
SIGPC/GOV		-0.63 (-1.52)		-0.39** (-2.76)	-0.24 (-0.34)
R-square	0.11	0.10	0.27	0.28	0.28

*significant at 10%
**significant at 5%

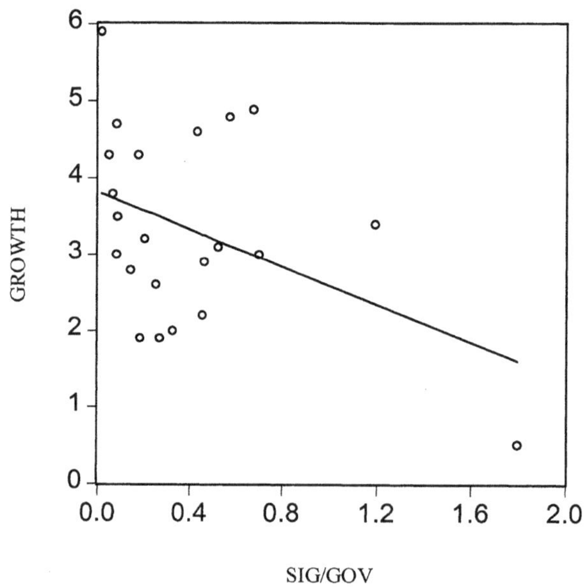

Fig. 8.2. Relative measure of special interest group effect

additional group have an equal marginal impact, may not be appropriate. A log specification would allow marginal effects to decline. In this way, the log form also reduces the influence of outlier observations.

Graphs for the log specifications are given in Figures 8.3 and 8.4, and regression statistics are shown in the 3rd and 4th columns of the upper panel in Table 8.2. Both the absolute and relative measures are statistically significant at the 5% level and the R^2s show improvement compared to the linear representations.[5] The significance of the relative measure again depends on the inclusion of Switzerland, but the absolute measure remains marginally significant at the 10% level (dropping Austria has no effect either by itself or along with Switzerland). The log form dictates that the marginal impacts depend on the number of *SIGPC* in the nation. For comparison to the linear measures, the partial derivatives for the log specification are calculated in Table 8.3. For the absolute effect, the average marginal impact is slightly smaller than the linear estimate suggesting the statistical significance is strictly through improved estimation precision.

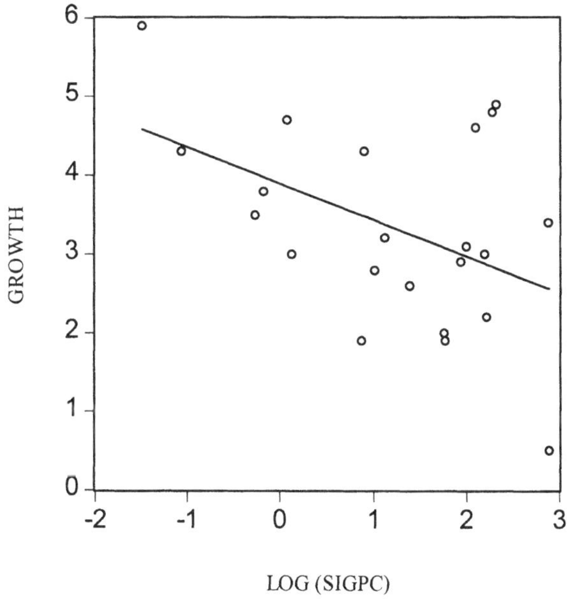

Fig. 8.3. Absolute measure of special interest group effect (log form)

[5] Since the *SIGPC* measure is in per capita terms, there is the potential that the negative coefficient is picking up a positive association between population and growth, rather than the presumed negative relation between the number of special interest groups and growth. As a check, we used the total number of special interest groups and population as separate independent variables. None of the results were affected by this change.

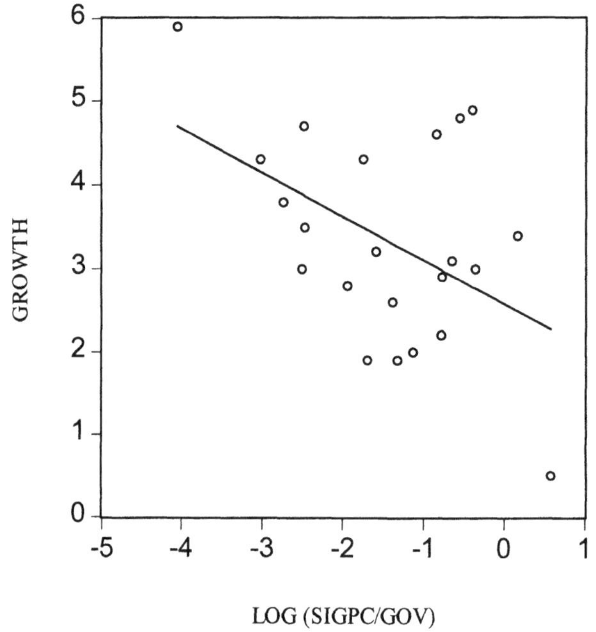

Fig. 8.4. Relative measure of special interest group effect (log form)

Gray and Lowery include both absolute and relative measures in their regressions. They find support for the relative measure but not the absolute measure. We include both measures simultaneously in the last column in Table 8.2. Neither variable is significant and in fact the coefficient on the absolute measure changes sign. But care is required in analyzing the regression because this procedure alters the interpretation of the coefficients. In the regression

$$GROWTH = a + bSIGPC + c(SIGPC/GOV) + u \quad (1)$$

the coefficient c measures the relative impact ($dGROWTH/d(SIGPC/GOV)$). The absolute impact of *SIGPC* is not simply b, however, but is given by $dGROWTH/dSIGPC = b + c/GOV$. In fact, the inclusion of *SIGPC* as a separate variable is simply a nuisance parameter since the absolute impact can be determined from *SIGPC/GOV* alone. Note that if *SIGPC* is dropped from equation (1), then the absolute impact is found by $dGROWTH/dSIGPC = c/GOV$, whereas the relative impact is still measured by c alone. Thus, no additional information is gained by including *SIGPC* as an additional variable by itself.

The marginal impacts of the absolute and relative effect are given in the last column of Table 8.3. The impact from the absolute measure is statistically significant, but the relative measure is not. The interpretation of the c coefficient is also slightly altered. Since we are controlling for the number of *SIGPC*, most of the variation in the relative measure must be from altering the size of government.

Since the relative impact is not significant in the joint regression, this suggests there is less impact if the relative changes are due to *GOV*, but changes are important when due to *SIGPC*. Thus, statistical significance of the relative measure in the bivariate regression is primarily due to its incorporation of the absolute effect.[6]

Table 8.3. Average marginal impact of log form SIGPC measures on growth (t-statistics)

	Measure(s) used in regression		
	Absolute only	Relative only	Both
		Growth 1970-1980	
Absolute	-0.080**		-0.092**
	(-2.27)		(-2.22)
Relative		-1.30**	-1.60
		(-2.36)	(-0.57)
		Growth 1980-1990	
Absolute	-0.061**		-0.066**
	(-2.74)		(-2.49)
Relative		-0.98**	-0.60
		(-2.76)	(-0.34)

Calculated from log measures columns in Table 8.2 and average GOV in Table 8.1.
**significant at 5%

How damaging are special interest groups to future growth? To answer this question, we considered the effect of the number of *SIGPC* in 1970 on growth over the 1980-1990 period. We expect that as new groups are created and fight for distributional gains, at different rates in each nation, the original groups in 1970 would still be harmful to growth but at a diminishing rate. Utilizing the same methodology as for the 1970-1980 period, we found similar, though smaller, effects, which suggests Pryor's (1983) concerns regarding the exact timing of Olson's hypothesized interest group effect on growth are not critical. Regressions results are presented in the lower half of Table 8.2.

First we considered the individual bivariate regressions for the absolute number of groups, and the relative size compared to government. The linear measures again were of the expected sign but not significant. Notice that the estimated coefficients are closer to zero although the absolute measure is of course not significantly different in the two time periods. As was true for the earlier period, logged representations represent a better fit than the linear measures. The log measures are statistically significant for both the absolute and relative measures, and the point estimates are smaller in absolute value compared to the earlier period. The average marginal impacts are presented in the bottom half of Table 8.3. The estimated average effect on growth in the second period is over 20% less compared to

[6] Further support for this interpretation is found in regressions using *SIGPC* and *GOV* as separate variables. Neither is individually significant but *SIGPC* has a t-statistic about 1.5 whereas *GOV* has a t-statistic of only about .4. Additionally, if one uses log (*SIGPC*) this variable has a t-statistic over 2 but *GOV* continues to have a t-statistic well below 1 in either its linear or log form.

the initial period. For the relative measure, the decline is just under 18%. Both measures are included in the final regression in Table 8.2. As for 1970-1980, neither coefficient is individually statistically significant, although the effect from the absolute number of *SIGPC* given by (*b* + *c*/*GOV*) is significant. When controlling for the relative measure, the estimated impact of the absolute measure is again enhanced, although by a smaller difference compared to the earlier period, and is still smaller in total effect. None of the conclusions are dependent on the inclusion of Switzerland.

The results presented above may be spurious if the number of special interest groups is highly correlated with other variables not included which impact growth. Given the small number of countries in the OECD, we are unable to present a fully specified growth model. Instead, we ran additional regressions including various combinations of additional explanatory variables for initial GDP, investment as a percentage of GDP, and urbanization rate, all for 1970, taken from World Bank (1984). In each case, controlling for these additional variables reduced the coefficient on the log of *SIGPC*, but it remained statistically significant with a t-statistic above 2. Among these additional controls, only urbanization was found to also be (negatively) significant. The same results hold for the 1980-90 growth rate, except here even the urbanization rate in 1970 no longer significantly affects future growth. Thus, our reported results and interpretation for the log of *SIGPC* remains robust.

8.4 Conclusion

Our findings support Olson's concept of a negative influence of special interest groups on economic growth. There is more evidence of an absolute effect from the number of groups than a relative effect of the number of groups compared to the size of government. When controlling for the absolute number of groups, the relative measure has no additional impact, but controlling for the relative measure increases the estimated average effect of the absolute number of groups, lending little support for Gray and Lowery's contention that government takes a pro-growth approach as the largest encompassing interest group. The marginal effects are nonlinear, as additional group formation is less harmful the more groups that already exist, although total growth would still be further limited by their presence. Finally, holding constant the number of groups, we find the estimated effects are still present in later years but are smaller in every specification of the measures. These results hold for both bivariate and multivariate specifications.

9 If I Had a Hammer: Mancur Olson as an Economic Historian*

Robert Whaples

Mancur Olson is primarily regarded as a pioneer of public choice theory, but he was also keenly interested in how political and economic forces interacted to influence the *historical* performance of the economy and society. This chapter examines the evolution of Olson's contributions to economic history, beginning with his early work on Britain's wheat market and wartime food shortages and culminating with *The Rise and Decline of Nations* and the work related to it. It maps the evolution of the field of economic history during Olson's career; examines Olson's historical methods, arguments, and findings; and brings these two together by analyzing the reception of Olson's ideas by economic historians.

Olson and mainstream economic historians had a mutual attraction but they also, at times, repelled one another. Olson fell in love with the study of economic history while earning his M.A. and read widely in the field, carefully considering the ideas and comments of a broad range of economic historians.[1] Economic historians also fell in love with Olson, thrilled and flattered that this engaging, energetic, inventive, well-read, well-regarded, original theorist cared about their research, struggled with their subject matter and sought their feedback. However, they were often uneasy with Olson's style of argumentation and standards of evidence, especially what they regarded as a penchant for overstatement and his unwillingness to test his ideas using the field's quantitative, econometric, cliometric approach. They never embraced him as one of their own, nor did Olson seek this goal or see economic historians as his reference group. Instead, he increasingly reached out to a much broader audience, rather than confining himself within a subdisciplinary cul-de-sac.

---

* I thank two of Mancur Olson's former colleagues, John Wallis and John Adams, for insightful comments.

[1] Olson explained that while studying at University College, Oxford as a Rhodes Scholar (1954-56) "he first acquired an interest in the economic history of Great Britain" (Olson 1963a, p. v).

9.1 The Field of Economic History in the United States: A Partial Map of the Terrain

Although the field of economic history changed considerably during the twentieth century and in the four decades of Mancur Olson's professional career, the one constant in the field has been a love affair with quantification. Edwin F. Gay, the Economic History Association's first president and "the first real American economic historian" (Cole 1946, p. 1), set this tone. Gay's research on enclosures overturned the received wisdom of the day, which argued that the enclosure movement had robbed the laborer of his land, causing massive displacement, depopulation and landlessness in England between the late 1400s and early 1600s. Gay believed that this conclusion rested on flimsy, anecdotal foundations and tested this contention by collecting archival data and computing the amount of enclosures during this period. "Inclosures in England in the Sixteenth Century" (1903), which presented Gay's dissertation findings, was a milestone. Analyzing data broken down by county and subperiod, it showed that the rate of enclosure was significantly slower than had been heretofore believed, and concluded that "An agricultural change affecting 2.76 per cent, or even 5 per cent, of the total land area of twenty-four counties in a century and a half, is surely nothing very alarming" (Gay 1903, p. 588). Gay imbued this "zest for the measurement" (Heaton 1949, p. 5) upon his doctoral students at Harvard University, who constituted a virtual "Who's Who" in economic history from the middle decades of the twentieth century.[2]

Gay was also active in establishing the National Bureau of Economic Research (NBER) and its program of data collection and analysis. He served as its first president (from 1920 to 1921) and helped direct the Bureau's survey for the Committee on Recent Economic Changes of the President's Unemployment Conference in 1929. In his presidential address to the American Economic Association, he explained the value of collecting historical data, which he called a "relatively dependable causeway" to be "thrown over the morasses of earlier economic history" (Gay 1930, pp. 2-3).

By the time Mancur Olson reached graduate school in the late 1950s, young scholars complained that many important economic issues were misinterpreted because of a failure to unite explicit economic theory to this rapidly accumulating mound of quantitative historical data. They pushed their older colleagues to employ formal economic theory along with measurement in order to better assess the historical performance of the economy.

The value of the new approach was convincingly displayed in Alfred Conrad and John Meyer's "The Economics of Slavery in the Ante Bellum South," (1958), one of the first papers of the "New Economic History" – or "cliometrics," as it

---

[2] They include four presidents of the EHA: Arthur Cole, Earl Hamilton, Anne Bezanson, and Harold Williamson; and other notables, such as Abbott Payson Usher, Blanche Hazard Sprague, Chester W. Wright, Louis C. Hunter, N.S.B. Gras, and Elizabeth Waterman Gilboy.

soon came to be known. It approached the subject as an investment problem to determine if slavery was profitable and whether or not it would have toppled under its own weight without the necessity of a Civil War. Conrad and Meyer modeled slaveowners as investors with a capital asset subject to depreciation and maintenance costs. They examined historical data on cotton yields, slaves' average life spans, and prices of inputs and output, calculating that owning slaves was more profitable than other potential investments.

Instead of imprecise qualitative statements such as "it is difficult to exaggerate the importance of this," cliometrics began to provide precise (though not necessarily accurate) estimates of historical economic relationships. Cliometricians were the first historians to harness computers, allowing them to estimate economic models and their marginal effects, which had been hidden in voluminous but previously mute and unusable bodies of archival data. Shortly after Olson completed his dissertation in 1963, the trickle of "new economic history" became a torrent, spurred on by growing interest among those in economics departments, who eagerly hired the hordes of new cliometricians (Williamson and Whaples forthcoming).

One way to gauge the progress of the cliometric revolution is to examine the pages of the leading economic history journal. In the early 1950s less than two percent of the pages in the *Journal of Economic History* were in cliometric articles, those which used measurement (tables) and explicit economic theory. This figure subsequently climbed to ten percent in the late 1950s, sixteen percent in the early 1960s, forty-three percent in the late 1960s, and seventy-two percent in the early 1970s (Whaples 1991). In the late 1950s, many scholars had derided cliometrics as a new fad, but by the 1970s it was the standard operating procedure for American economic historians. The success and influence of cliometrics is attested to by the fact that in 1993 the Royal Swedish Academy cited two cliometricians, Robert Fogel and Douglass North, for "for having renewed research in economic history by applying economic theory and quantitative methods in order to explain economic and institutional change" and awarded them the Nobel Prize in Economics, as "pioneers in ... cliometrics."

The cliometric revolution left behind a sizeable group of economic historians who were not trained in the new statistical techniques, especially older economists and those in history departments. Over the course of the next few decades the proportion of economic historians employed in history departments plummeted. Simultaneously, history departments in the United States took a turn to the left. At many schools the only economic historians left in history departments were radicals, who rarely interacted with the field's mainstream. With the waning influence of professional historians, economic historians tailored their product to suit a narrower audience of economists and began to focus on topics that interested economists more, especially the causes of economic growth – one of Olson's favorite topics.[3]

[3] The fraction of *JEH* pages concerned with economic growth more than doubled from the 1950s to the 1960s (Whaples 1991, p. 290).

Date of birth had an important influence on whether or not an economic historian used the cliometric approach. Although about twenty percent of authors publishing in the *Journal of Economic History* who were born in the early 1920s can be classified as cliometricians, this share rises to almost fifty percent for those born in the early 1930s and about seventy-five percent among those born in the early 1940s (Whaples 1991, p. 296). As these results suggest, many economic historians above a certain age drifted away from the field. Mancur Olson, who was born in 1932, was one of those authors in the majority of his cohort who would never be identified (or identify himself) as a cliometrician. However, rather than abandoning the field, he maintained his interest and research in economic history, while swimming against the strengthening cliometric tide.

Among the most successful missionaries of the new cliometric methodology was Douglass North. His short textbook, *Growth and Welfare in the American Past* (1966), which used simple economic theory and tables of quantitative data to challenge conventional views on many important topics in American economic history, charted the course for much additional research. However, after publishing *Growth and Welfare*, North decided to switch from American to European economic history, and became convinced that the conventional static neoclassical economic theory used by most cliometricians was incapable of explaining longer-term economic change, which required the modeling of institutions, property rights and government. As reflected in his EHA presidential address, "Beyond the New Economic History" (1974), North sought to move beyond economic growth's *proximate* causes (such as improvements in technology and increases in inputs such as labor, capital and raw materials) and criticized those unconcerned with explaining economic change's *ultimate* causes.

Over the next couple of decades, North (with help from others including co-authors Lance Davis and Robert Paul Thomas) tried to establish a new theoretical paradigm that could explain long-term economic change's underlying causes. Each of his books became more ambitious than the one that preceded it. By 1981, in *Structure and Change in Economic History*, North had abandoned the idea that institutions were efficient and began explaining why inefficient arrangements would tend to exist and be perpetuated. Mancur Olson had reached the same conclusion and was attacking the same set of problems. The building blocks of North's overarching theory included theories of property rights, the state and ideology. This book was incredibly ambitious, acknowledged as a treasury of bold generalizations and provocative insights, and applauded for directing attention toward important phenomena. However, reviewers warned that North had overstated, oversimplified and disregarded conflicting evidence, and that such grand theorizing eliminated the textures of historical economic systems. Similar reactions greeted North's *Institutions, Institutional Change and Economic Performance* (1990).[4] These two books were almost completely devoid of quantitative data – there is not a single table in either book, but North had effectively refocused the field's attention toward explaining the underlying causes of broader historical change. Olson's historical work from the same period, especially *The Rise and*

[4] For example, see Pryor (1982) and Field (1991).

Decline of Nations, was in many ways similar to North's and elicited many of the same reactions.

Despite North's efforts and influence, however, few economic historians adopted his big think, non-quantitative approach. The number of tables per page in the *Journal of Economic History*, for example, continued its upward trend.[5] The work of economic history's other Nobel laureate, Robert Fogel, exemplified this *increasingly* quantitative, number-crunching approach which aimed more and more at answering the "how big?" question.

In 1960 economic historian W.W. Rostow argued that a leading sector was needed to push the rest of the economy into a "take-off" to sustained growth and that the railroads had fulfilled this function in the United States in the nineteenth century. Fogel (1964) tested this hypothesis, expending an entire book to calculate a single number, the "social savings" (or increase in national income) generated by the decrease in transportation costs from the railroad industry. Fogel's breakthrough was in comparing the costs of railroad transportation with alternative forms of transportation. He estimated that the social savings from hauling freight via railroads in 1890 could not have been higher than 4.7 percent of GDP, refuting Rostow's conclusion that railroads were indispensable to American economic growth. Fogel demonstrated that the American economy was full of substitution possibilities and implicitly argued that the sources of growth were manifold.

Fogel's findings were initially greeted skeptically and sparked a flood of highly quantitative research and many attempts at refutation. His lengthy EHA presidential address, "Notes on the Social Saving Controversy" (1979), effectively rebutted these criticisms. A recent survey shows that the overwhelming majority of economic historians now agree with Fogel's underlying conclusion that railroads were *not* indispensable to nineteenth-century American economic growth (Whaples 1995). Perhaps because of the initial skepticism, Fogel's extended effort also convinced many of the power of theory-based quantitative economic history.

Reactions and attention to Fogel's railroad study were mild compared to responses to his next book (with Stanley Engerman) *Time on the Cross* (1974). Its most original findings were that material standards of living of American slaves were not as low as most had imagined and that slave plantations were considerably more efficient than Northern farms and free Southern farms at turning the inputs of land, labor, and capital into output and revenue. Several leading economic historians dropped their research projects to take up the challenge of assessing and refuting these findings.[6] The intense debate over slavery's efficiency, similar to the debate about the railroads, essentially boiled down to a single number – slave farms' relative total factor productivity – to answer the "how big?" question.

Thus, while economic historians increasingly entertained questions about institutions and politics in explaining the fundamental causes of economic growth and development (a la Douglass North), they continued to insist that, if possible, such

[5] Tables per page rose from 0.05 in the early 1950s, to 0.15 in the early 1960s, to 0.22 in the late 1980s and 0.28 since 1999 (Whaples 1991, p. 293).

[6] The most important of these works is David, Gutman, Sutch, Temin and Wright's *Reckoning with Slavery* (1976) whose authors included four future EHA presidents.

inquiries answer the "how big?" question. To achieve this, American economic historians adapted the cliometric approach to a set of broader questions and increasingly exported their methodology, as the 1980s and 1990s saw the cliometric approach sweep European economic history and begin to make major inroads among economic historians of Latin America, Asia and Africa. Some stalwarts continued to resist or ignore the cliometric approach. These included a few eminent figures such as David Landes; as well as those in fields abutting economic history, including many business historians; and radical historians. However, they were the exception, as was Mancur Olson.

9.2 The Early Historical Work of Mancur Olson

Mancur Olson's early historical work centered on the economics of the British grain trade in the nineteenth century and the first half of the twentieth century. His first article, "Free Trade in 'Corn': A Statistical Study of the Prices and Production of Wheat in Great Britain from 1873 to 1914" (1959), was written with Curtis C. Harris, Jr. and published four years before the completion of his dissertation. It was an atypical paper for Olson, a cliometric investigation (aided by Harris's statistical expertise), which attempted to measure the elasticity of the supply of wheat in Great Britain between 1873 and 1914. Regressing wheat acreage on various measures of lagged prices, it estimated a lower bound for this supply elasticity at 1.6 from 1873 to 1894 and 1.9 from 1895 to 1914 – unexpectedly high figures.[7] It concluded that British farmers quickly substituted from wheat to other products as wheat's price dropped by two-thirds, in an era in which Britain eschewed the protectionism of other European nations and imported a growing fraction of its food.

This was followed by *The Economics of the Wartime Shortage: A History of British Food Supplies in the Napoleonic War and in World Wars I and II* (1963a). In each of these wars the capacity of the British economy to survive and to counter the shortages it suffered surpassed the expectations of those concerned. Olson sought to explain why and to draw lessons from this history. He concluded that "the extent to which an economy can substitute for shortages of raw materials or food, or for that matter anything else, is quite remarkable," (1963a, p. 14) and

[7] More recent estimates put the short-run elasticity at 0.63 and the long-run elasticity at 1.11 (Floud and McCloskey 1994, Vol. 2, p. 151). There appears to be a conceptual flaw in Olson and Harris's estimation, which assumes that the supply curve (price vs. quantity) is captured by the price vs. acreage relationship. This implicitly assumes that the relationship between output and acreage was constant in this period, but the discussion in the article notes a couple of land-saving innovations – new methods of seeding and chemical fertilizers – which increased output per acre. Technological gains would make the supply curve shift out and down (i.e., lower costs per unit), while the price-acreage curve would shift in (less acreage is needed to produce the desired quantity). This may explain why Olson and Harris's "upper bound" is higher than later estimates. In addition, the work has been criticized for using nominal, rather than real, prices in its analysis (Williamson 1965, p. 429).

demonstrated how the British managed to avoid food shortages, despite the policies of their enemies designed to cut off their traditional foods imports.[8] These solutions included diverting food (and cargo space) that would have gone to livestock, switching to crops that yielded more calories per acre, reducing nonfood uses of crops, and, of course, expanding acreage devoted to producing food. These results were achieved by a combination of market forces and government fiat.

Perhaps most surprisingly, Olson concluded that Britain's strategy of free trade in the era before World War I served it better in wartime than did its enemy's policy of strategically protecting agriculture. Before the war Britain produced only about one-third of its calories, while Germany produced about four-fifths of its caloric requirements, yet during the war Britain enjoyed an adequate and healthful diet, while Germany lost about three-quarters of a million civilians because of its severe food shortages. "The British had only to plow their grassland to tap a reserve of fertility that had accumulated over many years, while German agriculture had been fully extended, in some sense even overextended, before the war, and could not increase output in the face of wartime shortages and adversities" (1963a, p. 114). Olson thus turned the traditional protectionism-for-national-security argument on its head.

This book set the tone for Olson's later historical work, tackling a big question with important policy implications. It is written in the classic pre-cliometric style, a wonderfully readable book that mixes the history of economic and popular thought, with a careful recounting of policies and events on a year-by-year basis, non-technical economic theory, and a liberal sprinkling of available official statistics.

The last of Olson's early studies on Britain and the grain market is "The United Kingdom and the World Market in Wheat and Other Primary Products, 1885-1914." Although published in 1974, it was written primarily in the mid-1960s, and argued against Ragnar Nurske's then-influential thesis, which attributed the development in the late 1800s of recently settled regions (such as Argentina, Australia, Canada, New Zealand, South Africa, the US, and Uruguay) to the extensive British demand for primary products. The crux of Olson's argument was that Britain's share of rising demand was minuscule. Simple statistics show that the increase in British wheat imports during this period was only about six percent of the total increase in wheat production in exporting countries. In many ways, this article parallels Fogel's debunking the indispensability of the American railroad system, downplaying the possibility of a razor's edge advancement of the world economy and big spillovers from British wheat purchases. As in *Wartime Shortage*, Olson argued persuasively that removing one factor, be it food imports or food exports, cannot block the growth and health of a robust economy.

This trio of historical studies by Olson was greeted with a collective shrug of indifference by the profession. Reviews of *Wartime Shortage* were appreciative, but not necessarily encouraging. David Wightman, reviewing for the *Economic*

[8] A related argument ran through an article Olson published a year earlier. "The Economics of Strategic Bombing in World War II" (1962a) argued that substitution throughout the economy rendered strategic bombing relatively ineffective.

History Review, concluded that "Olson's neatly argued thesis falsifies the notion that a nation will strengthen itself in a future war by reducing its dependence on foreign supplies" (Wightman 1964, p. 169), but Parzival Copes, a food economist, writing in the *Canadian Journal of Economics and Political Science* (1966), disagreed, noting that "the author applies his argument convincingly to the British case, though one is left wondering how general the conclusions are that one may draw."

The *Journal of Economic History*'s review and a second review in the *Economic History Review* were by two freshly-minted cliometricians, Jeffrey Williamson and Paul David, who would go on to become leading economic historians. Williamson's review (1965, p. 428) expressed disappointment that Olson's book was not a well-rounded cliometric monograph: "the core theory ... proves to be too naïve. The book depends in large measure on dated secondary sources for quantitative information when in many cases more ample and authoritative underlying data are available. Nowhere does the author present summary data on prices, aggregate trade figures, commodity trade breakdowns, imports by national sources, and so on. ... Not only does Olson fail to make full use of available data, but he very often makes poor use of the quantitative information which he does present." Despite closing by stating "it is encouraging to note yet another example of the conscious effort to bring economic theory to bear upon historical problems," the message was clear.

David praised *Wartime Shortages* as "an interesting little book," but complained that "Olson's reliance upon the movements of the absolute level of grain prices to indicate the magnitude of the scarcity ... is needlessly crude," and admonished that "a search for budget information on alterations in household consumption patterns during the war period might have proved fruitful," before concluding that "the economic historian will put it down with the feeling that a comparative historical study of wartime agriculture in Britain might have been made to yield a richer set of observations about the course of economic change than that which the author has extracted" (David 1965, pp. 168-69).

Williamson and David wanted Olson to become a cliometrician – extracting new data from the archives and using cutting-edge economic models and econometric techniques to test theories – and a more well-rounded historian. Olson wanted to test theories, but – partly because he was "totally bereft of econometrics"[9] – never in the systematic way of the new economic historians. Moreover he showed no willingness to muck about in archives, preferring to use official statistics and read secondary sources, even literary sources such as Rudyard Kipling and Arthur Conan Doyle, who are cited in *Wartime Shortage*.

Overall, the demand for Olson's early historical work was fairly meager and this largely explains his inability to keep his post as Princeton's economic historian. The *Social Science Citation Index* (which commenced in 1974) records twenty-three citations to *Wartime Shortage*, three citations to "Free Trade in

[9] This anonymous quote came in response to a query I posted on EH.NET.

'Corn'," and two to "The UK and the World Market in Wheat."[10] In comparison, Olson's path-breaking *The Logic of Collective Action* (1965) has been cited an astounding 4,845 times. It was obvious to Olson and to others that his comparative advantage was not in writing narrow, detailed studies in economic history.

The last of Olson's early historical works, however, was the exception that became the new rule. "Rapid Growth as a Destabilizing Force" (1963b), an invited paper presented at the Economic History Association's annual meetings, argued that, paradoxically, a good thing can be a bad thing. Olson argued convincingly that the presumption that economic growth brings political stability was unproved. But, instead of trying to carefully weigh the evidence for and against the proposition, Olson "put together" – or perhaps "piled up" (Goodrich 1963, p. 555) – a "bold and sustained argument in the opposite direction" (p. 530) of the prevailing wisdom.

Olson asserted "economic growth means vast changes in the income distribution. The fact that some gain a lot and others lose a lot, in a rapidly growing economy, means that the bonds of class and caste are weakened" (p. 532). Probably the most insightful part of the argument is that both gainers and losers will be ill-adjusted to the existing order. *Nouveaux riches* will be put into socially ambiguous situations that may leave them alienated from society, while *nouveaux pauvres* will be much more resentful of their poverty than those who have known nothing else. In addition, a "revolution of rising expectations," is apt to involve rising expectations about what the government should do, and "can awaken people to the possibilities of further improvement and thereby generate additional discontent" (p. 542).

The paper never attempts to define or quantify rapid economic growth. In lieu of historical data, the argument is sustained with wide-ranging historical examples drawn from secondary sources. Key supporting statements, such as "It is clear, first, that the Reformation followed a period of economic growth" (p. 545) and "It has been argued ... that the French Revolution also followed upon a period of economic growth" (p. 546) are not backed by quantitative estimates. One can imagine what Edwin Gay would have thought of this non-quantitative "morass." The paper is either a cliometrician's dream – a new, sweeping theory on a subject of overwhelming historical importance and contemporary concern, just waiting to

[10] One of the two citations to "The UK and the World Market in Wheat" is in Jeffrey Williamson's (1980) "Greasing the Wheels of Sputtering Export Engines." Williamson briefly mentions Olson's article and then uses a computable general equilibrium model to tackle the issue of how export trade affected the American Midwestern grain market. Olson's article warns that approaching the issue with such a general equilibrium approach "strains the capability of current theoretical and mathematical tools" (Olson 1974, p. 335). Ironically, Olson's comment was published in the same year as Williamson's *Late Nineteenth Century American Development: A General Equilibrium History*, from which "Greasing the Wheels" was developed. Williamson's computable general equilibrium modeling was regarded highly enough to secure his move from the University of Wisconsin to Harvard in 1983.

be empirically tested – or a nightmare – a bold, potentially incorrect restatement of history, replete with alluring anecdotes, impossible to adequately test and refute.[11]

In his comments on "Rapid Growth," Carter Goodrich, diplomat and former president of the EHA, noted that Olson's paper did not conform to the discipline's "strong current tendency ... to do economic history as much as possible – or indeed almost entirely – in quantitative and mathematical terms" (1963, p. 554). Goodrich, known for careful scholarship that combined simple quantification and detailed institutional analysis, genially discussed the calculated "overstatements" in this "challenging paper" (p. 555, 558).

Economic historians did not pay much attention to Olson's argument in this article. It has not been cited in either the *Journal of Economic History* or the *Economic History Review* since its publication. Elsewhere, however, it has been immensely influential, becoming the fourth most frequently cited article ever published in the *Journal of Economic History* (Whaples 2002), appealing to a broad range of political scientists.[12] Olson's influential *Rise and Decline of Nations* would follow the pattern set in "Rapid Growth." Instead of concentrating on statistics and the mundane concerns of so many other economic historians, Olson's comparative advantage was in applying his own sweeping theories and observations about human interaction to the widest possible range of historical circumstances.

9.3 The Rise and Decline of Nations and Related Work

After turning away from economic history for about a decade, Olson returned to the field from a position of great strength. Because of the success of *The Logic of Collective Action*, he was now an eminently respected scholar. He had become intrigued and "puzzled by the striking differences in postwar rates of economic growth in different countries" (Blaug 1999, p. 851), which led him to develop the theory and observations in *The Rise and Decline of Nations*. Similar to Douglass

[11] As Olson explained, "A final judgment, if one could ever be made, would have to rest on detailed historical studies of a vast variety of cases. These historical studies would have to be so careful and so detailed that they looked, not only at the connection over time between economic and political change, but also at the complex of detailed economic, social and political changes. They would have to identify both the gainers and the losers from rapid economic growth and all of the other factors affecting political stability, and then attempt to come to a judgment about the role of the economic changes. A massive set of historical studies of the kind needed, covering all historical periods and countries in which there has been rapid economic growth or political instability, is obviously out of the question in a brief paper, even if it were within my competence, which it is not" (1963b, p. 544).

[12] A search on JSTOR showed no citations to "Rapid Growth" in either the *Journal of Economic History* or the *Economic History Review*. JSTOR's coverage of these journals stops in 1997. JSTOR shows 27 citations to "Rapid Growth" in the political science journals archived there, but only three citations in economics journals.

North, his goal was to explain the *ultimate* forces at work in the economy. The cliometric, number-crunching growth accounting methodology of researchers such as Edward Denison, Dale Jorgenson, Paul David and Moses Abramovitz served well in discovering *proximate* causes. However, these efforts "do not trace the sources of growth to their fundamental causes; they trace the water in the river to the streams and lakes from which it comes, but they do not explain the rain" (Olson 1982, p. 4).

Rise and Decline was an immensely successful book, selling over 45,000 copies. Table 9.1 charts its influence by comparing its total citations in the *Social Science Citation Index* to those of the most important economic history books published in the same era.

Table 9.1. Citations to influential books in economic history

Author, *Title*	Year Published	Number of Citations
Alfred Chandler, *The Visible Hand: The Managerial Revolution in American Business*	1977	1832
Mancur Olson, *The Rise and Decline of Nations: Economic Growth, Stagflation, and Social Rigidities*	1982	1573
W.W. Rostow, *The Stages of Economic Growth: A Non-Communist Manifesto*	1960	1489
Douglass North, *Institutions, Institutional Change, and Economic Performance*	1990	1456
Milton Friedman and Anna Schwartz, *A Monetary History of the United States, 1867-1960*	1963	1170
Ester Boserup, *The Conditions of Agricultural Growth: The Economics of Agrarian Change under Population Pressure*	1965	1097
Robert Fogel and Stanley Engerman, *Time on the Cross: The Economics of American Negro Slavery*	1974	939
Douglass North, *Structure and Change in Economic History*	1981	746
David Landes, *The Unbound Prometheus: Technological Change and Industrial Development in Western Europe from 1750 to the Present*	1969	729
Simon Kuznets, *Modern Economic Growth: Rate, Structure, and Spread*	1966	663
Douglass North and Robert Paul Thomas, *The Rise of the Western World: A New Economic History*	1973	547
Robert Fogel, *Railroads and American Economic Growth: Essays in Econometric History*	1964	306

Source: *Social Science Citation Index*, as of May 30, 2002. http://isiknowledge.com

After recapitulating the logic of *The Logic of Collective Action*, *Rise and Decline* derived nine implications, which it then applied to historical problems ranging from the post-World War II economic "miracles" of West Germany and Japan, Britain's simultaneous relative economic decline and the rapid growth of the American South in the same period, to class, caste, and racial discrimination in Britain, India, and South Africa, and even the dynamics of the Great Depression and the emergence of "stagflation" in the 1970s.

Its most influential argument was that because "distributional coalitions" can induce democratic governments to grant them favors – favors which create economic inefficiencies – and because these interest groups take time to form, political stability can generate "institutional sclerosis" – putting in place incentives that sap economic growth. Paralleling the reasoning in "Rapid Growth as a Destabilizing Force," Olson argued that a good thing – peace and stability – can yield bad results; while a bad thing – war – seemed to have powerfully good economic effects.[13] Applying this logic to the recent history, Olson contended that the massive institutional shake ups of West Germany and Japan after World War II gave them clean slates and that the clearing away of these impediments to growth – interest groups such as cartels and labor unions – was the key to their unprecedented economic advance. Conversely, stable Britain (and to a lesser extent the United States) had grown slowly because stability had allowed interest groups the time to eutrify, thus choking growth.[14]

Olson gave some credit to alternative theories, especially the catch-up and convergence theory – "a particularly congenial partner to the present theory" (p. 114). However, only his argument had the power to explain why nations could both rise and decline – changing positions within the international hierarchy – without resort to ad hocery.

The book's only quantitative section (written with the statistical assistance of Kwang Choi) tested this theory on the United States. It argued that the length of time that interest groups had to coalesce could be proxied by the "age" of a state – the time elapsed since it entered the union, or *re-entered* in the case of the former Confederate states. A series of bivariate regressions found a consistent positive relationship between state age and measures of *recent* economic growth (from 1965 to shortly before the book's publication). A second set of regressions found that unionization rates, a measure of special interest group strength, were positively associated with state age. Olson concluded that "there is not only statistically significant evidence of the connection between the duration of stable freedom of organization and growth rates predicted by our model, but also ... distinct and statistically significant evidence that the process the model predicts is going on, that is, that the accumulation of special-interest organization is occurring, and that such organizations do, on balance, have the hypothesized negative effect on growth" (1982, p. 107-108).

Despite the previous quote, Olson was not entirely pleased with his own explanation that the South's catch-up to the rest of the country was due to its youthful institutions, because the timing was not very compelling. If the South's distributional coalitions had been wiped away during the Civil War and Reconstruction (as implied by his measure of state "age"), why had the South lagged for generations before suddenly catching-up almost a century later? In "The South Will Fall Again," Olson criticized his earlier work as "oversimplified," and for failing to

[13] Olson had essentially inverted his earlier inquiry. First he asked if growth was destabilizing, now he asked if stability was degrowthifying.

[14] An additional argument explained the relative success of Sweden and Norway due to the existence of "encompassing" interest groups there.

explain the timing of events (1983b, p. 19). In the refined argument, Olson essentially redefined the starting point of the South's institutional makeover as the New Deal and World War II, rather than the Civil War, stressing the importance of the Wagner Act in ossifying the North, but sparing the South, as well as other changes including falling transportation costs.

9.4 The Initial Response of Economic Historians to *The Rise and Decline of Nations*

As the ideas of *The Rise and Decline* gestated, Olson was encouraged, helped and criticized by a wide range of economic historians, whose reactions he sought as he worked to hone his argument. A dozen economic historians are thanked in the book's acknowledgements.[15] Despite all of this feedback, the immediate reaction of economic historians to *The Rise and Decline* was decidedly mixed. This reaction partly reflects differences between Olson's non-cliometric methods and the practice of mainstream economic history, and is also tied to the power of competing historical explanations and Olson's proclivity for exuberantly overselling his theory.

Olson was very impressed with the power of his theory and the range of its implications. "Of course … it would be preposterous to offer the present argument as a monocausal explanation," he admitted. "It is, nonetheless, remarkable how well the theory fits the patterns of growth across different nations as well as the pattern of growth within countries" (1982, p. 129). Most economic historians showed great appreciation for the insights of Olson's central arguments, but many felt that he pushed their explanatory power too far. Charles Kindleberger "welcomed" the "application of Olson's theory of collective interests applied to growth, decline, stagflation and the like … as a useful addition to the toolkit of the economist, political scientist, and economic historian, but one which complemented rather than replaced the others." To this Olson impishly replied, "To the kid with a hammer, the whole world looks like a nail" (Kindleberger 1983, p. 10).

This was the crux of the matter. Olson's method was that of a theorist developing new tools and then testing them out on *everything*. Kindleberger and other economic historians preferred the goal of explaining history to using it as a testing ground. Olson's goal seemed to them to be to develop a simple ingenious theory to explain all of history, but history wasn't simple and defied easy explanation. Economic historians had a track record of taking big, simple explanations of growth (the centrality of railroads and the role of British free trade, for example) and finding the factors they invoked to have smaller, more marginal effects than

[15] They are Moses Abramovitz, Alec Cairncross, Stephen DeCanio, Jan de Vries, Dudley Dillard, Stanley Engerman, Raymond Goldsmith, John Hicks, R.C.O. Matthews, Cynthia Taft Morris, Douglass North, and Frederic Pryor. Abramovitz, Hicks and Pryor participated in the 1978 conference held at the University of Maryland to assess Olson's ideas, which resulted in Mueller (1983).

had been claimed, and which depended on the institutional and historical setting. The economic history discipline made its advances more slowly and carefully, steadily fitting together pieces of the historical record. As Claudia Goldin put it at the time of Fogel and North's Nobel Prize, the award was a triumph for a discipline peopled by "clever little rodents" who discover ingenious methods for unearthing historic truths (Chandler 1993, p. C1). The rodents of the economic history profession carefully built their dams twig by twig, and quivered when Olson came along swinging a sledge hammer (or was it an axe?) attempting to fell one mighty tree across the entire river. One theory alone could *never* work. Douglass North patiently reminded Olson of the need to add theories of the state and ideology to his incomplete theory of self-interested individuals (North 1983).

Olson was pleased that his hammer had "implications for such an incredibly wide array of phenomena in different countries and historical periods that a thorough and meticulous testing (would be) out of the question" (p. 146) in a short book. Many, however, complained that Olson wasn't using his hammer properly, admonishing that his characteristic method was to look for confirmatory cases rather than to try to test the theory in Popperian style (Barry 1983, p. 19). They demanded that the theory be operationalized, so that it could be rigorously, statistically tested *against* competing theories. As Moses Abramovitz explained, "The influence of common-interest groups in governing growth rates of productivity needs to be tested jointly with many factors. ... For that purpose, direct measures of size, strength, and character of common-interest groups need to be derived." Abramovitz argued that the measure of interest-group strength proposed by Olson – the number of years of peaceful political development – made it difficult to separate the effects of differences in growth potential from the impacts of common-interest groups, and suggested many "reasons why the duration of uninterrupted periods of peaceful development is likely to prove a confusing proxy" (Abramovitz 1983, p. 88).[16] R.C.O. Matthews concurred that the statistical tests of the theory were inadequate and feared that they *never* could be, warning that it "is difficult to see how one or a few statistical measures could capture adequately both the strength of common interest groups and their noxiousness" (Matthews 1983, p. 920).

The hammer was just right for some jobs, but too clumsy for others. John Wallis (soon to become one of Olson's colleagues) praised him for using his theory "with considerable ingenuity and dexterity," but concluded that "it is possible, in almost every case, to think of a more plausible explanation of the behavior in question than Olson's coalition theory. ... On the other hand, the diversity of applications is overwhelming, and in several instances his theory appears to be the best available explanation" (Wallis 1983, pp. 566-67). Olson had used his hammer to knock down some nails that had defied the efforts of other tools, but he didn't seem to notice that many of the nails he hit didn't do the job very well – that the

[16] The state-age variable was particularly troublesome to many. For example, at my first EHA meeting as a graduate student in 1985, a wave of incredulity swept the crowd when a paper by Clark Nardinelli on "The Determinants of American Child Labor Laws" used the state-age variable to test Olson's hypothesis.

hold was "flimsy" (Maddison 1988, p. 25), and that other tools could be used to drive them in farther and more securely.

John Othick found Olson's argument "lucid and compelling," but warned that the "historical case studies which follow are less convincing" (Othick 1983, p. 325). Taking this cue, reviewer Jan de Vries (1983), an economic historian with a degree in history, rejected Olson's simple, almost anecdotal, claim that the Dutch Revolt against Spain's Philip II swept away distributional coalitions, arguing on the contrary that it was an effort to protect them from Philip's attempts at destruction. Likewise, Kindleberger picked apart Olson's explanation of the Great Depression. These critiques were tossed into a growing pile of bent nails.

Many (perhaps most) economic historians found Olson's explanation of postwar growth patterns to be "quite plausible," (Maddison 1988, p. 26) but they wanted more. Although the explanation elicited nods of conditional acceptance, it was handicapped by "vague measurement" and the statistical analysis contained in *Rise and Decline* was seen by some as "irrelevant" (Maddison, p. 29).[17] The early line was that, as always, economic historians wanted to know "how big?" but Olson's book, despite its many charms, provided no magnitudes or marginal impacts.

9.5 Longer-term Reactions by Economic Historians to Olson's Historical Work

The Rise and Decline of Nations continues to enjoy considerable influence among some economic historians. Joel Mokyr lauds it as a "classic" and identifies Olson and North as the "two giants of reintroducing the idea of institutions into the story of modern economic growth" (1999, pp. 1241, 1244). However, others are less enthusiastic and many economic historians have simply ignored it.

One way to gain an overall picture of this oft-cited book's status within the field is to examine publications in the field, especially textbooks, to see what they make of its arguments.

Mancur Olson's arguments in *The Rise and Decline of Nations* have, twenty years later, made scarcely a dent in American economic history texts and surveys. Among nine recent textbooks in American economic history, *Rise and Decline* is mentioned only twice. Ratner, Soltow and Sylla include it on a list of suggested readings "for important insights on postwar economic changes and rigidities" (1993, p. 512) and French (1997) briefly mentions it along with "The South Will Fall," giving a mild endorsement of the argument.[18] Other surveys mirror this find-

[17] Maddison complained, "He does not tell us how to measure the strength of distributive coalitions, how to measure the degree to which they are encompassing, or how to measure allocative efficiency. He does not tell us how to rebut alternative explanations of the growth phenomena he discusses" (p. 29).

[18] Cain and Hughes (1998) discuss Olson's ideas for a couple of paragraphs in a section on "Collective Goods and Resistance to Technological Change," but reference only *The Logic of Collective Action*.

ing. There is not a single citation to Olson in Engerman and Gallman (editors), *Long-Term Factors in American Economic Growth* (1986), nor in Bordo, Goldin, and White (editors), *The Defining Moment: The Great Depression and the American Economy in the Twentieth Century* (1998). In Engerman and Gallman's massive 2700-page, three-volume collection, the *Cambridge Economic History of the United States* (1996, 2000), *Rise and Decline* is mentioned briefly twice.[19] Thus mainstream, economic historians have paid scant attention to *The Rise and Decline* when analyzing the economic history of the United States.

Checking twenty-eight recent monographs in U.S. economic history yielded only eight that even referred to *Rise and Decline* – all but one fairly briefly.[20] The exception is Wright's *Old South, New South*, which lists Olson's "clean slate" dynamism story as among the most prominent explanations of the South's post-World War II "takeoff" – describing the thesis as "forcefully presented" (Wright 1986, pp. 239, 300). However, although Wright credits Olson's account as having "an important component of truth," he concludes that it misses "the historical context and the background developments...Thus the metaphor of the 'clean slate' has basic appropriateness for the postwar South. But the South did not start over with a clean slate all at once as of any precise date. History seldom works that way, and it certainly didn't in this case" (p. 241). Wright's complaint against Olson's overarching theory is effectively the same charge that was leveled against North's *Structure and Change in Economic History* – taking the history out of history.

However, *Rise and Decline* has cut a much higher profile among those studying the rest of the world. Of thirty-six non-US books surveyed, fifteen cite *Rise and Decline*. Olson's views are often left out of the picture when the story is *very* long-term economic growth; however *Rise and Decline* is very likely to be discussed, with great interest, in histories of more recent twentieth-century economic history, *especially* those focused on Britain and Europe.[21]

A telling example is Floud and McCloskey's three-volume *Economic History of Britain since 1700* (1994). Four of its chapters – three of them from the final volume on the economy between 1939 and 1992 – discuss *Rise and Decline*. No

[19] Lindert argues that the protectionism of the 1920s owed much to a "mixture of new shocks and the slow buildup of old redistributive coalitions," as the "long period of institutional stability from the Civil War to 1929 helped the coalition harden" (p. 458). Olmstead and Rhode reject the hypothesis: "recent attempts to explain the pattern and level of agricultural subsidies, employing Olson's theory of collective action ... to date have borne little fruit" (p. 738).

[20] I selected these works and the others mentioned below from among recent works reviewed on EH.NET and by browsing the Wake Forest University library shelves. This includes a book on the exact topic – Bernstein and Adler (editors), *Understanding American Economic Decline* (1994) – a radical work which never mentions *Rise and Decline*.

[21] Among the authors of recent books on long-run economic growth who omit any reference to *Rise and Decline* are Alfred Chandler, Rondo Cameron, Richard Easterlin, Deepak Lal, David Landes, Angus Maddison, Julian Simon, and Jeffrey Williamson.

consensus seems to have been reached, however, on the applicability of the argument to Britain versus the rest of Western Europe. While many authors conclude with Olson that "British society became highly sclerotic, with growth slowed down by entrenched interest groups" (Floud and McCloskey 1994, Vol. 3, p. 213), others reject it completely. They follow Moses Abramovitz's rejection of the theory because "the territorial, political and financial convulsions following World War I were on a scale commensurate with those after World War II, but they did not set off a comparable European growth boom" (Abramovitz 1989, p. 74), a point that Booth (2001, p. 39) echoes.

Ultimately, it is Abramovitz's alternative explanation to postwar growth patterns that may have done the most to divert interest from *The Rise and Decline*'s argument. In 1986 Abramovitz used Angus Maddison's newly constructed data set on historical income levels to test the "widely entertained" hypothesis that productivity growth rates tend to vary inversely with productivity levels.[22] He developed the theory that among nations with the same "social capability" laggards would be able to adopt the technologies and institutions of the leaders and quickly "catch-up" to them. The result would be a convergence toward the leader, provided that conditions of stability sustaining the catch-up were present. The article presented statistical evidence that supported the hypothesis and accorded well with historians' sense of what had occurred. Abramovitz's article has become the most frequently cited article ever published in the *Journal of Economic History* (Whaples 2002).

Among the reasons that economic historians and economists were attracted to Abramovitz's argument were that, unlike Olson's theory, it was very easy to operationalize by simply measuring the per capita income gap between the laggard and the leader. The model answered the "how big?" question in a straight-forward manner by estimating the rate at which a typical laggard would grow as a function of its distance from the leader. As importantly, Abramovitz paid close attention to the historical record, spending much time exploring the historical conditions that promoted catch-up and convergence and those that didn't. Abramovitz tried to tell a complete story, uniting other theories and factors to his new theory, in the classic cliometric style. Finally, as the historical record of the late twentieth century unfolded several countries followed the pattern predicted by the catch-up model – once these countries met the preconditions, they began by growing at phenomenal rates, decelerating as they neared the leader (Barro 1997). The brute historical facts of the long-run trend toward greater political and social stability *and* more economic growth were hard to ignore.

On the other hand, continued statistical tests of Olson's model proved to be less successful (Quiggin 1992). Booth, Melling, and Dartmann concluded "despite initial optimism, empirical verification of Olson's hypothesis has proved elusive ...Even when separate calculations are made of convergence ... Olson's institutional structures appear to explain little in the variation in national growth rates

[22] Baumol (1986) simultaneously developed a very similar argument and test.

(1997, pp. 417-18).[23] Olson appeared to reach the same conclusion in a later paper. "Big Bills Left on the Sidewalk," (1996) gives considerable credit to the catch-up thesis, spelling out its logic in detail, seemingly elevating it above the importance of the historical arguments in *Rise and Decline* and noting the benefits of democratic stability without worrying much about its negative side effects.

Thus, the longer-term reaction to *Rise and Decline* is that Olson's theory is insightful and important, but not as important as it was originally made it out to be. It is acknowledged that Olson had probably purposefully overstated his case to get it on the map, a practice that has an honorable academic tradition, but which could be pushed too far.

This can be seen in responses to a query about Olson that I posted on EH.NET. Ironically, the economic historians who responded were more likely to have been influenced and convinced by *The Logic of Collective Action* than Olson's explicitly historical work, although most had read and wrestled with *The Rise and Decline*. Several of the respondents reported that the insights in Olson's historical writings were excellent for generating classroom discussion and that these ideas have spurred their own thinking about economic history, especially in developing countries.

Some economic historians warmly embrace Olson – "we need big thinkers to generate interesting hypotheses even if they are proven too simple" and ignore the finer contours of history. However, a former president of the EHA turned this dictum on its head, bemoaning Olson's abandonment of the solid empirical work of his earlier career – the argument of *The Rise and Decline* "always seemed dubious ... He certainly didn't provide evidence ... He wasn't a good economic historian ... he was too interested in being an economic scientist to ... meet the standards of proof of historians and economic historians." Others, including another former president of the EHA split the difference – Olson's arguments were "not wholly convincing but there is an element of truth" and he "should have been awarded the Nobel Prize."

In many ways the reaction of economic historians to Olson's later historical work – interest in the big ideas but caution about the details and worries about magnitudes and testability – parallels their reaction to Douglass North's later work, but with some important differences. North's later work (as well as his earlier work) became part of the main corpus of economic history. One of his later, institutional books was named to EH.NET's list of the dozen "most significant works in twentieth-century economic history," and another made a follow-up list of twelve "important and influential works."[24] In contrast, Olson's *Rise and De-*

---

[23] In addition, they argued that Olson's simple story about the development of collective interest groups in postwar Britain, Germany and Sweden was oversimplified, painting a historical picture in which these developments were dependent on the specific economic and political environment of the postwar period.

[24] See EH.NET's Project 2000 and Project 2001 at http://www.eh.net/project2000/. The selections by North are *Institutional Change and American Economic Growth* (with Lance Davis 1971) and *The Rise of the Western World.* Fogel's *Railroads and American Economic Growth* and *Time on the Cross* also made the lists.

cline was not nominated for either of these distinctions, despite the fact that (as Table 9.1 shows) its overall citation counts match up very well in comparison to North's books.

One difference between North and Olson that cannot be overlooked is that North was an "insider" – editor of the profession's journal, president of the discipline's professional association, author of a leading textbook, and teacher of a cadre of students who became noted economic historians – while Olson never was. Although Olson studied under economic historian Alexander Gerschenkron at Harvard, published in both the *Journal of Economic History* and *Explorations in Economic History*, and exchanged ideas with many economic historians, most economic historians would not classify him as a full-fledged economic historian. He only occasionally attended the meetings of the EHA, appearing on its program just twice. He never served as an officer of the association or on its journal's editorial board. North, however, was a fixture in the field, did his share of theory-driven historical number-crunching exercises, including the well-regarded "Sources of Productivity Change in Ocean Shipping, 1600-1850," (1968), and as editor of the *Journal of Economic History* was credited with successfully battling the old guard and opening the floodgates to the onrush of cliometric studies. Thus when North became somewhat critical of mainstream cliometrics and began working to lead his colleagues over the next vista to institutional economic history, the profession gave him a wide berth and kept a watchful eye. Perhaps only a reborn insider could be widely accepted despite the often-problematic fit of his speculative, nonquantitative line of research with the numerical core of the field. A dabbler, an outsider, such as Olson – even one whose work was widely-read and similar to North's – could never be given as much leeway or have as much influence as a leader of the club.

Part III

Market Augmenting Government

10 Social Polarization, Political Institutions, and Country Creditworthiness*

Philip Keefer and Stephen Knack

A key issue in political economy and development is, under what conditions can governments commit themselves credibly to policy promises and respond flexibly to crisis? The answer to this question should depend on both institutional and societal characteristics, but the literature generally treats these factors separately. One literature has found that social polarization (in the form of income inequality, ethnic tensions or other differences) undermines both the credibility of government promises and the ability to respond to crisis. This research, however, abstracts from the role of political institutions and treats all forms of social polarization identically. Another literature finds that institutions, particularly the number of veto players in a country (or checks and balances), are key to credibility, but pays less attention to social characteristics such as polarization. In this paper we revisit these linkages.

We examine the creditworthiness of countries, a variable that is uniquely sensitive to both the credibility and the ability of governments to respond promptly to shocks, to illuminate three issues left open in the existing literature. First, it is difficult to draw conclusions from the literature on the net effect of characteristics of countries that affect both credibility and flexibility, but in opposite directions. This is particularly important for institutions such as checks and balances, which have been found to increase the first at the expense of the second. In a first approximation to this issue we find that checks and balances have a weak positive effect on creditworthiness – that is, the positive credibility effects outweigh the negative rigidity effects of multiple veto players.

Second, although many results on polarization depend on assumptions about institutions, and vice versa, there has been no systematic investigation of how the effects of one depend on the other. This chapter examines the effects of social polarization under different political conditions, including elections and checks and balances. We find that the effects of polarization depend strongly on the competitiveness of elections and the number of veto players.

Finally, Mancur Olson's work firmly establishes that the influence of special interests depends in part on their ability to overcome problems of collective action. The literature on polarization implicitly assumes that different forms of po-

* The authors are grateful to Christopher Clague and Dennis Coates for helpful comments and suggestions. The conclusions of this paper are not intended to represent the views of the World Bank, its Executive Directors, or the countries they represent.

larization (e.g., income, ethnic, or linguistic) have identical effects on society. We speculate, however, that the effects of ethnic and linguistic social groupings are likely to differ from those of income-based groupings. Olson (1982, ch. 6), for example, observed that successful distributional coalitions are often based on encouragement of ethnic prejudice and endogamy. In fact, we find that political institutions interact with these two dimensions of social polarization in opposite ways. Namely, an increase in income or wealth inequality makes it more likely that countries will default on their debt obligations, but this effect is *strongest* when democratic institutions such as checks and balances or competitive elections are most prevalent. However, although an increase in ethnic or linguistic polarization also increases the probability of default, this effect is *weakest* when democratic institutions are most prevalent.

10.1 The Literature on Polarization, Institutions, Credibility and Delay

Creditworthiness is a function both of the credibility of governments – the likelihood that they will honor their lending agreements – and of their flexibility – the likelihood that, in response to negative fiscal shocks, they will adapt fiscal policy to new exigencies and continue servicing their debt. Thus, creditworthiness captures two qualities of government that have been the focus of substantial research. One literature looks at the security of property and contractual rights, including the risk that government will expropriate illiquid assets. Svensson (1998) argues that a conflict of interest between two polarized parties that alternate in office will lead them to under-invest in a secure legal environment. Easterly and Levine (1997) conclude that ethnic polarization undermines economic growth, in part through adoption of less efficient economic policies which presumably contribute to reduced creditworthiness.

Keefer and Knack (2002) appeal to social choice reasoning to argue that increased polarization among decision makers can produce larger swings among different policies. Polarization has the effect of expanding the set of alternative policies that decision makers can propose to replace the current policy (e.g., the current policy to repay a loan that the government has received). Their argument shows immediately the effects of institutional assumptions. If multiple polarized groups vote, using majority rule, increased polarization increases policy instability and makes current government promises less credible. If multiple polarized groups each have veto power, then no change in policy can occur unless all agree, and increased polarization has no effect on policy instability.

North and Weingast (1989) specifically examine the effect of multiple veto players on the credibility of loan agreements. They show that the risk that the English Crown would not repay loans extended by Dutch lenders was significantly dampened by the presence of multiple veto players – the checks and balances introduced by a newly powerful parliament following the Glorious Revolution. They do not ask what happens when polarization of preferences increases. Keefer and

Stasavage (2000) do consider the interaction of polarization and the number of veto players, but in a specific application, the credibility of monetary policy.

Another literature has analyzed why governments sometimes respond with significant delay to crisis. Alesina and Drazen (1991) assume that polarized decision makers also exercise veto power over government decision making. They find that polarized interests who are each unsure about the costs delay imposes on the others have an incentive to delay reform even when doing so leaves everyone worse off. Rodrik (1999) argues that countries recover faster from inflation shocks if they have "consensus-building" institutions. However, rather than model such institutions politically – the extent of elections, checks and balances, etc. – he uses the security of property rights and similar variables to proxy for consensus-building institutions.

Creditworthiness is also affected by the sheer volume of country borrowing. Holding constant moral hazard problems and the likely response of countries to fiscal crisis, countries that have a higher demand for loans, and therefore more debt, are likely to be less creditworthy. Alesina and Gatti (1995) and Berg and Sachs (1988) both link polarization to the magnitude of government spending and, by implication, to indebtedness. Alesina and Gatti (1995) assume, like Svensson (1998), that there are no checks and balances, but rather two political parties that alternate in power. They show that if these parties have polarized preferences over government spending, they are likely to raise spending (or incur debts) in order to reduce the fiscal discretion of their successors.[1] Berg and Sachs (1988), on the other hand, argue that in more unequal societies, in which the rich control both economic and political life, pressures for redistribution are likely to lead to higher borrowing and therefore higher interest rates.[2]

These different contributions imply that polarization should have little or no effect on government response to crisis if polarized groups are not also veto players (Svensson 1998, Keefer and Knack 2002, Alesina and Drazen 1991) – in fact, Alesina and Drazen specifically point to cases where the unified control of government by a single partisan interest led to a quick resolution of crisis. Assuming polarization, the literature suggests that multiple veto players will increase credibility (North and Weingast 1989, Keefer and Stasavage 2000), but provides argu-

[1] McGuire and Olson (1996) show formally that the mere presence of instability, independent of preference differences over government spending, encourages governments to take actions in the present with high future costs.

[2] In their argument, it is not clear why the rich, politically powerful by assumption, would accede to more redistribution in the first place, and why redistributive pressures, *per se*, would lead to larger debt. However, in a recent paper, Acemoglu and Robinson (2001) argue that the threat of insurrection leads the rich elite to democratize (expand the franchise), leading to more political pressures to redistribute. In more unequal countries, larger amounts of redistribution are triggered by democratization, giving elites a larger incentive to stage counter-coups. Evidence in support of the theory is mixed: they point effectively to a number of country case studies, but cross-country evidence reveals little association between either redistribution and inequality or between inequality and political violence.

ments both in favor and against the proposition that they will reduce flexibility. While multiple veto players are a necessary condition for a delayed response to crisis in Alesina and Drazen (1991), multiple veto players may be precisely the sort of "consensus-building" institution that yields the faster response to crisis in polarized countries that Rodrik (1999) predicts. In any case, the literature provides no prediction as to which effect -- credibility or delay -- will dominate. Finally, all of these studies treat polarized groups as being identical in their internal characteristics. The next section asks how predictions about the effects of social polarization should be modified if the internal characteristics of the polarized groups are heterogeneous.

10.2 The Effects of Polarization when Polarized Groups are Heterogeneous

A substantial literature points to the importance throughout history and across many cultures of intra-ethnic social and economic exchange, ranging from marriage to trade. Intra-ethnic exchange may be driven by cultural mores and the prejudices of or about other ethnic groups, but it is also catalyzed by the greater possibilities of credible contracting within an ethnic group (Landa 1981, Greif 1989). Not all ethnic groups in all places and times exhibit dense patterns of social and economic exchange. The point is only that they are more frequent features of ethnic or linguistic groups than of income groups (although social exchange is often restricted across classes).

A dense pattern of exchange is likely to support the credibility of intra-group promises. For example, as Greif (1989) demonstrates, the threat of future exclusion from these exchanges is a powerful device for the deterrence of reneging. Ethnic groups, relative to income-based groups, are therefore more likely to overcome obstacles to collective action since, as Olson (1965) first pointed out, groups that cannot enforce contribution commitments by all members to the cause of the group are unlikely to be effective special interests. To the extent that intra-ethnic group ties are stronger than intra-income group ties, we would therefore expect ethnolinguistic groups to be more successful "special interests". Therefore, we would expect an increase in ethnolinguistic polarization to most reduce creditworthiness in those institutional environments that are most permeable to special interests rather than the interests of the "median voter": where elections are non-competitive, and where checks and balances are absent that might otherwise serve to pit competing special interests against each other.

If intra-group promises are significantly more credible than inter-group promises across ethnic groups, but not across income groups, then there are also important implications for the strategies of politicians. In particular, promises made to a particular ethnic group by competing candidates from that ethnic group are more credible than promises made by those candidates to other ethnic groups. The consequences of reneging on those promises include restricted access to the wide range of interactions that characterize membership in the ethnic group. Within income groups, in contrast, this threat is less severe and the credibility of promises of politicians from any one income group is likely to be similar across interest groups.

Where candidate promises are credible, and there are no information or other problems, candidates converge on the median voter's preferred outcome. Although the median voter has no particular reason to prefer high levels of spending that fund current consumption at the expense of future consumption, this restraint disappears if candidate promises are only credible to part of the electorate. In that case, Keefer (2002) argues that candidates will tilt their promises in favor of the group to which credible promises can be made, at the expense of the remainder of society. Since all of society bears the costs of low creditworthiness, but the ethnic group gets all of the benefits of increased spending, the median ethnic group "voter" will prefer high spending, and creditworthiness drops. This effect should be greatest, however, when:

- only one ethnic group is represented in government – when there are no checks and balances;
- voters from other ethnic groups have the least influence on selecting government officials – reducing the penalty that members of non-favored ethnic groups can impose on leaders from other ethnic groups who drive down country creditworthiness.

Perhaps most importantly, when institutions themselves provide a basis for credible promises by politicians across all ethnic groups, the incentive for differential treatment of ethnic groups dissipates. This is most likely to happen when institutions such as multiple checks and balances are in place, which increase the credibility of all government decisions, reducing the commitment advantage that some government decision makers or candidates have because of personal ties to some voters or groups of voters.

When politicians emerge from different income groups, a different dynamic is at work. In this case, the ability of politicians to make credible promises to specific constituencies, such as the poor or the rich, depends much more on the institutional environment. When it does not support credible promises, politicians gain nothing by pitting the rich against the poor, since the poor do not believe the politicians will help them, once in office. However, as elections grow more competitive and checks and balances provide greater assurances about the credibility of government decisions, the incentives to seek out and develop such constituencies grows. It is in these circumstances, then, that we expect income and wealth-based polarization to matter most.[3]

There is substantial, though non-systematic evidence that parties organized around "class" or income are not common in developing countries. Haggard and Kaufman (1992), in an examination of many episodes of high inflation in a number of countries, found very little evidence that parties and political conflict were

[3] Similarly, income polarization slows growth most in democracies in the model of Persson and Tabellini (1994), but for a different reason: in democracies (but not in non-democracies) policymakers act to satisfy the median-income voter.

organized by income groups. Inflation in most cases was driven by governments that spent excessively on infrastructure and development; independent groups representing the interests of the poor, whether political parties or not, were weak prior to the shifts in spending strategy. Only in a few of the countries that they studied, Argentina, Chile and Brazil, were there well-organized "worker" parties.

10.3 Summarizing the Testable Predictions

Taken altogether, the foregoing arguments yield a dense but clear-cut set of predictions.

- Given multiple veto players, social polarization should reduce the ability of countries to respond to shocks (Alesina and Drazen 1991), and therefore reduce creditworthiness.
- Provided there is some polarization of veto players, checks and balances should increase the credibility of agreements to repay loans and therefore increase creditworthiness (North and Weingast 1989).
- The effects of income-based polarization should be *greater* and the effects of ethno-linguistic polarization *smaller* when political promises are more credible – when there are more checks and balances, and more competitive elections.

Some of these hypotheses have already received empirical attention. With respect to veto player type arguments, most evidence has focused on political "fragmentation", defined in various ways. Haggard and Kaufman (1992) and Veiga (2000) present evidence that countries with more fragmented political systems are less likely to embrace stabilization programs after plunging into a period of high inflation. Haggard and Kaufman, in their case studies, find however that fragmentation affects country responses to hyperinflation, but not to other high but non-hyperinflationary episodes. These experimental settings allow the authors to evaluate the combined effect of polarization and checks and balances on responsiveness to crises, but do not allow them to disentangle the two effects nor to examine their influence on government credibility.

Haggard and Kaufmann do not directly take the number of veto players in a government into account in their analysis, although they do consider polarization, elections and the policy orientation of the ruling government. Their "polarization" variable comes closest to the hypotheses above, but does not take into account the number of veto players. On a three point scale, a one is assigned to countries with exclusive one party systems; a two to systems with inclusive or corporatist one-party systems or two-party systems with broad catch-all parties; and a three to polarized or fragmented party systems. They do not consider whether or not these parties control veto gates.

Alesina and Drazen or Rodrik type arguments are more plausible when applied to broad social polarization than to the polarization of elites. Alesina and Drazen rely on assumptions about information asymmetry that are easier to justify in reference to broad groups; similarly, Rodrik relies on assumptions about the enforceability of inter-group agreements that are less plausible when the agreements are between different segments of the elite. Their arguments are best tested with information both about political or partisan polarization (the polarization of political parties), and about social polarization. Haggard and Kaufman seem to rate as "most" polarized those countries in which both parties and society at large are polarized, where social polarization seems to be captured by the existence of organized groups in society that seem to be in conflict with each other. In this sense, their definition of polarization is partially driven by the contentiousness of the policy debate, so that causality is clouded. In the empirical work below, we use only a priori definitions of polarization (ethno-linguistic or income cleavages), as well as taking explicit account of the number of institutional veto players.

Veiga pays more attention to the number of veto players and their partisan affiliations, encapsulated in his "fragmentation" variable, also trichotomous, like Haggard and Kaufman's "polarization" measure. Fragmentation is "one" if there are no parties or an exclusive one party system; a two if there is a one-party majority parliamentary government, or a presidential government with one-party control of the legislature and presidency; and "greater than two" for other systems. While useful, this variable groups quite disparate countries into similar categories. For example, legislatures in presidential systems may act with greater independence, even when the president's party controls them, than parliaments with a one party majority. This is the case if one compares the US with Great Britain, for example. The category "greater than two" embraces a large number of disparate systems, ranging from divided presidential government to highly fractionalized government coalitions in parliamentary systems. Again, we might expect differences among these. The empirical work below uses a more fine-grained measure of veto players, which also takes into account partisan control of the veto gates; we also take social polarization explicitly into account.

Berg and Sachs (1988), Rodrik (1999) and Quinn and Woolley (2001) are all concerned with the effect of social polarization, and the latter two papers with the interactive effects of institutions and social polarization. Berg and Sachs (1988) look at 35 countries for which there was information on sovereign debt discount rates. Unlike later researchers, their focus is not institutional and they do not consider the differential effects of inequality under different institutional arrangements. They find that countries with greater income inequality have a higher likelihood of rescheduling debt, and a higher rate of discount on the debt. We are able to replicate their results, but for a larger sample of countries, since our creditworthiness ratings are more widely available. Apart from considering the institutional dimension, we also use a larger set of polarization variables, representing not only inequality in income but landholding and also ethnic fractionalization.

Rodrik (1999) and Quinn and Woolley (2001) are concerned with broader economic outcomes, growth before and after the oil crisis in the case of Rodrik and the volatility of economic growth in the case of Quinn and Woolley (2001). Their work examines indirectly the hypotheses that structure this chapter. Rodrik (1999) finds that the impact of trade shocks on economic performance is worse in the presence of ethnic fractionalization or income inequality and in the absence of democracy. This supports his contention that social conflict constitutes a barrier to adapting policy to external shocks unless there are institutions that moderate conflict and make agreements between contending groups more credible. This result potentially contradicts the conclusions of Alesina and Drazen, however, since democracies are characterized in part by their multiplicity of veto players, which (given social polarization) should delay rather than accelerate a country's response to growth. Quinn and Woolley (2001) find different results, however. Democracy (captured, as in Rodrik (1999), by Freedom House indices of political freedoms and civil liberties) makes economic growth less volatile. Ethnic fractionalization has neither a direct effect on volatility, nor does it influence the effect of democracy. Their results thus fail to support either model of bargaining, reform and delay. Unlike Rodrik, they permit democracy and ethnic fractionalization to enter independently, as well as in a multiplicative term, making theirs a more reliable test.

Persson and Tabellini (1994) examine the effect of income inequality on growth, conditional on regime type. Building on median voter models of income taxation and redistribution (e.g., Meltzer and Richard 1981), they argue that inequality should slow growth more in countries where median voters are more decisive, i.e. in democracies. Persson and Tabellini present cross-country evidence finding that a significant and negative relationship between inequality and growth exists only in their sub-sample of democracies, and not in the non-democracies. Knack and Keefer (1997a) show, however, that these results are an artifact of measurement error in the inequality data and regime type classifications used by Persson and Tabellini. Using more standard data sources on inequality and regime type, the link between inequality and growth is equally strong in democracies and non-democracies. Creditworthiness is more directly linked than economic growth to the decisions of government. Its use in the work below therefore provides a more direct test of the different hypotheses surrounding the influence of institutions and polarization on government credibility and response to crisis. In addition, we use institutional variables that allow a more fine-grained examination of how institutions mediate social polarization and growth, and we address a broader range of institutional conditions that might influence creditworthiness.

10.4 Data

Our measure of the creditworthiness of nations is based on a survey of leading international banks conducted every six months by Institutional Investor. Bankers are not permitted to rate their home countries. The sample ranges from 75 to 100 banks, with responses weighted to give more importance to the views of banks with greater worldwide exposure and more sophisticated country-analysis systems. It is scored on a 0-100 basis, with 0 representing the greatest chance of defaulting on the sovereign debt, and 100 assigned to countries with the lowest risk of default. The mean value among the 106 countries included in our empirical analyses is 38.8, with a standard deviation of 25.7. Ratings exceed 60 for most of the OECD countries, with Japan, Switzerland, Germany and the US the only nations above 90. The bottom of the distribution is dominated by conflict-ridden African and Latin America nations such as Sudan, Sierra Leone, Liberia, Zaire, Haiti and Nicaragua, all scoring below 10. (Data Appendix Table 10.A1 lists ratings from lowest to highest for all countries included in empirical tests.)

The accuracy of this creditworthiness index is supported by two statistical analyses. A study of 78 Euromarket loans for 34 countries found that the interest rate spread was strongly and inversely correlated with the creditworthiness ratings, controlling for maturity and length of the grace period (Feder and Ross 1982). A GAO study (1994) found that the creditworthiness index was similarly strongly related to the discount on 38 sovereign debt instruments, owed by 21 countries, traded on secondary markets.

In contrast to the limited number of countries for which data are available on interest rate spreads, or on discounts on debt traded in secondary markets, the Institutional Investor index is available for about 130 countries. Use of this subjective index is preferable to objective indicators on other grounds. Interest spreads are only a rough reflection of risk, as low interest rate spreads may be offset by high fees or special tax concessions, which are difficult to measure. Data are available for a large sample of countries on the debt-service ratio (interest plus repayment obligations relative to export revenue), or the stock of external debt relative to GDP. However, the debt-service ratio is a misleading gauge of creditworthiness, and is not a significant predictor of debt rescheduling (Rahnama-Moghadam and Samavati 1991). Using the stock of debt as our dependent variable would require attempting to control for various factors that might affect a country's ability to repay a large debt. The subjective index we use instead implicitly adjusts for these factors already -- and probably far more effectively than we could using statistical controls.

We use the mean value of the creditworthiness measure over the 1986-95 period. Using data over the ten-year period ensures that values are not unduly influenced by business cycle effects or by short-term fluctuations in the prices of petroleum or other key imported or exported commodities. We control for the log of initial (1985) per capita income and for growth in per capita income from 1980-85, just prior to the period of analysis, as higher values of these may improve the ability of governments to finance their debts. Since larger economies tend to be more diverse, and less subject to terms of trade or other shocks that can suddenly worsen a government's fiscal position, we also control for the ratio of a country's aggregate GDP to US GDP. Finally, we control for shifts in the net barter terms of trade, which represent exogenous changes in a country's ability to pay back debt denominated in foreign currencies. The terms of trade shift is constructed as the ratio of the 1986-95 average value, to the 1980-85 average value, of the ratio of the export price index to the corresponding import price index. Improvements in the terms of trade over the period for which our dependent variable is measured, relative to the preceding period, are reflected by values exceeding unity.[4] Since it

---

[4] In most cases, these shifts are unlikely to be unanticipated. To the extent they are anticipated, the relationship of shifts to creditworthiness may weaken as countries expecting improvements (deteriorations) may borrow more (less) in the current period.

is precisely through their policy decisions about fiscal and monetary policy that countries influence their creditworthiness, we do not attempt to control for endogenous variables such as inflation or deficit spending.

We assess the impact of three kinds of polarization and three variables that describe the political environment. With respect to polarization, we use a measure of income inequality, inequality in land ownership, and ethno-linguistic polarization. Although these measures have been used in other contexts in the literature, only Keefer and Knack (2002) justify their usage in view of the theoretical literature on polarization. We briefly review that discussion here, especially to explain our use of the ethnic fractionalization data.

Esteban and Ray (1994, p. 824) point out that commonly used measures of polarization may not, in fact, capture polarization in society – they may do just the opposite. They argue that groups in society are polarized with respect to any set of attributes when they exhibit the following three characteristics: the members of each group are homogeneous with respect to the set of attributes; different groups are heterogeneous with respect to these attributes; and the groups are relatively uniform in size. Esteban and Ray conclude that polarization is greatest when society is divided into two similarly sized groups, each internally homogeneous but significantly different from the others on all possible attributes.

As they observe, most measures of income inequality and ethnic fractionalization do not correspond to these definitions of polarization. Theoretically appropriate measures of income-based polarization should be sensitive to the degree of clustering of the population, which inequality measures derived from the Lorenz curve are not. Similarly, societies that are completely ethnically fractionalized could be regarded as completely non-polarized by their definition.

In Keefer and Knack (2002), we justify the use of Gini measures of inequality by showing that theoretical objections may not be empirically important. Using data available from a few countries that includes the percentage of the population at each income level, one could construct a theoretically robust measure of income polarization that turns out to be strongly correlated with the Gini coefficient calculated from the same data.

It turns out to be a simpler matter to transform measures of ethno-linguistic fractionalization into a theoretically adequate measure of ethnic polarization. We use Sullivan's (1991) measure of the fraction of the population belonging to the largest ethnic, linguistic or religious group (whichever cleavage is judged by Sullivan to be most salient in a society).[5] As Keefer and Knack (2002) argue, following Horowitz (1985), polarization ought to be lowest when this fraction is either smallest (reflecting many very small groups) or highest (reflecting only one

[5] An index of "ethno-linguistic fractionalization" reported in Taylor and Hudson (1983), has been widely used in the economics and political science literature. The Sullivan measure has substantially greater country coverage, as the fractionalization index is not reported for many African and other countries which were not yet independent when the variable was constructed in about 1960. The homogeneity variable and the fractionalization index are correlated at -.60.

group). To capture this non-linearity, we include a quadratic ethnic fractionalization term in the first sets of regressions below.

The quality of income inequality data is a second concern. As in Keefer and Knack (2002), we use the income inequality data compiled by Deininger and Squire (1996). This dataset has greater coverage over time and across countries than any previous compilation. In addition, and more importantly, they identify a "high quality" subset of observations. Deininger and Squire conclude that many observations in previous compilations fail to meet the minimum standards of quality required for inclusion in their dataset. Because our empirical tests examine inequality's impact on creditworthiness over the 1986-95 period, we chose inequality observations as close to 1985 as possible.[6] The mean year for observations is 1985, with a standard deviation of 4.8 years.

Societies can also be polarized according to holdings of assets. Land inequality is the only measure of asset inequality with broad country coverage. Gini coefficients for land inequality circa 1960 and 1970 are available from Taylor and Jodice (1983); Muller and Seligson (1987) include some additional values for circa 1970. Jazairy et al. (1992) report observations for more recent years for many countries. All of the land inequality observations are based on official agricultural censuses undertaken by the UN Food and Agriculture Organization, although they have not been subjected to the level of scrutiny Deininger and Squire (1996) have applied to income inequality data.

Finally, we use two political variables from the Database of Political Institutions (Beck et al. 2001). The number of veto players is captured by the variable *Checks*, which counts as veto players the president and each legislative chamber in a presidential system. The variable is incremented by one unless the president's party has a majority in the lower house *and* there is a closed list system (by which legislative candidates must be selected by party leaders) that weakens legislator autonomy from the president. In parliamentary systems, the prime minister and each coalition party that is not his or her own count as veto players. If there is no closed list electoral rule, the prime minister's party counts as a veto player, and *Checks* is incremented by one. *Checks* is set to one automatically in any country in which presidential elections are not competitive, on the presumption that formal institutional checks and balances are unlikely to operate in practice. We use the mean value for each country over the 1986-95 period.

Our second political variable, the competitiveness of executive elections, is based on another variable from the Database on Political Institutions which is coded from one to seven. Where there is no functioning executive, countries are coded 1. Where executives are unelected, they are coded 2. Where elections are not open to multiple candidates or parties, countries are coded in the 3-5 range

[6] Where no measure was available for 1985, a decision rule was consistently applied for selecting between available observations. This rule treated the possibility of reverse causation introduced from selecting later years as a more serious problem than increased measurement error resulting from the selection of earlier years. Specifically, the rule was to choose the year satisfying the function: min [2(year - 1985); 1985 - year]. Ties were resolved in favor of selecting the earlier year (for example, 1983 over 1986).

(See Data Appendix for details.) Countries in which multiple parties can and do compete and present candidates, but the winning candidate receives more than 75 percent of the vote are coded 6; a 7 is assigned if the winner receives less than 75 percent of the vote.

We create a dichotomous variable from this scale, with countries in which multiple candidates from multiple parties compete classified as having competitive elections and all other countries classified as non-competitive. Specifically, countries assigned to either the 6 or 7 category for the majority of years during the 1986-95 period were classified as competitive and all others as non-competitive. (Summary statistics for all variables are presented in Data Appendix Table 10.A2.)

10.5 Results

The regressions in Table 10.1 address whether social polarization reduces creditworthiness, abstracting from political institutions. The first three regressions examine income polarization (income inequality). All show that income inequality increases the likelihood of default on debt. In the first equation, the coefficient on income inequality suggests that each two point increase in Gini is associated with a 1.2 point decline in the creditworthiness index. Each standard deviation increase in income inequality (i.e. an increase of 9.5 in Gini) reduces creditworthiness by more than one-fifth of a standard deviation (*beta* = .2), or 5 points. This effect is comparable to that of income growth, and exceeds the effects of higher aggregate income (*beta* = .12) or improvements in the terms of trade (*beta* = .15).[7]

Equation 2 differs from equation 1 by weighting observations by aggregate GDP, instead of weighting all observations equally. The relationship between inequality and creditworthiness is even stronger in this test than in equation 1, indicating that the strong effect of inequality is not driven merely by a few very small countries.[8] Equation 3 differs from equation 1 by using median regression analysis rather than OLS. In median regression (see Gould and Rogers 1994), observations lying far from the regression line are weighted less heavily than in OLS. The inequality coefficient is nearly identical to that in equation 1, indicating that the relationship is not produced by a small number of extreme cases.

[7] In all regressions, the four control variables are positively and significantly related to creditworthiness. Income per capita is the strongest of the four: each standard deviation increase is associated with an increase of more than three-fifths of a standard deviation in creditworthiness in equation 1. Each 4 percentage-point increase in aggregate GDP (as a percentage of U.S. GDP) is associated with a 1-point increase in the creditworthiness index. Each 1 percentage-point increase in annual per capita income growth is associated with a 2-point increase in the index. Each 7 percentage-point improvement in the terms of trade (e.g. from 1 to 1.07) is associated with a rise of 1.4 points in creditworthiness.

[8] The aggregate GDP of the U.S. is 20,000 times that of Seychelles. The logic for treating each country equally is that they each represent a single natural experiment in economic policy making.

Table 10.1. Polarization and creditworthiness

Equation	1	2	3	4	5	6	7
Method	OLS	WLS	Median	OLS	OLS	OLS	OLS
Constant	-81.25 (14.20)	-88.36 (11.39)	-90.18 (21.91)	-119.44 (12.42)	-82.82 (13.31)	-107.09 (11.86)	-82.55 (14.64)
GDP per capita 1985	16.52** (1.43)	19.00** (1.00)	17.30** (2.12)	19.18** (1.36)	18.17** (1.43)	19.22** (1.36)	19.62** (1.47)
Growth 1980-85	2.04** (0.64)	1.47# (0.75)	2.08** (0.72)	1.48** (0.52)	1.56** (0.57)	1.77** (0.46)	1.83** (0.60)
Aggregate GDP 1985	0.24** (0.09)	0.09** (0.02)	0.26# (0.15)	0.29* (0.12)	0.26** (0.09)	0.29* (0.12)	0.24** (0.09)
Terms of trade shift	13.68** (4.40)	17.73** (3.78)	15.91** (6.21)	12.86* (5.90)	11.06* (4.90)	15.12** (5.51)	14.34* (5.63)
Gini: income inequality	-0.60** (0.16)	-0.94** (0.16)	-0.59** (0.21)		-0.54** (0.16)		-0.49** (0.16)
Gini: land inequality				-0.12 (0.08)	-0.20** (0.07)		-0.18* (0.07)
Ethnic homogeneity						-0.70** (0.23)	-0.52 (0.33)
Ethnic homogeneity squared						.005** (.002)	.003 (.002)
N	76	76	76	84	64	105	64
R^2/ Pseudo R^2	.83	.94	.60	.80	.87	.79	.87
S.E. of est.	11.0	6.3	--	12.3	10.2	12.0	10.0
Mean, D.V.	42.4	72.2	42.4	41.2	44.0	39.0	44.0

Dependent variable = International Investor Index of Creditworthiness, averaged over 1986-95. Inequality measures are circa 1985. Standard errors are calculated using White's (1980) heteroskedastic-consistent variance-covariance matrix. A #, * or ** indicates significance at .10, .05, or .01 level respectively for two-tailed tests. Note R^2 does not have its usual interpretation in WLS (equation 2).

Table 10.2. Checks and balances, polarization, and creditworthiness

Equation	1	2	3	4	5	6
Constant	-76.21 (15.35)	69.09 (15.31)	-107.39 (13.25)	-103.60 (13.00)	-120.00 (11.21)	-125.99 (11.48)
GDP per capita 1985	15.21** (1.80)	14.71** (1.77)	17.31** (1.70)	17.02** (1.63)	17.19** (1.47)	18.07** (1.50)
Growth 1980-85	2.11** (0.66)	2.15** (0.63)	1.31* (0.53)	1.27* (0.52)	1.70** (0.46)	1.70** (0.45)
Aggregate GDP 1985	0.23** (0.08)	0.24** (0.08)	0.28* (0.11)	0.31* (0.12)	0.29** (0.11)	0.27* (0.12)
Terms of trade shift	12.65** (4.45)	11.42* (4.55)	9.88# (5.74)	9.60# (5.59)	12.23** (4.72)	12.83** (4.61)
Gini: income inequality	-0.55** (0.17)	-0.58** (0.17)				
Gini: land inequality			-0.13 (0.08)	-0.15# (0.08)		
Ethnic harmony					0.24** (0.08)	0.18* (0.09)
Checks (# of veto players)	1.47 (1.15)	0.96 (1.40)	2.02# (1.10)	1.98# (1.09)	1.64# (0.92)	1.31 (0.92)
Inequality *Checks		-0.18# (0.11)		-0.06 (0.06)		
Ethnic harmony * Checks						-0.12* (0.06)
N	76	76	84	84	105	105
R^2	.84	.85	.81	.81	.80	.81
S.E. of est.	10.9	10.7	12.2	12.1	11.9	11.7
Mean, D.V.	42.4	42.4	41.2	41.2	39.0	39.0

Dependent variable = International Investor Index of Creditworthiness, averaged over 1986-95. Inequality measures are circa 1985. Standard errors are from White's (1980) heteroskedastic-consistent variance-covariance matrix. A #, * or ** indicates significance at .10, .05, or .01 level respectively for two-tailed tests. Inequality**Checks* = (deviation of Gini from sample mean)*(deviation of *Checks* from 3). Ethnic harmony **Checks* = (deviation of homogeneity from 70%, in absolute value)*(deviation of *Checks* from 3).

Equations 4-7 report results using the alternative measures of polarization or specifications. The results for land inequality, in equation 4, exhibit the right sign (more land inequality undermines creditworthiness), but the coefficient is not significant at conventional levels. However, controlling for income inequality, in equation 5, both land and income inequality are shown to have a significant negative effect on creditworthiness. Each one-unit increase in the Gini for land inequality reduces creditworthiness by one-fifth of one point.

Ethnic homogeneity is entered in equation 6 in quadratic form, to better capture the theoretical relationship between ethnic homogeneity and ethnic polarization, as discussed above. Consistent with that discussion, both ethnic homogeneity and its square are significant at the .01 level. Creditworthiness declines as the percent belonging to the largest group increases, up to about 70 percent, and increases thereafter. Equation 7 examines all of the polarization measures jointly.[9] Income and land inequality both remain strongly significant. Coefficients on homogeneity and its square decline somewhat relative to equation 5, and are not statistically significant in this smaller sample.

Table 10.2 tests the hypotheses that social polarization reduces creditworthiness, that checks and balances increases it, and that the effects of each are dependent upon the other. The coefficient estimates on *Checks* (the number of veto players) indicate that the number of veto players has a positive effect on creditworthiness. In the larger samples (equations 3 and 5), this effect is marginally significant, with each extra veto player associated with an improvement of about 2 points in the 100-point creditworthiness index. That is, the credibility effects of checks and balances appear to outweigh the responsiveness effects in the assessments of creditworthiness.

The effects of social polarization depend significantly on the number of veto players. Equation 2 of Table 10.2 shows that the negative effects of income inequality are significantly greater when there are more checks and balances.[10] The coefficient of the interaction between land inequality and *Checks* is also negative in equation 4, but not significant. Equation 6, which looks at ethnic polarization and its interaction with *Checks*, demonstrates the contrary result: ethnic harmony improves creditworthiness most when there are fewer veto players, and this beneficial effect *diminishes* significantly as the number of veto players increases. This is the first piece of evidence for the final hypothesis, that the nature of polarized

[9] Low correlations among income inequality, land inequality, and ethnic homogeneity suggest that societies are in general polarized in different ways across different dimensions. Income and land inequality are correlated at only .09 among the 64 nations in our sample with data available on both variables. Ethnic homogeneity is correlated with income and land inequality, respectively, at only -.25 (N = 75) and .03 (N = 84). Quadratic associations between inequality and homogeneity are even weaker: homogeneity and homogeneity squared explain only 7% of the variation in income inequality, and 0.1% of the variation in land inequality.

[10] The interaction terms in equations 2 and 4 are constructed as the deviation of the inequality variables from their sample means, multiplied by the deviation of checks from its mean value of 3.

Table 10.3. Electoral competitiveness, polarization, and creditworthiness

Equation	1	2	3	4	5	6
Constant	-99.47 (12.55)	-103.17 (15.04)	-128.90 (13.11)	-135.58 (14.48)	-136.73 (11.31)	-142.76 (11.45)
GDP per capita 1985	18.21** (1.60)	17.33** (1.66)	20.28** (1.54)	19.59** (1.52)	19.88** (1.46)	20.22** (1.42)
Growth 1980-85	2.06** (0.61)	2.02** (0.59)	1.65** (0.56)	1.45** (0.53)	1.81** (0.45)	1.80** (0.45)
Aggregate GDP 1985	0.24** (0.09)	0.24** (0.09)	0.27* (0.12)	0.31* (0.12)	0.30* (0.13)	0.29* (0.13)
Terms of trade shift	14.81** (4.31)	15.22** (4.22)	15.24** (5.67)	15.88** (5.57)	16.89** (4.85)	17.22** (5.01)
Gini: income inequality	-0.55** (0.16)	-0.19 (0.24)				
Gini: land inequality			-0.09 (0.08)	0.13 (0.12)		
Ethnic harmony					0.20** (0.08)	0.32** (0.09)
Electoral Competitiveness	-5.94 (3.97)	-4.57 (3.99)	-5.23 (4.03)	-4.95 (3.82)	-5.66# (3.27)	-5.74# (3.23)
Inequality * Competitiveness		-0.55* (0.27)		-0.40* (0.18)		
Ethnic harmony* Competitiveness						-0.23 (0.15)
N	76	76	84	84	105	105
R^2	.84	.85	.80	.81	.80	.80
S.E. of est.	10.8	10.6	12.3	12.0	11.9	11.9
Mean, D.V.	42.7	42.7	41.2	41.2	39.0	39.0

Dependent variable = International Investor Index of Creditworthiness, averaged over 1986-95. Inequality measures are circa 1985. Standard errors are calculated using White's (1980) heteroskedastic-consistent variance-covariance matrix. A #, * or ** indicates significance at .10, .05, or .01 level respectively for two-tailed tests. Inequality*competitiveness = (deviation of Gini from sample mean)*(competitiveness). Ethnic harmony*competitiveness = (deviation of homogeneity from 70%, in absolute value)*(competitiveness).

groups influences their effects on policy.

Table 10.3 pursues this theme, adding the competitiveness of executive elections and interacting it with the social polarization variables. Electoral competitiveness is negatively but (generally) not significantly associated with creditworthiness. We would expect that more organized groups would have a greater effect on policy when voters are least "empowered", as when elections are non-competitive. If ethnic groups are more organized than income groups, we would expect the effects of ethnic harmony on creditworthiness to be greatest when elections are least competitive. In contrast, the distribution of income should affect creditworthiness more when elections are more competitive. Equations 2, 4 and 6 provide evidence that this is the case. In equations 2 and 4, the interaction of land or income inequality with electoral competitiveness is negative and significant, indicating that inequality has a stronger negative effect on creditworthiness when elections are more competitive.[11] However, the negative coefficient on the ethnic harmony interaction in equation 6 signifies the opposite: more ethnic harmony (larger deviations from 70% belonging to the largest group) is less beneficial to creditworthiness – or, ethnic strife is less damaging -- when elections are more competitive. This interaction term is significant only at the .12 level, however, for a two-tailed test.

Table 10.4 provides a summary of the effect of changes in the social polarization variables, conditional on different levels of *Checks* and electoral competitiveness. The pattern of asterisks underlines the stark differences between ethnic polarization and income inequality. The impact of ethnic polarization is greatest (i.e. ethnic harmony is most beneficial, or ethnic divisions most damaging) at low levels of both *Checks* and electoral competitiveness. It is not significant where elections are competitive or where there are four or more checks. In contrast, inequality is most damaging at high levels of both *Checks* and electoral competitiveness. Both land and income inequality are significant only where elections are competitive. Income inequality is significant except where there are no checks on the executive (i.e. *Checks* equals one). Land inequality is significant only where checks is less than three.

[11] The interaction terms in equations 2 and 4 are constructed as the deviation of inequality from their sample means, multiplied by the electoral competitiveness dummy.

Table 10.4. Conditional coefficients and standard errors

		Impact on creditworthiness of 1-unit increase in		
		Gini (income)	Gini (land)	Ethnic harmony
Conditional on:				
Checks =	1	-0.23	-0.02	0.41**
		(0.25)	(0.13)	(0.10)
	2	-0.41*	-0.08	0.29**
		(0.19)	(0.09)	(0.08)
	3	-0.58**	-0.15#	0.18*
		(0.17)	(0.08)	(0.09)
	4	-0.76**	-0.21*	0.06
		(0.21)	(0.10)	(0.13)
	5	-0.93**	-0.27#	-0.05
		(0.29)	(0.15)	(0.18)
	6	-1.11**	-0.33#	-0.17
		(0.38)	(0.19)	(0.23)
	7	-1.29**	-0.39	-0.28
		(0.48)	(0.25)	(0.29)
Electoral competitiveness =	0	-0.19	0.13	0.32**
		(0.24)	(0.12)	(0.09)
	1	-0.74**	-0.27*	0.09
		(0.16)	(0.11)	(0.12)

A #, * or ** indicates significance at .10, .05, or .01 level respectively for two-tailed tests. Note the maximum value for *Checks* is 7.65 (the average for France over the period) and the minimum value is 1.

10.6 Summary

Our finding that social polarization is associated with reduced creditworthiness is consistent with the Alesina and Drazen (1991) model of delayed stabilizations. Our results, using a different dependent variable, corroborate those of Berg and Sachs (1988), who found inequality was associated with a greater likelihood of defaulting on debt, and a higher discount on debt in secondary markets. We find that on average, more veto players are associated with improved creditworthiness, consistent with the analysis by North and Weingast (1992) of English sovereign borrowing in the 17th and 18th centuries. This result is somewhat contradictory to those of Veiga (2000) and Haggard and Kaufman (1992), who find that fragmented political systems slow responses to inflation crises; however, our dependent variable reflects both credibility and responsiveness to crisis. Our results also show that the effects of social polarization and institutions are highly interdependent, providing a unifying basis for assessing the implications of these different strands of the literature.

Finally, results of our interaction tests are consistent with our claim that Olson's insights regarding the importance of the internal organization of groups are important to consider in evaluating the effects of social polarization. Where elections are not competitive and there are few checks on executive power, a candidate's promises will be less credible to members of other ethnic groups, and the candidate will have an incentive to promise higher spending that benefits his or her own group. Accordingly, ethnic divisions undermine (or, ethnic harmony enhances) creditworthiness more where checks are few and elections are less competitive. In contrast to the high social and economic costs of reneging on promises to one's own ethnic group, the costs to reneging on promises made to income groups appear to be relatively low. Those promises will be more credible when competitive elections and checks and balances increase the predictability of government decision making. Accordingly, inequality undermines creditworthiness more where checks are more prevalent and elections are competitive.

Data Appendix

Table 10.A1. Countries in sample (with creditworthiness values)

Country	Value	Country	Value	Country	Value	Country	Value
Sudan	5.9	Dominican Republic	17.6	Gabon	30.3	Malta	60.1
Nicaragua	6.9	Bangladesh	18.9	Uruguay	31.4	Malaysia	61.4
Uganda	6.9	Jamaica	19.3	Papua NewGuinea	32.6	Portugal	61.5
Sierra Leone	7.2	Senegal	19.3	Trinidad & Tobago	33.6	New Zealand	65.2
Haiti	8.3	Nigeria	19.7	Venezuela	36.1	Korea	66.4
Liberia	8.4	Syria	20.4	Algeria	36.1	Ireland	67.1
Mozambique	8.8	Cote D'Ivoire	20.8	Barbados	36.3	Australia	70.8
Zaire	9.0	Swaziland	21.5	Guinea-Bissau	36.4	Spain	74.2
Ethiopia	9.2	Ecuador	21.9	South Africa	37.0	Denmark	74.3
Zambia	11.1	Costa Rica	22.1	México	37.2	Finland	75.2
Tanzania	11.8	Panama	23.1	Israel	37.4	Italy	76.5
El Salvador	11.9	Nepal	23.5	Tunisia	38.7	Taiwan	77.1
Angola	12.3	Iran	24.3	Colombia	39.0	Singapore	78.1
Iraq	12.8	Sri Lanka	24.9	Chile	39.4	Sweden	78.1
Guinea	13.7	Philippines	26.3	Turkey	41.7	Belgium	78.5
Bolivia	13.9	Argentina	26.3	Mauritius	43.4	Norway	79.6
Honduras	14.1	Egypt	26.4	Botswana	43.8	Canada	84.0
Myanmar	14.2	Zimbabwe	26.6	India	44.7	Austria	84.4
Congo Republic	14.7	Ghana	27.5	Cyprus	45.9	Luxembourg	84.5
Peru	14.9	Cameroon	27.5	Greece	48.0	UK	86.4
Benin	16.2	Kenya	27.7	Indonesia	48.5	France	86.5
Mali	16.5	Paraguay	28.2	Oman	51.1	Netherlands	87.8
Guatemala	16.5	Jordan	28.2	Iceland	54.2	USA	90.4
Togo	16.8	Morocco	29.1	Kuwait	54.2	Germany	91.9
Malawi	16.9	Pakistan	29.4	Saudi Arabia	59.2	Switzerland	93.3
Seychelles	17.1	Brazil	29.6	Thailand	59.5	Japan	93.4
Burkina Faso	17.2	Mauritania	30.1				

Table 10.A2. Summary Statistics

	N	Mean	Std. dev.	Min.	Max.
Creditworthiness index	106	38.8	25.7	5.9	93.4
Gini income inequality	76	41.7	9.5	25.2	63.2
Gini land inequality	84	55.1	16.1	8.0	95.6
Ethnic homogeneity	105	68.5	25.0	17	100
Ethnic harmony	105	21.0	13.5	0	53
Log GDP per capita 1985	106	7.97	1.06	5.70	9.72
Per capita annual growth 1980-85	106	-0.1	3.3	-10.7	6.9
Aggregate GDP 1985 (% of US)	106	3.5	10.8	0.005	100
Net barter terms of trade shift	106	0.94	0.27	0.41	1.95
Electoral competitiveness (0-1)	106	0.62	0.49	0	1
Checks (number of veto players)	106	2.89	1.74	1	7.64

Coding of Political Institutional Variables

Table 10.A3. Coding of executive index of electoral competitiveness (EIEC)

	Value assigned
No executive	1
Unelected executive	2
Elected, 1 candidate	3
1 party, multiple candidates	4
multiple parties are legal	5
multiple parties with multiple candidates, and	
the winner received more than 75% of the votes	6
the winner received less than 75% of votes	7

- Executives who are elected directly by population, or elected by an electoral college that is elected by the people *and* has the sole purpose of electing the executive, are scored on the above scale.
- Executives elected by bodies other than these are given the same score that the electing body would get. Even if the electing body is not the actual "legislature" (such as an appointed electoral college), the competitiveness of that body is used to score the executive.
- This means that competitively elected prime ministers get 6 or 7. The chief executives of Communist nations (the chairman of the Communist Party) are given a 3, because they are elected by the Party Congress, electing bodies which they do not appoint. Executives elected by small, appointed juntas or by appointed electoral colleges get 2.
- Rival chief executives in one country, particularly in the setting of armed conflicts, are counted as No executives, and thus score a 1.
- Referenda and votes by "popular acclamation" on unelected executives are scored as 3.

- If executives unilaterally extend their terms of office, they get a 2 starting in the year they should have held elections. Any executive elected for life, even by the people or an elected assembly, gets a 2. This elected-for-life rule is slightly different from that followed for legislatures that unilaterally extend their rule.

Checks

Checks equals one if the above index (EIEC), or the legislative index of electoral competitiveness (LIEC, also from Beck et al. 2000), is less than 5: countries where legislatures are not competitively elected are considered countries where only the executive wields a check. In presidential systems: (1) if EIEC is greater than 6, *Checks* is incremented by one to distinguish countries with competitively elected presidents and no other checks (see (2) and (3)) from countries with non-competitively elected presidents; (2) if the opposition controls the legislature, *Checks* is incremented by one; (3) *Checks* is incremented by one for each chamber of the legislature UNLESS the president's party has a majority in the lower house AND a closed list system is in effect (implying stronger presidential control of his/her party, and therefore of the legislature); (4) if the first government party has a position on economic issues closer to the largest opposition party than to the party of the executive, *Checks* is incremented by one. In parliamentary systems: (1) if LIEC is greater than 6, *Checks* is incremented by one, to establish equivalence with presidential checks counting; (2) if the opposition controls the legislature, *Checks* is incremented by one; (3) for every party in the government coalition, up to the largest three parties, *Checks* is incremented by one; (4) *Checks* is incremented by the number of "other" government parties if the total number of government seats in the legislature without taking those parties into account is less than 50 percent; (5) for every party in the government coalition that has a position on economic issues closer to the largest opposition party than to the party of the executive, *Checks* is incremented by one.

11 The International Campaign against Corruption: An Institutionalist Perspective

Christopher Clague

The 1990s could well be called the "Decade of Corruption Awareness." A survey of the Economist, the Financial Times and the international coverage of the New York Times revealed that articles mentioning corruption quadrupled between 1985 and 1995 (Leiken 1997, cited in Quah 1999, p. 245). The end-of-the-year editorial in the Financial Times on December 31, 1995 characterized 1995 as the year of corruption (cited in Tanzi 1998, p. 560). International organizations have recently addressed the issue, including the UN, the OECD, the WTO, and the Council of Europe. In 1996, under the auspices of the Organization of American States, 23 countries signed the *Inter-American Convention Against Corruption*, under which the signatory states agreed to take measures against certain defined corrupt practices (Shihata 1997, pp. 469-73). Transparency International (TI) was formed in the early 1990s by several World Bank employees who felt that the Bank and the rest of the development community were not devoting sufficient resources to addressing the problem. TI has developed into a large and influential organization with chapters in over 70 countries.[1]

Why has corruption become such a prominent issue in development circles? Has the problem actually gotten worse, or is it simply getting more attention?[2] There are some reasons for thinking that corruption became more common in many newly independent countries in Africa and Asia after World War II. Colonial administrators were replaced by locals who had much less education and had not absorbed the administrative practices of their European masters. Fragile new governments, whether democratic or authoritarian, lacked institutions of accountability that could have constrained politicians from engaging in massive corrup-

---

[1] Some observers think that this flurry of international activity presages a turning point in the world's historical struggle against corruption. Glynn et al. (1997, p. 8) state: "...Nonetheless, there is reason to believe we may be at a historical turning point in humanity's long wrestle with corruption. A new global standard appears to be taking shape in human consciousness, with potentially major ramifications for our institutions as well as our political and business lives. The 1990s, we would predict, are unlikely to pass without the achievement of significant legal and institutional anticorruption reforms." On p. 26 they say, "But when a future historian writes the long and ugly story of human corruption, there is reason to suppose the 1990s could be to corruption what the 1850s were to slavery: a decade of irreversible change."

[2] See Tanzi (1998) for a discussion of this question.

tion. Many less-developed countries, including those not newly independent, embarked on *dirigiste* programs of industrialization, which created multiple opportunities for the exchange of bribes and favors (Krueger 1993). Part of the expanding role of the state was the proliferation of state enterprises, a fertile source for nepotism and other corrupt practices; ironically, recent privatizations in both less-developed and transition economies have channeled large assets to insiders. The rise of international trade in narcotics has greatly increased the rewards for corruption in both producing countries and countries used for transit on the way to the markets in the rich countries. On the other hand, there are reasons for thinking that longstanding corrupt practices have recently been exposed more frequently and are more often the object of public criticism. The wave of democratization in Latin America removed constraints on freedom of expression, so that the peculation of newly democratic governments got a full airing in the local media. A similar breakdown of the barriers on expression occurred in post-communist Europe, which also witnessed the collapse of the old economic system and with it respect for rules of any kind. There seems to be no compelling reason to think that corruption in Sub-Saharan Africa has increased in the last decade, but foreigners have been more willing to raise the issue, and it has been described as one of the factors in the region's continuing economic deterioration. Italy's explosive political scandals of the early 1990s have increased public appetite in that country for cleaning up politics and punishing the guilty (della Porta and Vannucci 1999). Finally, media and popular concern with corruption tends to occur in waves, and during an upswing the popular perception is that corruption has never been as bad as it is now. Kaufman (1998, p. 76) reported on a 1996 survey of elites in 63 developing and formerly communist countries, in which almost half the respondents thought that corruption had increased in their country over the past ten years, and another third believed that it had stayed roughly the same.[3]

International corporations have long paid bribes to host countries in connection with exports and foreign investments. In most of the rich countries, until recently these bribes were regarded as part of the cost of doing business and were even deductible on income tax forms. The United States, in the wake of the Watergate scandal, passed the Corrupt Practices Act in 1977, which criminalized these bribes and precluded their deductibility. Subsequently, U.S. companies complained that they were losing business to European and Japanese competitors because they were unable to pay the "commissions" demanded by host country officials and politicians. Partly as a result of pressure on this issue from business interests, the U.S. Government in the 1990s urged the international community to take up the issue of corruption more generally.

[3] But it is not clear that public opinions have really changed. Geddes (1994, pp. 25-26) reports some survey results from Brazil and Argentina. "When asked whether 'the only really important problem in Brazil is the problem of lack of character and honesty,' only 15 per cent of those who had an opinion disagreed." "...when Argentines were asked, 'Do you believe that today in this country one can get or cover up anything if one has money or influence?' 93 per cent answered yes and only 1.7 per cent answered no." These surveys were conducted in 1965-66 and 1963.

The discipline of economics seems to have arrived at the corruption issue on its own. At the theoretical level, the emergence of principal-agent theory in the 1970s provided a useful tool for thinking about corruption. Principal-agent theory provides guidelines and strategies for political leaders and top-level bureaucrats to combat corruption by government employees (Klitgaard 1988). In the 1980s the New Institutional Economics put institutional questions at the heart of the emergence of capitalism in the West and governance failures in the Third World. Corruption is just one example of a broader failure of institutions to harmonize private and social interests. The literature on property rights and contract enforcement led to the search for measures of rule of law, integrity of courts, bureaucratic efficiency, and corruption, and such measures turned out to be important determinants of investment and growth (Mauro (1995) and Keefer and Knack (1995) are two seminal articles in this now burgeoning literature). The literature on cooperation and social order developed game-theory models with multiple equilibria, some with high levels of rule obedience and cooperation, and others with low levels of rule obedience and high levels of corruption (Andvig and Moene 1990; Clague 1993). These models seem to support the notion that an aggressive anti-corruption campaign may enable a society or a single organization to move from a low level of cooperation to a high level, or from rampant corruption to pervasive rule obedience. However, the evidence does not generally support the hope that rapid turnarounds in the level of corruption occur, or that they are sustainable when they do occur. Other models, based on learning and collective reputations (described in Bardhan 1997 for example), help to explain why corruption is resilient to reform campaigns.[4]

On the whole, the international development community has become much less tolerant of corruption in less-developed countries. In the 1960s and 1970s, practitioners and observers of development politely refrained from raising the issue of corruption forcefully (Myrdal 2002 [1968] criticized this practice). The academic literature was also ambivalent about whether corruption was really very harmful for development (Leff 1964; Huntington 1968). Both of these attitudes had changed dramatically by the 1990s (see, for example, Johnston (1986), Klitgaard (1988, pp. 27-48) and Theobald (1990, pp. 107-131) for a critique of earlier views). To quote two members of Transparency International:

> When TI was launched, the World Bank had just published *Governance*, a treatise on the four constitutive elements of 'good governance': (1) public sector management, (2) accountability, (3) the legal framework for development, and (4) information and transparency. Very little specific reference to corruption was made in this document.... An internal memorandum referred to corruption as the

[4] However, Andvig et al. (2000, p. 132) point out that even a successful campaign may leave an organization vulnerable to relapse because the "memory" of corruption remains and old partners in corruption can find one another. According to these authors, all of the success stories cited in Klitgaard (1988) have turned out to be unsustainable (Andvig et al. 2000, p. 130). Klitgaard, et al. (2000, pp. 105-109) describe the resurgence of corruption in La Paz following the first term of the reformist mayor Roberto MacLean Abaroa.

'C' word, symptomatic of the taboo within the institution and much of the multilateral development community for this issue. (Galtung and Pope 1999, p. 263)

As mentioned above, this taboo has now been lifted (partly through the efforts of Transparency International), and less-developed countries have come in for harsh criticism for their failures to combat corruption (Riley 1998). TI emphasizes public awareness and civic activism as strategies for combating corruption, and the World Bank has to some extent shifted its strategies in response to the TI critique (Shihata 1997, Riley 1998). It is perhaps not an exaggeration to say that TI and some parts of the donor agencies have launched an Anti-Corruption Crusade (if not a jihad). How successful is this international effort likely to be? Which seem to be the most promising ways in which the international community can assist in combating corruption? What should be the role of anti-corruption programs in international assistance?

Exposure of corruption arouses strong moral condemnation in most people. It is difficult to read or hear the details of particular instances of corrupt behavior without feeling a rising sense of indignation that the perpetrators are getting away with it. The moral outrage at perceived corruption has on many occasions led to various forms of political activity, such as voting the rascals out, street demonstrations, and riots and looting. Political science, however, teaches us that such spontaneous actions typically have little effect on this or other political issues, unless they are combined with sustained, organized political activity. It is difficult to sustain a political organization based solely on moral outrage. Established political actors (political parties, various interest groups) can sometimes use the public's moral outrage to complement other forms of political pressure, but these actors have their own agendas, not always coincident with the public welfare. In fact, charges of corruption against one's opponents are a commonly used weapon in the struggle for political power, and such charges may be used cynically to weaken a fundamentally reformist government (Anechiarico and Jacobs 1996; Singh 1997). Moreover, progressive leaders in democratic or semi-democratic polities often have to resort to bribery, patronage, or other corrupt practices in order to win approval of modernizing measures. Thus an international campaign to draw attention to corruption in government may have adverse as well as positive effects on political systems in less-developed countries.

This chapter will explore some issues surrounding the international campaign against corruption. I first address (in section 11.1) the question of which types of corruption seem to be the most harmful to development. I argue that the types that attract the most attention in the media are not necessarily those that do the most damage. This section also discusses the ambiguous relationship between democracy and the control of corruption. Section 11.2 describes different strategies for combating corruption, including economic liberalization, technocratic reforms (these are changes in organizational structures and practices, inspired in large part by principal-agent theory), and greater accountability through strengthened civil society. In light of the limitations of each of these strategies, section 11.3 assesses the role of donor agencies and the international community in fighting corruption. In section 11.4, to put some meat on these general observations, I shall consider some examples of efforts to control corruption. I look at attempts to establish a civil service in mid-20th century Brazil, civil service reform in 19th-century America, and the remarkably clean civil service in contemporary Botswana. The first two examples involve efforts by middle- and upper-class reformers to enlist moral outrage in their campaigns against corruption. Section 11.5 offers some concluding comments.

I had the privilege of working in the same Economics Department with Mancur Olson for thirty years, and his ideas pervade this chapter. A starting point is the importance of governance institutions, as opposed to resource endowments, for economic growth and prosperity (Olson 1996). An earlier article on "Diseconomies of Scale and Development" (Olson 1987) pointed out that organizational deficiencies, including corruption, in poor countries were a major obstacle to development. In the last years of his life, Olson thought and wrote about the complex relationship between power and economic prosperity (Olson 2000). He pointed out that on the one hand, the separation of powers (or checks and balances) in modern democracies provides more secure growth-enhancing institutions of property rights and contract enforcement than an autocratic regime can possibly provide (Olson 1992). On the other hand, the consolidation of the power of coercion in the hands of a single ruler gives him an incentive to establish property and contract rights and to provide public goods that would not be provided when coercive power is widely dispersed (Olson 1993). Similarly, the concentration of political power in the hands of a group with an encompassing interest in the performance of the economy provides that group with incentives for growth-enhancing policies. These Olsonian ideas relate closely to two of the themes of this chapter. One theme is that the available avenues for controlling or moderating corruption can be quite different in the developed democracies, which have rather good institutions overall, than in the poor countries with largely dysfunctional institutions. In other words, I shouldn't let the pursuit of the ideal block such modest ameliorations as may be feasible (see Olson's opinion on "when to demand democracy and when not to" in Olson (1997, pp. 59-61)). Another theme is that proposed remedies for corruption must take account of power relationships in society, and how these might be changed by feasible interventions. This requires paying more attention to the realities of different political configurations than economists are accustomed to doing.

11.1 Types of Corruption and Consequences for Development

A great deal has been written about definitions of corruption and different ways of classifying corrupt practices. For our purposes a simple definition and a simple tripartite classification will be sufficient. Corruption is defined as "the abuse of public office for private gain." This definition assumes the existence of the concepts of the public sphere and the private sphere and a boundary between them. Corruption consists of the failure to abide by the rules of this boundary. The tripartite classification distinguishes three ways in which public officials fail to respect this boundary: illicit exchange of favors by public officials, extortion by public officials, and theft of public assets. A further distinction is between grand and petty corruption. Following a brief discussion of these distinctions, I describe the commonly used measures of corruption and the degree to which they capture important distinctions among types of corruption. Subsequently, I discuss corruption in autocracies and democracies.

The term "abuse" in the definition of corruption implies a legal or moral judgment about what is legal or proper. The term "corruption" carries with it moral overtones that are absent from terms such as "poor governance," and "administrative incapacity." If acts of corruption are identified, individual people are guilty of them, as opposed to poor governance or administrative incapacity, which may be attributed to prevailing practices and institutions. Corrupt acts or practices of course can be regarded as more or less serious, or more or less important. One way to judge their importance is by the degree to which they violate ethical or legal norms, or to put it another way, by the degree of moral outrage that they provoke. On the other hand, another way of judging their seriousness or importance is by the degree to which they impede economic and social development. A major theme of this chapter is that these two ways of judging the seriousness of corruption are not necessarily congruent. That is, the types of corruption that inspire the strongest moral outrage are not necessarily those that do the most harm to economic development. This point will be brought out in the discussion of the three types of corruption.

11.1.1 Types of Corruption

11.1.1.1 Illicit Exchange

This type of corruption is a trade of favors between a public official and a private interest (which may be an individual or a group). The public official makes a decision partly or wholly based on the favor he receives from the private interest. The decision may affect procurement, hiring, allocations of credit or foreign exchange, regulatory exceptions, and so on. The moral outrage is likely to depend mainly on the magnitude of the bribe or favor received by the public official, and also by the clarity of the connection between the favor and the decision. The consequences for development, on the other hand, are strongly influenced by the precise nature of the decision. Does the preferred contractor do the job correctly? Is the employee hired through nepotism competent? A substantial part of the poor governance in most Third World countries is the failure to provide and maintain physical infrastructure at adequate levels. If the only problem were that the cost to the public purse of infrastructure were inflated by 10 percent due to bribes, the consequences for development would not be serious. On the other hand, some of the most harmful forms of illicit exchange for development do not provoke much moral outrage because their consequences are not apparent to the public. For example, the public official may protect a local company's domestic monopoly simply by prohibiting the entry of foreign competitors.

11.1.1.2 Extortion by Public Officials

This type of corruption differs from illicit exchange in that the public official threatens others with positive harm, whereas in illicit exchange, the public official is offering a positive benefit to the favored individual or group. An example is the shaking down of wealthy individuals or companies by the threat of regulatory burdens, tax audits, or even violence. This kind of extortion can have a devastating effect on property rights and the incentive to invest. It would also be severely morally condemned if it were made public, but the victims may well keep it secret out of fear of even worse consequences for themselves.[5]

11.1.1.3 Theft of Public Assets

This type of corruption differs from the trade of favors and from extortion in that a private interest is not directly involved. The public official steals from the public purse. One form of theft is being on the public payroll and not doing one's job. The public is outraged at the discovery of ghost workers on the payroll, but the public is ill equipped to judge whether employees who show up are putting forth much effort. In fact, laziness of public employees is seldom what survey respondents have in mind when asked about corruption, although incompetence due to laziness is surely "an abuse of public office for private gain." Embezzlement is of course another form of theft, and it certainly occurs, but it is probably much less important than illicit exchange, because without protection from the political authorities, bureaucrats cannot steal on a large scale. Another form of theft that has acquired prominence in recent years arises in the privatization of government assets; government officials purchase assets at below-market prices, in situations where the true value of the assets is very difficult to assess (for examples in Latin America, see Manzetti 2000). This behavior provokes great moral outrage; it may or may not have severe adverse consequences for development. Those consequences depend in large part on the structure of property rights and incentives facing the newly privatized company.

Another distinction is that between grand and petty corruption.[6] Grand corruption refers to corruption on the part of the top political leaders of the society, while

[5] The distinction between illicit exchange and extortion is somewhat blurred at the edges. In my conception, while illicit exchange may be initiated by either party, the failure of the exchange to take place does not imply ruin for the private party. Extortion by public officials is always initiated by the officials, and the term suggests that failure of the private party to comply with the demands would impose adverse consequences so severe that his very survival would be threatened. Thus the term extortion suggests that power lies exclusively with the public official, and this situation is generally very bad for business.

[6] According to Galtung and Pope (1999, p. 279), the expression "grand corruption" was coined by George Moody-Stuart in 1993.

petty corruption is that conducted by lower-level public officials. These may not be separate, as the higher-level officials may tolerate or encourage petty corruption in order to extract resources from lower-level officials, as by the sale of offices. Grand corruption generally provokes more moral outrage than petty corruption, but it is not necessarily more harmful for development. The secure, developmentally minded autocrat may skim off enough money to make himself and his clique fabulously wealthy, but their extractions can easily constitute only a small tax on the economy. If the regime provides a good economic environment, the country can prosper and poverty can be diminished (Suharto's Indonesia comes to mind). Grand corruption can also exist in democracies, when the leaders of dominant political parties conspire with business interests to run a political machine. Such a regime may or may not be harmful for economic development, depending on country characteristics too numerous to mention (compare Italy's rapid development in the early postwar decades with India's relative stagnation in the same period). Petty corruption may be small scale, decentralized, and relatively harmless, but when it paralyzes the public bureaucracy, the consequences for development may be very serious.[7] For example, the government may be severely impeded in its delivery of educational, health, and rural development services. Some countries with extensive grand corruption have nevertheless done a good job of delivering these services (for example, Japan, Taiwan, and Korea during the "miracle" years).

11.1.2 Measures of Corruption

Recently, data on corruption have become available and have been widely reported in the media and employed in academic research. Transparency International has put together a "corruption perception index" (CPI), which is an average of some ten different surveys and ratings (Lambsdorff 2001). Some of the sources are formal surveys of business executives, while others provide ratings by experts. The questions asked in the different sources differ somewhat but they generally ask about the "extent of corruption," "frequency of corruption or bribery," "level of corruption," "corruption as a constraint on business," etc. Lambsdorff (2001) observes that the different sources give quite similar rankings for particular countries, despite the variety of types of respondent and wording of the questions. Even a Gallup survey of ordinary citizens yielded scores that correlate rather highly with the other sources (Treisman 2000). Lambsdorff argues that the high correlations indicate that the different sources are tapping the same phenomenon. While this may be true, it seems clear that the CPI does not accurately measure the de-

[7] A related distinction is between "state capture" and "administrative corruption," which is being employed by the World Bank and the European Bank for Reconstruction and Development in their large-scale study of Business Environment and Enterprise Performance (BEEP) in transition economies. The concept of capture is that private business uses corrupt means to influence the rules under which business operates, while administrative corruption in their study refers to bribery to affect specific procurement decisions.

gree to which corruption constrains economic development in particular countries. Many of the sources are explicitly attempting to assess the degree to which foreign corporations are hampered by corruption, and the emphasis is on the frequency and size of bribes demanded by public officials (that is, the focus is mainly on illicit exchange). The questions don't get at the possible adverse effects of corruption on the quality of public infrastructure, or the harmful effects of legal regulations that might have been put in place by corrupt exchanges. An important distinction in the theoretical literature on corruption is whether the briber "gets what he pays for," or in other words, whether having paid the bribe, the business person enjoys security of property rights and contract enforcement (Shleifer and Vishny 1993). These considerations probably help to explain why the CPI and its component indexes display very high levels of corruption in some countries that have been very successful developers, such as Indonesia under Suharto (1970-1997), China since 1978, and Thailand in recent decades.[8] By the wording of the questions, it is also evident that the CPI components do not reflect bureaucratic ineptitude and laziness that is not manifested in bribery but in the failure to deliver public services to ordinary citizens, such as health and education services.

11.1.3 Corruption in Democracies and Autocracies

Corruption takes somewhat different forms in democratic and authoritarian regimes. In the former type of regime, the process of getting elected often involves the corrupt exchange of favors with private interests. While the private interests basically seek financial benefits, the political and bureaucratic actors are interested in power as well as money. Political corruption is best visualized not as an exchange between two actors but as a complex web of exchanges, involving politicians, party leaders (who may not hold office), bureaucrats, and businesses. In well-functioning democracies, elected officials are constrained by a free press, an active civil society, an independent judiciary, an insulated civil service, and the will of the voters. Even in such societies, the financing of political parties is a fertile source of exchanges that the public regards as corrupt (even if some of the practices are legal). However, democracies need strong political parties to communicate and enforce the will of voters. Labels of corruption are often applied to political parties from the implicit perspective of an ideal political system, rather than from a comparison of feasible alternatives. With a few exceptions (mainly in Scandinavia), politicians in almost all democracies engage in exchanges that offend the moral sensitivities of the public. Whether this political corruption is seriously harmful to governmental performance is another matter. Some democratic regimes widely perceived as corrupt presided over rapid economic development

[8] Grand corruption has been quite large in Korea, as described by Wedeman (1997), who also explains why corruption in Korea was not very damaging to economic growth, in contrast to the corruption in Zaire and the Philippines. His explanation has to do with property rights and the incentives to keep capital at home. See also Campos et al. (1999) for econometric evidence that the predictability of corruption matters for investment.

(19th-century America, Brazil in the 1950s, Italy in the postwar, etc.). On the other hand, massive political corruption in many Third-World semi-democracies (i.e. electoral democracies with poorly functioning institutions of accountability (Schedler et al. 1999)) has severely undermined public administration and economic performance.

In authoritarian regimes the electoral process is not a source of corruption, but political leaders are not constrained by democratic political institutions. Dictators may have a great deal of discretion, and in that case the nature of the regime will depend on the personal goals of the dictator (the "developmental state" versus the "kleptocratic state" (Evans 1992)). In addition, authoritarian leaders vary greatly in their security of tenure. Politics is generally a highly competitive game, and most authoritarian leaders have to be concerned about being replaced by violence. The need to buy off potential rivals may severely constrain the dictator's freedom of action. However, some authoritarian leaders have established secure regimes and have used their discretion to build economically advantageous institutions of property rights, contract enforcement, and strong public administration. As was famously pointed out by Mancur Olson (1993), if a secure authoritarian leader aims to maximize his extraction of revenue from his domain, he would establish such economic rights and would provide a substantial amount of public infrastructure[9] (see also McGuire and Olson 1996). An insecure dictator, on the other hand, has a short time horizon and may have strong incentives to abrogate property rights, break contracts, and seize whatever resources he can to buy off threatening competitors or to provide for a comfortable retirement in exile. In Olson's terms, he becomes a roving rather than a stationary bandit. At the present time, all too many poor countries are in the grip of leadership groups that are not secure in their positions of power. With very short time horizons, these leaders do not try to institutionalize the rules of the economic game, but instead they grab what they can while they are in power. This type of "hand-over-fist" corruption channels the proceeds outside the country, where property rights are more secure. The loss of resources is likely to be less damaging to development than the insecure property rights and weak contract enforcement that such a regime provides.

There has been much discussion in the political science literature on the relationship between corruption and democracy.[10] A long tradition in political science regards corruption as a symptom of a "democratic deficit," and the remedy for corruption is strengthening democratic political institutions. While it does seem to be true that the ultimate remedy for corruption is a well-functioning democracy with strong institutions of accountability, transitions from authoritarian rule to a regime of elections do not necessarily reduce the level of corruption. Transitions from authoritarian rule to electoral democracy may actually be accompanied by increases in corruption, partly because of the weaker political positions of the new leaders (and their shortened time horizons), and partly because of the competitive

[9] Note that in this conception the distinction between the public sphere and the monarch's private interest breaks down.

[10] A nice discussion of these debates is in Chapter 4 by Amundsen in Andvig et al. (2000).

pressure to raise money for campaigns.[11] This observation is consistent with Treisman's (2000) empirical finding that consolidated democracy (continuous democracy for 40 years) reduced the level of corruption (holding many other variables constant), but democracy of shorter duration had little effect.

In earlier decades, authoritarian rule was thought to have important advantages for development. While opinion on this point has changed dramatically in recent years, it should be conceded that a theoretical case can be made that the concentration of power in the hands of a strong ruler can improve economic policy and reduce corruption, at least in the short or intermediate run. The case is essentially the one made by Olson (1993), alluded to above. The point is that a strong, secure leader (or the social class that supports him) has an encompassing interest in the economy and the society and therefore has something to gain from building the institutions that encourage the subjects to be productive. These institutions include functioning bureaucracies and controls on petty corruption. Even an initially insecure dictator can strengthen his political position by encouraging economic growth and curbing visible corruption. Obviously most authoritarian leaders do not do this, but examples of ones that did include the rulers in Korea after 1962, Brazil after 1964, Indonesia after 1967, Chile after 1973, Ghana after 1983, and Uganda after 1986.[12]

11.2 Strategies for Controlling Corruption

There are many different ways in which government actions can affect the incentives of public officials to engage in corruption. For present purposes, these can be grouped into three categories: economic liberalization, technocratic reforms, and strengthening institutions of accountability.

11.2.1 Economic Liberalization

The bargaining position of public officials vis-à-vis the private sector is strengthened in an environment of extensive government controls over the private sector. When government officials are in a position to award extremely valuable privileges to individuals in the private sector, in circumstances in which the criteria for allocation are imprecise (i.e. officials have considerable discretion), the temptation

[11] Examples of transitions from autocracy to electoral democracy in Africa that seem to have been accompanied by an increase in corruption include Nigeria in the early 1980s, and Zambia, Kenya, and Ghana in the early 1990s, according to Riley (1998). Corruption did not seem to decrease under Corazon Aquino in the Philippines (Hutchcroft 2000, p. 208), and it increased with democratization in Thailand in the 1990s (Rock 2000, pp. 197-99).

[12] Despite economic and administrative reforms, institutions remain fragile in Ghana and Uganda, and corruption is still present (van de Walle 2001, p. 89; Watt et al. 2000, pp. 59-62).

for illicit exchange between the officials and private interests is extremely strong. In the case of goods and services under price controls, the magnitude of the temptation increases as the controlled prices deviate from market equilibria.[13]

Of course economic liberalization cannot solve the whole problem of corruption, because governments have important tasks to perform, such as providing health and education services and physical infrastructure, protecting the environment, securing property rights, enforcing contracts, and collecting taxes. In each of these areas, there remain ample opportunities for illicit exchanges and theft of public assets. Moreover, even a very minimal government can engage in extortion. Economists have a tendency to exaggerate the potential role of economic liberalization in combating corruption.

11.2.2 Technocratic Reforms

These reforms include setting up organizational structures, recruitment procedures, salary structures, accounting systems, and measures of performance so that employees are rewarded for serving the public well and penalized for engaging in corruption.[14] Also included in this category are training programs for the employees themselves and for auditors and inspectors who monitor their performance. These reforms are called technocratic because their effectiveness in controlling corruption depends on the absence of political obstacles to their implementation.

---

[13] For a statement stressing the importance of economic liberalization in combating corruption, see Kaufman (1998).

[14] A widely used formula for analyzing corruption control is Corruption = Monopoly + Discretion – Accountability (Klitgaard 1988). Corruption can sometimes be reduced by permitting competition among public agencies (in granting licenses or permits, for example). Corruption can also be controlled by limiting the discretion of public employees, for example by allowing an employee only certain types of actions. Accountability can be enhanced by inspections, audits, and follow-up procedures that result in penalties for discovered violations. It should be noted, however, that discretion is not necessarily the enemy of organizational efficiency. Organization theorists and practitioners have found that the most efficient organizations are not those that follow the rules rigidly in a Weberian manner, but those that permit and encourage their members to exert effort, exercise initiative, and take responsibility (as discussed in Clague 1993 and many other places). Understanding this type of behavior requires us to move away from the strictly rational self-interest assumption of principal/agent theory, and to recognize the possibility of group identity, internalization of group goals, and *esprit de corps*. Organizations that succeed in eliciting effort, initiative, and responsible behavior from their employees are found much more frequently in the private sector of developed countries than in their public sectors, and they are probably extremely rare in the public sectors of less-developed countries. But the possibility of creating such organizations in the public sectors of poor countries should not be ruled out, and this has implications for designing rules to curb corruption in these organizations (see the discussion of reforming the Mexican internal revenue service in Das-Gupta and Mookherjee 1998). See also Theobald (1999) on the departures from Weberian principles in developed-country bureaucracies.

In other words, these reforms are likely to be effective in controlling corruption if they can be fully implemented.

The following are examples of technocratic reforms[15]:

a. improved accounting systems, or financial management programs
b. improved procurement regulations, and no-bribery pledges
c. rules providing punishment for corruption (such as loss of job and pension)
d. meritocratic recruitment of employees (e.g. by examination)
e. training programs for auditors, accountants, and inspectors
f. adequate pay for civil servants
g. increased dispersion of salaries for civil servants (with promotion based on merit)
h. measures of individual or group output, with rewards tied to performance (e.g. in tax collection agencies)
i. establishment of an independent anti-corruption agency, with broad powers of investigation and punishment (perhaps modeled on such agencies in Hong Kong and Singapore).[16]

These reforms are easy to recommend, but often are difficult to implement. Their effectiveness in controlling corruption depends critically on how they are implemented in practice. Much of the public administration literature exaggerates the benefits of the formal enactment of these reforms.

11.2.3 Strengthening Institutions of Accountability

Schedler et al. (1999) and others distinguish two types of institutions of accountability: vertical and horizontal. Vertical accountability refers to the accountability of political leaders and public officials to the public. In democracies, political leaders are held accountable through elections. Even in less-than-democratic regimes, opinions of some political groups can lead to rewards and punishments for political leaders and public officials, so that some degree of vertical accountability may exist. Civic organizations and the media play an important role in vertical accountability in collecting and publicizing information on government performance and corruption. Horizontal accountability refers to accountability between government agencies, and it arises from the separation of powers. The executive is accountable to the legislature, and both are accountable to the judiciary. Other independent agencies such as ombudsmen, anti-corruption agencies, and auditing

[15] Robert Klitgaard is perhaps the foremost proponent of the application of institutional economics and new ideas in public management in the fight against corruption (and inefficiency) in less-developed countries. Many of his writings contain practical suggestions for reformers. See Klitgaard (1988, 1997a, 1997b) and Klitgaard et al. (2000).

[16] The reform literature often cites these success stories (and that of Botswana) as models for other less-developed countries, without drawing attention to the unusual political circumstances that made them possible. The politics of Botswana's administrative state are described in section 11.4 below.

offices hold government organizations accountable. The mechanisms of horizontal accountability are also influenced by civic organizations and the media.

Measures to strengthen institutions of accountability include the following.

a. laws protecting freedom of organization and of the media
b. training programs for civic organizers and journalists
c. laws strengthening electoral integrity
d. laws and practices strengthening the independence and integrity of the judiciary
e. programs to improve the administration of law courts and training of judges and other court personnel
f. public information campaigns to inform citizens of their rights and of ways in which they can make their voices heard
g. surveys of the public's experience with public services offered by particular agencies

The effectiveness of some of these measures depends of course on the degree to which the laws are respected, and this is precisely the problem of corruption in many countries: the laws are on the books but they are ignored. They are ignored precisely because those in power do not want to share it. Much of the anti-corruption literature exaggerates the impact on corruption of enacting laws that purport to strengthen accountability.

11.2.4 Civil Society as a Solution

Civil society has recently been rediscovered in the political science literature as a vital element in supporting democracy and checking the power of governments. It certainly plays this role in the developed democracies, and many reformers have looked to civil society to play the same role in less-developed countries. There is a tendency in the reform literature to regard civil society organizations as an abstract "good thing," which serves to prevent corruption and other abuses of public power, without paying attention to the social classes and economic interests that such organizations represent (Khan 1998, pp. 113-14). However, in many of the poorest countries, civil society organizations are part of the problem, not the solution. In Khan's words (p. 126):

> In the worst performing developing countries, the dominant organizations of civil society are deeply implicated in the political impasse and in the redistributive pressures which have prevented accumulation and growth. *Presenting the problem as one of bad states which have to be disciplined by good civil societies fundamentally misrepresents this historical reality.* (emphasis in original)

The fundamental problem is that good governance is a public good affecting so many people that each person's individual economic interest in it is miniscule. To be sure, people are motivated by moral considerations, and outrage over corruption has not infrequently led to voting the rascals out (in democracies) or violent replacement of governments perceived as excessively corrupt. The challenge, and it is a daunting one, is to channel people's morality-based motivations into enduring organizations and institutions. "People power" in the Philippines that drove Ferdinand Marcos from office was motivated in large part by outrage over corruption, but the new government of Corazon Aquino, despite her personal integrity, did little to combat deeply entrenched corruption (Hutchcroft 1998). Popular indignation at corruption contributed to driving from office Presidents Ferdinand Collor of Brazil, Carlos Andres Pastrana of Venezuela, and Abdala Bucaram of Ecuador without producing enduring institutional reforms. To quote Khan again (p. 125):

> In the eighties and nineties repeated anti-corruption movements emerged in India, Pakistan and Bangladesh which collected behind them a wide range of middle class-led groups united under the anti-corruption banner. In each case the anti-corruption movements were ostensibly successful, corrupt leaders were replaced but no lasting change in social organization emerged....On the other hand, society paid the costs of these movements in the form of years of political instability and the economic disruption caused by political logjam and (in the case of Bangladesh) repeated general strikes.

The political regimes of Sub-Saharan Africa have been characterized by van de Walle (2001), Medard (2002), and others as largely autonomous from societal influences. The countries are dominated by a small "political aristocracy" (often numbering no more than a few hundred individuals (van de Walle, 2001, p. 54), bound together by largely vertical rather than horizontal ties. There is clientelism, but in contrast to Latin America and Asia,[17] the recipients of official favors have little leverage against the political elite. In many African states, there is a rich associational life separate from the state, but the state has been able to "compel the 'departicipation' of nonstate actors that might threaten the state's dominance" (van de Walle 2001, p. 47). van de Walle judges that the recent wave of elections in Africa has not yet empowered civil society to challenge the state (van de Walle 2001, pp. 256-270).[18]

---

[17] An interesting comparison of corruption in Africa and Asia is in Sindzingre (2002). In Thailand, Malaysia, and Indonesia, the Chinese business community developed institutionalized patterns of exchange with politically dominant local ethnic groups. See also Hutchcroft (1998).

[18] The autonomy of the state from society, which elsewhere has been conducive to economic policy reform, has not been so in Africa, because African states generally lack the capacity to formulate and implement programs. In short, the state institutions are extremely weak, having been compromised by the patrimonial practices of the political elite. The elite would benefit from a more prosperous economy, but the radius of trust is so narrow that the political leaders find it in their interest to weaken rather than strengthen the state bureaucracy (see van de Walle, 2001, p. 135).

11.3 Donor Agencies and the International Community in the Fight against Corruption

How can donor agencies and non-governmental organizations (NGOs) promote economic liberalization, technocratic reforms, and greater accountability? They can work with existing government structures and try either (a) to persuade the authorities to see their interests differently or (b) to use financial leverage to alter their incentives. Alternatively, they can attempt (c) to support NGOs in their efforts to strengthen civil society organizations and institutions that can pressure government agencies to curb corruption. I shall consider the effectiveness of persuasion, financial leverage, and NGO activity in promoting the three types of reforms. Subsequently, I shall assess the prospects for success of comprehensive anticorruption campaigns, and then I comment on the donors' dilemma.

11.3.1 Economic Liberalization

Economic liberalization and stabilization have been pushed by donor agencies with some success in recent decades. Financial leverage has been a powerful tool, especially in countries suffering from debt crisis, financial collapse, and extreme shortage of government revenues with which to satisfy previously dominant economic interests. I believe that intellectual persuasion of elites has also played a significant role in many instances of economic policy reform,[19] and thus to the extent that liberalization has reduced corruption, intellectual persuasion can claim part of the credit. Strengthening civil society, however, if it were possible (see below), does not necessarily promote economic liberalization.[20]

11.3.2 Technocratic Reforms

Donor agencies can play a useful role in assisting political leaders who are genuinely interested in administrative reform and the control of corruption. Indonesia under Suharto (Crouch 1979; Hutchcroft 1998), Ghana under Rawlings (Leith and Lofchie 1993; Medard 2002, p. 395), and Uganda under Museveni (Coolidge and Rose-Ackerman 2000; Watt et al 2000) are examples of improvement in public administration (in autocratic regimes) with assistance from donor agencies. (Of course, autocratic political leaders do not always need donor assistance to implement technocratic reforms, as the examples of Singapore (Lee 2000) and Hong Kong (Quah 1999) illustrate.) But in most countries politicians and government officials generally see all too clearly that their political and financial interests are best served by continuing their corrupt practices, even while they sign on to anti-

[19] See Clague (2002) for a discussion.

[20] See Callaghy (1994), Bates (1994), and van de Walle (2001) on the characteristics of civil society in Africa, and Khan (1998) on the differences among civil societies in Malaysia, Thailand, Korea, India, Pakistan, and Bangladesh.

corruption campaigns. Intellectual persuasion of these leaders has a limited role to play, as they understand the situation all too well. Financial leverage by donors is not a very effective tool for combating corruption, because donors do not have sufficient information to know what is really going on. Donors frequently come upon instances of corruption, but they are not in a position to know with confidence that a particular set of corrupt practices has really been changed.

It is possible for donor agencies to punish countries by withdrawing funds when blatant instances of corruption are revealed,[21] either in a public scandal or privately to the donor agency. This strategy seems to be implicit in some of the anti-corruption literature.[22] A problem with this strategy is that the connection between the revelation of corruption and its ongoing level is tenuous. Assistance programs in government agencies should have long time horizons, and their interruption by extraneous events like corruption scandals elsewhere in the government is likely to be disruptive. These observations are not meant to deny that donor agencies can allocate more assistance to countries and agencies that make better use of the funds, so that there can be some connection between corruption control and assistance. But financial leverage in general does not seem to be very effective in curbing corruption.

An interesting comparison can be made between corruption control and election monitoring. International observers have played quite a useful role in monitoring elections and in providing technical expertise on anti-fraud voting procedures (Pastor 1999; Eisenstadt 1999). Official election outcomes can be checked against exit polls, and blatant intimidation of voters is much easier to observe than is financial corruption. More importantly, international election observers and NGOs providing technical assistance are natural allies of opposition politicians, who have a strong interest in preventing incumbents from manipulating the results. Out of the struggle between incumbent and opposition politicians may come agreement on institutional arrangements that promote fair elections. In the fight

[21] The World Bank's position on this issue is described in Riley (1998, pp. 136-38). "The evidence of systemic corruption in itself is not a reason to withdraw the Bank's support" (quote from a Bank memorandum of 1997). But "If corruption is systemic, is affecting the Bank's projects, and a government is unwilling to act to reduce corruption, the Bank now proposes to reduce sharply or stop lending to the government concerned, although it will continue its support for NGOs and civil society organizations." (quote from Riley, p. 137).

[22] Rose-Ackerman (1999) seems to suggest that the International Financial Institutions take a tough line. On pp. 196-97 she remarks that the Bank and the Fund have taken corruption more seriously, but she continues, "Yet doubts remain about the depth of these commitments. A serious attempt to deal with the subject will require confrontations with many borrowers and with lenders whose own firms pay bribes in developing countries. The World Bank's own difficulties are easy to see in their policy document *Helping Countries Combat Corruption*... No individual country is named in the entire document except for a brief reference to three that are starting to reform." I have doubts that the Bank should be as confrontational as this passage suggests. There is also the problem that Bank staff may not be able to gain the confidence of their counterparts in host countries if the Bank becomes aggressive in exposing corruption wherever it finds it.

against corruption, on the other hand, it is difficult for international actors to find domestic allies who have a strong interest in providing the public good of honest government.

11.3.3 Enhancing Accountability through Strengthening Civil Society

Reformers often seem to regard this avenue as the ultimate solution to the problem of corruption.[23] They attempt to support organizations and movements that have the public interest at heart, relying at least in part on moral outrage against corruption. TI has been extremely successful in drawing the attention of the media around the world to the problem of corruption (Galtung and Pope 1998).[24] TI's "Corruption Perception Index" has been widely reported and has even attracted the condemnation of politicians who did not like the results.

However, the limitations on the ability of international NGOs to foster public-spirited civil society organizations are obvious. Reformers claim that they raise public awareness of corruption as a problem, but it seems that most citizens in less-developed countries already have very little confidence in the integrity and benevolence of their governments[25], but they correctly perceive that there is little that they can do about it. Situations of course vary by country, but in a large part of the less-developed world, countries are run by autocratic governments. These governments in some cases tolerate expressions of dissent, but only if the dissenters remain largely powerless. Challenging such governments is dangerous and is likely to be undertaken mainly by those with a strong private interest in doing so (i.e. by those who hope to take power themselves). Moreover, most less-developed countries have fundamentally inegalitarian social structures. Attempts to organize the lowest classes threaten the dominance of local elites, who have many tools with which to retaliate against upstarts.[26] One hopes that in the long run as devel-

---

[23] See for example, Eigen (1998), the founder of Transparency International. He states that the fight against corruption requires the cooperation of government, the private sector, and civil society, but the emphasis that TI brings to the discussion is the potential role of public-spirited civil society organizations. See also Galtung and Pope (1998, p. 279): "In the end, TI's most significant contribution, however, has been to identify and assert the role of civil society – in a broad sense – as the missing factor in previous efforts to contain corruption..."

[24] Newspaper editors are natural allies of organizations attempting to expose corruption, because stories about corruption help to increase circulation.

[25] See footnote 3 above.

[26] Husted (1999 p. 343) in a statistical study of the determinants of corruption (as measured by TI's Corruption Perception Index) finds that per capita income is the main determinant, but he also finds a positive effect of some cultural variables, notable "power distance," which is "the extent to which the less powerful members of institutions and organizations within a country expect and accept that power is distributed unequally."

opment takes place, the political culture will become more egalitarian, but that is not something that can be changed in the near term.[27]

As discussed above, the effects of democracy and of democratic transitions on corruption in less-developed countries are ambiguous, but the promotion of democracy is desirable in its own right, and the international community may contribute to this goal. However, the comparative politics literature generally supports the view that establishing and maintaining democratic political institutions depends overwhelmingly on the motivations and interests of domestic political actors; the international community has at best a marginal influence on democratization. Financial leverage seems to be the main avenue through which the international community promotes democracy. Both by providing financial assistance to fledgling democracies and by threatening to cut off assistance to actual or potential dictators, international actors have on occasion influenced political outcomes. But the limitations of this tool are obvious; these occasions are the exception rather than the rule.

The vast literature on the determinants of democratic political institutions and on the conditions favoring transitions to democracy indicates that the prospects for democracy are extremely dim in countries with low incomes, high rates of illiteracy, and ethnic divisions accompanied by past violence between ethnic groups. To be sure, there are some exceptions to the general patterns, but these exceptional countries are almost all former British colonies that had some experience with the institutions of electoral democracy and judicial independence before decolonization (Clague, Gleason, and Knack 2001). In short, there are large parts of the Third World where the structural conditions of the economy do not favor democracy and where there is no institutional history on which to build; this applies to most of Sub-Saharan Africa. In addition, the Muslim Middle East has shown little receptivity to democracy, even in countries with relatively high levels of income and education. To think that the international community through its financial leverage, technical assistance, and NGO activity can construct democratic regimes in these countries is extremely unrealistic and naïve.

11.3.4 The Prospects for Anticorruption Campaigns

Anti-corruption reformers often present outlines of reform programs (e.g., Stapenhurst and Kpundeh 1999). These involve a great many different steps, as described above under the categories economic liberalization, technocratic reforms, and strengthening institutions of accountability. One of the themes that commonly appears is that the program must be comprehensive,[28] or it must involve "all the 'pil-

---

[27] A thoughtful and cautious statement of the case for "social empowerment" as a long-term strategy for combating systemic corruption is in Johnston (1998). However, Johnston (1997) suggests that corruption control may arise through a variety of circumstances, depending on political and economic configurations.

[28] Stapenhurst and Kpundeh (1999, p. 239) state: "Although anticorruption strategies should focus on priorities, they should be comprehensive. All the agencies designed to fight cor-

lars of integrity' if a government is seriously committed to reducing corruption." (Langseth, Stapenhurst and Pope 1999, p. 147). I think a realistic assessment of the nature of political regimes in Africa, Latin America, the Middle East, South Asia, and elsewhere indicates that reforms are not going to be methodical and comprehensive. The logic that comprehensive reform is needed to change people's expectations in a move from a high-corruption to a low-corruption equilibrium makes a great deal of sense, but the political conditions for such a transformation are extremely rare. It did happen in Singapore and Hong Kong, where corruption was indeed dramatically reduced by determined and enlightened governments, but the political configurations that underlay these achievements are generally not present elsewhere (Johnston 1999). The efforts of Rawlings in Ghana and Museveni in Uganda in economic policy reform and improvements in bureaucratic performance are noteworthy, but these have depended on these particular leaders, who have not in fact been able to institutionalize a new regime (Watt et al. 2000; van de Walle, 2001, pp. 186, 276-77).

Corruption is clearly linked to economic development; statistics confirm this association both over time in individual countries and in cross sections of countries. The causation undoubtedly goes both ways: clean government, property rights, and contract enforcement enhance economic growth, and on the other hand, higher incomes and education often (not always) improve government capacity and strengthen societal pressures on government to be less corrupt (Treisman 2000; Tanzi 1998; Whitehead 2000). The anticorruption reform literature stresses the first path of causality, and urges that donors and the international community attack corruption directly, in order to promote economic growth and poverty alleviation. If this is possible, there is much to recommend it. But some economic progress can take place despite corruption. It could well be that, in light of the political feasibility of different types of assistance, the donors and the international community can make more headway in promoting development by avenues other than a direct assault on corruption.

11.3.5 The Donors' Dilemma

Donor agencies and the international community continually confront the question of whether to support individual regimes in potential recipient countries. These outsiders inevitably must make judgments on whether their assistance goals would be better served by working with the existing regime or by waiting until a better one comes along. These judgments involve the democratic character of the regime, the apparent goals of its top leadership or of the social classes it represents, and the efficiency and integrity of its public administration. An international campaign to combat corruption is bound to opt for the strategy of strengthening democracy as a remedy for corruption. In view of the intellectual triumph of democ-

ruption – prevention, investigation, research, education, and enforcement bodies – have to work in concert, harmonize their efforts, and complement each other to develop one strategy."

racy, such an international movement has little choice. The international community can hardly come out in favor of authoritarian rule. However, in the real world of foreign assistance, it seems to me that donors will often have to work with existing regimes that have many shortcomings in terms of efficiency and accountability to their people. There certainly will be occasions in which the regime is so bad that the international community should withdraw its assistance. But making assistance conditional on high standards with respect to efficiency, anti-corruption, or democracy would simply not be helpful in many countries that are far from these ideals.

11.4 Some Examples of Efforts to Control Corruption

This section discusses three examples of efforts to control corruption: civil service reform in mid-20th-century Brazil, the civil service in 19th-century America, and the civil service in contemporary Botswana. I shall try to illuminate the strength of different forces promoting or hindering reform, including especially the potential role of citizen moral outrage at corruption.

11.4.1 Civil Service Reform in Brazil

An honest and efficient civil service is a public good for society, but as is typical of public goods, it faces serious free rider problems. A major beneficiary, the general public, can seldom be mobilized to exert pressure for civil service reform. The reason is obvious: each member of the public has little to gain by it and normally is too occupied with other matters to inform herself about the issue. Voters in the electoral democracies of the Third World are typically much more influenced by personal favors from local bosses than by considerations of the public good. Civil service reform also normally confronts determined opposition from politicians who use the public administration as patronage for their political supporters and as a tool to achieve other political goals.

A number of insights about civil service reform can be drawn from Geddes' (1994) study of building state capacity in Latin America, with an emphasis on Brazil in the 1930-64 period. She combines the theoretical insights from political science and economics with a detailed knowledge of Latin American politics. First, public opinion surveys from the 1960s and 1970s in Latin America indicate that the public was well aware of corruption in government and considered it to be a serious problem for national development (see footnote 3 above). In other words, there was (and is) a latent group in favor of administrative reform (pp. 25-26). Second, she finds that collective action problems are often solved by political entrepreneurs who do not share the interests of the latent group, but instead have their own incentives for providing the public good (p. 38). (This point is reminiscent of Mancur Olson's examples of collective goods being provided by organizations that offer selective incentives to members.) Third, however, because of informational and influence asymmetries, politicians normally have incentives to provide particular benefits to some politically useful citizens rather than general benefits distributed impartially (p. 41).

Summarizing this part of her study, Geddes states,

> Since 1930, development-oriented elites in Brazil, supported by public opinion, have attempted to increase state capacity by establishing competent bureaucratic agencies capable of contributing to economic growth. Throughout the period, however, tension has persisted between reform attempts aimed at increasing bureaucratic capacity, on the one hand, and pressures for the distribution of jobs and benefits, on the other. Where agencies have been insulated from these pressures, even temporarily, their effectiveness has improved....(p.78)
>
> ...[A]ll elected officials confronted incentives in the electoral game that undermined their commitment to administrative reform...No candidate in competition with other candidates could afford to eschew such exchanges..."(p. 80)

A particularly poignant illustration of the frustrations encountered by public-spirited reformist politicians is the fate of the National Democratic Union (UDN) party. The party was organized to combat corruption and clean up Brazilian politics, and it drew some of its electoral support from the educated middle class. In spite of its vigorous anti-corruption rhetoric, in order to win elections the party had to resort to the same tactics as the other parties: offering patronage and other particularistic benefits to party supporters. The party's only successful presidential candidate was Janio Quadros, whose symbol was the broom to sweep away corruption; he resigned in 1961 after seven months in office.

One sustained effort to establish a meritocratic civil service took place during the authoritarian Estado Novo period (1937-45) under President Getulio Vargas. Vargas had been frustrated by Congressional refusal to support reform in 1930-37. After dissolving the legislature, he established the Administrative Department of Public Service (DASP). This agency attempted to transform the public bureaucracy into a modern administration: it instituted entrance examinations for the elite civil service, established rigid controls over placement, transfer, and promotion of personnel, and audited purchases of material for government use. DASP encountered stiff resistance from the bureaucracy, partly because its authoritarian methods and rigid adherence to rules ran counter to Brazilian norms and culture, but it enjoyed the strong backing of President Vargas and was able to upgrade the standards and performance of the administration. Its employees developed a strong sense of mission and esprit de corps, such that in later years elite public agencies consciously sought out and hired former DASPistas. With the collapse of the Estado Novo in 1945, democratic politicians quickly emasculated the agency and again used patronage as a tool for rewarding political supporters. An observer might regard that development as an indication of moral failing on the part of Presidents Jose Linhares (1945-46) and Eurico Dutra (1946-51), but these presidents, even if they had wanted, could not have obtained Congressional approval for preserving the civil service insulation achieved by DASP.

11.4.2 Civil Service Reform in 19th-Century America

The public administration under Washington, Adams, Jefferson, and their immediate successors was, by the standards of the time, relatively efficient and honest. Commentators compared the American administration favorably with that of Britain, where aristocratic property in office permitted private appropriation of funds, nepotism, and indifference to public welfare on the part of administrators (Skowronek 1982, p. 31; Van Riper 1958, p. 27; Rubinstein 1983). The Federalists and the Jeffersonians recruited well-educated people of high social status into the administration, and these people developed a sense of professionalism and personal integrity (Van Riper 1958, Chap. 2). The upper classes that ran the country until the Jacksonian revolution were anxious to show that the new regime of electoral democracy (with a restricted franchise) would work, and one of the driving forces behind the revolution against England had been the abuse of power by colonial governors (Nelson 1982, pp.750, 757).

The election of Andrew Jackson in 1828 marked the triumph of ordinary people over the pretensions of the Eastern gentry to continue to rule and to perpetuate themselves in the public administration (Van Riper 1958, p. 33). While the practice of the spoils system had its origin before 1829, especially at the local level, Jackson and his supporters carried the system further, and they publicly endorsed the principle of partisan rotation of public offices. The gentry professed shock at the corruption of the spoils system, but in fact partisan pressures for the efficient delivery of services constrained the inefficiency and corruption (Van Riper 1958, p.36) and even led to a modernizing bureaucratization of the Postal Service under Jackson's Postmaster General, Amos Kendall (Nelson 1982, p. 762). Moreover, the democratizing of the public service under Jackson and his followers surely helped to legitimize the American form of government for the lower classes (Van Riper 1958, pp. 55-56).

Pressure to replace the partisan spoils system with a meritocratic civil service began to build after the Civil War. Thomas Jenckes in 1867 introduced a bill to establish a Civil Service Commission, patterned after the British reforms, which was empowered to administer examinations for entry into the federal service. The bill failed to gather much support, but a reform movement was launched in the newspapers (Van Riper 1958, p. 66). With support from President Grant, Congress in 1871 authorized the president to establish a civil service commission, and Grant appointed a leading reformer, George Curtis, as its chairman. The commission began to introduce examinations in a few federal facilities, but it encountered strong resistance from Congress and received only tepid support from the president. It soon ceased to function (Van Riper 1958, p. 71; Skowronek 1982, pp. 57-59). During the late 1870s reform of the spoils system became a prominent political issue, and the reformers started to organize civil service reform associations in many states and cities. Corruption scandals fueled the campaign. Success came with the enactment of the Pendleton Act in 1883, which laid the basis for the civil service system. The Act reinstated a Civil Service Commission, endorsed the principles of recruitment by examination and protection of civil servants from partisan removal from office, and contained provisions against the assessment of office holders.

The Pendleton Act of 1883 is widely regarded as the triumph of determined and enlightened reformers over entrenched political interests (and thus might serve as inspiration for anti-corruption activists today). In the words of Van Riper (1958, p.80):

> But, for the most part, the reform was initiated and carried through by a comparatively few individuals representing the top strata of politics, law, business, journalism, and education. These few used their unusually large personal influence, their avenues of publicity, their writing ability, and their oratory to bear down heavily upon the evils of the spoils system. Thus a small group of predominantly wealthy and politically conscious easterners with a philanthropic turn of mind, aided by an aroused public opinion, laid the basis for the Pendleton Act of 1883.

These "good people" (Mosher 1968, p. 64) were helped by some accidents of history. In July 1881, shortly after his inauguration, President Garfield was assassinated by a man who turned out to be a disappointed office seeker. The newly organized reformist associations mounted a massive publicity campaign against the spoils system (Van Riper 1958, p. 92), aided by a Supreme Court decision upholding a law forbidding the assessments of office holders. However, the Republican-dominated Congress remained unmoved, until the results of the November 1882 election showed that the politicians had misjudged public opinion: The Republicans lost control of the House, losing electoral support especially in the states where the reform organizations were strongest. In addition, the reformist Democrat Grover Cleveland was elected Governor of New York (Skowronek 1958, p.66). The lame-duck Congress, still dominated by Republicans, passed the Pendleton Act in January, 1883. Part of the Republicans' motivation came from the fact that they feared losing the presidency in 1884 for the first time since 1860, and the new act would limit the ability of the new president to use the spoils to strengthen his party (Skowronek 1982, p. 66). In fact, Grover Cleveland, the New York reformer, did win the presidential election in 1884, in "the crowning achievement of the new independent reform politics" (Skowronek 1982, p. 67).

There has been a great deal of debate over the relative importance of the moralistic campaigns of the reformers versus the hard political interests of politicians and interest groups in passage of the Pendleton Act and the subsequent expansion and strengthening of the civil service. The influence of the reformers has been emphasized in the accounts by political scientists Van Riper (1958), Hoogenboom (1961), Mosher (1968), and Maranto and Schulz (1991). Skowronek's (1982) analysis, which is influenced by the new institutionalist perspective in political science, puts more emphasis on the interests of federal politicians in limiting the power of local party bosses. Economists Johnson and Libecap (1994) draw heavily on the new institutionalist and public choice literature in economics and political science in an effort to explain most of what happened in terms of the interests of vote-maximizing politicians.

There is general agreement that the Pendleton Act was only a beginning for the civil service. Only 11% of federal employees were classified under the merit system in the original Act. The subsequent expansion in coverage, which reached over 60% by 1913, occurred primarily through presidential executive order and secondarily through growth in federal employment (Skowronek 1982, pp. 70-71; Johnson and Libecap 1994, p. 58). Political assessments of office holders did decline, but this was attributed in large part to the emergence of business sources of campaign finance rather than strict enforcement of Pendleton Act provisions (Skowronek 1982, p. 75). Moreover, the Civil Service Commission prior to 1900 was weak politically and was unable to establish control over promotions, which remained in large part under the control of party loyalists (Skowronek 1982, p. 77). Nevertheless, with all its limitations, the Pendleton Act was a landmark piece of legislation, under which there gradually occurred a major transformation of the national political system from one based on spoils to one with stronger national parties and a national administration.

How much credit should be given to the moralistic campaigns of the reformers? Van Riper (1958, p. 86) observes that the language of the reformers was consistent with American culture of the period. Moral choice based on religious obligation was part of everyday speech. It is interesting that the reformist campaigners placed greater emphasis on moral reform of the political system, so that decent people could once again return to politics without being ashamed, than on efficiency and economy in government. Van Riper claims, and Skowronek agrees, that moralistic reformers rather than business people played the leading role in the movement. Business people made up about half of the civil service reform associations, but the organizers and prominent spokesmen were lawyers, journalists, academics, and clergy (Skowronek 1982, p. 53).

On the other side of the debate, Johnson and Libecap (1994) make a persuasive case that federal politicians had strong incentives to curtail the spoils system. They stress the burdens placed on members of Congress and especially the president by the large volume of job-seekers, and the difficulty these politicians encountered in monitoring patronage employees as the federal service increased dramatically in size. The president had a strong interest in limiting the number of patronage positions, in order to increase his bargaining power with members of Congress. In addition, the president was responsive to a national constituency and the nationally organized interest groups pressing for a more efficient federal service. Although individual members of Congress could benefit from rewarding their supporters with patronage, as a group they had a collective interest in limiting patronage, which was largely controlled by local party bosses. By delegating the power to expand the civil service to the president, as provided for in the Pendleton Act, Congress was able to solve its collective action problem of restraining the patronage demands of individual members. Finally, many authors argued that the executive orders expanding the classified service at the expense of patronage positions (so-called "blanketing-in" orders) were in large part carried out by lame-duck presidents trying to limit their successors' use of spoils.[29]

Even though the new institutionalist analyses of Skowronek and Johnson and Libecap find substantial evidence that hard political interests of politicians were served by the Pendleton Act and subsequent measures, their interpretations leave room for a significant influence from the politically independent reformist movement. The scandals associated with the spoils system did influence the voters in 1882 and 1884. It is obvious that there was public dissatisfaction with the corruption and inefficiency of the spoils system, and this must have been influenced by the reformers' incessant hammering away in newspapers, pamphlets, sermons, and public speeches.

The story is interesting, but the implications for anti-corruption drives in today's less-developed world are probably limited. The political systems and the political cultures in the Third World are very different from those of America in the "age of reform".[30]

11.4.3 The Civil Service in Botswana

Botswana is an extraordinary country in many ways. It was one of the poorest and least educated countries in Africa at independence in 1966, but it has enjoyed one of the highest rates of economic growth of all the countries in the world. It has done this under a regime of multi-party electoral democracy, with free speech, a free press, and free and fair elections. These accomplishments would not have occurred had it not been for the highly efficient civil service, which has been remarkably free of corruption. The civil service has maintained its efficiency and integrity despite the fact that the mechanisms of accountability are quite weak in Botswana. How did this exceptional political and administrative regime come to be?

Prior to independence in 1966, British colonial authorities fostered the emergence of an alliance among cattle ranchers (both white and Tswana), a white cattle-marketing company, and a group of moderate Tswana politicians who formed the Bechuanaland Democratic Party (BDP) in 1962.[31] The cattle industry was the only economic asset of the territory, and a marketing crisis in the 1950s led to negotiations among these interests that simultaneously involved the development of this industry, new exports of beef to Europe, and the establishment of political institutions leading to an independent state. The new Tswana political elite saw the tremendous economic opportunities to be realized by cooperating with the white marketing company and the white ranchers (who also played an important role in

[29] Johnson and Libecap (1994, pp. 60-66) argue that this phenomenon has been overemphasized.

[30] See van de Walle (1994, pp. 132-4) for a comparison of African neopatrimonialism with New York's Tammany Hall.

[31] This paragraph is based on Parson (1984) and Morrison (1993). The party name was changed to Botswana Democratic Party at independence.

bringing black-owned cattle to market), and with the colonial authorities, who were offering substantial amounts of economic assistance (Holm 1988, p. 203). In 1960-63 a more radical political party, supported by returning emigrant workers from South Africa who were imbued with doctrines from the African National Congress, posed a threat that helped to persuade the white and black elites to work together. Thus there emerged in Botswana a political coalition in which the black politicians undoubtedly held the ultimate decision-making power, but in which they found it in their interest to take advantage of the administrative and commercial skills of resident whites and foreign donors.

At independence in 1966 the public administration was largely in the hands of expatriates (Parson 1984, p. 41), as there were very few native university and even secondary school graduates. The BDP moved only gradually to replace white civil servants with blacks, adopting a policy of not "lowering standards" (Picard 1987, p. 205). In the 1969 electoral campaign the opposition parties made localization of the civil service an issue, with the aid of the Botswana Civil Servants Association, but the BDP policy of maintaining high standards was not abandoned, even though of course natives did enter the administration in increasing numbers.

Unlike other developmental states, such as Taiwan and Korea from the 1960s to the 1990s and Meiji Japan, the government in Botswana has not suppressed the opposition by force. The BDP has been returned to power at the national level in every election since independence, and it has done so without abusing the democratic constitutional rules. The early strength of the party derived from traditional tribal authority. Traditional society was very hierarchical, both within the Tswana tribe and in the dominant relationship of the Tswana to subordinate peoples (Parson 1984, p. 18; Holm 1988, pp. 181-83; Datta and Murray 1989). The newly organized BDP in the mid-1960s was composed of high-ranking Tswana tribal members, both at the national and the district levels, and this was the main source of the BDP's command of the loyalty of the vast majority of the peasantry in the pre-independence elections of 1965, where it received a decisive majority. The leader of the BDP, Dr. Seretse Khama, had been the heir to the throne of the largest tribe of the Tswana people before being deprived of the right to the throne in a conflict with the colonial authorities (Parson 1984, pp. 29-30), but he still retained the aura of royal authority.

The authoritarian and hierarchical Tswana society did contain a tradition of openness to criticism in the *kgotla* or village assembly, at which the chief listened to opinions and complaints before making his decision. The institution continued to function under the colonial administration, even though the authority of the chiefs was weakened by decisions handed down from above. At times the British used the *kgotla* as a check on the chief or to ratify the appointment by the colonial authorities of a new chief or headman (Holm 2000, p. 291). The new national government skillfully made use of the *kgotla* to sell its programs. It became customary for bureaucrats to visit *kgotla* meetings as they drew up their plans, and it has become mandatory to obtain *kgotla* approval for rural development projects (Holm 2000, p. 292).

The electoral success of the new national government was not due entirely to traditional authority and the skillful adaptation of the *kgotla*. The leadership of the

BDP also derived prestige from their high levels of education and their commercial success. Dr. Khama assembled around him a group of "new men" possessed of a progressive, commercial outlook, many of whom did not enjoy tribal authority. In addition, the sound policies followed by the new administration led to rapid economic growth, which was assisted mightily by the discovery of diamonds and other minerals and their exploitation by efficient foreign companies (Holm 1988, p. 199). Foreign donors poured in money and expertise, which the competent administration was able to use effectively to build physical infrastructure and to expand education and health services (Harvey and Lewis 1990; Norberg and Blomstrom 1993). Finally, the BDP was well financed through contributions from commercial interests and was able to deliver extra material benefits to its supporters at all levels (Holm 1988, p. 190).

Thus a political coalition formed by a series of unusual historical circumstances created a strong administration leading to a rapidly growing economy. What has been the role of the civil service in Botswana's political regime? Botswana seems to have been a technocrat's dream. The civil service seems to manage the politicians and the electorate rather than the other way around. Patrick Molutsi is a native Botswanan with a PhD in sociology from Oxford, now teaching at the University of Botswana. In two papers (Molutsi 1994a, 1994b) he characterizes the ruling class as composed of five elements: elected representatives, traditional rulers, the bureaucracy (senior officials in the public, parastatal, and private sectors), the business elite, and livestock and crop farmers. His thesis is that the bureaucracy is dominant. The civil servants formulate policy, sell it to the Members of Parliament (whose educational level is not high and who are not well informed) and to the local councilors (who are much less educated than the MPs), and see to its implementation. Despite the upper class status of the top levels of the bureaucracy and the political elite, some important government programs have served the interests of the poorer segments of the population.

A complementary picture is painted by Holm and his co-authors (Holm 1988 and 2000; Holm et al. 1996; Somolekae 1994). Botswana's democracy is not based on vigorous civil society putting pressure on the government. Civil society organizations have emerged only slowly since independence, and a good share of them have relied on foreign funding. Government requirements that social groups must have a constitution, elect their leaders, and maintain records imposes impossible limits on organizations composed mainly of illiterates (Holm et al. 1996, p. 51) and favors educated communities. Some groups are formed to cooperate with government ministries in delivering services, and these are in no position to challenge the government. Civil servants insist that civil society groups approach the government through the bureaucracy rather than through the politicians (Holm, et al. 1996, p. 56). Civil society groups do not try to pressure politicians, and politicians do not attempt to mobilize civil society support (Holm 2000, p. 299).

Botswana's democracy is not based on vigorous inter-party competition, either. Opposition parties are free to criticize the government, and an opposition party has won control of some local councils and the mayoralty of the capital city, but their appeal has been limited to one or two ethnic groups (Holm 2000, p. 297). The more important political competition exists between two factions of the dominant

BDP (Holm 2000, p. 295); one faction supports civil-service domination of policy making, while the other, constituency-oriented faction seeks particularistic benefits, especially for local business interests. Policy, however, still seems to reflect the national orientation of the civil service.[32]

In short, mechanisms of vertical accountability in Botswana are weak. Civil society does not have much control over the politicians, and neither the politicians nor civil society groups control the civil service. However, some mechanisms of horizontal accountability are strong. The judiciary and the Attorney General are independent of the politicians, and they have investigated cases of corruption and made public their findings, resulting in the resignation of cabinet members (Holm 2000, p. 292). The land boards and the police are also independent and apparently quite free of corruption. The press has been free to criticize the government, and while the Attorney General has taken newspapers to court, he has never won (Holm 2000, p. 290).

It does not seem that Botswana's highly successful political and administrative regime offers much in the way of lessons for most other African countries. A series of historical accidents has permitted the creation (by enlightened political leadership) of a most unusual configuration of political and economic institutions. Social scientists have often argued that restraints on government and the rule of law have come about in the West through struggle between competing interests.[33] This idea underlies the strategy of combating corruption by strengthening civil society. But this is not how a relatively corruption-free regime has emerged in Botswana.

11.5 Concluding Comments

The anti-corruption campaign led by Transparency International and other reformers has succeeded in attracting a great deal of attention to corruption as an obstacle to economic development.[34] TI in particular has contributed to the collection and dissemination of new data on corruption. New research, much of it conducted by or under the auspices of the World Bank, has increased our knowledge about the causes and effects of corruption, and these advances are likely to continue as surveys become more detailed and sophisticated. In addition, the campaign by reformers has strengthened the resolve of the rich democracies to curtail the bribery offered by multinational corporations. However, the rhetoric of the campaign is extremely ambitious in its endeavor to reduce the level of corruption in the less-

---

[32] For example, foreign companies remain free to compete with local business on an equal footing.

[33] Schedler (1999, p. 304); see Collins (1980) on Weber's theory of the emergence of capitalism.

[34] In a speech to the International Monetary Fund on February 20, 2002, Cardinal Oscar Andres Rodriguez, the Bishop of Tegucigalpa, identified corruption as the number one global threat (IMF Survey, Feb. 25, 2002, p. 60).

developed world. Without wishing to deny that there have been some concrete improvements in governance resulting from the campaign, I have suggested in this chapter that the gains on the ground are likely to be modest in relation to the rhetoric.

My argument is not an apology for corruption. I don't deny that institutional deficiencies are the major obstacle to development in poor countries, and I applaud the increased emphasis that donors have given to governance and institutional reform in less-developed countries. My concern is with the methods for promoting this institutional reform. I have attempted in this chapter to make the following points. First, corruption is not the only problem (not even the only institutional problem) confronting less-developed countries, and it may be possible for donors and the international community to help some countries develop, even without directly attacking or significantly reducing the level of corruption. Some of the reform rhetoric suggests that corruption is so harmful that no progress in development can be achieved without drastically reducing the level of corruption.[35] While I agree that some countries are so badly governed that donors should withhold their assistance until there is a change in regime, there are many where this is not the case. Second, it is in the nature of reform campaigns (such as the one supporting the Pendleton Act) to arouse moral outrage in order to get citizens to act against corruption. Moral outrage often leads to bursts of citizen protests or voting the rascals out, but it forms a weak basis for sustained political activity. Moreover, by increasing the stridency of public discourse, anti-corruption rhetoric can contribute to political instability, with harmful economic consequences. Third, this chapter has argued that the forms of corruption that arouse the greatest moral outrage are not the same as those forms that most seriously impede economic and social development. Reform movements have their own logic; in order to gather support for their anti-corruption activities, public-interest organizations play up the issues that attract the most attention, rather than the ones that cause the most harm. Fourth, I think there is a tendency among anti-corruption activists to call for excessively high standards of integrity, especially in connection with the financing of political parties. Strong political parties are essential to well-functioning democracies, and political activists need to be rewarded for their efforts. Political patronage is not an unmitigated evil.[36] Fifth, history illustrates, as Mancur Olson ex-

[35] Doig and Theobald (2000, p. 7) state "Currently, the curtailment of grand corruption is seen as essential for good government which, in turn, is regarded as the *sine qua non* of sustainable economic development." Watt et al. (2000, p. 51) state "It is now widely accepted that in the absence of a vigorous civil society, administrative measures aimed at combating corruption will achieve little." However, Ghana improved the quality of its bureaucracy from 1 to 4 (on a 0 to 6 scale in the ratings by International Credit Risk Guide) from 1982 to 1990 (as cited in Easterly 2001, p. 251). Civil society was not active in the Rawlings regime (van de Walle 2001, p. 29).

[36] As Hutchcroft (2002 p. 506) put it, citing Huntington (1968): "...to the extent that corruption builds political parties, it undermines the conditions of its own existence..." [Historically, he continues, political parties of the West which were initially] "leeches on the bu-

plained, that there have been different routes to improved governance, some of which involve stronger civil society putting pressure on governments, and others of which involve the concentration of power and the controlling of corruption to serve the interests of a ruling group or class. Reform activists, often assuming that all good things go together, tend to push for the strengthening of civil society and for decentralization of government, even in societies with dismal prospects for such reforms. In the cases of the worst performing governments, ambitions need to be suitably modest. Finally, I suggest that donor agencies, in their dialogues with host governments, might consider returning to the more neutral terminology of "governance" and "public administration" rather than the inflammatory and polarizing rhetoric of corruption.

reaucracy in the end became the bark protecting it from the more destructive locusts of clique and family."

12 The Public Promotion of Private Interest (Groups)

John Joseph Wallis

Mancur Olson's work drew attention to two fundamental connections in the structure of human societies. In *The Logic of Collective Action* Olson described how individuals voluntarily come together to pursue common goals, when those goals included, at the limit, the provision of public goods that benefited everyone. In the *Rise and Decline of Nations* Olson described how these interest groups, once formed, exercise their organizational muscle to persuade governments to redistribute income and wealth in their favor at the expense of the larger society. The accumulation of these "redistributional coalitions" eventually slows the rate of economic growth. In his final years, Olson began grappling with how governments could promote economic development through "market augmenting" policies. It is interesting that, while Olson's stationary bandit and the encompassing interests of large democratic political coalitions share *the logic* of his earlier work, interest groups themselves play very little role in the process of promoting economic growth. Market augmenting government policies emerge from the fiscal interests of the state, not the interaction of voluntarily organized groups.

One of Mancur Olson's defining characteristics as a person and a scholar was burning intensity and focus. He followed his line of thinking with a single minded tenacity. His concentration on how individuals formed groups and how groups influenced governments led him to place less emphasis on the fact that governments form groups and groups influence individuals. This chapter explores the way in which governments promote or retard the formation of organizations of all types, public and private and extends what Olson might have said had his research moved in this direction. It builds on the salient historical fact that in those times and places when governments loosen their restrictions on the formation of organizations -- and the tendency for governments is almost universally to restrict rather than promote organizations within their midst -- and begin promoting the formation of a wide range of private and public organizations, then we observe rapid and sustained modern economic growth. The specific historical example is the early nineteenth century United States. The U.S. experienced an explosive proliferation of all types of organizations actively supported by governments, particularly state governments, at the same time that it began growing at the sustained and modern rate of 1.5 percent per year per capita. This chapter turns the prediction of *Rise and Decline* on its head: the onset of modern economic growth is associated with a rise in the number of organizations.

12.1 Some Propositions

The basic argument can be summarized in four related propositions:

1. The degree of economic productivity of any society is a function of the degree of specialization and division of labor.

The proposition could be stated in a stronger form as the major source of economic growth is specialization and division of labor. Such a claim would immediately become entangled in debate over the independent role of technology and factor accumulation (resources, physical capital, and human capital). As I will discuss later, the argument is not dependent on which source of growth dominates.

2. The degree of specialization and division of labor is limited by the extent of the market.
3. The extent of the market is limited by the nature of organizations operating within the market.

By "nature" I mean the scope, range, depth, and density of the existing organizations. Individuals in a state of nature rarely find themselves in face to face contact with other, unknown individuals with whom they wish to trade. Exchange requires either a framework of repeated interaction or third party enforcement of agreements before anything much of value can be traded. Organizations are a way to regularize repeated dealings through organizational forms such as partnerships and through specialization in trading which increases the number of interactions between a small number of traders. Organizations of all types, public and private, religious and secular, fraternal and competitive, also provide frameworks for third party enforcement of contracts. The extent of the market is limited by the extent of organizations operating in that market.

4. The nature and extent of organizations is limited by the government.

In most societies, governments place significant limits on what organizations are allowed to exist and further limits on what organizations are allowed to do. For much of human history, any organization of individuals was a potential military threat.[1] Throughout the middle ages, trade over any distance was carried out only by individuals operating in organizations who had obtained permission to enter into foreign domains. It was not until the 1820s that individuals were allowed to form organizations with the privileges of corporate status without applying to the crown or the legislature. As late as the 1770s, individuals who did not belong to a recognized church in Massachusetts were forced to support the state sponsored church, in Virginia the Anglican church was not disestablished until 1785, and in

---

[1] "P. Grierson has drawn attention to stipulations in the laws of Ine, king of Wessex which call for the following distinctions to be made among aggressors: if there are less than seven they are simply thieves; if they are more numerous, they constitute a band of brigands; but if there are over thirty-five, they may fairly be taken for an army" Duby (1974, p. 49).

their revolutionary constitutions several states still required office holders swear an oath that they were good protestant Christians.[2]

Together these four propositions can be combined into the following statement:

If governments limit the extent of organizations,
Then the extent of the market will be limited,
Then the degree of specialization and division of labor will be limited, and
The level of economic productivity will be reduced.

This statement is logically complete: if governments limit organizations they will lower the level of economic productivity. In logical terms, relaxing the limits that governments impose on organizations does not necessarily lead to an increase in the extent of the market, the degree of specialization and division of labor, and the level of economic productivity. Nonetheless, it is an intriguing possibility. Do economies grow and develop when governments allow more and more varied organizations to exist? It is a question that modern economics, economic development, and economic history have failed to ask.

12.2 A Framework

The concepts of individuals, organizations, governments, institutions and markets are generically defined, but what, if any, special connotations do they have here?

Individuals are individual human beings. They interact with each other in a number of different ways. Some interactions between individuals occur within markets, others occur in a variety of social environments.

Organizations are distinct from groups -- here I differ from Olson. A group is any number of individuals with a common interest. A group can be a crowd of people waiting at a bus stop (the bus being the common interest), tobacco farmers, or all people over seven feet tall. An organization is a group of people who act in a

---

[2] Article 22 of the Delaware constitution of 1776 required that:

> Every person who shall be chosen a member of either house, or appointed to any office or place of trust, before taking his seat, or entering upon the execution of his office, shall take the following oath, or affirmation, if conscientiously scrupulous of taking an oath, to wit: I, A B [name], will bear true allegiance to the Delaware State, submit to its constitution and laws, and do no act wittingly whereby the freedom thereof may be prejudiced.
>
> And also make and subscribe the following declaration, to wit:
>
> I, A B [name], do profess faith in God the Father, and in Jesus Christ His only Son, and in the Holy Ghost, one God, blessed for evermore; and I do acknowledge the holy scriptures of the Old and New Testament to be given by divine inspiration.
>
> And all officers shall also take an oath of office.

The passage of the "Statute of Religious Freedom" in Virginia on December 17, 1785 was the central act in providing religious freedom in Virginia, and also played a key role ion shaping Madison's thoughts about the organization of political society in America, as discussed by Banning (1995, pp. 84-97, 101-102).

coordinated manner.[3] Organizations can be as loosely organized as my wife's book group or as tightly organized as a football team. They range in size from the very small to the very large. Membership in an organization can be limited or completely open. The structure of an organization can be highly articulated, contractual, and enforced by legal systems or it can be casual and voluntary. In Olsonian terms, an interest group need not be an organization, it could simply be a group of individuals with a common interest, but only organizations pursue collective action – coordinated behavior.

In *The Logic,* Olson focused on a subset of organizations in which membership was voluntary and the coordinated action of the members was directed toward the production of a public good. He was uninterested in the existence of profit maximizing firms and why they were able to coordinate individual action through the use of wages and other economic incentives: there was no challenge in understanding why they existed. Given the focus of *The Logic* on the problem of collective action, this emphasis was appropriate. Although Olson continued to identify voluntary organizations as his focus *Rise and Decline,* he had, in fact, switched his focus. *Rise and Decline* is about the growth of redistributive coalitions, and many of those coalitions and actors are themselves profit maximizing firms or organizations. The distinction between profit maximizing firms and voluntary groups, even in Olson's own terms, is a matter of degree rather than structure. There is no bright line separating voluntary and profit maximizing firms in this chapter.

The limits to successful organization in pursuit of any collective goal, either public or private, depend on the size of the group and the availability of selective incentives. Members of small groups can more easily monitor each other's behavior and see that agreements are enforced. Selective incentives allow the group leaders to insure cooperation in the provision of the collective good by allowing access to valued group benefits that only cooperators can enjoy. Profit maximizing organizations have ready access to selective incentives – work or you do not get paid – and thus do not, in Olson's world, face the same problems as voluntary organizations. The recent spate of corporate accounting fraud a la Enron, however, highlights just how difficult in is for a profit maximizing organization to insure cooperative behavior. Some of Enron's owners, the stockholders, were unable to elicit appropriate behavior on the part of their partners, the stock option holding management. Selective incentives may always exist for profit maximizing firms, but they don't always work. In the absence of effective selective incentives, even profit maximizing firms will not come into existence.

I accept Olson's logical assertion that in the absence of small numbers or selective incentives organizations will not arise. But many of the selective incentives that organizations use to coordinate their members are not inherently incentive compatible, that is, they are not self-enforcing relationships. Many organizations rely on the use of third party enforced agreements to structure their internal affairs. To the extent that governments are the third parties used to enforce agreements, the range of selective incentives available to organizations depends on the range of

[3] So all organizations are groups, but not all groups are organizations, since not all groups act in a coordinated manner.

contractual arrangements that the government agrees to enforce. The existence of public and private organizations, of voluntary and for profit organizations depends on the policies of the government towards organizations.

What then is a government? Barzel (2002, p.22) defines a state as:

> The *state* consists of (1) a set of individuals who are subject to a single ultimate third party who uses violence for enforcement and (2) a territory where those individuals reside, demarcated by the reach of the enforcer's power.[4]

The government is the "single ultimate third party enforcer." While governments are not the only third party enforcer, they are the ultimate third party enforcer because of their superior access to violence.[5] No government agrees to be a third party enforcer to any and every agreement that individuals and organizations make. Governments limit the kind of contracts they will enforce.[6] Because they limit the kind of arrangements they will enforce, governments explicitly place limits on the selective incentives available to organizations.

The entirety of society – individual, organizations, and governments – operates within a set of endogenous institutions.[7] Institutions are the rules of the game: the social norms, laws, formal rules, and informal arrangements that structure human relationships. A full description of the institutions in a society would require descriptions of the institutions governing the autonomous behavior of individuals, organizations, and governments as well as descriptions of the interaction of those groups. The relationship between governments and organizations, that is, how governments constrain or promote the activities of organizations, is of particular interest in this chapter, but it is only one of six possible relationships.

My definition of a market again draws on Barzel (2002). He distinguishes between economic and legal rights. Economic rights are what you actually possess, legal rights are what a third party enforcer will delineate and enforce. "Contractual exchange" is the exchange of goods and services whose rights are legally defined and supported. The market is the sum of all contractual exchange between individuals, organizations, and governments. Many exchanges and interactions between individuals, between organizations, and between individuals and organizations do no involve contractual exchange and are thus outside of the market. For example, many of the activities within a church are reciprocal exchange, but not within the context of the market. In the early twenty-first century United States most impersonal exchange occurs within an explicit, if sometimes background, framework of third party enforcement, and thus is almost completely market exchange.

---

[4] Many of the ideas in this chapter are discussed in greater detail and sophistication in Barzel's excellent book.

[5] Barzel's discussion of power is especially interesting. Power is the ability to impose costs on other individuals. Governments, organizations, and individuals all possess power, governments just garner a larger share of theirs from the threat of violence.

[6] See Hurst's (1956) discussion of the development of American commercial law as an example of just this point.

[7] The concepts of institutions and organizations follow the lines suggested by North (1990).

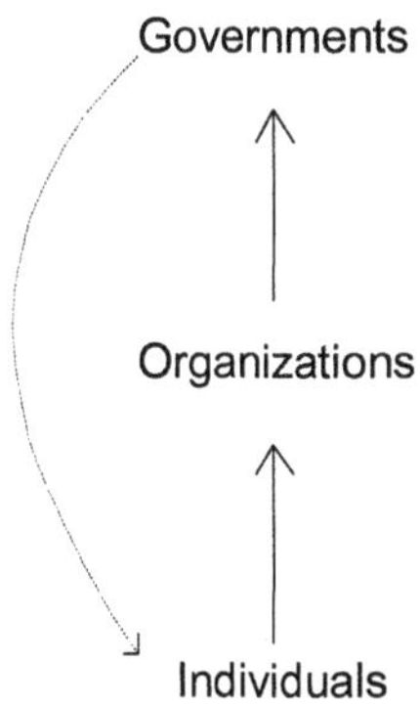

Fig. 1. Olson's framework

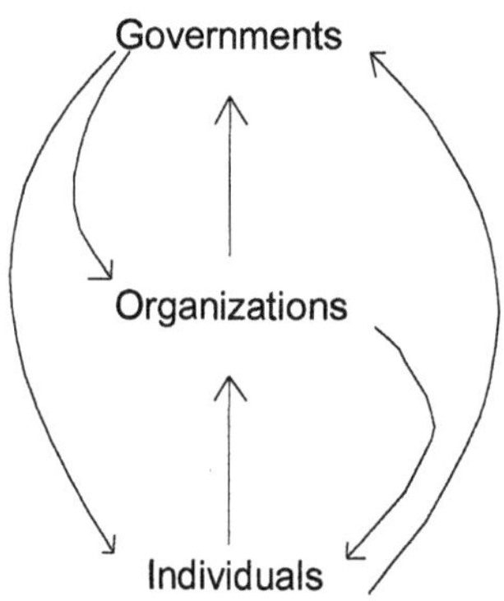

Fig. 2. Wallis's framework

12.2.1 Connections

Figure 12.1 depicts a stylized way to think about the connections between individuals, organizations, and governments. Olson focused on two of the possible six connections. *The Logic* examined how individuals came together to form organizations, *Rise and Decline* how those organization used their influence on governments to redistribute income to themselves.[8] In "Dictatorship, Democracy, and Development" and *Power and Prosperity*, Mancur began asking how government affected individuals, the dotted outside line in the figure. Figure 12.2 shows all of the relevant pairs are connected and their relationships should be examined.

Economics and political science usually focus on the pair of relationships between governments and individuals. In the simplest explanation for why economies grow, political systems become democratic and the interaction between the voters and the government lead the government to adopt policies that promote the well being of the voters in order to secure reelection. This virtuous cycle, however attractive, appears to be inconsistent with the logic of collective choice.[9] That is, there is no automatically self-enforcing political-economic equilibrium in which democracy leads to economic growth and happiness. A great deal of economic theory and its applications are about the effect of governments on individuals. A great deal of political theory and its applications are about the effect of individuals on government. For two centuries now, a primary concern of both disciplines has been to discover how governments can be constrained in their relationships with individuals to promote secure property rights, the rule of law, and the economic development that follows.

The second pair of relationships is between individuals and organizations. Economic theory posits rational individuals who interact via the market to maximize individual utility. Organizations (in this case firms) are just another kind of individual with slightly more complicated internal dynamics, but a much simpler objective function: firms maximize profits rather than utility. In the simplest of economic worlds there is only production and consumption. All decisions about the allocation of production and consumption, about the distribution of goods and services across individuals and firms are made impersonally by the market.

When individuals interact in a market, however, they face positive transaction costs. They do not have complete information about the nature of their trading partner, about all relevant prices, about the quality of the good or service they are purchasing or selling, and they cannot costlessly write enforceable contracts. People have developed millions of ways to deal with these problems, and we can heroically characterize them as one of two types. One solution to the problem of costly exchange is repeated interaction between individuals. At the simplest level, repeat dealing allows pairs of individuals to develop trust in one another. At a higher level, repeat dealing in the context of a community enables some individuals to develop a reputation for honesty, probity, product quality, trustworthiness, or some other desirable quality through repeated specialization in an activity. Individuals with, for example, a reputation for honesty earn rents from the perception that they can be honest third parties, and the loss of those potential rents in the future creates an incentive for the honest to remain honest. The second solution to the problem of costly exchange is the use of third party enforcement mechanisms. Parties to an exchange agree to involve a third party, who may be an individual,

[8] I do not mean to imply in any way that Olson was not aware that all of the connections were important, only that he focused on two in his work.

[9] See Buchanan and Tullock (1962) and Downs (1957).

organization, or government, to resolve disputes and disagreements over terms of their exchange.[10] Third party enforcement takes many forms and is ubiquitous in modern developed economies.

Individual people interacting through a primitive market with only individual participants (that is, without any organizations) face very high transaction costs. Goods cannot move across long distances because it is costly for individuals to develop reputations across long distances. We expect to see, and indeed do see historically, the emergence of individuals who specialize in creating relationships with like minded individuals across long distances. We call these people traders. In order to perform their task, traders must be heavily networked. They must possess reputational capital that allows them to enact trades in multiple geographic locations and they must be connected, at home, to a distribution network of "retailers and wholesalers" with whom they had reputational capital. At the heart of every trader's network are a set of durable, bilateral, and reciprocal relationships with people the trader trusts exceptionally: his partners. Partners act in a coordinated manner to pursue common goals. In a word, partnerships are organizations.

No market beyond a simple gathering place for local produce can function without the organizational support of partnerships. This is the canonical example of how the extent of organizations limits the extent of the market. It is possible for a ruby mined in India to end up in Britain through a long series of impersonal hand to hand exchanges, without the agency of an organization. Such links, however, are historically irrelevant. Trade over any substantial distance historically is always supported by organizations. In the beginning, trade is supported by simple organizations, such as partnerships, whose internal relationships are governed by self-enforcing reputational arrangements. By the end of the 18th and beginning of the 19th century, organizationally simple but economically sophisticated firms composed of a few partners, such as Barings and Browns, conducted extensive trade operations throughout the world. Moreover, long distance trade, from the earliest times, regulated and supported (or suppressed) by governments.

It would be exceedingly naive and narrow minded to argue that the origin of human organization is to be found in trade. People need to belong to organizations and groups. Human beings are social animals whose very utility/well-being/happiness is determined in part by the social relationships they maintain. People organize for many reasons other than the production and consumption of goods and services. Religion, procreation, mutual defense, and mutual interests head the list.[11] While participation in these organizations yields returns that can be physically measured, it also seems that belonging, in and of itself, is a valued activity. People define who they are in terms of the people they interact with and

[10] From the definition of a market given earlier, it is clear that all exchange enforced by a third party is market exchange, that is, contractual exchange, while reputation enforced exchange may or may not be market exchange.

[11] I am fully aware that all of these organizations can be thought to provide a good or service, and thus are "economic," but at that point what is economic versus what is sociological loses all meaning. All is economics.

how they interact.[12] The strongest evidence of this comes from studies of health in large organizations. Upper level managers, subject to the stress, strain, and long working hours of their jobs, live significantly longer than workers in low stress, low responsibility jobs: one's place in the organization even has biological implications. It must be acknowledged that organizations exert a tremendous influence on the behavior of their members. Comparing the behavior of individuals across geographic regions or across societies without reference to the organizations that constrain and shape their behavior, is certain to be a frustrating exercise.

How then do we explain the existence and structure of organizations? One approach is to focus on the connections between individuals and organizations. This is the approach of industrial organization and of Mancur Olson in *The Logic*. The other approach is to focus on the connections between governments and organizations, the last pair in the framework. This way of thinking about organizational development has been neglected. Based on the assumption that human organization is ubiquitous, the limited number of organizations that we find in undeveloped economies must be the result of some other constraint.[13] The constraints that government places on the number and type of organizations shape the existence and structure of organizations until that constraint is relaxed. Until the last two hundred years in the politically liberal democracies of the developed world, organizations have never been free to develop as they pleased. The "right to organize" was as severely restricted as any individual liberty.

An important element in the development of organizations and their relationship to government is the second solution to the problem of high transaction costs trade: third party enforcement. Parties to an exchange may significantly lower their transactions costs *ex ante* if they can agree on a third party who will, *ex post*, resolve disputes between the parties. The use of a third party involves several requirements: a third party whom both the first and second party trust (either because of the third party's inherent character or because the third party is himself constrained to be impartial and honest by reputational considerations or other third party arrangements); a willing third party; and an *ex ante* agreement on the jurisdiction of the third party and the rules under which decisions are to be rendered. The last requirement is enormously important. Third parties never agree to enforce any and all contracts. The type of contracts that third parties will and can enforce shapes the structure of individual contracting and market exchange, but it also shapes the structure of organizations.

Organizations are natural places for members to resolve their disputes and for third party enforcement arrangements to evolve. Grief's (1989) Mahgribi traders, for example, are an organization that developed sophisticated internal third party arrangements to enforce contracts between members, enforced by incentive compatible collective choice action on the part of the whole organization. Not only can

---

[12] For an attempt to understand some these issues in an economic framework see Akerlof and Kranton (2000).

[13] For evidence on the limited number of groups in developing countries relative to developed countries see Knack (2003), Knack and Keefer (1997b), and Coates and Heckelman (2003).

organizations provide third party services to their members, they can also market third party services to non-members. An integral part of the financial services of a firm such as Barings or Browns was assuring individuals who dealt with the firm that the contracts they were making through the agency of the firm, would be enforced with the resources of the firm. So a cotton grower in Mississippi selling to a textile firm in Manchester through Barings, could rely on Barings to see that the terms of the sale were met. An integral part of the services of an intermediary is the provision of third party enforcement.

Governments and organizations are always potential competitors in the provision of third party enforcement. Since governments are themselves organizations, any private organization is always a potential threat to the government. Following Barzel, governments are the ultimate third party enforcers who use, or threaten to use, violence to enforce their decisions. Governments never have a monopoly on power or violence (everyone has some power and any person can become violent), but governments that rule by force rather than agreement have strong incentives to minimize the amount of violence potential possessed by their subjects. Since the effective use of violence requires coordination and leadership, violence is always more effectively deployed by organizations. This leads to the following conjecture:

Conjecture 1: Under the right conditions, particularly when governments rule by force or their tenure as the government is uncertain, governments view all organizations as potential military threats. Under these conditions government will limit the number and type of organizations that are allowed to exist, will regulate the internal structure of the organizations that do exist, and will prohibit all other organizations from forming.

This conjecture is not absolute, nor everywhere binding. Yet, in many societies the level of development of organizations is quite limited. For most of human history, any significant number of organized men was a potential military force. American law inherited from British law the concept of "conspiracy": whenever two or more are gathered together a conspiracy is possible. For a time in the Soviet Union, in Communist China, and other statist societies the right to form any organization was monopolized by the state.

While states rarely monopolize all organizations, they do have an incentive to limit them. First, states themselves are organizations whose ability to create and project violence requires significant coordination. Military action requires a hierarchy of authority, thus a hierarchy of organization. Only modern nation-states find it feasible to maintain a large standing army. The government must possess a preponderance of military authority, but the leader's military authority is maintained through the allegiance and cooperation of lesser military leaders. The "king" creates or recognizes the military authority and organizations of his subordinates. He must continually devote his attention to maintaining incentive compatible arrangements with the lesser military leaders and stay on top of a constantly changing and evolving political/military situation.[14]

[14] I tend to think of this problem in terms of feudalism, but the problems described here are not unique to northwestern Europe.

In a parallel fashion, governments have an incentive to create organizations in order to obtain the resources necessary to rule. For the feudal king, fiscal and military requirements were identical: he raised an army directly in the form of the military service of earls, dukes, and knights rather than in the form of tax revenues to hire military labor. For all governments, however, access to tax revenues at relatively low costs requires physically tapping into the exchange of goods and services. Conceptually, governments have incentives to create markets by allowing organizations that promote market exchange to form, because the very existence of the organizations produces lower cost sources of revenue to the government. Historically, the commercial history of Europe in the Middle Ages is replete with examples where governments create and promote the existence of organizations whose primary use to the government is mobilizing fiscal and military resources. In northern Europe free towns with written charters developed when powerful lords granted the towns the physical and economic freedom from expropriation necessary to develop markets, in return for a steady flow of tax revenues from the town's markets. In Italy, city-states such as Venice and Genoa, developed where the state and the traders were identical. Within the "commune" of the political body the interests of the traders and the government were identical.

The fiscal side of the relationship between governments and organizations is of primary importance. North (1981) and Olson both begin their theories of the state with "revenue maximizing monarchs". Military considerations prevent any ruler from being strictly revenue maximizing, so a critical "ceteris paribus" condition always applies. Nonetheless, the fiscal interests of government are the place to investigate how and why governments create organizations.[15] The driving force in the relationship is a *quid pro quo*: the government grants a special privilege or franchise to a specific organization, in return for which the organization provides revenues to the government. Keep in mind that the historical, if not theoretical, starting point for this development is an economy with very limited markets, low levels of specialization and division of labor, very high transaction costs, and endemic violence, e.g. Europe around 1000 A.D. The *quid pro quo* leads directly to another conjecture:

Conjecture 2: When governments do not have access to broad, market based, low cost tax instruments (e.g. sales, property, or income taxes), it will often be in the government's interest to generate revenue by granting special privileges to a limited number of organizations. By their very nature, the value of these special grants of privilege, and thus the revenues that the government realizes from making the grants, is higher when the number of organizations receiving the grants is smaller. As a result, there is an inherent fiscal motivation to limit absolutely the number of organizations the government creates for fiscal purposes.[16]

---

[15] In my own work I have tried to develop a "fiscal interest" model of government behavior, and to tie that model to the behavior of American state governments in the 19th century. See Heckelman and Wallis (1997), Wallis, Sylla, and Legler (1994), and Wallis (2000, 2002).

[16] One can illustrate the conjecture with the granting of bank charters by American states in the early nineteenth century. States could sell bank charters to organizations, but the

This conjecture is the heart of the chapter. Governments have natural reasons to treat private organizations as potential competitors and so to limit their numbers and nature. At the same time, if the number of organizations is limited, there are substantial rents to be had by the organizations that do exist. The government taps into these rents by charging for the privilege of having an organization. The amount the government can charge for the privilege, however, is a decreasing function of the number of organizations the government creates, resulting in a "revenue maximizing" number of organizations that is less than we observe with free entry into organizations.

Tax farming is an obvious case of granting special privileges to a limited number of organizations, common in both England and France. Regulation of foreign trade was another source of rents. In England in the 14th, 15th, and 16th century, the monarch constantly attempted to maximize the value of the taxes imposed on wool exports, a policy that typically resulted in granting a monopoly on the wool staple (control over the export of wool to the continent).[17] Sometimes monopoly rights over foreign trade in England were granted to English merchants, but there were time when it was in the fiscal interest of the English king to grant the monopoly rights to German merchants.

The limitation of organizations, in turn, produces "rent seeking" behavior on the part of the organizations. There is both a supply and a demand side to this market. The organizations owe their existence not to the provision of low cost/high quality services to the market, but instead to the provision of revenues and political favors to the government. Pursuit of these rents creates an opportunity for incentive compatible relationships between the government and the organizations. Kings and dictators perpetually worry about assassination and coups. By creating rents for a small number of powerful associates, and surrounding oneself with those associates, the king purchases some modicum of security. Since contracts with the king, by their very nature, cannot be enforced by third parties, the rents created by limiting organizations open up the possibility for incentive compatible reputational relationships between the government and the limited organizations.[18]

As an example, in his history of British government finance in the 18th century, Brewer reaches the following conclusion about the nature of financial markets and the interaction between the government and financial markets in the 17th century:

value of the bank charter was a decreasing function of the number of banks chartered by the state. The revenue maximizing number of bank charters occurred where the demand for bank charters was unit elastic, and that number of banks was likely to be far less than the number of banks that would come into existence under a system of open entry with a fixed fee, such as the free banking systems that developed after the 1830s. For empirical substantiation of this assertion see Wallis, Sylla, and Legler (1994).

[17] See Postan's (1987) discussion in the *Cambridge Economic History*.

[18] Greif, Milgrom, and Weingast's (1994) characterization of the merchant guild in medieval Europe illustrates how limited organizations with special access to governments can arrange incentive compatible arrangements that constrain both the rulers and the traders.

Such seventeenth-century bankers had a way of worming themselves into the fabric of the state. In order to recoup their loans, or at least to protect their interest, they combined lending to the monarch with tax farming, the operation of monopolies granted by royal fiat, or the tenure of offices in the fiscal apparatus. All of these provided financiers with privileged access to royal income which thereby acted as collateral for the king's loans. This meant that it was difficult to identify clearly a 'financial interest' when the government's creditors were neither state fish nor society fowl. (Brewer 1990, p. 207)

This is the world Mancur Olson described in the *Rise and Decline of Nations*. A number of small, well organized groups used their collective weight to influence government to redistribute income to them at the cost of the larger public welfare. This predatory state was Olson's stationary bandit. It actively uses its ability to regulate the number and nature of organizations to create rents that it can tax, increasing its revenues at the same time that it reduces overall output (*ceteris paribus*). All of the predictions of *Rise and Decline* go through at this stage of economic development.

In addition, as is often the case when dealing with organizations, the social implications are more far reaching than the economic. Just as governments have an incentive to limit organizations to maximize revenues, governments (rulers) create and/or sustain social arrangements that limit access to the higher reaches of society to those that are politically connected, that is, to those from whom the government benefits. The noble aristocracy is a case in point.[19] The infinite shades of status and position in an aristocracy are, at root, planted in one's usefulness to the monarch. Much misery, suffering, and unhappiness would be eliminated if human societies did not separate those that are "in" from those that are "out," but such distinctions seem so ubiquitous as to be inevitable.

This brings us to the final conjecture:

Conjecture 3: While governments may limit the extent of organization for perfectly understandable economic reasons, they are unlikely to open up access to organizations to everyone in society simply for fiscal expediency. That is, governments only open up organizational forms if there is a strong social consensus for reducing or eliminating the social hierarchy and privileges that come from limited organizational forms.

So, for example, when in their search for revenues British and French kings began expanding the aristocracy by creating new peerages, the existing nobles and lords resisted. As already discussed, in societies where governments are not regularly replaced by electoral or other measures, rulers live in constant awareness of assassination and overthrow. A social hierarchy in which those who are near the ruler depend on the ruler for social status as well as economic well-being buys the leader some measure of insurance (not perfect). Social and economic privilege are a coin with which the ruler can purchase loyalty and safety, and no ruler can ever buy enough of those commodities. Privilege permeates most societies.

---

[19] Olson, for example, discussed the aristocracy in Europe and the caste system in India.

The existence of these privileges is perhaps the most fundamental problem in establishing a workable rule of law. In a privileged society, access to justice and other public services is limited by your position in the hierarchy. Not only is access to organizational forms limited, but only those individuals in certain organizations have access to justice. One's standing in the community was reflected in their standing in court. As North and Weingast (1989) point out, one of the major problems that debtors had in recovering their loans from the British Kings was that cases against the king were tried in the Star Court, whose judges were appointed by the king. The privilege of suing the king to recover your debts was unavailable to most people. The only creditors with a reasonable chance of repayment were those with the social and economic resources to make recourse to the courts immaterial, and their most effective threat was withholding future loans.

12.2.2 Technology and Capital

I have laid out a simple description of the economy, its principle elements, and their interactions, and a related set of propositions about division of labor, the extent of the market, the nature of organizations, and the limits put on organizations by government. The tendency is for government to limit organizations, limit the extent of the market, limit specialization and inhibit growth. In the historical section that follows, I will show how in the United States governments not only stopped limiting organizations, but actively began to promote private organizations: the public promotion of private interests of the title.

A key proposition is that a major source of economic growth is specialization and division of labor. I drew a distinction between increasing specialization, technological change, and factor accumulation as sources of growth, and asserted that it did not matter which source of growth dominated historically. It is now time to make good on the assertion.

The pace of technological change quickened rapidly in the late 18th and early 19th century, a story well known to all economic historians. The initial burst of technological change was intimately associated with a burst of entrepreneurial development. A group of innovators, who were not necessarily inventors, arose to bring new technologies to market. These entrepreneurs operated through the partnership and the corporation organizational forms. In the United States, general incorporation laws put the corporate form at the disposal of innovators by the 1820s and 1830s, without any of the limits imposed by political access required by special acts of state legislatures. The flexibility to choose corporate organization went hand in hand with the development of new technologies, indeed the implementation of new production and transportation technologies in railroads, steel, chemicals, and power generation and distribution played a critical role in the development of the corporation.[20] Not only were modern technologies inextricably linked

[20] The classic story of the endogeneity of technological change and organizational form is Chandler's (1997) *Visible Hand.* I am in debt to Ken Sokoloff who immediately grasped the implications of organizational freedom for technological change.

to increasing specialization, they were linked to growing organizational freedom as well.

The third fundamental source of economic growth is factor accumulation, particularly capital accumulation. Here again flexibility of organization played a critical role in the development of financial and capital markets. A central element of capital markets is pooling of resources: capital markets require coordinated group behavior in order to function. Loans, of course, are inherently incentive incompatible, borrowers always have some incentive to walk away from their obligations. Reputation can serve as a way to provide incentive compatible contracts, but third party enforcement is typically required for a capital market to function even at a primitive level.

As stressed earlier, most financial intermediaries provide explicit or implicit third party enforcement as a part of their services. Governments, however, are usually involved in the provision of third party enforcement in capital markets from very early on for three reasons. First, reputational enforcement of loan agreements, that is of contracts that span time, are always subject to default. Any private system of third party enforcement of loan contracts must ultimately rely on the reputation of a few large financiers or rely on the state for third party enforcement. Second, capital markets always develop in conjunction with goods markets. Capital markets exchange financial instruments tied to physical transactions, e.g. bills of exchange. This geographic movement of goods requires the development of reputations that extend over substantial geographic areas. The state has a comparative advantage in enforcing these types of contracts. Again, the merchant guild provides an example (Grief, Milgrom, and Weingast 1994). The guilds made arrangements for access to individual markets controlled by sovereigns who provided legal and physical protection for the markets. The guild ensured that sovereigns abided by their agreements by threatening to take guild business, and tax revenues, away from governments that would not play by the rules.

Third, the financial needs of the state often play a critical role in the development of financial markets. Governments are often the largest single borrowers in a financial system, and the availability of negotiable government debt issues provides a financial instrument that can be used in many types of exchange.[21] If the government actually fulfills its promises to repay its own debts, it is also in a stronger position to provide third party enforcement to other financial contracts.[22] Sylla (1969, 1985, 1998) has shown that the development of a very sophisticated financial system in the early 19th century United States was tied both to the ability

[21] Obviously, the usefulness of government securities as a "risk free" asset depends on the commitment of governments to pay back their debts. This, too, seems to be a feature of only some modern nation states.

[22] The logic here is less than transparent. Third party enforcement works best when the third party is impartial. Governments that unconditionally commit to pay their debts have some measure of impartiality. Governments that do not always pay their debts are always potentially subject to the influence of their creditors, and are thus not impartial with regard to those creditors.

of the federal government to commit itself to repay its debts and to the development of the corporate form, particularly in banking.

Expanding Proposition 1 to include technology and factor accumulation as sources of economic growth only strengthens the importance of organizations as catalysts for economic growth. It is now time to turn to a real historical example.

12.3 History

The main thesis of this chapter has two parts: 1) up to the 18th century in western Europe and throughout much of the world today, governments placed significant restrictions on the forms that private organizations could take and limited access to organizational forms to a narrow group of politically connected individuals; and 2) beginning in the 18th century, in Britain and the United States, then in France and spreading to the rest of northwestern Europe, governments began lifting restrictions on the form that organizations could take, what we can call passive promotion, and began actively promoting private organizations. The result of the change in government policy was to dramatically increase the number and complexity of organizations, expand the extent of the market, and promote economic development through increased specialization and division of labor, technological change, and factor accumulation. The hypothesis obviously requires two substantiating types of evidence. First, that before the 18th century governments everywhere restricted the number and form of private organizations.[23] Second, that countries liberalize their organizational forms before or as the process of modern economic development begins.[24] With the development of indexes of organization freedom or liberality, it should be possible to test the hypothesis quantitatively.[25]

Recent work on the number of interest groups and the rate of economic growth provide support for the argument. As Knack (2003), Knack and Keefer (1997b), and Coates and Heckelman (2003) clearly show, the number of organized groups is much higher in developed than in undeveloped or developing countries. This does not address the question of causation, perhaps development leads to more groups, but their data reflect the restrictions placed on organizations in most countries even today. Second, their work does not confirm the simple Olson hypothesis that the more organizations the slower the rate of economic growth and invest-

[23] Those restrictions are still common in most countries today, most particularly in countries that have not yet begun the process of modern economic development.

[24] It is easy to fall into the trap of creating absolute categories, such as governments restrict or don't restrict organizations, when in fact there are infinite gradations of restriction and liberality, and multiple dimensions upon which governments interact with organizations. The liberalization of organizational forms is a long process, contiguous with economic development.

[25] The modern panel growth regression studies, for all of their many flaws, seem to show clearly that countries with institutions that support organizational forms and transparency, for example rules that protect shareholders, are countries that experience higher rates of growth (Levine 1997).

ment. The results are decidedly mixed on this score. Coates and Heckelman find that increasing the number of organizations tends to reduce investment in OECD countries, but tends to raise investment in non-OECD countries.

Extending this research agenda is far more ambitious than I can hope to accomplish in the remainder of this chapter. Further evidence for the restrictive phase of government policy will not be discussed. The history of organizations in pre-18th century Europe is vast and I will not be convincing in a few short pages to those who are not already convinced that governments regularly limited organizations in the form of chartered companies, monopolies, and the like, only to the special friends of the government. Likewise I will not try to convince anyone that in most modern undeveloped countries the government restricts political, social, and economic organization and that governments are fundamentally "corrupt", by which I mean that only the government and its friends are given access to the organizations that control the economy and society. I will, however, show that the United States underwent an organizational revolution between 1776 and the 1840s. This revolution encompassed churches, political parties, and business firms. It touched on every aspect of American life.

12.3.1 Liberal Government: The Case of the United States

During and following the Revolution, government in the United States progressively opened access to organizational forms to ever wider segments of the population. I will not show that this is why the American economy grew steadily from the early 19th century onward. But I can document the deliberate and considered way in which American states pursued these policies, and try to indicate something of why they did so. My discussion will cover five areas: De Toqueville, churches, banks and other business corporations, political parties, and the Handlin's *Commonwealth*.

On of the most notable quotes in De Toqueville's study of *Democracy in America* highlights the importance of organization in the early 19th century United States, both in comparative terms with Europe and as a lynchpin of De Toqueville's argument about why democracy worked in America:[26]

> Americans of all ages, all stations in life, and all types of dispositions are forever forming associations. There are not only commercial and industrial associations in which all take part, but others of a thousand different types – religious, moral, serious, futile, very general and very limited, immensely large and very minute. Americans combine to give fetes, found seminaries, build churches, distribute books, and send missionaries to the antipodes. Hospitals, prisons, and schools take shape in that way. Finally, if they want to proclaim a truth or propagate some feeling by the encouragement of a great example, they form an association. In every case, at the head of any new undertaking, where in France you

[26] My colleague Jeff Smith suggested that this chapter might be entitled "Mancur Olson meets De Toqueville".

would find the government or in England some territorial magnate, in the United States you are sure to find an association. (p. 513)

De Toqueville had a dark vision of the growing power of the state, particularly of elected states, and he regretted the absence of an aristocracy, which protected liberty, at least the liberty of the aristocrats. He saw associations (organizations) as a bulwark against the growing power of the state:

I am firmly convinced that one cannot found an aristocracy anew in this world, but I think that associations of plain citizens can compose very rich, influential, and powerful bodies, in other words, aristocratic bodies.

By this means many of the greatest political advantages of an aristocracy could be obtained without its injustices and dangers. An association, be it political, industrial, commercial, or even literary or scientific, is an educated and powerful body of citizens which cannot be twisted to any man's will or quietly trodden down, and by defending its private interests against the encroachments of power, it saves the common liberties. (p. 697)

The advantages of free and unlimited association were paramount to De Toqueville, and in the first eight chapters of the second book of *Democracy* De Toqueville laid out how the United States was fostering and developing association. "Among laws controlling human societies there is one more precise and clearer, it seems to me, than all the others. If men are to remain civilized or to become civilized, the art of association must develop and improve among them at the same speed as equality of conditions spread." (p. 517)

12.3.1.1 Churches

Religious liberty played an important symbolic and substantive role in the American struggle to establish liberty and Republican government. Religious freedom also serves as an excellent example of how American government came early to a policy of promoting private organization. Churches are a particularly illuminating example, since by the 1770s in America there were limited fiscal implications of religious liberty.[27] Religious liberty required only that government allow people to worship as they pleased and to prevent private citizens from interfering in the religious beliefs and practices of others, within the limitations of acceptable social behavior.

But Americans went much farther than that. For example, in the colonial period in New York,

Churches of the established faith [Church of England] were freely chartered by the royal governors of New York, apparently finding no difficulty in securing corporate privileges there. By the end of the colonial period probably all, or nearly

[27] In colonial Massachusetts, Virginia, and perhaps other states, mandatory assessments for the support of religion were imposed by the government. It was the repeal of the assessments that lay at the heart of the Virginia Statutes for Religious Freedom.

all, of this faith were incorporated. A few of the Dutch Reformed denomination were also chartered, perhaps out of respect to a clause in the treaty of 1664 by which New Netherlands had been surrendered to the English. Other sects, on the other hand, – notably the Presbyterians, the French Protestants, and the Lutherans, – sought frequently but in vain for like advantages. (Davis 1917, p. 77)

Although colonial New York allowed religious freedom for Protestant Christians, the state would not extend to non-Anglican congregations the benefits of the corporate form. These benefits were of substantial advantages to a church, since recognition as a corporation allowed the church to hold real property and receive bequests and legacies.

At the state legislature's first peace time session, held in New York City in 1784, the legislature passed a general incorporation statute for churches:

The statute provided an equal opportunity for all religious denominations to secure the legal advantages of corporate ownership of their real property. It is noteworthy that the first enactment of a general incorporation law in New York made these advantages equally available by excluding partisan politics form the incorporation procedure. ... The great value of incorporation was that the trustees of a congregation could receive bequests and legacies, and the lands and buildings and other property owned by the congregation was [sic] secured by a corporate title that could be defended at law in the name of the congregation. Under common law, an unincorporated company could not legally possess property in its own name; its property had to be held in trust; and it could not defend its property at law in its collective capacity. (Seavoy 1982, pp. 9-10)

The New York statute did two very important things for churches. First, it granted every congregation that met the requirements of the statute access to the privileges of the corporate form. Second, it did not require congregations to acquire the approval of the state legislature to create a corporation. By creating an administrative process to approve applications for corporate status, New York took politics out of the chartering of congregations. New Jersey passed a general incorporation statute for religious organizations in 1786 (Cadman 1949, p. 5-6) and Pennsylvania in 1791. Between 1784 and 1830, New York passed twenty general regulatory statutes and general incorporations acts governing the establishment of churches, colleges and academies, municipal corporations, libraries, medical societies, turnpikes, manufacturing corporations, bible societies, agricultural societies, charitable societies, limited partnerships, and obituary societies (Seavoy 1982, pp. 283-5).

Religious freedom required more than a general incorporation act for churches, of course, and extending the corporate form was not the only way that governments could promote organizations. Laws governing corporations, however, are easily observed, and any state allowing any religious groups access to the corporate form was unlikely to be suppressing religious organizations on other dimensions. The early 19th century witnessed an upsurge of religious organization, the second "great awakening".[28] The new religious awareness brought social as well as spiritual changes, as the new religious activism played a central role in political developments in the mid-19th century. The widespread formation of churches and congregations also contributed to an extensive "organizing" of communities, organization that could and did spread into other areas of life. As Putnam has emphasized, "Faith communities in which people worship together are arguably the single most important repository of social capital in America" (Putnam 2000, p. 66).

Churches certainly were one of the organizations Olson intended to explain in *The Logic*. Note that the New York law supplies selective incentives to a church incorporating under the general statute. The statute gives the church as a corporate body the legal right to hold property, to write contracts, and to sue and be sued. The 1818 constitution of Connecticut took this one step further:

ARTICLE SEVENTH: OF RELIGION

SECTION 1. It being the duty of all men to worship the Supreme Being, the Great Creator and Preserver of the Universe, and their right to render that worship in the mode most consistent with the dictates of their consciences, no person shall by law be compelled to join or support, nor be classed with, or associated to, any congregation, church, or religious association. But every person now belonging to such congregation, church, or religious association, shall remain a member thereof until he shall have separated himself therefrom in the manner hereinafter provided. And each and every society or denomination of Christians in this State shall have and enjoy the same and equal powers, rights, and privileges; and shall have power and authority to support and maintain the ministers or teachers of their respective denominations, and to build and repair houses for public worship by a tax on the members of any such society only, to be laid by a major vote of the legal voters assembled at any society Meeting, warned and held according to law, or in any other manner.

SECTION 2. If any person shall choose to separate himself from the society or denomination of Christians to which he may belong, and shall leave a written notice thereof with the clerk of such society, he shall thereupon be no longer liable for any future expenses which may be incurred by said society.

This clause of the Connecticut constitution enabled congregations to lay taxes on the members "by a major vote of the legal voters assembled." This was public support of private organizations indeed.

[28] See Fogel (2000, pp. 21-22) and Johnson (1978) for a discussion of the second great awakening in upstate New York.

12.3.1.2 Banks and other Corporations

Banks were the most valuable business organizations created in the early United States. Beginning with the Bank of North America, states began chartering banks in the 1780s, until by 1830 there were over 600 chartered banks in operation. Banks were initially regarded as public utilities. A relatively small number of charters were issued to banks in major urban centers. A bank charter, however, was literally a license to print money, and charters were aggressively sought by groups who hoped to start their own bank.

Pennsylvania chartered the Bank of North America (BNA) in 1781.[29] The BNA successfully resisted an attempt to charter a second bank, the Bank of Pennsylvania in 1784, largely by promising the state that it would broaden its shareholder base and allow the promoters of the Bank of Pennsylvania to get in on the BNA. After the creation of the national Bank of the United States in 1791, based in Philadelphia, there was an attempt to charter a second Bank of Pennsylvania in 1794. This time the new bank was successful in out bidding the BNA for a new charter. The BNA offered the state the opportunity to buy BNA stock at a preferential price, but the Bank of Pennsylvania offered the state a better deal in its own shares. The scenario was repeated again in 1803 when the Bank of Philadelphia applied for a charter, again opposed by the existing banks. The state, mindful of its investment in the Bank of Pennsylvania, was leery of chartering a new bank and reducing the value of its stock and dividends, but the new bank offered substantial inducements. After a long negotiation, a charter was issued to the Bank of Philadelphia for which the bank paid the state $135,000 in cash; the state had the right to subscribe to $300,000 in stock by tendering U.S. bonds, which would be returned to the state should the bank fail; the state had additional rights to purchase stock in the future; and the bank incurred the obligation to loan the government up to $100,000 at 5 per cent for a period not exceeding ten years.[30] Another bank was chartered in 1809, again in the face of opposition by existing banks and in return for a substantial charter fee. Schwartz (1987, p. 15) concluded:

> The offer of monetary inducements for the granting of a charter, which began as a voluntary solicitation of the legislature [by the bank promoters], came to be looked upon as a necessary accomplishment of a petition for incorporation. The committee reported that since the petitioners sought a charter for profit-making purposes, the state had a right to require a payment for the privileges it conferred.

For the next four decades Pennsylvania would continue to sell bank charters, collect dividends, and restrict the number of banks in order to protect its fees and dividends. Pennsylvania is a perfect example of how the fiscal interests of a government can lead it to restrict entry when the state is selling monopoly/oligopoly rents.

---

[29] The discussion of Pennsylvania, Massachusetts, and banking in general is taken from Wallis, Sylla, and Legler (1994).

[30] The discussion of Pennsylvania banking is based on Schwartz (1987, pp. 6-15).

Massachusetts began in much the same way, chartering a relatively small number of banks, owning stock in a number of them, and closely identifying the fiscal interest of the state with the banks. With most of the existing bank charters up for renewal in 1812, the state planned to expand its already large holdings in the banking system by chartering the Bank of Massachusetts, with a capital of $3 million of which the state subscribed a third.[31] In 1812, the state also imposed an annual, one per cent tax on bank capital (Handlin and Handlin 1969, p. 120).[32] Unlike Pennsylvania, where banks paid large charter fees, political competition in Massachusetts had resulted in more liberal chartering at lower fees, over the strenuous opposition of the existing banks. When revenues from the tax on bank capital began flowing into the Treasury, the state saw that its fiscal interest lay in increasing the number of banks. By 1820, the state had liquidated all of its bank stock and was liberally providing charters. In 1829 "a general act was passed prescribing the powers and duties and internal organization of all banks that might thereafter be incorporated and also of those existing banks whose charters should be extended or capital increased" (Dodd 1954, p. 211). This was a general regulatory statute, chartering still required a special act of the legislature, but the structure of charters was set and the state essentially incorporated all the banks that applied and met the requirements.

By the 1820s, Massachusetts had created unlimited entry into banking. The free banking acts passed in Michigan in 1838 and New York in 1839, created similar situations in those states. By the late 1840s, many states had adopted some form of free banking law. Free entry into banking was far from universal, Indiana and Missouri would have state owned banking monopolies into the 1850s. But there was a strong general trend to opening banking up to new organizations, with free entry, and eliminating the political system from the creation of organizations through special chartering. This was not only a northern phenomenon. States throughout the south began chartering banks in earnest in the 1830s. Many banks in the south and west failed in the crisis from 1837 to 1843, and banking in those parts of the country was less developed than in the northeast, but states continued to promote banking throughout the south and west up to the Civil War.[33]

A similar movement swept through business incorporation in general. Between 1842 and 1852, twelve states adopted new constitutions. In eleven of those states the new constitutions mandated general incorporation laws be written for business. As in free banking, these general incorporation laws guaranteed free entry to all prospective corporations and prohibited the political system from restricting charters. By the 1850s, anyone who sought a corporate charter for legitimate business purposes could find a state that would support them. On Olsonian terms, the states

---

[31] The state already had substantial bank holdings; Handlin and Handlin (1969) report a total of $1.8 million in 1812.

[32] The discussion of Massachusetts is based on Handlin and Handlin (1969, pp. 113-121) and Dodd (1954, pp. 201-218).

[33] For a southern banking see Schweikart (1987) and for free banking see Shade (1972). It is impossible to characterize ante-bellum American banking with any simple generalizations.

had extended the opportunity for nascent business organizations to take advantage of the significant selective incentives offered by the corporate form.[34]

12.3.1.3 Political Parties

From the beginning of the 18th century, through the revolution, and on into the early 19th century, Americans were suspicious of political parties and the evil of faction. In the words of Bernard Bailyn (1967, pp. 36-37):

> Parties, to almost every political writer of the eighteenth century, were indisputably evil. The ancient ideal of an organic polity whose parts, operating independently within their assigned spheres, fitted together harmoniously, persisted. The King, it was universally allowed, made national policy and chose ministers as his servants to execute it, and the King would do no wrong; active opposition to the king's government, therefore, could only be a design to impose upon the King, and was hence improper, unconstitutional, and if persisted in, seditious. Party rivalries signified illness within the body politic, malfunctions within the system, not because all interests were expected to harmonize with each other automatically but because right-minded men – men motivated not by private but by public interests – would naturally find ways of reconciling them. Parties – defined in Walpole's time precisely as Madison would define them over half a century later in *The Federalist* – were the malign result of "the gratifying of private passion by public means," and "faction is to party," Bolingbroke wrote, "what the superlative is to the positive; party is a political evil, and faction is the worst of all parties."

Even De Toqueville, with his love of association, is leery of political associations and the dangers they might bring. How then did American politics come to be governed by political parties?

It is well to note that the first past the post electoral system for President created conditions under which a two party system was probably inevitable. But Americans were reluctant to embrace parties, even at the national level, and were constantly aware and ever vigilant of the dangers to their liberties posed by political corruption. Corruption has many facets, but fundamental corruption of the political system occurred when politicians responded only to the interests of their faction, of their party, or of their constituents, rather than answering to the public good.

Balanced against the fear of faction was the need for access to the political system. Had the Alien and Sedition Acts of 1798 gone unchallenged, effective political opposition would have been difficult, if not impossible. While party politics under Jefferson played an important role in his triumph over Adams and the Revolution of 1800, a era of party politics was not ushered in by Jefferson. Permanent national political parties did not form until the Democrats under Jackson in 1828. Jackson's election was aided by the public perception that he had lost the 1824

[34] The discussion of corporations is elaborated in much more detail in Wallis (2000, 2002). For a discussion of the number of corporations and the adoption of general incorporation laws by state see Evans (1948).

election because of the "corrupt bargain" between John Quincy Adams and Henry Clay, and Jackson's appeal as a politician and a party leader was immensely strengthened by his ability to communicate the idea that he, and his party, stood for the people *against* the government. The two-decade long conflict between the Whigs and Democrats strengthened this tenet of Jackson, that parties were a necessary bulwark of the people against the depredations of government.

The nature and structure of American political organizations has changed perpetually since the early 19th century. The key element for my argument is that political organizations (with the exception of those that are clearly criminal or seditious) have been allowed to self-organize with very little interference from the government. Americans, despite a predisposition to oppose political parties, have managed to allow political organizations to flourish in the same way that they have allowed religious and economic organizations to flourish.

12.3.1.4 The Handlins

Oscar and Mary Flug Handlin's book *Commonwealth: A Study of the Role of Government in the American Economy: Massachusetts, 1774 - 1861* was one of a number of books commissioned and supported by the Committee on Research in Economic History to investigate the role of the government in promoting economic development in the early nineteenth century. The committee was particularly interested in the importance of laissez faire policies. The Handlins quickly discovered that states did not follow laissez faire policies in Massachusetts or anywhere else. States everywhere deliberately and actively promoted economic development. The theme of their book is the role of association, organization, and incorporation in the economy of Massachusetts, and the role of government in promoting organizations, as well as restricting and shaping them. They found that the state's most important role was helping the economy organize itself:

> The public purpose which justified extension of government powers to a bank, to bridges, and to a factory soon comprehended a wide and ever widening circle of enterprises. The Commonwealth's concern with the entire productive system, its solicitude for the welfare of many diverse activities, all interdependent and all adding to the strength of Massachusetts, quickly put the corporate form to the use of many new ventures. The political balance defeated any notion of keeping the device exclusive; the expansive thinking, the excited spirits of the young state, brooked no casual denial. Charters in steadily mounting volume clothed with living tissues the skeletal hopes for an economy to serve the common interest.
> (Handlin and Handlin 1969, p. 106)

The Handlins' book is full of marvelous examples of how the state came to the aid of organizations. Chapters 4 and 5, "The State in Association" and "Commonwealth and Corporation", are a litany of state promotion of private and public interests through assisting organizations. For example, "The lumberman who had, without success, attempted to control the flow of logs at the head of tide on the Androscoggin River, in 1788 asked for and secured incorporation as a 'Body Politick, with all the Power & Authority that other Bodies Pollitick do Enjoy'" (p.

106). Two aspects of the Massachusetts experience provide a revealing light on the argument of this chapter, beyond establishing the fact that Massachusetts was willing to promote private organization in a wide variety of ways.

First, the Massachusetts legislature was not wild about corporations and associations in general.[35] They were quite willing to assist organizations that would benefit the citizens and economy of the state, but their generosity stopped at the border: "Incorporation was easy to come at when it seemed to serve the interests of Massachusetts, but only in such cases. The legislature opposed projects that operated to the advantage of out-of-state ports, refusing, for instance, to charter John Brown's Blackstone Canal in 1796 lest it draw trade to Providence" (p. 109). Although the enthusiasm for economic development seemed to heed no bounds, government promotion of private associations was conscious and calculating. Politicians supplied public support because it was good politics, not because of ideological predisposition.

Second, consistent with the historical view of the corporation as a grant of privilege motivated by an explicit *quid pro quo* that created rents for the organizations and revenues or power for the government, Massachusetts struggled mightily with the idea of the corporation as "special" privilege:

> The areas of economic activity into which the corporate technique did not reach in this period throw further light upon the presumptions essential to grant of the privilege...commerce also witnessed no incorporations. At the existing stage of development the only privilege of value to it – monopoly – was beyond the scope of state action after 1789... Most important, the fact that trading operations were already well established and spread wide among many individuals, partnerships and joint stock companies made it difficult to justify special privileges for a single group. Unlike the activities which involved innovation or some special public service, incorporation in the field of trade seemed to close rather than open new opportunities. The corporation could not extend into this area so long as the Commonwealth purpose was primary, the private interests secondary. (pp. 131-32)

Massachusetts felt strongly that the government should not create special privileges. They feared the old political order that used state sanction to limit organizational access to those with special relationships with the government would lead directly to corruption:

> Monopoly was an instrument of government even less susceptible of adaptation to the new purposes. Once an obvious and legitimate technique of patronage, this now seemed outside the scope of proper state action and at the root of a whole roster of evils – high prices, short supply, and restricted markets... The corporation, object of the same unfriendliness encountered by monopoly, nevertheless possessed the resiliency to adjust to new circumstances and new uses. (pp. 212-3)

The resiliency of the corporation would depend on "the gradual elimination of privileges from the nature of the corporation." That is, corporations could not be

[35] See Maier (1992, 1993) for a more detailed discussion of Massachusetts corporations in this period.

created for one group that were not available for every group. This was the principle embodied in the New York general statute for churches in 1784 and in the widespread adoption of general incorporation acts that allowed anyone who met the minimum requirements to obtain a corporate charter. In Olsonian terms, these collective action organizations were given the special incentives they need to mold their group into an effective organization, but were stripped of any special privileges unique to their group or their charter.

12.4 Conclusions

This chapter began by questioning Mancur Olson's conclusions about the role of organizations and economic development. Just as the American economy was beginning to "take-off" into sustained modern economic growth, there was a proliferation of organizations. Not only did the number of organizations increase exponentially, the growth was spread across the entire social spectrum. It occurred in banks, manufacturing firms, and business corporations; in churches, bible societies, and missionary societies; and in funeral societies, fire protection societies, and lumberman's associations. The spread of associations was universal in the United States, as celebrated by De Toqueville.

Many of these organizations tried to act as pure redistributional coalitions, in pure Olsonian terms. Famously, the Charles River Bridge Company attempted to use its corporate charter to preclude other companies from bridging the Charles. The Bank of North America tried to prevent the state of Pennsylvania from establishing more banks in Philadelphia. In my favorite example, the state of New Jersey awarded the Camden and Amboy railroad the monopoly rights to the direct rail route between New York and Philadelphia (Cadman 1949), a privilege the railroad held for forty years and for which the company amply compensated the taxpayers of New Jersey. Unfortunately, freight shippers between New York and Philadelphia paid monopoly rates for the entire forty years. Americans created thousands of redistributional coalitions in the early 19th century, states even gave many of them corporate charters to help solve the free rider problem, and still the American economy grew.

While I reach a different conclusion about the relationship between the number of organizations and the rate of economic growth, nothing in this chapter is inconsistent with the conceptual ideas in *The Logic* or in *Rise and Decline,* or with "Democracy, Dictatorship, and Development". I have extended Olson's approach by incorporating explicitly the decision by government to regulate the number and type of organizations that are allowed to exist in society. The world prior to the 18th century was one largely described by *Rise and Decline*. Governments were predatory. They severely limited the number of organizations that were allowed to form. They restricted organizations to those who had a close relationship, socially and fiscally, with the government. This produced incentive compatible arrangements between kings and lords, or in modern terms between rulers and elites. This kind of crony capitalism (or not capitalism if you prefer another economic system) is a political economy equilibrium in which governments limit organizations; the limited number of organizations limits the extent of the market; the limited extent of the market limits the degree of specialization of labor, technological and entrepreneurial development, and capital accumulation; and economic growth stagnates.

England in the 18th century, America in the 18th and early 19th century, northwest Europe in the mid-19th century began breaking out of this mold. Governments began allowing a wider range of private organizations to exist. In the United States, the state governments began an active program of promoting private organization in economic, political, social, and religious realms of society. While I have drawn my evidence for the United States largely from the experience of corporations, it cannot be doubted that organizations of all forms and structures were allowed much freer development in the early 19th century.

I have not explained how the England of the 17th century that beheaded kings, packed Parliaments, and repudiated debts came to be the England of the 18th century that defeated France by borrowing at 4%, paid all of its obligations, and established a political ideology of republican liberty that still governs all of us today. Nor have I explained how the United States – in 1776, on the periphery of the British system, a land rich agricultural nation doomed to be crushed in the European wars of colonization and global dominance, and with only a dim vision of what a democratic republic should look like, much less how it would function – within 50 years adopted universal white male suffrage, developed general incorporation laws for business and churches, and nurtured a national system of finance and transportation that rivaled and then exceeded anything the Europeans had done.

There are some hints contained in this chapter. First, we should look more carefully at the fiscal interest of governments. The fact that in our world most government revenue is raised by general tax instruments like the income tax, should not blind us to the fact that government finance was much more idiosyncratic just two centuries ago (or less) and that it remains so for the majority of the world's population. These idiosyncrasies have real implications for how governments behave with respect to the economy and organizations. Second, we need to be more creative in the way we think about organizations. Organizations are malleable creatures shaped by the institutional environment in which they originate. For most of the world's history their development was shaped primarily by the constraints imposed on them by government. Third, organizations are the primary determinant of how well markets work. If I am right about the importance of organizations and their ties to government, then we have dramatically reduced the problem of understanding how economies make the transition from the low output/restricted organizations/bad government equilibrium to the high output/liberal organization/good government equilibrium. The number of important organizations in a pre-modern economy is relatively small. We should be able to study them and eventually come to understand why some economies produce so many organizations in the process of economic development.

13 Macroeconomic Policy and Collective Action

David C. Colander, Kenneth J. Koford, and Jeffrey B. Miller

An individual cannot by saving more protect himself from the consequences of inflation if others do not follow his example: just as he cannot protect himself from accidents by obeying the rule of the road if others disregard it. We have here the perfect opportunity for social action, where everyone can be protected by making a certain rule of behavior universal. Keynes (1940)

In his posthumously published book, *Power and Prosperity* (2000), Mancur Olson returned to his long concern with why some countries are rich and others poor, and pushed his analysis a bit further. As seen from his early work, *The Logic of Collective Action* (1965), he focused on the ability of small groups to come together to obtain special-interest benefits and the failure of government to provide genuine public goods. In his Presidential address to the Eastern Economic Association (1995), he made a similar argument and pointed out that small-scale market activity flourishes everywhere; it is the effectiveness of large-scale economic activity that determines whether an economy is prosperous or not.

Effective large-scale economic activity requires, according to Olson, that there are powerful political interests that focus on the overall gains to society--what he called in another context "market-augmenting government." It is these "encompassing interests" in a democratic society that assure that complex institutions can arise and produce effectively. These "encompassing interests" also fight against the tendency of narrow special interests to obtain benefits for themselves at a cost to society.

Our argument in this chapter is that macro policy can be usefully conceived of within a general Olsonian framework emphasizing the fight between special interests and encompassing interests.[1] The policy question in macro is the same as it is in micro: how to encourage "encompassing interests" in a society to reign in the many special interests and provide the true public goods that are necessary for an economy to function effectively. There are many ways to do this, and, as Olson emphasized in his *Power and Prosperity*, one important way is the establishment of secure property rights and their boundaries to the exercise of power. We argue that thinking of macro policy as the development of "property rights rules" in variables that affect macroeconomic outcomes provides useful insight into macro policy debates, and is a natural extension of the Olsonian framework.

---

[1] Mancur Olson and David Colander followed this same approach in their jointly written paper (Olson and Colander 1984).

13.1 Macroeconomic Externalities and Coordination Failures

In the past two decades a body of work has developed that describes macroeconomic microfoundations with Keynesian properties. This approach is often called "New Keynesian" (Phelps 1985; Colander 1986; Romer 2001). Similar to New Classical or Real Business Cycle work, New Keynesian work has adopted a dynamic general equilibrium modeling approach. The key elements include:

1. a general equilibrium framework;
2. analysis of the aggregate economy from a microeconomic perspective with rational maximizing agents;
3. a form of incomplete markets or an externality that lead to Keynesian properties.[2]

We refer to this approach as "New Keynesian" while agreeing that many authors in the Real Business Cycle tradition are doing similar work.

Most New Keynesian research has focused on particular sub-areas, such as the labor or credit market; this research has shown how small changes from the market-clearing assumption change the stylized properties and policy conclusions from Classical full-employment general equilibrium to Keynesian. This work is not especially compatible with Olson's approach. However, one branch of that work, notably the coordination failure branch, is highly compatible with Olson's encompassing interest approach. This literature shows how coordination failures can lead to less than optimal macroeconomic outcomes.[3]

This coordination failure approach structures the macroeconomic problem as one quite compatible with Olson's framework. Individuals are assumed to follow their own self-interest against the collective good, which, for macro externalities is achieving one of the standard macroeconomic goals—stabilization, growth, and a relatively stable price level. If the economy does not achieve these goals, the rea-

---

[2] For discussions of this approach see Colander and Koford (1985) and Andrew John (1995). David Romer's (2001) textbook has an up-to-date general review of "New Keynesian" work.

[3] Prominent examples are Bryant (1983), Cooper and John (1988), and Cooper (1999). Considerable work has been done to obtain empirical evidence on macroeconomic coordination failures, which also go under the name of strategic complementarities. Bils and Klenow (1998) show that models of cyclical utilization do perform better in explaining consumer sales than several real business cycle approaches. Cooper and Haltiwanger (1993) and Cooper (1996) provide evidence of a specific macroeconomic complementarity in automobile sales in the interwar period, while Cooper and Haltiwanger (1990) find evidence of co-movements in output consistent with macroeconomic complementarities. Levine and Zervos (1998) find that developed stock markets and banks increase growth and productivity, holding constant other factors, in a large sample of countries; these are means of improving coordination. Rotemberg and Woodford (1995) show that "stylized" empirical results fit macroeconomic complementarities well in dynamic general equilibrium growth models, in contrast to traditional real business cycle approaches.

son it does not can be seen as resulting from individuals following their own self-interest and not taking the broader collective good into account. Thus, for example, when individuals on average respond more quickly to opportunities to raise their price than they do to lower their price, the result is an unsustainable rise in the price level, which would blow up if it were not anchored. Under current policy rules, in which limiting the money supply growth is required to maintain a price level anchor, this requires markets, on average, to be kept in a position of excess supply, to the detriment of the collective good.[4]

One useful outcome of framing the macro problem in this way is that it directs one toward a taxonomy of "microeconomic" approaches to macro problems, which essentially involve requiring agents to take the collective good into their decision making process. For example, by creating property rights in prices, one can force individuals to take into account any effect their actions have on the aggregate price level, and thereby guide individuals to work for the collective good even as they follow their specific interest. Alternatively, one can achieve the same ends by tax and subsidy incentives, or by modifying the incentives in existing institutions.[5]

As suggested in the introductory quote, which is from Keynes' *How to Pay for the War* (1940), this coordination failure approach to macro policy has Keynesian roots. It sees the underlying cause of the macro problem as the existence of a macroeconomic externality, in which individual decisions do not lead to desirable results for the entire society. The approach can also be seen in the work of Baumol (1950) and Lerner (1960), but it disappeared during the golden years of neo-Keynesian macroeconomics, the 1960s, when it was just *assumed* that active monetary and fiscal policies were needed to stabilize the economy, without any highly developed formal micro foundation for these policies. By the 1970s, the rise of inflation and continued high unemployment led to a breakdown of the neo-Keynesian synthesis, leading theorists to explore alternative approaches. These included the new microeconomic foundations and rational expectations theories, which undercut the neo-Keynesian model and required a microeconomic rationale for Keynesian-type policies. The coordination failure approach answered these challenges to Keynesian policy thinking and provided a microeconomic rationality in a way that nicely fits Olson's general framework.

To demonstrate that relationship, in this chapter we relate the general idea of macroeconomic externality models found in strategic complementarities to Olson's ideas, arguing that his general approach fits not only micro issues, but macro issues too. In doing so we provide an organizing structure for thinking about macro policy within a special interest/collective good framework. Macro policy

4 For a discussion of this issue see Colander (1992).

5 In other work we have shown how this coordination failure work provides a theoretical foundation for a set of policies that use the creation of property rights or tax incentives to deal directly with macroeconomic problems. Specifically we have shown that the Cooper and John (1988) model can be extended to include methods of "solving" the macroeconomic problem (Koford, Miller, and Colander 2001). In this chapter we concentrate on relating the approach to Olson's ideas.

problems can be thought of as being created by macro externalities—results of individual decisions on macroeconomic variables, such as inflation, growth and stabilization—that are not taken into account by the decision maker. Given a macroeconomic externality, the macro policy problem in a collective interest framework is to find a method of internalizing the externality that provides greater gains than costs.

Once macro policy is placed within this broad special interest/collective good framework, one can move on to the real policy questions of determining the costs, administrative and other, including the costs of errors, of each specific policy, and of determining whether these costs are less than the benefits. By placing macro policy within Olson's framework one sees that economists differ on macro policy far more because of different estimates of these costs and far less because of differences in theory.

13.2 A System of Market Rights in Macroeconomic Variables

If negotiations over macroeconomic variables were cheap it would be relatively easy for the encompassing interests to develop institutions to guide special interests toward the collective good. One could easily allow interagent negotiation, and, following Coase's argument, arrive at an acceptable solution. But negotiations are not cheap; they have very high transactions costs, since an individual's effect on key macro variables are widespread and small, although in the aggregate these effects can be substantial. The problem facing encompassing interests is to design institutions to force individuals to undertake actions that lead to desirable macroeconomic results.

Designing those institutions presents what might be called the Olsonian trap. Even though one knows that these are problems where the collective good is great, in any negotiations about the design of the program special interests will have incentives to prevent the encompassing interests from winning, and to design the program to their benefit. For an economy to succeed, the encompassing interests must design enforceable rules, which limit special narrow interests and direct individual's actions toward the collective good, but those rules must be accepted by the special interests. The need is to pit one special interest against another and to maintain as much transparency in the negotiations as possible in the initial establishment of property rights, which then become embodied into the institutions of the economy.

The role of government in guiding the development of such property rights is becoming more and more accepted in microeconomics. For example, air pollution rights have been developed by government during the past decade in an attempt to deal creatively with the pollution problem. Each firm is allowed to pollute at specific levels. If a firm generates more pollution than it has rights to, additional rights must be purchased from other firms, which then must reduce their pollution. The price of the rights varies with supply and demand. By controlling the overall supply of pollution rights the government can, in effect, control the market price. Such systems have worked quite effectively in the Midwest and in Southern California (Schmalensee et al. 1998).

However, in macroeconomic variables, the potential role of property rights in allowing the encompassing interests to prevail is still seen as somewhat strange. Macro externalities are seen as somehow more esoteric because macro policy has seldom been thought of in this way. However, what matters for policy is not how esoteric the idea of rights in something is, but how easily the rights are made into property; the problems that exist in creating property rights to deal with some types of macroeconomic variables, such as inflation, are less difficult than the problem of turning air or water rights into property rights because the dimensionality of what is being controlled is less. With inflation one is only worried about the composite price level, not with the many different types of pollution that can exist, making the technical measurement, and definitional problems of establishing such property rights, much less daunting.[6]

The existence of the macro externalities can be seen through backward induction. If the price level should optimally remain relatively constant, then firms' price-changing decisions that affect the price level can be see as creating an external effect. Similarly if growth and stabilization are desirable goals, then individuals' decisions that work against achieving those goals can be seen as creating an externality. The policy question is how to get the encompassing political interests to require individuals to make decisions compatible with the collective good. One way of doing that is to create a market in rights to those macro externalities.

In order to create a market to solve a macroeconomic externality problem, two basic issues must be resolved: (1) The rights must be defined in some measurable way; and (2) The quantity of available rights must be fixed by the government (by law or regulation).[7] It is important to point out the different incentives of private actors once the property rights in the externality have been established compared to the incentives before they had been established. Consider the market for pollution. Under a system of market rights to pollution, each firm defends politically *its* fixed amount of pollution rights and opposes politically every *other* firm's efforts to expand its rights, or to cheat on those rights. If other firms expand their rights, this reduces the market value of each firm's rights. The same incentives exist with inflation. Under a system of market rights to prices, each firm defends politically

[6] The method in which one defines these property rights in prices is key to the administrative feasibility. Lerner and Colander (1980) argue that by defining property rights in value added per unit inputs the administrative problems can be far less than those in defining pollution rights.

[7] Chari and Jones (2000) show that markets in pure public goods, even when fully defined, are unlikely to operate well. The alternative approach, which we follow, is for a government to determine the size of the external effect and from it the socially optimal level of the pure public good. The rights established in the activity are for this amount. These rights are then valuable *private* goods to the firms, just as pollution rights are valuable private rights.

its fixed amount of rights, and opposes politically every other firm's effort to expand on those rights.

Before a market in pollution rights was established, firms individually had incentives to lobby for the legal right to expand their own pollution. These were "stationary bandits", in that everyone saw the harm they were doing, and could impose some costs on them. Also, each polluter saw benefits from cheating without being caught (the "midnight pollution"). Similarly with inflation; firms will lobby hard for the right to raise their price, but will also lobby hard for the Fed to hold down inflation, which means limiting other firms from raising price. The reality is that to solve externality problems, we need both an economically efficient result, and a political balance of forces that will maintain the economically efficient result. Market-based systems with enforceable property rights can help fulfill this requirement.

Of course, setting them up presents serious political problems and brings with them significant administrative costs. The desirability of any policy depends on whether the benefit from internalizing the externality outweighs the administrative costs of a system, and on whether the policy is politically sustainable. These issues in turn depend on the current institutional structure. For example, countries that already measure firms' revenues in the form of a tax on value added, have much of the administrative machinery already in place, and will find it much easier to establish such policies than other countries.

13.3 The Range of Policy Alternatives

Macroeconomic goals are generally considered to be stabilization, growth, and maintaining a relatively constant price level. In our framework each of these can be seen as a collective good that is not reached because special interests do not take the collective good of achieving them into account in the decisions they make. Not achieving these collective goods has negative consequences for the economy that the encompassing interests have an incentive to see are offset. For example, inflation destroys the usefulness of money as a medium of exchange and thus reduces the trading efficiency of the economy.[8] Thus, ultimately, in a reasonably functioning economy, encompassing interests must win out over special interests and see that the goal is achieved. The policy question is how to do so.

There are four basic ways to achieve a policy goal within this framework:

1. Create a market in the interaction so that individuals internalize the externality in their market decisions;
2. Tax or subsidize the interaction so that the outcome mirrors the market result;
3. Change the institutional setting (the game) within which individuals interact;
4. Have the government act to offset the externality.

[8] Okun (1981, Ch. 7) concludes that the optimal inflation rate is "very low--close to zero," after discussing these various costs.

Each of these requires encompassing interests to achieve them. The hardest solution to implement, but also the solution that most deeply builds the solution into the institutional structure, is the creation of a market that guides special interests into decisions that contribute to the collective good. This involves encompassing interests using their political capital to establish the market. In macro policy it would mean creating property rights in prices, or in some variable related to fluctuations in output and growth, and establishing a set of enforceable rules that could maintain the market. The most developed of these proposals in regard to inflation is the MAP proposal (Lerner and Colander 1980) which creates property rights in nominal value added, so that any firm increasing its nominal value added per unit input would need to buy the right to do so by buying rights to do so generated by other firms decreasing their nominal value added per unit input by an offsetting amount.[9]

In most cases the creation of a market will be impractical, but thinking about establishing such a market can still be useful as a method of shedding light on the effectiveness of other policies that are designed to achieve the same end. It allows one to see whether the chosen policy properly internalizes external effects, and attains the optimal outcome, on both the aggregate and disaggregated level. Taxes and subsidies require less initial political capital, but are more susceptible to continual changes and political forces, and rent seeking. The most developed of these in regard to inflation are the tax-based incomes policy (TIP) proposals in which firms raising their wages or value added per unit input are subject to a tax.

Changing the institutional structure is easier than the previous two methods, but it, too, requires significant political capital by encompassing interests. An example in regard to inflation would be some of the deregulatory policies that established stronger competition in various industries. Having the government act to directly offset the externality is politically less difficult, but it requires continual action and thus is difficult to maintain. Functional finance, in which monetary and fiscal policy are used in a predetermined counter cyclical fashion, and discretionary monetary and fiscal policies, are examples of such a policy for the stabilization goal.

13.4 Monetary and Fiscal Policy from a Macro Externality Perspective

Looking at standard monetary and fiscal stabilization policies in reference to a market solution to the stabilization problem, it is clear that these policies deviate significantly from that market solution. A market solution would require anyone changing his or her output level more or less than the collectively desired amount to enter the market and "buy" the right to do so by finding someone who internalizes the externality that decision creates by offsetting the effect of that change on the socially desired output level.

---

[9] Below we explain the MAP proposal in more detail.

In principle, the net effect of these stabilization externalities could be either excessive unemployment or labor shortages (Malinvaud 1976).[10] Traditional macroeconomic policy has tried to find an aggregate demand policy that will move the economy only to the optimal *aggregate* output level, not worrying about sectoral imbalances that are created by the policy. That model was extended to determine optimal aggregate investment and consumption using monetary policy. Yet neither policy acts directly on the individual external effects, and so while an aggregate optimum might be reached, it is very unlikely that the individual agents are at the social optimum when monetary and fiscal policy are used. In addition, the forecasting requirements for aggregate demand policy are daunting.[11]

Another insight provided by the macro externality approach is to remind us that when there is too little spending in the economy, there is no reason to believe that it is just the government that is doing too little spending; it is the entire economy. Fiscal policy is a solution in which the government attempts to make up the majority of the externality; in terms of the market to internalize externalities, the use of fiscal policy implicitly corresponds to a market solution in which government faced a low price, and the private sector faced a high price, of internalizing the externality.

Fiscal policy also operates extremely slowly relative to how the market solution would operate. In a democratic country, taxes and expenditures are determined by the legislature, and this process typically takes months (in the U.S., normally a year from the OMB budget review in December to the budget passage in October or November). Special interests tend to dominate, such as occurred with the Agricultural Support Act of 2002. Spending policy always hits some sectors strongly and others weakly, in the effort to affect the whole economy. Tax policy typically does so as well.

Another advantage of a relatively "automatic" market-based policy is that it reduces the opportunities for rent seeking. Fiscal policy in the U.S. has traditionally been captured by such rent-seeking groups, while both monetary and fiscal policies in less-developed countries have been captured by special interest groups. When a crisis develops, special interests can often find a way to manipulate that crisis to make quick gains, as seen in the numerous groups demanding tax cuts or spending increases in the U.S. in 2001-2.

A useful outcome of viewing fiscal policy from a macro externality framework is that it guides us in thinking about ways in which fiscal policy can be made more like the market—to make it more automatic; to reduce the possibility for rent-seeking associated with it; and to smooth out the adjustment among various sec-

[10] In more fully specified macroeconomic environments, where there are job search costs (Pissarides 1990), disutility of labor, and reasons for other resources to be unemployed, the individual choices are even more important. The same would be true if credit market externalities were considered.

[11] Bernanke et al. (1999) and Bernanke and Gertler (1999) propose that monetary policy focus only on inflation, giving up a concern both for output levels and the long-run price level. In contrast, Svensson (1999) broadly favors keeping the price level constant, as a more "fundamental" approach.

tors of the economy. How easily it will be to do so depends in part upon existing institutions. For example, countries with a Value-Added Tax may be in a better position to change taxes than countries with an individual income tax, where the initial incidence of the tax is on the individual rather than the firm. For spending, the issue is more difficult, since changes in the appropriation of money for specific projects are hard to make "automatic". Three year moving average budgets and large rainy day (or better yet, rainy season) funds as standard budgeting procedure can also help.

Turning our attention to monetary policy we see many of the same issues. Monetary policy works through some subsectors of the financial sector, particularly those that borrow from banks and also home-buying. These feed strongly into construction, and in the U.S., to smaller businesses. This is an effect on output. But, when a contraction in money is needed by the economy, it is not just the interest sensitive sectors where the contraction needs to take place. Any effect on the price level requires that these sectors' demands fall enough to bring about a significant overall decline in aggregate demand.

Monetary policy is currently typically made by an "independent central bank". This can isolate the decision makers from special-interest groups. But giving discretion to unelected experts has serious weaknesses as well. If a pure price-level rule were socially optimal and could be carried out using technical means, the political problem could be solved. New Zealand has followed this approach, and the European Central Bank is attempting a similar policy.

In general, monetary and fiscal policies affect some sectors of the economy strongly and others weakly, so they cannot mimic the uniform incentive effect that is appropriate to correct for macroeconomic externalities. Also, monetary and fiscal policy affects some parts of the economy more quickly than others, creating a new, intertemporal externality. Finally, neither fiscal nor monetary policy deals directly with the price-level externality.

One should also note the distinction between adjustment to numerous small shocks that have a similar nature, and adjustment to a variety of possibly large and idiosyncratic shocks. Policy rules are typically aimed at the "typical small shock" while it may be the truly large novel shock that does the most damage. A policy to "expect the unexpected" is hard to develop, but this is a useful goal. But since a market in changes in output variables is generally seen to be impossible, such proxies may well be the best we can do. However, care must be taken to prevent their use as a means to build short-term political support at the expense of long-run stability, as is often the case, particularly in developing and transition countries.

Markets in externalities would avoid the distorting effects of monetary and fiscal policy but would also have both administrative and "divergence-from-optimality" costs. But even if these costs are manageable, the existence of the market must be supportable politically. Most observers do not see the existence of such a market in variables that affect output stability as politically possible, so, despite the problems with monetary and fiscal policy, we must accept the current policies as substitutes.

The bottom line is that for any policy there is a trade-off between administrative costs and effective implementation. In general, it is not optimal to design policies that are first best, given many margins that require costly administration.[12] Wherever possible, tax systems could be designed with these problems in mind so that they can be offset to the greatest degree possible.

When the economy is viewed in a more dynamic context, one concern is whether policy interventions are destabilizing. A policy of government compensation for shocks requires recognizing a shock quickly, plus the political ability to respond appropriately. The monetarist view is that since an optimal policy requires policymakers to continually respond optimally to dynamic disturbances, optimal policy is impossible. However, if the economy is more stable under an optimal policy, policymakers may be able to follow a simple, stable rule. Our impression, viewing macroeconomic fluctuations and financial crises around the world, is that sources of fluctuations tend to vary unpredictably, so that "each source of fluctuation is different" (Caprio and Klingabiel 1997). This suggests making institutional frameworks as stable as possible, and then tying down aggregate price and output levels so that the unpredictable shocks or fluctuations cannot push these aggregates far from their long-run equilibrium values.

13.5 A Market in Rights to Change Prices

Let us now turn to the price-level change externality, which has been more extensively discussed in the literature than other types of macro externalities. The most developed of these proposals, the MAP proposal, recommends the creation of a market in the right to change value added input prices. If a firm wishes to raise its "price", the right must be purchased from another firm that is lowering its "price". In the MAP proposal, price changes are determined by changes in nominal value added units, which makes the property right in a uniform commodity. Thus, for example, a change in the price of cars which raised a firm's value added per unit input could be offset by a change in the price in the opposite direction of varieties of other goods—paper clips, TVs or computers, whatever—which when they are combined, create sufficient value added to offset the change in the price of cars.[13]

The market in rights to change prices that internalizes the macro externality is different than a market in pollution rights, because the policy goal with inflation is not to reduce the price level, but is, instead, to create a relatively stable price level. Therefore the market in rights to change prices is symmetric, and the price of rights to change price could be positive or negative depending on whether there is inflationary or deflationary pressure. Thus, if there were deflationary pressure in

[12] Sah (1987, p. 75) discusses ways of including administrative costs in optimal incentive schemes.

[13] One can think of the process of prices and quantities reversing places. Prices are weighted by value added quantities.

the economy, firms wanting to lower their prices would have to buy the right from firms wishing to raise their prices by an offsetting amount.

There are many technical problems with creating such a market, which have been discussed in the literature.[14] The literature concludes that it is possible to do so, but would have technical problems such as exist with the establishment of any property rights. We will not discuss those problems here other than to note that all supporters have the control variable to be "value added per unit input", not output prices. This is done for both theoretical and practical reasons. Firms would determine their value added in a manner similar to the manner in which the value added tax is determined. Their property rights base would be their initial value added at the level of inputs they are currently using. This base would rise by the average productivity increase in the economy.

Firms would then calculate an index of their real inputs, which would be primarily labor and new investment. When they increase their inputs they would gain value added rights equal to the real value of that input. For example, if a firm hired a worker for $14 per hour who was previously earning $12 per hour, it would gain value added equal to $12 per hour times the number of hours he works but would have to buy rights for the added $2 per hour times the number of hours he works minus the average productivity increase in the economy. To make the program manageable, it need only be operative for firms above a certain size, since if they hold their prices down, smaller firms will be forced to hold their prices down to be able to compete.

While the administrative costs of the plan are substantial, it is important to remember that the gains are also substantial. Moreover, the administrative costs of enforcing the property rights vary directly with the gains in preventing inflation that the plan provides. This is because the administrative costs are only large to the degree that there is a significant price for changing price. If there is little inflationary pressure, the price of raising price will be close to zero, and firms will not be overly concerned with the market. The program will only provide a coordination role, allowing a direct measure of the degree of inflationary or deflationary pressure in the economy. Moreover, the Fed can use that price of changing price as a guide to its monetary policy. If it sees a rise in the price of raising price, it knows to reduce the money supply to offset it, thereby reducing the price of raising price. The market makes the pressures for inflation transparent and in doing so helps make it possible for the encompassing interests to control inflation.

Could such a market be established? Currently, U.S. Policymakers have become convinced that the administrative costs of programs such as wage-price controls are very high. However, we believe that the answer is yes, precisely because of the strong encompassing interests in having a relatively stable price level. Stable prices are a politically potent value among the public and also among bondholders. Economists have also argued effectively that stable prices, guaranteed over the long run, are an important value. So there is both a political and economic constituency for stable prices. That constituency has supported the creation of re-

[14] See, for instance, Lerner and Colander (1980) and Colander (1986).

cessions to prevent accelerating inflation and the maintenance of a higher level of unemployment than would be the case to prevent inflation from occurring. Under current institutions the costs of doing that fall upon the unemployed. After a market in changing prices is established, the costs fall more directly on the individuals raising their prices.

13.6 The Real Policy Debate

Often, debates about macro policy are presented in the texts as differences in theory. Within our structure, that is not the case. The coordination failure approach can fit all groups. When looked at from the special interests/collective good framework, differences in macroeconomic policy no longer stem from basic theoretical differences as to whether external effects might exist in macro economies, since all major streams of research allow for externalities. Rather they come from differences in assessing their size and nature, and the implementation and political incentive problems and administrative costs of effective policy solutions. The question is whether the admitted incomplete markets can be made "complete" by government policy. Thus the debate can be joined directly taking the agreed-upon theoretical foundations, identifying the incomplete markets and determining the costs of these "market failures", and then examining the effectiveness and costs of potential policy solutions.

The Olsonian special interest/collective good framework presented in this chapter interprets differences between New Keynesian and New Classical policy as differences in views about costs of offsetting macroeconomic externalities. Keynesians regard excessive unemployment as extremely costly--*more* than proportional to the loss of jobs. This is consistent with models in which workers want, but cannot find, work. In Akerlof and Yellen's (1985) terms, while the external effects for the firms are second-order, the workers who lose their jobs suffer first-order losses. Real business cycle modelers, to the contrary, have treated unemployment as search activity, with excessive unemployment a merely second order effect. That is, workers should be essentially indifferent between working and unemployment (errors are all at the margin) and it is only the curvature of the utility hill that causes losses.[15]

By structuring the macro policy debate within this Olsonian special interest/collective good framework, assessing these costs becomes fundamental to choosing appropriate policy. The issues separating economists are then empirical, not theoretical. It is in the assessment of these costs that policy differences really

[15] Lucas (1987, p. 27) sees the only gains from optimal policy to be assuring a "perfectly smooth consumption path," not an increase in consumption. The value of this gain is small; "less than one tenth of a percentage point." In contrast, Okun (1981) calculates that the costs of unemployment are nearly proportional to the percentage loss of GNP below full-employment GNP. For 1976-1985, Gordon (1987) calculates this gap to average 3.6% of full-employment GNP.

are based. Since macro researchers all accept the same modeling approach, it is surprising how little analysis has gone into this debate. New Classicals still fall into the old Chicago approach to externalities ("In theory they might exist, but in practice I have yet to find one"). New Keynesians minimize the costs of internalizing the externality.

The real macro policy question has less to do with theory, and much more to do with practical and political problems of implementation. Do the encompassing interests have the power to win out over the special interests? By bringing these questions to the forefront, Olson's approach to economics sheds important light not only on microeconomic policy issues, but on macroeconomic policy issues as well.

References

Aarts, C., Lieshout, R. (1986) Size or Heterogeneity? A Contribution to a More Complete Analysis of the Likelihood of Collective Action, unpublished manuscript

Abramovitz, M. (1983) Notes on International Differences in Productivity Growth Rates, in Mueller, D. (ed) The Political Economy of Growth, Yale University Press, New Haven, 79-89

Abramovitz, M. (1986) Catching Up, Forging Ahead, and Falling Behind, Journal of Economic History 46, 385-406

Abramovitz, M. (1989) Thinking about Growth and other Essays on Economic Growth and Welfare, Cambridge University Press, New York

Acemoglu, D., Robinson J. (2001) A Theory of Political Transitions, American Economic Review 91, 938-963

Akerlof, G., Kranton, R. (2000) Economics and Identity, Quarterly Journal of Economics, 115, 715-754

Akerlof, G., Yellen, J. (1985) Can Small Deviations from Rationality Make Significant Differences to Economic Equilibria? American Economic Review 75, 708-20

Alesina, A., Drazen, A. (1991) Why are Stabilizations Delayed? American Economic Review 81, 1170-1188

Alesina, A., Gatti, R. (1995) Independent Central Banks: Low Inflation at no Cost? American Economic Review Papers and Proceedings 85, 196-200

Alston, L., Thráinn, E., North., D. (1996) Empirical Studies in Institutional Change, Cambridge University Press, Cambridge

Alt, J. (1999) Thoughts on Mancur Olson's Contribution to Political Science, Public Choice 98, 1-4

American Trucking Associations (1986-1988 Editions) Motor Carrier Annual Report, American Trucking Associations, Arlington, VA

Andersen, H. (1837, 1948) The Emperor's New Suit, in Andersen, H., Shorter Tales (tr. Hersholt, J.), Heritage Press, New York, NY

Andreoni, J. (1988) Privately Provided Public Goods in a Large Economy: The Limits of Altruism, Journal of Public Economics 35, 57-73

Andvig, J., Feldstad, O., Amundsen, I., Sissener, T., Soreide, T. (2000) Research on Corruption: A Policy-Oriented Survey, Chr. Michelsen Institute and Norwegian Institute of International Affairs, Bergen/Oslo

Andvig, J., Moene, K. (1990) How Corruption May Corrupt, Journal of Economic Behavior and Organization 13, 63-76

Anechiarico, F., Jacobs, J. (1996) The Pursuit of Absolute Integrity: How Corruption Control Makes Government Ineffective, University of Chicago Press, Chicago

Appelbaum, E., Katz, E. (1987) Seeking Rents by Setting Rents: The Political Economy of Rent Seeking, The Economic Journal 97, 685-699

Archer, K., Gibbins, R., Knopff, R., Pal, L. (1995) Parameters of Power: Canada's Political Institutions, Nelson Canada, Toronto

Aug, S. (1976) Truckers Pay $20 Million for Licenses of Associated, Washington Star, July, B-6

Bailyn, B. (1967) The Ideological Origins of the American Revolution, Harvard University Press, Cambridge

Baldwin, R. (1989) The Political Economy of Trade Policy, The Journal of Economic Perspectives 3, 119-135

Balinski, M., Young, H. (1982) Fair Representation, Yale University Press, New Haven

Banning, L. (1995) Sacred Fire of Liberty: James Madison & the Founding of the Federal Republic, Cornell University Press, Ithica, NY

Banting, K., Simeon, R. (1983a) Federalism, Democracy and the Constitution, in Banting, K., Simeon, R. (eds) And No One Cheered: Federalism, Democracy and the Constitution Act, Methuen, Toronto, 2-26.

Banting, K., Simeon, R. (1983b) Federalism, Democracy and the Future, in Banting, K., Simeon, R. (eds) And No One Cheered: Federalism, Democracy and the Constitution Act, Methuen, Toronto, 348-359

Bardhan, P. (1997) Corruption and Development: A Review of Issues, Journal of Economic Issues 35, 1320-1346

Barnes, T. (1995) There'll Always Be a Canada and a Canadian Constitutional Crisis, Annals of the American Academy of Political and Social Science 538, 27-39

Barro, R. (1991) Economic Growth in a Cross Section of Countries, Quarterly Journal of Economics 106, 407-444

Barro, R. (1997) Determinants of Economic Growth: A Cross-Country Empirical Study, MIT Press, Cambridge, MA

Barry, B. ([1970] 1988) Sociologists, Economists and Democracy, University of Chicago Press, Chicago

Barry, B. (1983) Some Questions about Explanation, International Studies Quarterly 27, 17-27

Barzel, Y. (2002) A Theory of the State, Cambridge University Press, New York

Bates, R. (1994) The Impulse to Reform in Africa, in Widner, J. (ed) Economic Change and Political Liberalization in Sub-Saharan Africa, Johns Hopkins University Press, Baltimore, 13-28

Baumol, W. ([1952] 1969) Welfare Economics and the Theory of the State, Harvard University Press, Cambridge, MA

Baumol, W. (1950) Welfare Economics and the Theory of the State, Princeton University Press, Princeton

Baumol, W. (1986) Productivity Growth, Convergence, and Welfare: What the Long-Run Data Show, American Economic Review 76, 1072-1085

Beck, T., Clarke, G., Groff, A., Keefer, P., Walsh, P. (2001) New Tools in Comparative Political Economy: The Database of Political Institutions, World Bank Economic Review 15, 165-176

Becker, G. (1974) A Theory of Social Interactions, Journal of Political Economy 82, 1063-1093

Bemheim, B. (1986) On the Voluntary and Involuntary Provision of Public Goods, American Economic Review 76, 789-793

Bentley, A.F. ([1908] 1967) The Process of Government, Belknap Press, Cambridge, MA

Berg, A., Sachs, J. (1988) The Debt Crisis: Structural Explanations of Country Performance. Journal of Development Economics 29, 271-306

Bergstrom, T., Blume, L. and Varian, H. (1986) On the Private Provision of Public Goods, Journal of Public Economics 29, 25-49

Bernanke, B., Gertler, M. (1999) Monetary Policy and Asset Price Volatility, in New Challenges for Monetary Policy, Federal Reserve Bank of Kansas City

Bernanke, B., Laubach, T., Mishkin, F., Posen, A. (1999) Inflation Targeting: Lessons from the International Experience, Princeton University Press, Princeton

Bernstein M., Adler, D. (eds) (1994) Understanding American Economic Decline, Cambridge University Press, New York

Bils, M., Klenow, P. (1998) Using Consumer Theory to Test Competing Business Cycle Models, Journal of Political Economy 106, 233-261

Blaug, M. (ed) (1999) Who's Who in Economics, third edition, Edward Elgar, Cheltenham, UK

Booth, A. (2001) The British Economy in the Twentieth Century, Palgrave, Houndsmill, UK

Booth, A., Melling, J., Dartmann, C. (1997) Institutions and Economic Growth: The Politics of Productivity in West Germany, Sweden, and the United Kingdom, 1945-1955, Journal of Economic History 57, 416-447

Bordo, M., Goldin, C., White, E. (eds) (1998) The Defining Moment: The Great Depression and the American Economy in the Twentieth Century, University of Chicago Press, Chicago

Boserup, E. (1965) The Conditions of Agricultural Growth: The Economics of Agrarian Change under Population Press, Aldine, Chicago

Bowen, H. (1943) The Interpretation of Voting in the Allocation of Economic Resources, Quarterly Journal of Economics 58, 27-48

Bowen, R., Noreen, E., Lacey, J. (1981) Determinants of the Corporate Decision To Capitalize Interest, Journal of Accounting and Economics 3, 151-179

Brand, D. (1983) Corporatism, the NRA, and the Oil Industry, Political Science Quarterly 98, 99-118

Breen, D. (1977) The Monopoly Value of Household-Goods Carrier Operating Certificates, Journal of Law and Economics 20, 153-185

Brewer, J. (1990) The Sinews of Power: War, Money and the English State, 1688-1783, Harvard University Press, Cambridge, MA

Brozovsky, J., Sopariwala, P. (1995) The Determinants of Performance Plan Adoptions, Journal of Accounting, Auditing, and Finance 10, 655-676

Bryant, J. (1983) A Simple Rational Expectations Keynes-Type Model, Quarterly Journal of Economics 98, 525-528

Buchanan, J. (1965) An Economic Theory of Clubs, Economica, 35, 1-14

Buchanan, J. (1999) Mancur Olson. The Region, Minneapolis Federal Reserve Bank

Buchanan, J. Tullock, G. (1962) The Calculus of Consent, Logical Foundations of Constitutional Democracy, University of Michigan Press, Ann Arbor

Cadman, J. (1949) The Corporation in New Jersey: Business and Politics, 1791-1875, Harvard University Press, Cambridge

Cain, L. Hughes, J. (1998) American Economic History, fifth edition, Addison-Wesley, Reading, MA

Callaghy, T. (1994) Civil Society, Democracy, and Economic Change in Africa: A Dissenting Opinion About Resurgent Societies, in Harbeson, J., Rothchild, D., Chazan, N. (eds.) Civil Society and the State in Africa, Lynne Reiner Boulder, CO, 231-254

Campos, J., Lien, D., Pradhan, S. (1999) The Impact of Corruption on Investment: Predictability Matters, World Development 27, 1059-1067

Caprio, G., Klingebiel, D. (1997) Bank Insolvency: Bad Luck, Bad Policy, or Bad Banking? in Bruno, M., Pleskovic, B. (eds) Annual Bank Conference on Development Economics, 1996, World Bank, Washington, D.C.

Carter, N., James, P. (2002) What Game Did They Play, After All? Long Knives, Long Memories and the Constitutional Negotiations of 1981, presented at the biannual meeting of the Association for Canadian Studies in the United States, San Antonio, TX

CBOS (1993) Preferencje polityczne spoleczenstwa trzy tygodnie przed wyborami (Political Preferences of Polish Society Three Weeks Before the Elections), CBOS, Warszawa

Central Europe Online (CEO) (June 19, 1997), Internal Feud Rocks Main Polish Opposition Group, www.centraleurope.com

Chamberlain, N. (1966) The Logic of Collective Action, (book review) American Economic Review 56, 603-605

Chamberlin, J. (1974) Provision of Collective Goods as a Function of Group Size, American Political Science Review 68, 707-716

Chandler, A. (1977) The Visible Hand: The Managerial Revolution in American Business, Belknap Press, Cambridge, MA

Chandler, C. (1993) Two Americans Given Nobel in Economics, Washington Post, October 13, C1

Chari, V., Jones, L. (2000) A Reconsideration of the Problem of Social Cost: Free Riders and Monopolists, Economic Theory 16, 1-22,

Choi, K. (1983) A Statistical Test of Olson's Model, in Mueller, D. (ed) The Political Economy of Growth, Yale University Press, New Haven, CT, 57-78

Clague, C. (1993) Rule Obedience, Organizational Loyalty, and Economic Development, Journal of Institutional and Theoretical Economics 149, 393-414

Clague, C. (2002) Economic Policy Reform: Analytical Approaches from Economics and Political Science, in Grosbard-Shechtman, S., Clague, C. (eds) The Expansion of Economics: Toward a More Inclusive Social Science, M.E. Sharpe, Armonk, NY, 68-98

Clague, C., Gleason, S., Knack, S. (2001) The Determinants of Lasting Democracy in Poor Countries: Institutions, Culture, and Economic Development, Annals of the American Academy of Political and Social Science January, 573, 16-41

Coates, D., Heckelman, J. (2003) Interest Groups and Investment: A Further Test of the Olson Hypothesis, Public Choice, forthcoming

Colander, D. (1992) A Real Theory of Inflation and Incentive Anti-Inflation Plans, American Economic Review 82, 335-40,

Colander, D. (ed) (1986) Incentive Based Incomes Policies, Ballinger, Cambridge, MA

Colander, D., Koford, K. (1985) Externalities and Macroeconomic Policy, in Maital, S., Lipnowski, I. (eds) Macroeconomic Conflict and Social Institutions, Ballinger, Cambridge, MA

Cole, A. (1946) An Approach to the Study of Entrepreneurship: A Tribute to Edwin F. Gay, Journal of Economic History 6, Supplement, 1-15

Cole, A. (1970) The Committee on Research in Economic History: An Historical Sketch, The Journal of Economic History 30, 723-741

Collins, R. (1980) Weber's Last Theory of Capitalism: A Systematization, American Sociological Review 45, 925-42

Commons, J. ([1950] 1970) The Economics of Collective Action, University of Wisconsin Press, Madison

Commons, J. (1934) Institutional Economics: Its Place in Political Economy, The Macmillan Company, New York

Conrad, A., Meyer, J. (1958) The Economics of Slavery in the Ante-Bellum South, Journal of Political Economy 66, 95-130

Coolidge, J., Rose-Ackerman, S. (2000) Kleptocracy and Reform in African Regimes: Theory and Examples, in Hope, K., Chikulo, B. (eds), Corruption and Development in Africa, Macmillan, London, 57-86

Cooper, R. (1996) Evidence on Macroeconomic Complementarities, Review of Economics and Statistics 77, 78-93

Cooper, R. (1999) Coordination Games: Complementarities and Macroeconomics, Cambridge University Press, Cambridge

Cooper, R., Haltiwanger, J. (1990) Inventories and the Propagation of Sectoral Shocks, American Economic Review 80, 170-190

Cooper, R., Haltiwanger, J. (1993) Autos and the National Industrial Recovery Act: Evidence on Industry Complementarities, Quarterly Journal of Economics 108, 1043-1072

Cooper, R., John A. (1988) Coordinating Coordination Failures in Keynesian Models, Quarterly Journal of Economics 103, 441-464

Copes, P. (1966) Review of The Economics of Wartime Shortage, Canadian Journal of Economics and Political Science 32, 128

Cornes, R., Sandler, T. (1985) The Simple Analytics of Pure Public Good Provision, Economica 52, 103-116

Cornes, R., Sandler, T. (1986) The Theory of Externalities, Public Goods and Club Goods, Cambridge University Press, Cambridge

Cotta, M. (1996) Structuring the New Party Systems after the Dictatorship: Coalitions, Alliances, Fusions and Splits During the Transition and Post-Transition Stages, in Pridham, G., Lewis, P. (eds) Stabilizing Fragile Democracies: Comparing New Party Systems in Southern and Eastern Europe, Routledge, London, 69-99

Crouch, H. (1979) Patrimonialism and Military Rule in Indonesia, World Politics 31, 571-89

Dahl, R. (1956) A Preface to Democratic Theory, University of Chicago Press, Chicago

Das-Gupta, A., Mookherjee, D. (1998) Incentives and Institutional Reform in Tax Enforcement, Oxford University Press, New Delhi

Datta, K., Murray, A. (1989) The Rights of Minorities and Subject Peoples in Botswana: A Historical Evaluation, in Holm, J., Molutsi, P. (eds), Democracy in Botswana, Ohio University Press, Athens, OH, 58-74

David, P. (1965) Review of The Economics of Wartime Shortage, Journal of Economic History 25, 167-169

David, P., Gutman, H., Sutch, R., Temin, P., Wright, G. (1976) Reckoning with Slavery: A Critical Study in the Quantitative History of American Negro Slavery, Oxford University Press, New York

Davis, J. (1917) Essays in the Earlier History of American Corporations, Harvard University Press, Cambridge

Davis, L., North, D. (1971) Institutional Change and American Economic Growth, Cambridge University Press, Cambridge

De Toqueville, A. (1966) Democracy in America, (translated by Lawrence, G.), Harper and Row, New York

de Viti de Marco, A. ([1932] 1936) First Principles of Public Finance, (translated by Marget, E.), Harcourt Brace and Co, New York

de Vries, J. (1983) The Rise and Decline of Nations in Historical Perspective, International Studies Quarterly 27, 11-16

Deininger, K., Squire, L. (1996). Measuring Income Inequality: A New Data Set, World Bank Economic Review 10, 565-591 della Porta, D., Vannucci, A. (1999) Corrupt Exchanges: Actors, Resources, and Mechanisms of Political Corruption, Aldine de Gruyter, New York

DeVany, A., Savings, T. (1977) Product Quality, Uncertainty, and Regulation: The Trucking Industry, American Economic Review 67, 582-594

Dixit, A., Olson, M. (2000) Does Voluntary Participation Undermine the Coase Theorem? Journal of Public Economics 76, 309-335

Dodd, E. (1954) American Business Corporations until 1860, with Special Reference to Massachusetts. Harvard University Press, Cambridge

Doig, A., Theobald, R. (2000) Introduction: Why Corruption? in Doig, A., Theobald, R. (eds) Corruption and Democratisation, Frank Cass, London, 1-12

Dotto, L., Schiff, H. (1978) The Ozone War, Doubleday, Garden City, NJ

Dougherty, K. (2001) Collective Action under the Articles of Confederation, Cambridge University Press, New York

Dougherty, K. (2002) Madison's Theory of Public Goods, in Kernell, S. (ed) James Madison: The Theory and Practice of Government, Stanford University Press, Stanford (forthcoming)

Dowding, K. (1997) Olson, Mancur, in Parker, N., Stuart S. (eds) The A-Z Guide to Modern Social and Political Theorists, Prentice Hall, New York, 270-273

Downs, A. (1957) An Economic Theory of Democracy, Harper and Row, New York

Duby, G. (1974) The Early Growth of the European Economy: Warriors and Peasants from the Seventh to the Twelfth Century, (translated by Clarke, H.), Cornell University Press, Ithaca, NY

Easterly, W. (2001) The Elusive Quest for Growth: Economists' Adventures and Misadventures in the Tropics, M.I.T. Press, Cambridge, MA

Easterly, W., Levine, R. (1997) Africa's Growth Tragedy: Policies and Ethnic Divisions, Quarterly Journal of Economics 112, 1203-1250

Eigen, P. (1998) The Role of Civil Society, in Corruption and Integrity Improvement Initiatives in Developing Countries, United Nations Development Program, New York, 83-90

Eisenstadt, T. (1999) Off the Streets and into the Courtroom: Resolving Post-Electoral Conflicts in Mexico, in Schedler, A., Diamond, L., Plattner, M. (eds) The Self-Restraining State: Power and Accountability in New Democracies, Lynne Reiner, Boulder, CO, 83-104

Ely, K. (1991) Interindustry Differences in the Relation between Compensation and Firm Performance Variables, Journal of Accounting Research 29, 37-58

Engerman, S., Gallman, R. (eds) (1986) Long-term Factors in American Economic Growth, University of Chicago Press, Chicago

Engerman, S., Gallman, R. (eds) (1996, 2000) The Cambridge Economic History of the United States, three volumes, Cambridge University Press, New York

Enis, C., Morash, E. (1986) Market Protection, Deregulation, and the Question of Industry Losses, Transportation Law Journal 15, 89-104

Epstein, E. (1989) Deception: The Invisible War between the KGB and the CIA, Simon & Schuster, New York, NY

Esteban, J., Ray, D. (1994). On the Measurement of Polarization, Econometrica 62, 819-851

Esteban, J., Ray, D. (2001) Collective Action and the Group Size Paradox, American Political Science Review 95, 663-672

Evans, G. (1948) Business Incorporations in the United States, 1800-1943. NBER, Waverly Press, Baltimore

Evans, P. (1992) The State as Problem and Solution: Predation, Embedded Autonomy, and Structural Change, in Haggard, S., Kaufman, R. (eds) The Politics of Economic Adjustment, Princeton University Press, Princeton, NJ, 139-181

Feder, G., Ross, K. (1982). Risk Assessments and Risk Premiums in the Eurodollar Market. Journal of Finance 37, 679-691

Field, A. (1991) Review of Institutions, Institutional Change and Economic Performance, Journal of Economic History 51, 999-100

Filippov, M., Ordeshook, P., Shvetsova, O. (1999) Party Fragmentation and Presidential Elections in Post-Communist Democracies, Constitutional Political Economy 10, 3-26

Flanagan, T. (2002) Canada's Three Constitutions: Protecting, Overturning, and Reversing the Status Quo, in James, P., Abelson, D., Lusztig, M. (eds) The Myth of the Sacred: The Charter, the Courts and the Politics of the Constitution in Canada, McGill-Queen's University Press, Montreal and Kingston

Floud, R., McCloskey, D. (eds) (1994) The Economic History of Britain since 1700, three volumes, Cambridge University Press, New York

Fogel, R. (1964) Railroads and American Economic Growth: Essays in Econometric History, Johns Hopkins University Press, Baltimore, MD

Fogel, R. (1979) Notes on the Social Saving Controversy, Journal of Economic History 39, 1-54

Fogel, R. (2000) The Fourth Great Awakening & the Future of Egalitarianism, University of Chicago Press, Chicago

Fogel, R., Engerman, S. (1974) Time on the Cross: The Economics of American Negro Slavery, Little, Brown and Company, Boston

French, M. (1997) U.S. Economic History since 1945, Manchester University Press, Manchester

Friedman, M., Schwartz, A. (1963) A Monetary History of the United States, 1867-1960, Princeton University Press, Princeton

Frohlich, N., Oppenheimer, J. (1970) I Get by with a Little Help from my Friends, Journal of World Politics 23, 104-120

Galtung, F., Pope, J. (1999) The Global Coalition Against Corruption: Evaluating Transparency International, in Schedler, A., Diamond, L., Plattner, M. (eds) The Self-Restraining State: Power and Accountability in New Democracies, Lynne Reiner, Boulder, CO, 257-282

GAO (1994) Credit Reform: U.S. Needs Better Method for Estimating Cost of Foreign Loans and Guarantees, Washington, DC: U.S. General Accounting Office

Gay, E. (1903) Inclosures in England in the Sixteenth Century, Quarterly Journal of Economics 17, 576-597

Gay, E. (1930) Historical Records, American Economic Review 20, 1-8

Geddes, B. (1994) Politician's Dilemma: Building State Capacity in Latin America, University of California Press, Berkeley

Gibbins, R. (1983) Constitutional Politics and the West, in Banting, K., Simeon, R. (eds) And No One Cheered: Federalism, Democracy and the Constitution Act, Methuen, Toronto, 119-132.

Gilpin, R. (1987) The Political Economy of International Relations, Princeton University Press, Princeton, NJ

Glynn, P., Kobrin, S., Naim, M. (1997) The Globalization of Corruption, in Elliott, K. (ed) Corruption and the Global Economy, Institute for International Economics, Washington, D.C., 7-27

Goodman, J., Dolan, E. (1982) Economics of Public Policy: The Micro View, 2nd edition, West, St. Paul, MN

Goodrich, C. (1963) Rapid Growth as a Destabilizing Force: Discussion, Journal of Economic History 23, 553-558

Gordon, R. (1987) Macroeconomics, Addison Wesley, Reading, MA

Gould, W., Rogers, W. (1994) Quantile Regression as an Alternative to Robust Regression, Proceedings of the Statistical Computing Section, American Statistical Association, Alexandria, VA

Graniszewski, L. (1997) Akcja Wyborcza Solidarnosc - sojusz prawicy demokratycznej (Electoral Action Solidarity - the Coalition of Democratic Right), in Gebethner, S. (ed) Wybory '97. Partie i Programy Polityczne, Dom Wydawniczy Elipsa, Warsaw

Gray, V., Lowery, D. (1988) Interest Group Politics and Growth in the U.S. States, American Political Science Review 82, 109-131

Greif, A. (1989) Reputation and Coalitions in Medieval Trade: Evidence on the Maghribi Traders, Journal of Economic History 49, 857-882

Greif, A., Milgrom, P., Weingast, B. (1994) Coordination, Commitment, and Enforcement: The Case of the Merchant Guild, The Journal of Political Economy 102, 745-776

Grofman, B., Mikkel, E., Taagepera R. (2000) Fission and Fusion of Parties in Estonia, 1987-1999, Journal of Baltic Studies 31, 329-357

Haggard, S., Kaufman, R. (eds) (1992) The Politics of Economic Adjustment: International Constraints, Distributive Conflicts and the State, Princeton University Press, Princeton, NJ

Handlin, O., Handlin, M. (1969) Commonwealth: A Study of the Role of Government in the American Economy: Massachusetts, 1774-1861. Harvard University Press, Cambridge, MA

Hardin, R. (1982) Collective Action, Johns Hopkins University Press, Baltimore, MD

Harper, D. (1980) The Federal Motor Carrier Act of 1980: Review and Analysis, Transportation Journal 20, 6-7

Harvey, C., Lewis, S. (1990) Policy Choice and Development Performance in Botswana, St. Martin's Press, New York

Head, J. (1962) Public Goods and Public Policy, Public Finance 27, 197-219

Healy, P. (1985) The Effect of Bonus Schemes on Accounting Decisions, Journal of Accounting and Economics 7, 85-107

Healy, P., Kang, S., Palepu. K. (1987) The Effect of Accounting Procedure Changes on CEO's Cash Salary and Bonus Compensation, Journal of Accounting and Economics 9, 9-34

Heaton, H. (1949) The Making of an Economic Historian, Journal of Economic History 9, Supplement, 1-18

Heckelman, J. (2000) Consistent Estimates of the Impact of Special Interest Groups on Economic Growth. Public Choice 104, 319-327

Heckelman, J., Wallis, J. (1997) Railroads and Property Taxes, Explorations in Economic History 34, 77-99

Heckelman, J., Wood, J. (1999) Federal Reserve Membership and the Banking Act of 1935: An Application to the Theory of Clubs, in Heckelman, J., Moorhouse, J., Whaples, R.

(eds) Public Choice Interpretations of American Economic History, Kluwer Academic Press, Boston, MA
Heckman, J. (1976) A Life-Cycle Model of Earnings, Learning, and Consumption, Journal of Political Economy 84, S11-S44
Hiebert, J. (1993) Rights and Public Debate: The Limitation of a Rights Must be Paramount Perspective, International Journal of Canadian Studies 7-8, 117-135
Hinich, M., Munger, M., Marchi, S. (1998) Ideology and the Construction of Nationality: The Canadian Elections of 1993, Public Choice 97, 401-428
Hirschman, A. (1970) Exit, Voice, and Loyalty, Harvard University Press, Cambridge, MA
Holm, J. (1988) Botswana: A Paternalistic Democracy, in Diamond, L., Linz, J., Lipset, S. (eds) Democracy in Developing Countries, v.2: Africa, Lynne Reiner, Boulder, CO, 179-218
Holm, J. (2000) Curbing Corruption through Democratic Accountability: Lessons from Botswana, in Hope, K., Chikulo, B. (eds) Corruption and Development in Africa, Macmillan, London, 288-304
Holm, J., Molutsi, P., Somolekae, G. (1996) The Development of Civil Society in a Democratic State: The Botswana Model, African Studies Review 39, 43-69
Holthausen, R. (1981) Evidence on the Effect of Bond Covenants and Management Compensation Contracts on the Choice of Accounting Techniques: The Case of the Depreciation Switch-Back, Journal of Accounting and Economics 3, 73-109
Hoogenboom, A. (1961) Outlawing the Spoils: A History of the Civil Service Reform Movement 1865-1883, University of Illinois Press, Urbana, IL
Horowitz, D. (1985) Ethnic Groups in Conflict, University of California Press, Berkeley, CA
Hume, D. ([1739-40], 1978) A Treatise of Human Nature, Selby-Bigge, L. (ed), Clarendon Press, Oxford, UK
Huntington, S. (1968) Political Order in Changing Societies, Yale University Press, New Haven, CT
Hurst, J. (1956) Law and the Conditions of Freedom in the Nineteenth Century United States, University of Wisconsin Press, Madison
Husted, B. (1999) Wealth, Culture, and Corruption, Journal of International Business Studies 30, 339-360
Hutchcroft, P. (1998) Booty Capitalism: The Politics of Banking in the Philippines, Cornell University Press, Ithaca, NY
Hutchcroft, P. (2000) Obstructive Corruption: The Politics of Privilege in the Philippines, in Khan, M., Jomo, K. (eds) Rents, Rent-Seeking and Economic Development: Theory and Evidence from Asia, Cambridge University Press, Cambridge, 199-227
Hutchcroft, P. (2002) The Politics of Privilege: Rents and Corruption in Asia, in Heidenheimer, A., Johnston, M. (eds) Political Corruption: Concepts and Cases, Transaction Publishers, New Brunswick, NJ, 489-512
IMF (International Monetary Fund) (2002) Survey, IMF, Washington, D.C
Interstate Commerce Commission (1980) Annual Report, U.S. Government Printing Office, Washington, D.C.
Interstate Commerce Commission (1981) The Effect of Regulatory Reform on the Trucking Industry: Structure Conduct, and Performance, U.S. Government Printing Office, Washington, D.C.
Interstate Commerce Commission (1984) Annual Report., U.S. Government Printing Office, Washington, D.C.

Jack, B. (1990) The Coumot-Nash Alliance Public Good Model: An Integrated, Diagrammatic Approach to the Free-Riding, Multilateral Contribution and Neutrality Results, University of Maryland Department of Economics, Working Paper 90-16

James, P. (1993) Energy Politics in Canada, 1980-1981: Threat Power in a Sequential Game, Canadian Journal of Political Science 26, 31-59

James, P., Lusztig, M. (2002) Say Goodbye to the Dream of One Canada: The Costly Failure to Purchase National Unity, in Lazar, H., Telford, H. (eds) Canada: State of the Federation 2001, Queen's University Institute of Intergovernmental Relations, Kingston, forthcoming

Janis, I. (1972) Victims of Groupthink: A Psychological Study of Foreign Policy Decisions and Fiascoes, Houghton Mifflin, Boston, MA

Jankowski, R. (2001) Conditional Economic Convergence: A Theoretical and Empirical Analysis, presented at Public Choice Society conference, San Antonio, TX

Jazairy, I., Alamgir, M., Panuccio, T. (1992) State of World Rural Poverty: An Inquiry into its Causes and Consequences, International Fund for Agricultural Development.

Jensen, M. (1989) Eclipse of the Public Corporation, Harvard Business Review 67, 61-74

Jensen, M., Meckling, W. (1976) Theory of the Firm: Managerial Behavior, Agency Cost and Ownership Structure, Journal of Financial Economics 3, 305-360

Jensen, M., Murphy, K. (1990) Performance Pay and Top-Management Incentives, Journal of Political Economy 98, 225-264

John, A. (1995) Macroeconomic Externalities, in Dixon, H., Rankin, N. (eds) The New Macroeconomics: Imperfect Markets and Policy Effectiveness, Cambridge University Press, New York

Johnson, P. (1978) Shopkeeper's Millenium: Society and Revivals in Rochester, New York, 1815-1837, Hill and Wang, New York

Johnson, R., Liebecap, G. (1994) The Federal Civil Service System and the Problem of Bureaucracy, University of Chicago Press, Chicago

Johnston, M. (1986) The Political Consequences of Corruption: A Reassessment, Comparative Politics 18, 459-78

Johnston, M. (1997) Public Officials, Private Interests, and Sustainable Democracy: When Politics and Corruption Meet, in Elliott, K. (ed) Corruption and the Global Economy, Institute for International Economics, Washington, D.C., 61-82

Johnston, M. (1998) Fighting Systemic Corruption: Social Foundations for Institutional Reform, in Robinson, M. (ed) Corruption and Development, Frank Cass, London, 85-104

Johnston, M. (1999) A Brief History of Anti-Corruption Agencies, in Schedler, A., Diamond, L., Plattner, M. (eds) The Self-Restraining State: Power and Accountability in New Democracies, Lynne Reiner, Boulder, CO, 217-226

Jones, T., Hill, C. (1992) Stakeholder Agency Theory, Journal of Management Studies 29, 131-154

Jovanovic, B. (1979) Job Matching and the Theory of Turnover, Journal of Political Economy 87, 972-990

Kaminski, M. (1998) Strategiczne konsekwencje laczenia sie i dzielenia: Analiza konsolidacji polskiego systemu partyjnego pomiedzy 1993 a 1997 rokiem (Strategic Consequences of Splits and Mergers: Analysis of the Consolidation of the Polish Party System between 1993 and 1997), Studia Socjologiczne 150, 19-47

Kaminski, M. (2001) Coalitional Stability of Multi-Party Systems: Evidence from Poland, American Journal of Political Science 45, 294-312

Kaminski, M., Lissowski, G., Swistak, P. (1998) The Revival of Communism or the Effect of Institutions? The 1993 Polish Parliamentary Elections, Public Choice 97, 429-449

Kaufman, D. (1998) Revisiting Anti-Corruption Strategies: Tilt Towards Incentive-Driven Approaches, in Corruption and Integrity Improvement Initiatives in Developing Countries, United Nations Development Program, New York, 63-82

Keefer, P. (2002) Credibility, Clientilism and the Fiscal Impact of Political Institutions, presented at the Public Choice Society meetings, San Diego, CA

Keefer, P., Knack, S. (2002) Polarization, Property Rights and the Links between Inequality and Growth, Public Choice 111, 127-154

Keefer, P., Stasavage, D. (2000) Bureaucratic Delegation and Political Institutions: When are Independent Central Banks Irrelevant? World Bank Policy Research Working Paper 2356

Keynes, J. (1940) How to Pay for the War, Harcourt, Brace, New York

Khan, M. (1998) The Role of Civil Society and Patron-Client Networks in the Analysis of Corruption, in Corruption and Integrity Improvement Initiatives in Developing Countries, United Nations Development Program, New York, 111-128

Kindleberger, C. (1981) Dominance and Leadership in the International Economy: Exploitation, Public Goods, and Free Rides, International Studies Quarterly 25, 242-254

Kindleberger, C. (1983) On the Rise and Decline of Nations, International Studies Quarterly 27, 5-10

Klitgaard, R. (1988) Controlling Corruption, University of California Press, Berkeley, CA

Klitgaard, R. (1997a) Information and Incentives in Institutional Reform, in Clague, C. (ed) Institutions and Economic Development: Growth and Governance in Less-Developed and Post-Socialist Countries, Johns Hopkins University Press, Baltimore, MD, 292-315

Klitgaard, R. (1997b) Cleaning Up and Invigorating the Civil Service, Public Administration and Development 17, 487-509

Klitgaard, R., MacLean-Abaroa, R., Parris, H. (2000) Corrupt Cities: A Practical Guide to Cure and Prevention, ICS Press, Oakland, CA

Knack, S. (2003) Groups, Growth and Trust: Cross Country Evidence on the Olson and Putnam Hypotheses, Public Choice forthcoming

Knack, S., Keefer, P. (1995) Institutions and Economic Performance: Cross-Country Tests Using Alternative Institutional Measures, Economics and Politics 7, 207-227

Knack, S., Keefer, P. (1997) Does Inequality Harm Growth Only in Democracies? A Replication and Extension, American Journal of Political Science 41, 323-332

Knack, S., Keefer, P. (1997) Does Social Capital Have an Economic Payoff? A Cross-Country Investigation, Quarterly Journal of Economics 112, 1251-1288

Koford, K., Miller, J., Colander, D. (2001) Macroeconomic Externalities: New Keynesian Theory and Policy, University of Delaware Working Paper

Kopecky, P. (1995) Factionalism in Parliamentary Parties in the Czech Republic: A Concept and Some Empirical Findings, Democratization 2, 138-151

Krueger, A. (1993) The Political Economy of Economic Policy Reform in Developing Countries, MIT Press, Cambridge, MA

Krzaklewski, M., Raina, P. (1997) Chcemy byc narodem z przyszloscia (We Want to Be a Nation with the Future), Ksiazka Polska, Warsaw

Kuran, T. (1991) Now out of Never: the Element of Surprise in the East European Revolution of 1989, World Politics 44, 7-48

Kuznets, S. (1966) Modern Economic Growth: Rate, Structure, and Spread, Yale University Press, New Haven

Laaksa, M., Taagepera, R. (1979) The 'Effective' Number of Parties: A Measure with Application to West Europe, Comparative Political Studies 12, 3-27

Lambsdorff, J. (2001) Background Paper to the 2001 Corruption Perceptions Index, Transparency International and Gottingen University (www.transparency.org)

Landa, J. (1981) A Theory of the Ethnically Homogeneous Middleman Group: An Institutional Alternative to Contract Law, Journal of Legal Studies 10, 349-362

Landau, D. (1985) Government Expenditure and Economic Growth in the Developed Countries: 1952-1976, Public Choice 47, 459-477

Landes, D. (1969) The Unbound Prometheus: Technological Change and Industrial Development in Western Europe from 1750 to the Present, Cambridge University Press, Cambridge

Langseth, P., Stapenhurst, R., Pope, J. (1999) National Integrity Systems, in Stapenhurst, R., Kpundeh, S. (eds) Curbing Corruption: Toward a Model for Building National Integrity, World Bank, Washington, 127-150

Larcker, D. (1983) The Association Between Performance Plan Adoption and Corporate Capital Investment, Journal of Accounting and Economics 5, 3-30

Larcker, D. (1987) Short-Term Compensation Contracts and Executive Expenditure Decisions: The Case of Commercial Banks, Journal of Financial and Quantitative Analysis 22, 33-50

Lee, Y. (2000) From Third World to First: The Singapore Story, HarperCollins, New York

Leff, N. (1964) Economic Development through Bureaucratic Corruption, American Behavioral Scientist 8, 8-14

Leiken, R. (1997) Controlling the Global Corruption Epidemic, Foreign Policy 105, 55-73

Leith, J., Lofchie, M. (1993) The Political Economy of Structural Adjustment in Ghana, in Bates, R., Krueger, A. (eds) Political and Economic Interactions in Economic Policy Reform: Evidence from Eight Countries, Basil Blackwell, Oxford, 225-293

Lenz, R., Lyles. M. (1986) Managing Human Problems in Strategic Planning Systems, Journal of Business Strategy 6, 57-66

Lerner, A. (1960) On Generalizing the General Theory, American Economic Review 50, 121-43

Lerner, A., Colander, D. (1980) MAP: A Market Anti Inflation Plan, Harcourt Brace, New York

Levine, R. (1997) Financial Development and Economic Growth: Views and Agenda, Journal of Economic Literature 35, 688-726

Levine, R., Zervos, S. (1998) Stock Markets, Banks, and Economic Growth, American Economic Review 88, 537-558

Lewellen, W., Loderer, C., Martin K. (1987) Executive Compensation and Executive Incentive Problems: An Empirical Analysis, Journal of Accounting and Economics 9, 287-310

Lindahl, E. ([1919] 1967) Just Taxation: A Positive Solution, in Musgrave, R., Peacock A. (eds) Classics in the Theory of Public Finance, St. Martin's Press, New York, 168-176

Lindahl, E. ([1928] 1967) Some Controversial Questions in the Theory of Taxation, in Musgrave, R., Peacock A. (eds) Classics in the Theory of Public Finance, St. Martin's Press, New York, 214-232

Lindert, P. (2000) U.S. Foreign Trade and Trade Policy in the Twentieth Century, in Engerman, S., Gallman, R. (eds) The Cambridge Economic History of the United States, Vol. 3, The Twentieth Century, Cambridge University Press, New York

Lomax, B. (1994) Elections in Hungary: Back to the Future or Forward to the Past? The Journal of Communist Studies and Transition 10, 125-137

Loury, G. (1993) Self-Censorship, The Partisan Review 60, 608

Lucas, R. (1987) Models of Business Cycles, Oxford: Basil Blackwell

MacDonald, G. (1980) Person-Specific Information in the Labor Market, Journal of Political Economy 88, 578-597

Maddex, R. (1995) Constitutions of the World, Washington, DC: Congressional Quarterly, Inc.

Maddison, A. (1988) Ultimate and Proximate Growth Causality: A Critique of Mancur Olson on the Rise and Decline of Nations, Scandinavian Economic History Review 36, 25-29

Maier, P. (1992) The Debate Over Incorporations: Massachusetts in the Early Republic, in Wright, C. (ed) Massachusetts and the New Nation, Massachusetts Historical Society, Boston

Maier, P. (1993) The Revolutionary Origins of the American Corporation, William and Mary Quarterly, 3d series, Vol L, 51-84

Malinvaud, E. (1976) The Theory of Unemployment Reconsidered, Halsted

Manfredi, C., (2001) Judicial Power and the Charter: Canada and the Paradox of Liberal Constitutionalism, 2nd. ed., Oxford University Press, Don Mills, Canada

Manzetti, L. (2000) Market Reforms without Transparency, in Tulchin J., Espach, R. (eds) Combating Corruption in Latin America, The Woodrow Wilson Center Press, Washington, D.C., 130-172

Maranto, R., Schulz, D. (1991) A Short History of the United States Civil Service, University Press of America, Lanham, MD

March, J., Simon, H. (1958) Organizations, John Wiley and Sons, New York

Marschak, J. (1955) Elements for a Theory of Teams, Management Science 1, 127-137

Marsh, D. (1976) On Joining Interest Groups: An Empirical Consideration of the Work of Mancur Olson Jr., British Journal of Political Science 6, 257-271

Martin, R. (1996) Reconstituting Democracy: Orthodoxy and Research in Law and Social Science, in Peacock, A. (ed) Rethinking the Constitution: Perspectives on Canadian Constitutional Reform, Interpretation, and Theory, Oxford University Press, Toronto, 249-270.

Matthews, R. (1983) Review of The Political Economy of Growth, Economic Journal 93, 919-920

Mauro, P. (1995) Corruption and Growth, Quarterly Journal of Economics 110, 681-712

McCallum, J., Blais, A. (1987) Government, Special Interest Groups, and Economic Growth, Public Choice 54, 3-18

McGuire, M. (1974) Group Size, Group Homogeneity and the Aggregate Provision of a Pure Public Good under Cournot Behavior, Public Choice 18, 107-126

McGuire, M., Olson, M. (1996) The Economics of Autocracy and Majority Rule: The Hidden Hand and the Use of Force, Journal of Economic Literature 34, 72-96

McKelvey, R., Ordeshook, P, (1984) Rational Expectations in Elections: Some Experimental Results Based on a Multidimensional Model, Public Choice 44, 61-102

McLean, I. (2000) The Divided Legacy of Mancur Olson, British Journal of Political Science 30, 651-668

McMenemy, J. (2001) The Language of Canadian Politics: A Guide to Important Terms and Concepts. 3rd. ed. Waterloo, Canada: Wilfred Laurier University Press

Medard, J. (2002) Corruption in Neo-Patrimonial Regimes of Sub-Saharan Africa, in Heidenheimer, A., Johnston, M. (eds) Political Corruption: Concepts and Cases, Transaction Publishers, New Brunswick, NJ, 379-402

Meekison, J. (1993) Canada's Quest for Constitutional Perfection, Constitutional Forum 4, 55-59.

Meltzer, A., Richard, S. (1981) A Rational Theory of the Size of Government, Journal of Political Economy 89, 914-927

Mill, J. ([1848] 1965) Principles of Political Economy, 7th Edition, University of Toronto Press, Toronto

Mitchell, W. (2001) The Old and New Public Choice: Chicago versus Virginia, in Shughart, W., Razzolini, L. (eds) The Elgar Companion to Public Choice, Edward Elgar, Cheltenham, UK

Moe, T. (1980) The Organization of Interests, University of Chicago Press, Chicago

Moe, T. (1997). The Positive Theory of Public Bureaucracy, in Mueller, D. (ed) Perspectives on Public Choice, Cambridge University Press, Cambridge

Mokyr, J. (1999) Eurocentricity Triumphant, American Historical Review 104, 241-446

Molutsi, P. (1994a) The Ruling Class and Democracy in Botswana, in Holm, J., Molutsi, P. (eds) Democracy in Botswana, Ohio University Press, Athens, OH, 103-117

Molutsi, P. (1994b) Whose Interests Do Botswana's Politicians Represent? in Holm, J., Molutsi, P. (eds) Democracy in Botswana, Ohio University Press, Athens, OH, 120-133

Moore, T. (1978) The Beneficiaries of Trucking Regulation, Journal of Law and Economics 21, 327-343

Morrison, J. (1994) Botswana's Formative Late Colonial Experiences, in Stedman, S. (ed) Botswana: The Political Economy of Democratic Development, Lynne Reiner, Boulder, CO, 27-50

Mosher, F. (1968) Democracy and the Public Service, Oxford University Press, New York

Mueller, D. (1989) Public Choice II, Cambridge University Press, Cambridge

Mueller, D. (1993) The "Virginia School" and Public Choice, in The Public Choice Approach to Politics, Edward Elgar, Brookfield, VT

Mueller, D. (ed) (1983) The Political Economy of Growth, Yale University Press, New Haven, CT

Mueller, D. (ed) (1999) Perspectives on Public Choice: A Handbook, Cambridge University Press, Cambridge

Muller, E., Seligson, M. (1987) Inequality and Insurgency, American Political Science Review 81, 425-451

Murphy, K. (1985) Corporate Performance and Managerial Remuneration: An Empirical Analysis, Journal of Accounting and Economics 7, 11-42

Murrell, P. (1984) An Examination of the Factors Affecting the Formation of Interest Groups in OECD Countries, Public Choice 43, 151-171

Musgrave, R. (1939) The Voluntary Exchange Theory of Public Economy, Quarterly Journal of Economics 53, 213-237

Musgrave, R. (1959) The Theory of Public Finance, McGraw-Hill, New York

Musgrave, R., Peacock A., (eds) (1967) Classics in the Theory of Public Finance, St. Martin's Press, New York

Myrdal, G. ([1968] 2002) Corruption as a Hindrance to Modernization in South Asia, in Heidenheimer, A., Johnston, M. (eds) Political Corruption: Concepts and Cases, Transaction Books, New Brunswick, NJ, 265-280

Nelson, M. (1982) A Short, Ironic History of American National Bureaucracy, Journal of Politics 44, 747-78

New York Times (1997) Tobacco's Crumbling Barricades, March 22, p. 22

Nitzan, S. (1994) Modelling Rent Seeking Contests, European Journal of Political Economy 10, 41-60

Norberg, H., Blomstrom, M. (1993) Dutch Disease and Management of Windfall Gains in Botswana, in Blomstrom, M., Lundahl, M. (eds) Economic Crisis in Africa: Perspectives on Policy Responses, Routledge, London, 162-180

North, D. (1966) Growth and Welfare in the American Past, Prentice-Hall, Englewood Cliffs, NJ

North, D. (1968) Sources of Productivity Change in Ocean Shipping, 1600-1850, Journal of Political Economy 76, 953-970

North, D. (1974) Beyond the New Economic History, Journal of Economic History 34, 1-7

North, D. (1981) Structure and Change in Economic History, Norton, New York

North, D. (1983) A Theory of Economic Change, Science 219 (January 14), 163-164

North, D. (1990) Institutions, Institutional Change and Economic Performance, Cambridge University Press, New York

North, D., Thomas, R. (1973) The Rise of the Western World: A New Economic History, Cambridge University Press, Cambridge

North, D., Weingast, B. (1992) Constitutions and Commitment: The Evolution of Institutions Governing Public Choice in Seventeenth-Century England, Journal of Economic History 49, 803-832

OBOP (1994) Na kogo glosowaliby Polacy w wyborach parlamentarnych? (Who Would the Poles Vote for in the Parliamentary Elections?), OBOP, Warsaw

OBOP (1995) Na kogo glosowaliby Polacy w wyborach parlamentarnych? (Who Would the Poles Vote for in the Parliamentary Elections?), OBOP, Warsaw

OBOP (1996a) Preferencje partyjne Polakow w lutym 1996 roku (Political Preferences of the Poles in February, 1996), OBOP, Warszawa

OBOP (1996b) Preferencje partyjne Polakow w koncu sierpnia 1996 roku (Political Preferences of the Poles in late August, 1996), OBOP, Warszawa

OBOP (1997) Preferencje partyjne Polakow w czerwcu 1997 roku (Political preferences of the Poles in June, 1997), OBOP, Warszawa

Okun, A. (1981) Prices and Quantities: A Macroeconomic Analysis, Brookings

Olmstead, A., Rhode, P. (2000) The Transformation of Northern Agriculture, 1910-1990, in Engerman, S., Gallman, R. (eds) The Cambridge Economic History of the United States, Vol. 3, The Twentieth Century, Cambridge University Press, New York

Olson, M. (1962a) The Economics of Strategic Bombing in World War II, The Airpower Historian 2, 121-127

Olson, M. (1962b) The Calculus of Consent (book review), American Economic Review 52, 1217-1218

Olson, M. (1963a) The Economics of the Wartime Shortage: A History of British Food Supplies in the Napoleonic War and in World Wars I and II, Duke University Press, Durham, NC

Olson, M. (1963b) Rapid Growth as a Destabilizing Force, Journal of Economic History 23, 529-552

Olson, M. (1965) The Logic of Collective Action, Harvard University Press, Cambridge, MA

Olson, M. (1974) The United Kingdom and the World Market in Wheat and Other Primary Products, 1885-1914, Explorations in Economic History 11, 325-55

Olson, M. (1982) The Rise and Decline of Nations: Economic Growth, Stagflation, and Social Rigidities, Yale University Press, New Haven, CT

Olson, M. (1983a) Political Economy of Comparative Growth Rates, in Mueller, D. (ed) The Political Economy of Growth, Yale University Press, New Haven, CT

Olson, M. (1983b) The South Will Fall Again: The South as Leader and Laggard in Economic Growth, Southern Economic Journal 49, 917-932

Olson, M. (1986) Why Some Welfare-State Redistribution to the Poor is a Great Idea, in Rowley, C. (ed) Public Choice and Liberty: Essays in Honor of Gordon Tullock, Basil Blackwell, Oxford

Olson, M. (1987) Diseconomies of Scale and Development: Essays in Honor of Peter Bauer, Cato Journal 7, 77-97

Olson, M. (1990) The Logic of Collective Action in Soviet-type Societies, Journal of Soviet Nationalities 1, 8-33

Olson, M. (1992) The Hidden Path to a Successful Economy, in Clague, C., Rausser, G. (eds) The Emergence of Market Economies in Eastern Europe, Basil Blackwell, Cambridge, MA, 55-76

Olson, M. (1993) Dictatorship, Democracy, and Development, American Political Science Review 87, 567-76

Olson, M. (1995) Why the Transition from Communism Is So Difficult, Eastern Economic Journal 21, 437-462

Olson, M. (1996) Big Bills Left on the Sidewalk: Why Some Nations are Rich, and Others Poor, Journal of Economic Perspectives 10, 3-24

Olson, M. (1997) The New Institutional Economics: The Collective Choice Approach to Economic Development, in Clague, C. (ed) Institutions and Economic Development: Growth and Governance in Less-Developed and Post-Socialist Countries, Johns Hopkins University Press, Baltimore, 37-66

Olson, M. (2000) Power and Prosperity: Outgrowing Communist and Capitalist Dictatorships, Basic Books, New York

Olson, M., Colander, D. (1984) Coalitions and Macroeconomics, in Colander, D. (ed) Neoclassical Political Economy, Ballinger, Cambridge, MA

Olson, M., Harris, C. (1959) Free Trade in 'Corn': A Statistical Study of the Prices and Production of Wheat in Great Britain from 1873 to 1914, Quarterly Journal of Economics 73, 145-168

Olson, M., Kähkönen, S. (eds) (2000) A Not-So-Dismal Science: A Broader View of Economies and Societies, Oxford University Press, Oxford

Olson, M., Sarna, N., Swamy, A. (2000) Governance and Growth: A Simple Hypothesis Explaining Cross-Country Differences in Productivity Growth, Public Choice 102, 341-364

Olson, M., Zeckhauser, R. (1966) An Economic Theory of Alliances, Review of Economics and Statistics 48, 266-279

Oneal, J., Elrod, M. (1989) Nato Burden Sharing and the Forces of Change, International Studies Quarterly 33, 435-456

Othick, J. (1983) Review of The Rise and Decline of Nations, Economic History Review 36, 324-325

Parson, J. (1984) Botswana: Liberal Democracy and the Labor Reserve in Southern Africa, Westview Press, Boulder, CO

Pastor, R. (1999) The Third Dimension in Accountability: The International Community in National Elections, in Schedler, A., Diamond, L., Plattner, M. (eds) The Self-Restraining State: Power and Accountability in New Democracies, Lynne Reiner, Boulder, CO, 123-142

Peacock, A. (1996) Introduction: The Necessity of Rethinking the Constitution, in Peacock, A. (ed) Rethinking the Constitution: Perspectives on Canadian Constitutional Reform, Interpretation, and Theory, Oxford University Press, Toronto, vii-xxix

Perlman, S. (1949) A Theory of the Labor Movement, Augustus M. Kelley, New York

Persson, T., Tabellini, G. (1994) Is Inequality Harmful for Growth? American Economic Review 84, 600-621

Phelps, E. (1985) Political Economy, Norton, New York

Picard, L. (1987) The Politics of Development in Botswana: A Model for Success? Lynne Reiner, Boulder, CO

Pissarides, C. (1990) Equilibrium Unemployment Theory, Basil Blackwell, Oxford

Postan, M. (1987) The Trade of Medieval Europe: The North, in Postan, M., Miller, E. (eds) Cambridge Economic History of Europe, 2nd edition, Cambridge University Press, New York

Pryor, F. (1982) Review of Structure and Change in Economic History, Journal of Economic History 42, 986-89

Pryor, F. (1983) A Quasi-test of Olson's Hypotheses, in Mueller, D. (ed) The Political Economy of Growth, Yale University Press, New Haven, CT

Putnam, R. (2000) Bowling Alone: The Collapse and Revival of American Community, Simon and Schuster, New York.

Quah, J. (1999) Combating Corruption in South Korea and Thailand, in Schedler, A., Diamond, L., Plattner, M. (eds) The Self-Restraining State: Power and Accountability in New Democracies, Lynne Reiner, Boulder, CO, 245-256

Quiggin, J. (1992) Testing the Implications of the Olson Hypothesis, Economica 59, 261-77

Quinn, D., Woolley, J. (2001) Democracy and National Economic Performance: The Preference for Stability, American Journal of Political Science 45, 634-657

Raciborski, J. (1997) Polskie wybory (Polish Elections), Wydawnictwo Naukowe "Scholar", Warszawa

Rahnama-Moghadam, M., Samavati, H. (1991) Predicting Debt Rescheduling by Less-Developed Countries: A Probit Model Approach, Quarterly Review of Economics and Business 31, 3-14

Ratner, S., Soltow, J., Sylla, R. (1993) The Evolution of the American Economy: Growth, Welfare, and Decision Making, second edition, Macmillan, New York

Riker, W., Ordeshook, P. (1968) A Theory of the Calculus of Voting, American Political Science Review 62, 25-42

Riley, S. (1998) The Political Economy of Anti-Corruption Strategies in Africa, European Journal of Development Research 10, 129-159

Roberts, R. (1984) A Positive Model of Private Charity and Public Transfers, Journal of Political Economy 92, 136-148

Rock, M. (2000) Thailand's Old Bureaucratic Polity and Its New Semi-Democracy, in Khan, M., Jomo D. (eds) Rents, Rent-Seeking, and Economic Development: Theory and Evidence in Asia, Cambridge University Press, New York, 182-206

Rodrik, D. (1999) Where Did All the Growth Go? External Shocks, Social Conflict, and Growth Collapses, Journal of Economic Growth 4, 385-412
Romer, D. (2001) Advanced Macroeconomics, McGraw-Hill, New York
Rose-Ackerman, S. (1999) Corruption and Government: Causes, Consequences, and Reform, Cambridge University Press, New York
Rostow, W. (1960) The Stages of Economic Growth: A Non-Communist Manifesto, Cambridge University Press, Cambridge
Rotemberg, J., Woodford, M. (1995) Dynamic GE Models with Imperfectly Competitive Product Markets, in Thomas F. Cooley (ed) Frontiers of Business Cycle Research, Princeton University Press, Princeton, NJ
Rubinstein, W. (1983) The End of 'Old Corruption' in Britain 1780-1860, Past and Present 101, 55-86
Sah, R. (1987) Queues, Rationing, and Markets: Comparisons of Outcomes for the Poor and the Rich, American Economic Review 77, 69-77
Samuelson, P. (1954) The Pure Theory of Public Expenditures, The Review of Economics and Statistics 36, 387-389
Samuelson, P. (1955) Diagramatic Exposition of a Theory of Public Expenditures, Review of Economics and Statistics 37, 350-356
Samuelson, P. (1958) Aspects of Public Expenditure Theories, Review of Economics and Statistics 40, 332-338
Sandler, T. (1992) Collective Action: Theory and Applications, University of Michigan Press, Ann Arbor
Sandler, T. (2001) Economic Concepts for the Social Sciences, Cambridge University Press, Cambridge
Sax, E. ([1924] 1967) The Valuation Theory of Taxation, in Musgrave, R., Peacock, A. (eds) Classics in the Theory of Public Finance, St. Martin's Press, New York, 175-189
Schedler, A. (1999) Restraining the State: Conflicts and Agents of Accountability, in Schedler, A., Diamond, L., Plattner, M. (eds) The Self-Restraining State: Power and Accountability in New Democracies, Lynne Reiner, Boulder, CO, 333-350
Schedler, A., Diamond, L., Plattner, M. F. (eds) (1999) The Self-Restraining State: Power and Accountability in New Democracies, Lynne Reiner, Boulder, CO
Schelling, T. (1978) Micromotives and Macrobehavior, Norton, New York NY
Scheppele, K. (1988) Legal Secrets: Equality and Efficiency in the Common Law, University of Chicago Press, Chicago, IL
Schmalensee, R., Bailey, E., Ellerman, A., Joskow, P., Montero, J. (1998) An Interim Evaluation of Sulfur Dioxide Emissions Trading, Journal of Economic Perspectives 12, 53-68
Schmid, A. (1996) Mancur Olson, Jr., in Samuels, W. (ed) American Economists of the Late Twentieth Century, Edward Elgar, Brookfield, VT
Schrader, S. (1991) Informal Technology Transfer Between Firms: Cooperation through Information Trading, Research Policy 20, 153-170
Schwartz, A. (1987) Money in Historical Perspective, NBER, University of Chicago Press, Chicago
Seavoy, R. (1982) The Origins of the American Business Corporation, 1784-1855, Greenwood Press, Westport, CT
Shibata, H. (1971) A Bargaining Model of the Pure Theory of Public Expenditure, Journal of Political Economy 79, 1-29

Shihata, I. (1997) Corruption: A General Review With an Emphasis on the Role of the World Bank, Dickinson Journal of International Law 15, 451-486

Shleifer, A., Vishny, R. (1993) Corruption, Quarterly Journal of Economics 108, 599-617

Shughart, W., Razzolini, L. (eds) (2001) The Elgar Companion to Public Choice, Edward Elgar, Brookfield, VT

Sidgwick, H. ([1901] 1969) The Principles of Political Economy, 3rd ed., Kraus Reprint Company, New York

Sigurdson, R. (1993) Left- and Right-Wing Charterphobia in Canada: A Critique of the Critics, International Journal of Canadian Studies 7-8, 95-115.

Sindzingre, A. (2002) A Comparative Analysis of African and East Asian Corruption, in Heidenheimer, A., Johnston, M. (eds) Political Corruption: Concepts and Cases, Transaction Publishers, New Brunswick, NJ, 441-460

Singh, G. (1997) Understanding Political Corruption in Contemporary Indian Politics, in Heywood, P. (ed) Political Corruption, Blackwell Publishers, Oxford, 210-222

Skowronek, S. (1982) Building A New American State, Cambridge University Press, New York

Smiley, D. (1983) A Dangerous Deed: The Constitution Act, 1982, in Banting, K., Simeon, R. (eds) And No One Cheered: Federalism, Democracy and the Constitution Act, Methuen, Toronto, 74-95

Smith, A. ([1776] 1985) An Inquiry into the Nature and Causes of the Wealth of Nations, Teichgraeber, R. (ed), Modern Library, New York

Smith, C., Watts, R. (1982) Incentive and Tax Effects of Executive Compensation Plans, Australian Journal of Management 7, 139-157

Smithey, S. (2002) Cooperation and Conflict: Group Activity in R. v. Keegstra, in James, P., Abelson, D., Lusztig, M. (eds) The Myth of the Sacred: The Charter, the Courts and the Politics of the Constitution in Canada, McGill-Queen's University Press, Montreal and Kingston

Snow, J. (1977) The Problem of Motor Carrier Regulation and the Ford Administration's Proposal for Reform, in MacAvoy, P., Snow, J. (eds), Regulation of Entry and Pricing in Truck Transportation, American Enterprise Institute for Public Policy Research, Washington, D.C., 3-43

Social Science Citation Index (http://isiknowledge.com)

Somolekae, G. (1994) Bureaucracy and Democracy in Botswana: What Type of Relationship? in Stedman, S. (ed.) Botswana: The Political Economy of Democratic Development, Lynne Reiner, Boulder, CO, 113-122

Stapenhurst, R., Kpundeh, S. (eds) (1999) Curbing Corruption: Toward a Model for Building National Integrity, World Bank, Washington, D.C

Stretton, H., Orchard, L. (1994) Public Goods, Public Enterprise, Public Choice: Theoretical Foundations of the Contemporary Attack on Government, St. Martin's Press, New York

Sulek, A. (1995) Do czego sluza sondaze? Wykorzystanie badan opinii publicznej w kampanii wyborczej 1993 (What is the Purpose of Polls? The Use of Polls in the Campaign of 1993), Kultura i Spoleczenstwo 38, 103-17

Sullivan, M. (1991) Measuring Global Values, Greenwood, New York

Sutter, D. (2002) Constitutional Prohibitions in a Rent Seeking Model, Public Choice 111, 105-125

Svensson, J. (1998) Investment, Property Rights and Political Instability: Theory and Evidence, European Economic Review 42, 1317-1342

Svensson, L. (1999) How Should Monetary Policy Be Conducted in an Era of Price Stability? in New Challenges for Monetary Policy, Kansas City: Federal Reserve Bank of Kansas City

Sylla, R. (1969) Federal Policy, Banking Market Structure, and Capital Mobilization in the United States, 1863-1913, Journal of Economic History 29, 657-686

Sylla, R. (1985) Early American Banking: The Significance of the Corporate Form, Business and Economic History, 2nd series, 14, 105-123

Sylla, R. (1998) U.S. Securities Markets and the Banking System, 1790-1840, Federal Reserve Bank of St. Louis Review 80, 83-98

Taagepera, R., Shugart, M. (1989) Seats and Votes: The Effects and Determinants of Electoral Systems, Yale University Press, New Haven, CT

Tanzi, V. (1998) Corruption Around the World: Causes, Consequences, Scope, and Cures, International Monetary Fund Staff Papers 45, 559-594

Taylor, C., Jodice, D. (1983) World Handbook of Political and Social Indicators, 3rd ed. Yale University Press, New Haven, CT

Tehranian, H., Waegelein, J. (1985) Market Reaction to Short-Term Executive Compensation Plan Adoption, Journal of Accounting and Economics 7, 131-144

Theobald, R. (1990) Corruption, Development, and Underdevelopment, The Macmillan Press, London

Theobald, R. (1999) So What Really is the Problem with Corruption? Third World Quarterly 20, 491-502

Tiebout, C. (1956) A Pure Theory of Local Expenditures, Journal of Political Economy 64, 416-424

Treisman, D. (2000) The Causes of Corruption: A Cross-National Study, Journal of Public Economics 76, 399-437

TRINC's Blue Book of the Trucking Industry (1959-1985) Annual Editions, TRINC Transportation Consultants, Division of Dun and Bradstreet, Inc., Washington, D.C.

Truman, D. (1951) The Governmental Process: Political Interests and Public Opinion, Adolph Knopf, New York

Tullock, G. (2001) Rent Seeking, in Michie, J. (ed) Reader's Guide to the Social Sciences, Volume 2, Fitzroy Dearborn Publishers, London and Chicago, 1410-1411.

Tversky, A., Kahneman, D. (1974) Judgment Under Uncertainty: Heuristics and Biases, Science 185, 1124-1131

U. S. Congress (1935) Motor Carrier Act of 1935, 49 U.S. Code 301-27, 74th Congress

U. S. Congress (1980) Motor Carrier Act of 1980, 49 U.S. Code 10101, 96th Congress

U. S. Congress (1981) The Economic Recovery Tax Act of 1981, 97th Congress

U. S. Department of Justice (1994) The Charlestown Code of Silence, www.usdoj.gov/dea/major/charlestown.htm

U. S. Department of State (1998) Military Expenditures and Arms Transfers, Washington, DC

U. S. General Accounting Office (1987) Fact Sheet for the Chairwoman, Subcommittee on Government Activities and Transportation, Committee on Government Operations, House of Representatives, Truck Safety: Deposition of Allegations Concerning Three Safety Audits, GAO, Resources, Community and Economic Development Division, Washington, DC

U. S. General Accounting Office (1989) Report to Congressional Requesters, Truck Safety: Implementation of the Single Driver's License and Notification Requirements, GAO, Resources, Community and Economic Division, Washington, DC

U. S. General Accounting Office (1990a) Report to Congressional Requesters, Truck Safety: States' Progress in Testing and Licensing Commercial Drivers, GAO, Resources, Community and Economic Development Division, Washington, DC

U. S. General Accounting Office (1990b) Report to Congressional Requesters, Truck Safety: Need to Better Ensure Correction of Serious Inspection Violations. GAO, Resources, Community and Economic Development Division, Washington, DC

U. S. General Accounting Office (1991) Report to Congressional Requesters, Freight Trucking: Promising Approach For Predicting Carriers' Safety Risks. GAO, Resources, Community and Economic Development Division, Washington, DC

U. S. Senate (1976) Testimony Before the Subcommittee on Antitrust and Monopoly of the Committee on the Judiciary, Concerning Economic Regulation of the Motor Carrier Industry

United States v. Houlihan (1996), 92 F.3d 1271, United States Court of Appeals for the First Circuit

van de Walle, N. (1994) Neopatrimonialism and Democracy in Africa, with an Illustration from Cameroon, in Widner, J. (ed) Economic Change and Political Liberalization in Sub-Saharan Africa, Johns Hopkins University Press, Baltimore, 129-157

van de Walle, N. (2001) African Economies and the Politics of Permanent Crisis, 1979-1999, Cambridge University Press, New York

Van Riper, P. (1958) History of the United States Civil Service, Row, Peterson and Company, Evanston, IL

Veiga, F. (2000) Delays of Inflation Stabilizations, Economics and Politics 12, 275–295

Waegelein, J. (1988) The Association Between the Adoption of Short-Term Bonus Plans and Corporate Expenditures, Journal of Accounting and Public Policy 7, 43-63

Waller, M. (1995) Making and Breaking: Factions in the Process of Party Formation in Bulgaria, Democratization 2, 152-167

Wallin, T. (1975) Alternatives in Transportation Policy: A Matrix Approach, Transportation Journal 15, 43-53

Wallis, J. (1983) Review of The Rise and Decline of Nations, Journal of Business 56, 566-568

Wallis, J. (2000) State Constitutional Reform and the Structure of Government Finance in the Nineteenth Century, in Heckelman, J., Moorhouse, J., Whaples, R. (eds) Public Choice Interpretations of American Economic History, Kluwer Academic Publishers, Boston, 33-52

Wallis, J. (2002) Market Augmenting Government? The State and the Corporation in 19th Century America, in Azfar, O., Cadwell, C. (eds) Market Augmenting Government, Center for Institutional Reform and the Informal Sector, University of Michigan Press, Ann Arbor

Wallis, J., Sylla, R., Legler, J. (1994) The Interaction of Taxation and Regulation in Nineteenth Century Banking, in Goldin, C., Libecap, G. (eds) The Regulated Economy: A Historical Approach to Political Economy, University of Chicago Press, Chicago, 121-144

Warr, P. (1982) Pareto Optimal Redistribution and Private Charity, Journal of Political Economy 19, 131-138

Warr, P. (1983) The Private Provision of a Public Good is Independent of the Distribution of Income, Economics Letters 13, 207-211

Watt, D., Flanary, R., Theobald, R. (2000) Democratisation or the Democratisation of Corruption? The Case of Uganda, in Doig, A., Theobald, R. (eds) Corruption and Democratisation, Frank Cass, London, 37-64

Watts, R., Zimmerman, J. (1978) Towards a Positive Theory of the Determination of Accounting Standards, The Accounting Review 53, 112-134

Wedeman, A. (1997) Looters, Rent-Scrapers, and Dividend-Collectors: Corruption and Growth in Zaire, South Korea, and the Philippines, Journal of Developing Areas 31, 457-478

Whaples, R. (1991) A Quantitative History of the Journal of Economic History and the Cliometric Revolution, Journal of Economic History 51, 289-302

Whaples, R. (1995) Where Is There Consensus Among American Economic Historians? The Results of a Survey on Forty Propositions, Journal of Economic History 55, 139-154

Whaples, R. (2002) The Supply and Demand of Economic History: Recent Trends in the Journal of Economic History, Journal of Economic History 62, 524-532

White, H. (1980) A Heteroskedasticity-consistent Covariance Matrix Estimator and a Direct Test for Heteroskedasticity, Econometrica 48, 817-838

Whitehead, L. (2000) High-Level Political Corruption in Latin America: A 'Transitional' Phenomenon? In Tulchin, J., Espach, R. (eds) Combating Corruption in Latin America, The Woodrow Wilson Center Press, Washington, D.C., 107-129

Wicksell, K. ([1896] 1967) A New Principle of Just Taxation, in Musgrave, R., Peacock A. (eds) Classics in the Theory of Public Finance, St. Martin's Press, New York, 72-118

Wightman, D. (1964) Review of The Economics of Wartime Shortage, Economic History Review 17, 168-69

Williamson, J. (1965) Review of The Economics of Wartime Shortage, Economic History Review 18, 428-29

Williamson, J. (1974) Late Nineteenth-Century American Development: A General Equilibrium History, Cambridge University Press, Cambridge

Williamson, J. (1980) Greasing the Wheels of Sputtering Export Engines: Midwestern Grains and American Growth, Explorations in Economic History 17, 189-217

Williamson, S., Whaples, R. (forthcoming) Cliometrics, in Mokyr, J. (ed) Oxford Encyclopedia of Economic History, New York

Wilson, G. (1980) Economic Analysis of Intercity Freight Transportation, Indiana University Press, Bloomington, IN

Wright, G. (1986) Old South, New South: Revolutions in the Southern Economy since the Civil War, Basic Books, New York

Yates, A., Heckelman, J. (2001) Rent Setting in Multiple Winner Rent Seeking Contests, European Journal of Political Economy 17, 835-852

Zdort, M. (1997a) ROP z AWS o wyborach (ROP and AWS on Elections) Rzeczpospolita 134 (06/11), Warsaw

Zdort, M. (1997b) Nocne ultimatum (A Nightly Ultimatum), Rzeczpospolita 140 (06/18), Warsaw

Zdort, M. (1997c) KPN czeka na decyzje AWS (KPN Awaits the AWS' Decisions), Rzeczpospolita 153 (07/13), Warsaw

Zeckhauser, R., Marks, D. (1996) Signposting: The Selective Revelation of Product Information, in Zeckhauser, R., Keeney, R., Sebenius, J. (eds) Wise Choices: Decisions, Games, and Negotiations, Harvard Business School Press, Boston, MA, 22-41

Zielinski, J. (2000) On Political Parties in Eastern Europe: Why do Party Systems Fragment? Ohio State University working paper

Zielinski, J. (2002) Translating Cleavages into Party Systems: The Significance of New Democracies, World Politics 54, 17-33

Contributors

Christopher K. Clague is Professor Emeritus, University of Maryland, and Lecturer in Economics, San Diego State University

Dennis Coates is Professor of Economics, University of Maryland at Baltimore County

Cary Coglianese is Associate Professor of Public Policy, John F. Kennedy School of Government, Harvard University

David Colander is Christian A Johnson Distinguished Professor of Economics, Middlebury College

Keith L. Dougherty is Assistant Professor of Political Science, Florida International University

Charles R. Enis is Associate Professor of Accounting, Pennsylvania State University

Jac C. Heckelman is Associate Professor of Economics and McCulloch Family Fellow, Wake Forest University

Bryan C. Jack was Director of Programming and Fiscal Economics, U.S. Dept. of Defense

Patrick James is Professor of Political Science, University of Missouri

Marek M. Kaminski is Assistant Professor, Department of Political Science and Institute for Mathematical Behavioral Science, University of California – Irvine

Philip Keefer is Lead Economist, The World Bank

Stephen Knack is Senior Research Economist, The World Bank

Kenneth Koford is Professor of Economics, University of Delaware

Jeffrey Miller is Professor of Economics, University of Delaware

Mancur Olson was Distinguished Professor of Economics, University of Maryland, and Chair and Principal Investigator, Institutional Reform and the Informal Sector

Edward A. Parson is Associate Professor of Public Policy, John F. Kennedy School of Government, Harvard University

John J. Wallis is Professor of Economics and Director of Undergraduate Studies, University of Maryland

Robert Whaples is Associate Professor of Economics, Wake Forest University, and Associate Director of EH.NET

Richard J. Zeckhauser is Frank Plumpton Ramsey Professor of Political Economy, John F. Kennedy School of Government, Harvard University

Author Index

Subject Index

MIX
Papier aus verantwortungsvollen Quellen
Paper from responsible sources
FSC® C105338

If you have any concerns about our products,
you can contact us on
ProductSafety@springernature.com

In case Publisher is established outside the EU,
the EU authorized representative is:
Springer Nature Customer Service Center GmbH
Europaplatz 3, 69115 Heidelberg, Germany

Printed by Libri Plureos GmbH
in Hamburg, Germany